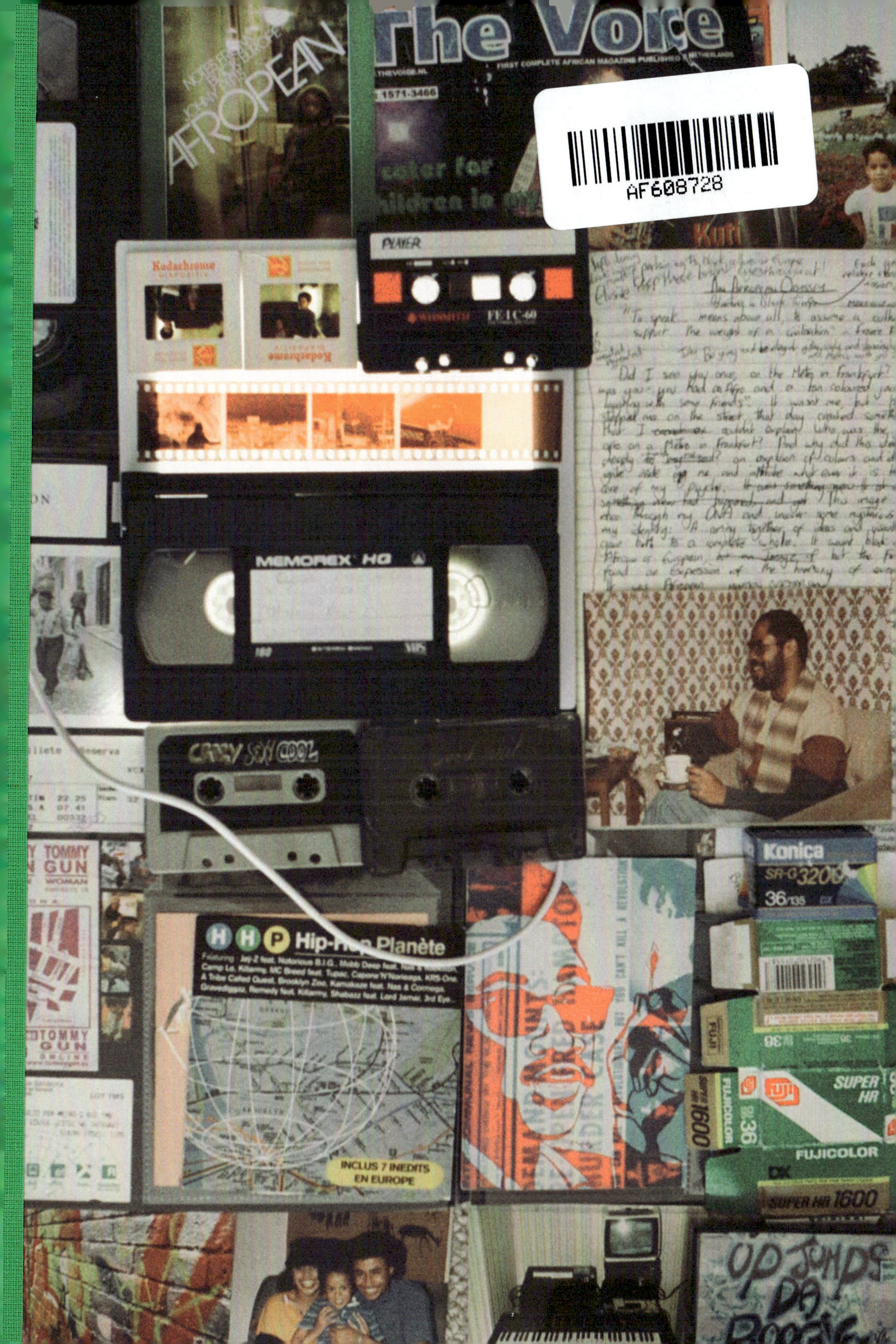
AFROPEAN
The Voice
AF608728
Kodachrome
PLAYER
MEMOREX HQ
Konica
SR-G 3200
36/135
TOMMY GUN
Hip-Hop Planète
INCLUS 7 INEDITS EN EUROPE
FUJICOLOR
SUPER HR
SUPER HR 1600

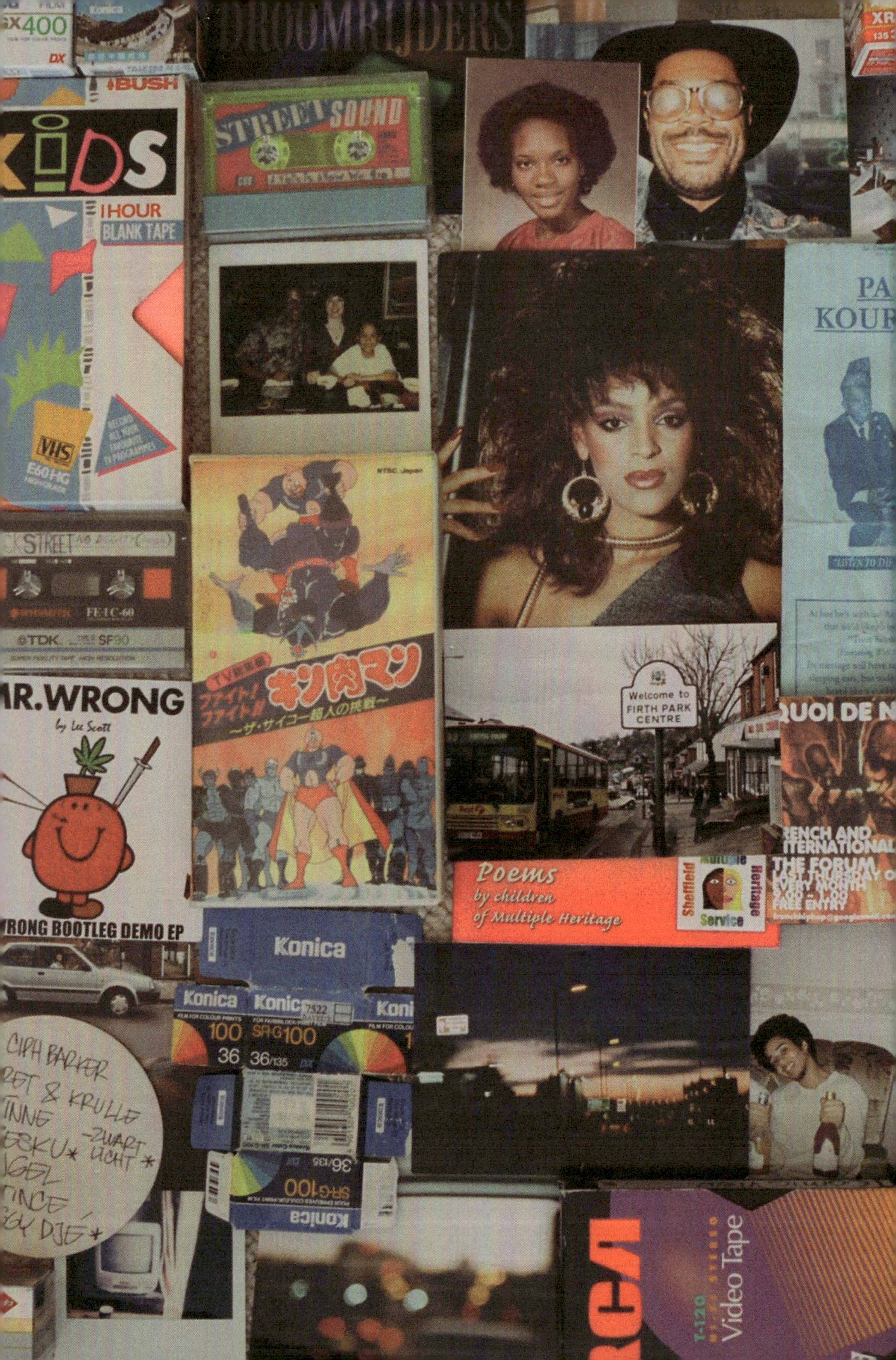

GX400
Konica
DROOMRIJDERS
BUSH
KIDS
1 HOUR
BLANK TAPE
VHS
E60 HG
STREET SOUND
TDK SF90
FE-I C-60
MR.WRONG
by Lee Scott
RONG BOOTLEG DEMO EP
NTSC Japan
ファイト！ファイト!!
キン肉マン
～ザ・サイコー超人の挑戦～
Welcome to
FIRTH PARK
CENTRE
Poems
by children
of Multiple Heritage
Sheffield
Multiple
Heritage
Service
PA
KOUR
QUOI DE N
RENCH AND
INTERNATIONAL
THE FORUM
LAST THURSDAY O
EVERY MONTH
9.00 - 1.00
FREE ENTRY
Konica
SR-G100
36
CIPH BARKER
RET & KRULLE
ZWART
LICHT
RCA
T-120
Video Tape

CONTENTS



© Johny Pitts, *The B-Side*, 2021 (for *The Eyes* magazine). A collection of ephemera from a personal archive, documenting Johny Pitts' multicultural, working-class family home.

Taous Dahmani

# B—SIDE

Dear readers,

This new issue in your hands looks at how artists and photographers portray the plurality of identities. In that regard, this year *The Eyes* seeks to explore the possibility of a "fusion" of Africa and Europe and more specifically the characteristic "in-betweenness" of diasporic identities.[1] A strange phenomenon of cohabitation of unity and fraction: the promiscuity of differences.

This internal conflict and its conciliations are the main theme of Paul Gilroy's *The Black Atlantic: Modernity and Double Consciousness* (1993).[2] This is also what Johny Pitts focused on in *Afropean: Notes from Black Europe* (2019). An English writer and photographer from Sheffield, in the North of England, Johny Pitts was born into two cultures – African American and white British. In the multiple renditions of his work, he addresses the interaction of Black and European culture; in his book he states: "When I first heard [this word], it encouraged me to think of myself as whole and unhyphenated: *Afropean*. Here was a space where blackness was taking part in shaping European identity at large. It suggested the possibility of living in and with more than one idea: Africa and Europe, or, by extension, the Global South and the West, without being mixed-this, half-that or black-other."[3] Of course, we wanted to invite Johny Pitts to think about this theme with us. This issue is the result of this collaboration, which he proposed to title *B-Side*.

In a context of creative (in)visibility and event-driven over-visibility, the contributors to this issue discuss the experiences of Europeans of African Caribbean heritage and more broadly global majorities that are minorities in Europe. Invented in the early 1990s by the music group Zap Mama, Afropeanity has its roots in the musical realm, and it is therefore quite natural that we drew on this for inspiration for this issue. In his book *Afropean*, Johny Pitts wrote that he wished to "sing something into visibility".[4] With *B-Side*, we invited him to explore the photographic aspects of this journey.

Records have two sides – A and B – and traditionally the second one has usually been dedicated to secondary recordings that have generally received less attention. The B-side thus becomes an active concept for us to revisit works by photographers who are less seen or overlooked and new photographic endeavours that have not yet found their audience. On the B-side of *A Love Supreme* by John Coltrane, we can find the song title "Pursuance", which means the action of trying to achieve something. If the B-side receives less attention, it also allows for more freedom to experiment, to produce something different and unique. So symbolically, the B-side offers a metaphor for possibilities. It becomes, for us, a space of photographic exploration where images and operators take up their right to document the under-documented and to visualize Afropean experiences and subjectivities – and, by extension, those that are considered marginal.

Thus, this collection navigates between selected historical pieces and more contemporary proposals: it seeks both to highlight the issues under debate today and to emphasize their genealogy. In these pages you will find the work of James Barnor and Maud Sulter, but also Zineb Sedira, Délio Jasse and Mohamed Bourouissa, as well as a new generation represented by Sofia Yala Rodrigues, Marvin Bonheur, Tabita Rezaire, Jazz Grant and Cédrine Scheidig. Across time and geographical areas, visual or referential traditions are emerging and urgent innovations are created.

John Berger, in his essay "Uses of Photography" (1978), wrote: "There are photographs which belong to private experience and there are those which are used publicly."[5] Although this dichotomy is interesting in many ways, it seems to be debunked by the work of photographers from the African Caribbean diasporas presented in this issue. Here, the photographers draw on their personal experiences to make them public: not in an act of exhibitionism but rather of affirmation. In 1995, in her book *Art on My Mind*, the North American feminist intellectual and activist bell hooks wrote: "Cameras gave to black folks, irrespective of class, a means by which we could participate fully in the production of images."[6] When bell hooks wrote those words she was speaking of the gesture of speaking up and out through the photographic act. She then added how essential it was "that any theoretical discussion on the relationship of black life to the visual, to art making, makes photography central".[7] Afropean photographers, as full actors in the social world, propose through their image making a cultural counter-hegemony, a visual resistance. This is also what the North American author and professor Sarah Lewis developed in her project "Vision and Justice", defending a right to fair representation, thinking of a democratization of visualities and an emancipation through images.[8]

This speaking out, this seizing of one's own freedom, is further discussed by the Nigerian writer Chinua Achebe in his book *Hopes and Impediments*, a collection of essays published in 1988 in which he states: "Art is man's constant effort to create for himself a different order of reality from that which is given to him; an aspiration to provide himself with a second handle on existence through his imagination."[9] It is these "other-realities" that this issue explores. It is a proposal that keeps in mind the urgent necessity for critical vigilance towards photographic images as they exist in our visual world. It is also a project that asks questions about the role of photography in our society, whose recent history has seen, to name but a few, the UK's exit from the European Union in December 2020 – an expression of all kinds of retrenchment – and the murder of George Floyd on 25 May 2020, provoking a wave of uprisings for rights and freedoms. "Every human problem cries out to be considered on the basis of time, the ideal being that the present always serves to build the future,"[10] wrote Frantz Fanon. And so we hope to bring to you a topical issue, reflecting the times, with the hope that the future will make it obsolete.

1 Find out more: Leonora Miano, *Afropea: Utopie post-occidentale et post-raciste*, Grasset, Paris, 2020.
2 Paul Gilroy, *The Black Atlantic: Modernity and Double Consciousness*, Harvard University Press, Cambridge (MA), 1995.
3 Johny Pitts, *Afropean: Notes from Black Europe*, Allen Lane, London, 2019, p. 11.
4 Ibid.
5 John Berger, "Uses of Photography: For Susan Sontag" (1978), *Understanding a Photograph*, Penguin, London, 2013.
6 bell hooks, *Art on My Mind: Visual Politics*, The New Press, New York, 1995, p. 57.
7 Ibid.
8 For more information, visit https://visionandjustice.org.
9 Chinua Achebe, *Hopes and Impediments: Selected Essays*, Anchor Books, New York, 1990 [1st ed. 1988].
10 Frantz Fanon, *Black Skin, White Masks*, Grove Press, New York, 1967, p.25.

# JAZZ GRANT

Jazz Grant was born in 1992 in London and grew up in Brighton. Her paternal grandparents arrived from Jamaica in 1957 and 1959, a decade after the *Empire Windrush* – the term "Windrush generation" was coined to describe the Caribbean immigrants who came to Britain at that time. Having dreamed of becoming a fashion designer since childhood, she studied fashion design at the London College of Fashion, graduating in 2016. Her discovery of the practice of collage dates from these formative years. On the advice of her teachers, she favours this technique to present her ideas and concepts.

Handmade collages became a hobby and then a means of expression in their own right. Jazz Grant is "fascinated by the creation of new worlds" that collage allows. She cuts out and scans directly from books and printed ephemera, exploring and distorting perception and depth found within imagery.


*Father's Son*, 2021
*Indentations*, 2020
*Athulya*, 2020
*Small Axe 1*, Steve McQueen for *The Face Magazine*, 2020
*BLM*, photography by Sophie Jones, 2020
*Small Axe 2*, Steve McQueen for *The Face Magazine*, 2020
*Woman Walking 2*, 2019

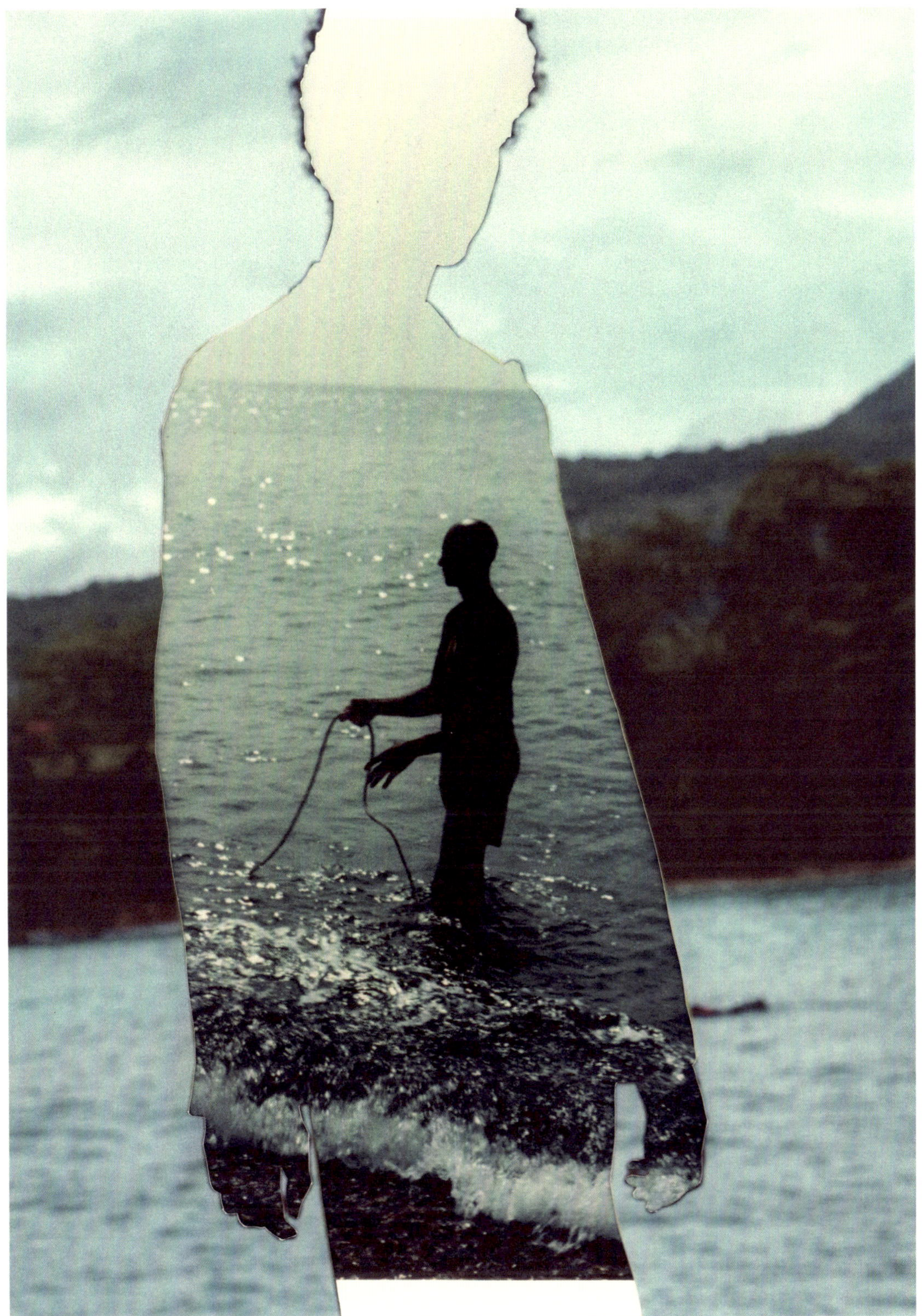

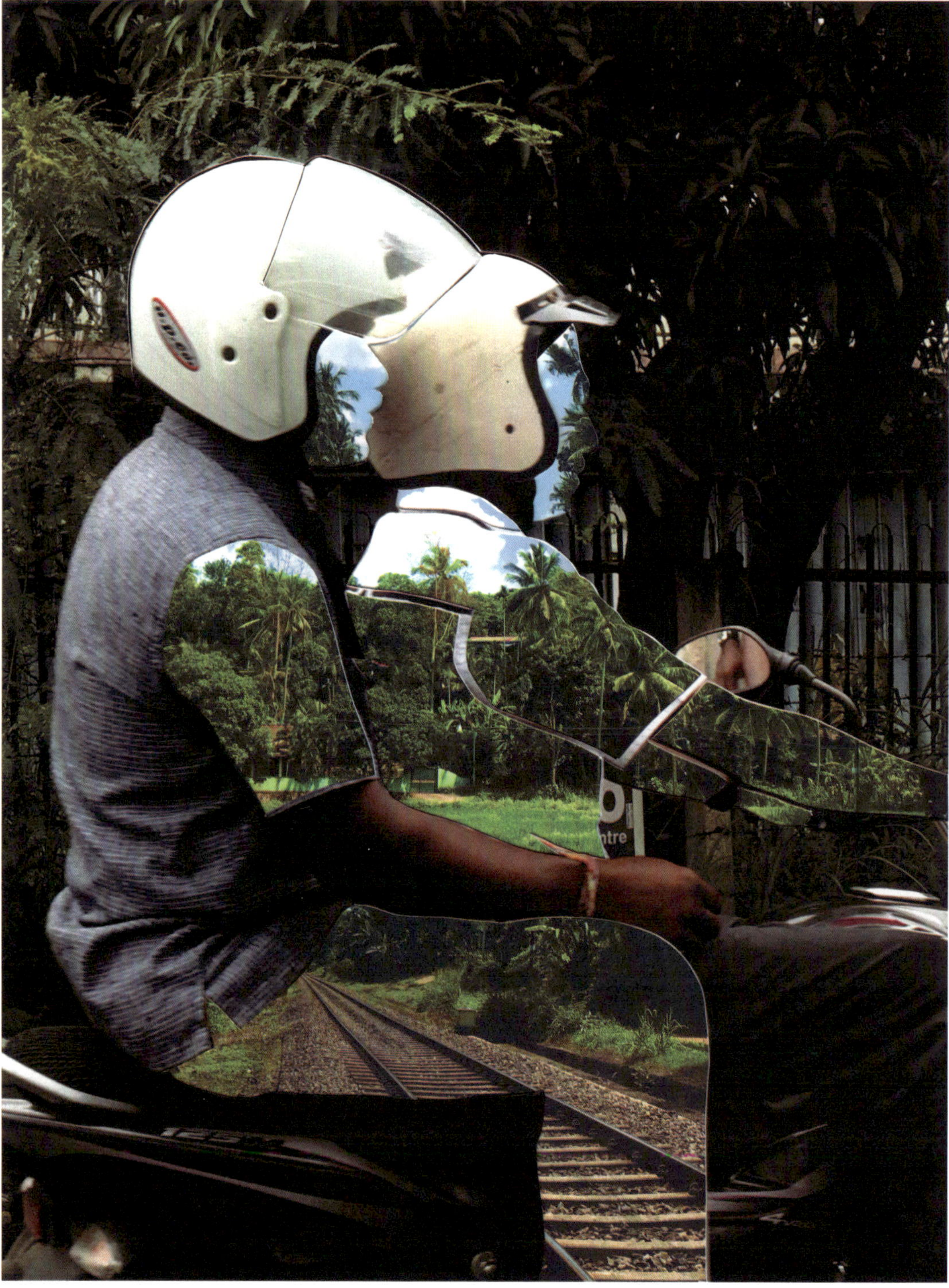

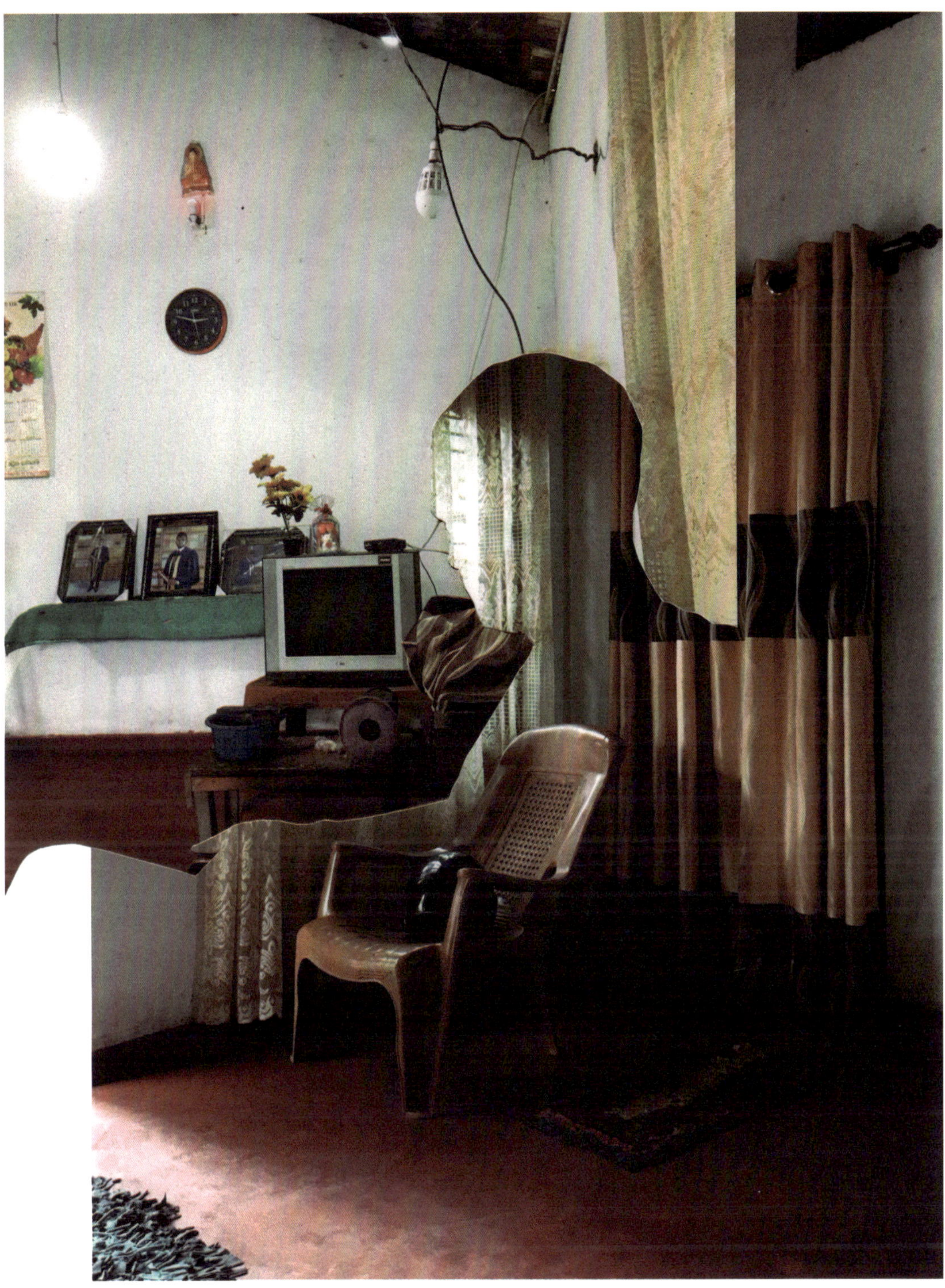

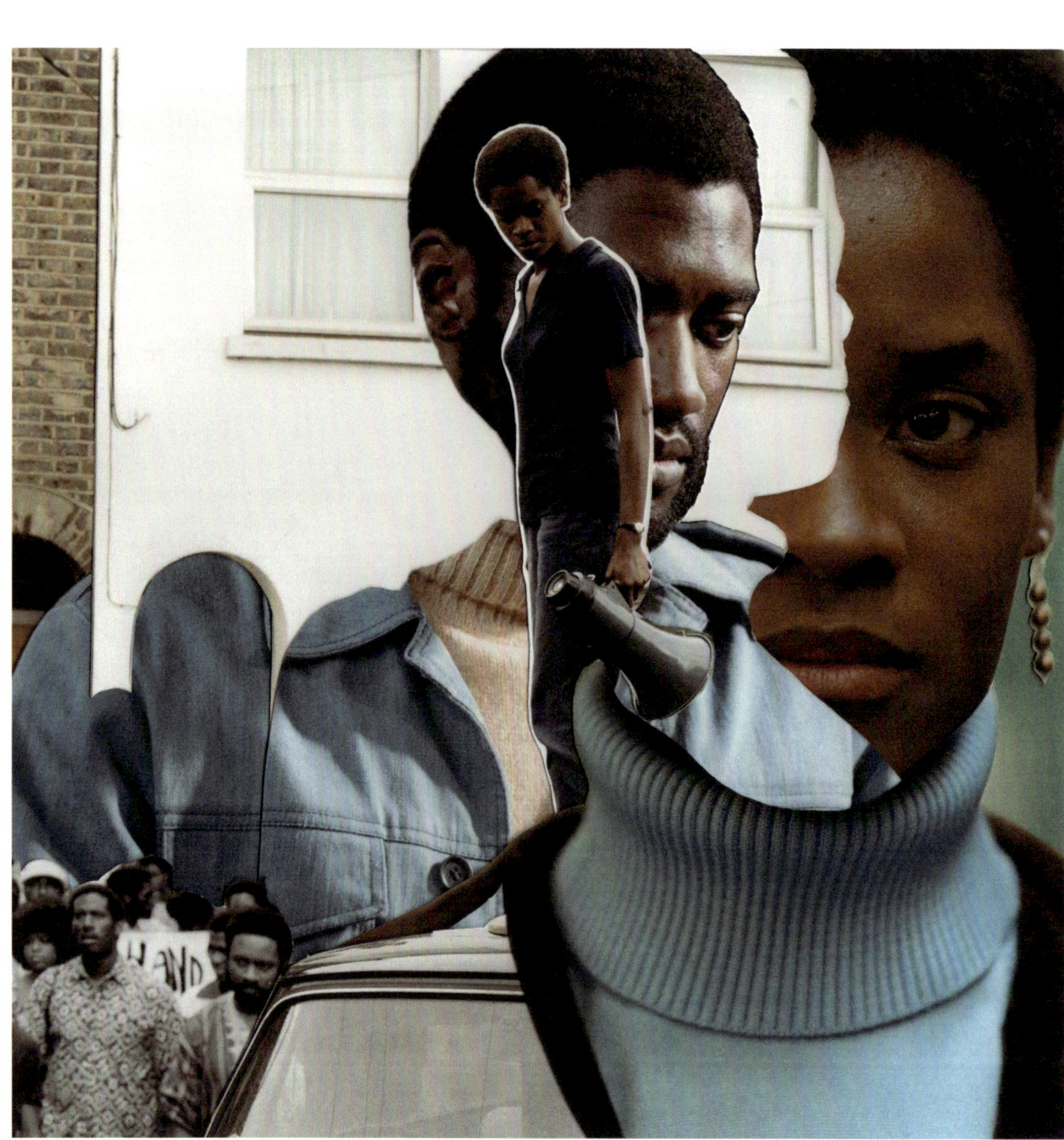

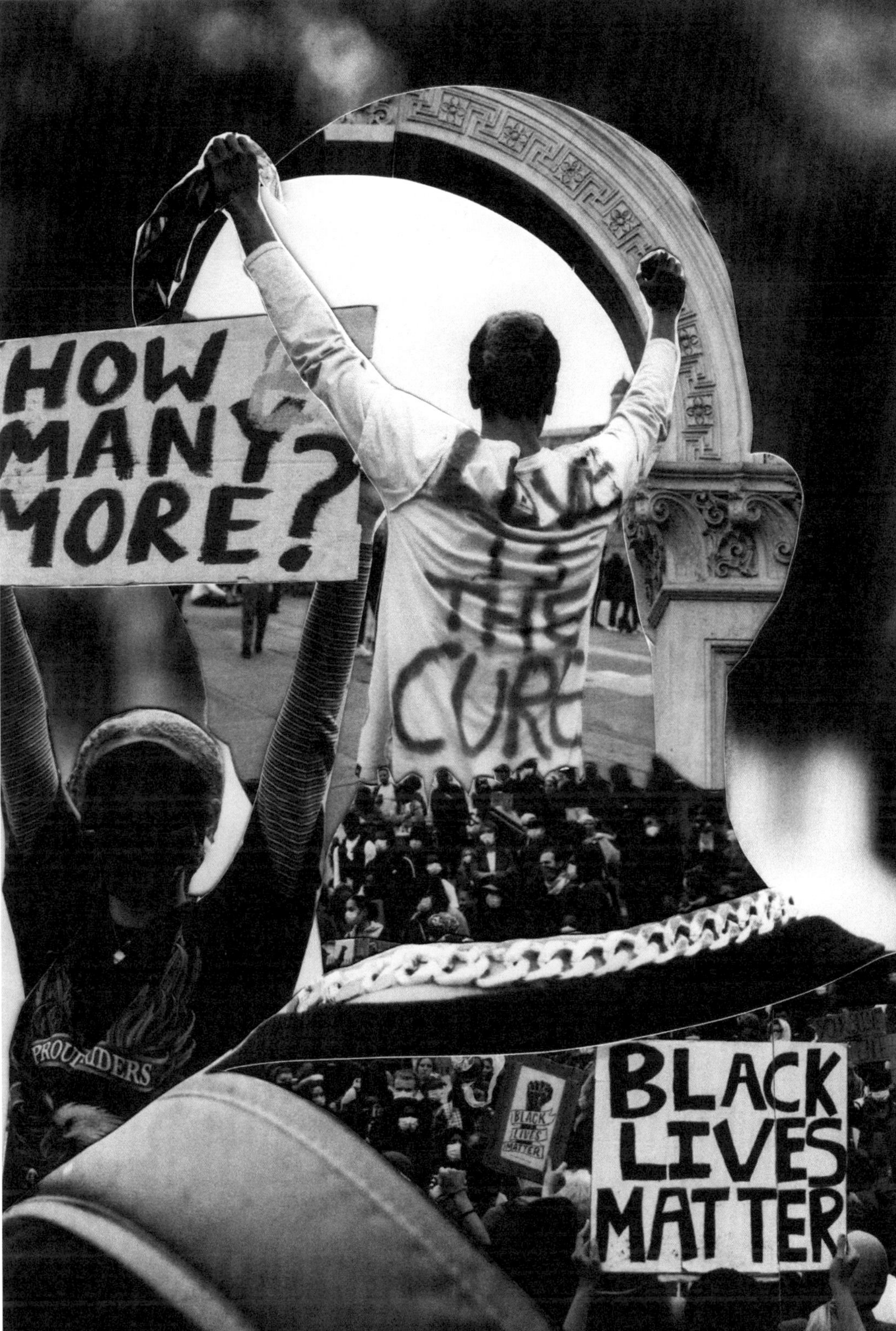
HOW
MANY
MORE?
BLACK
LIVES
MATTER

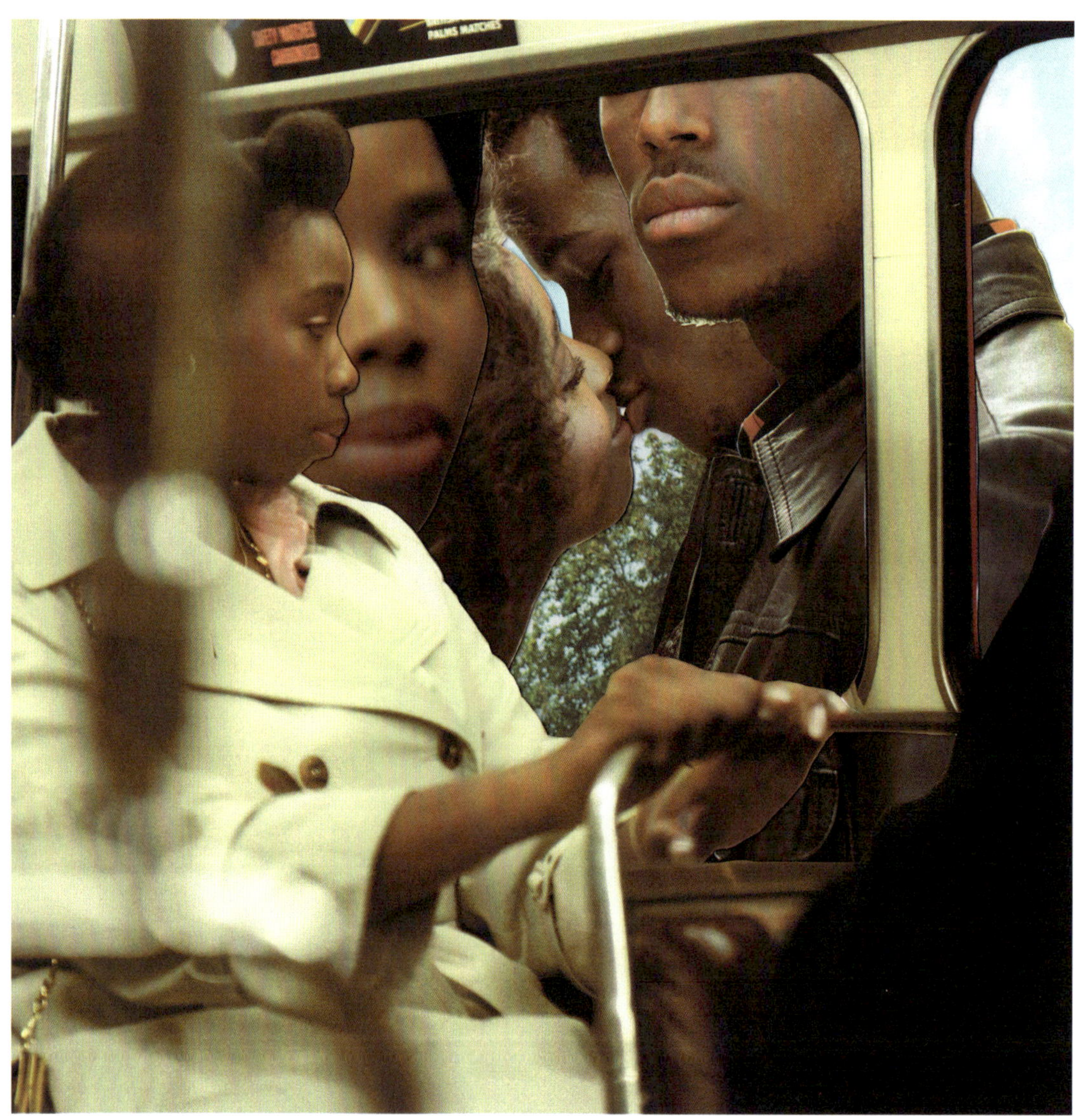
PALMS MATCHES

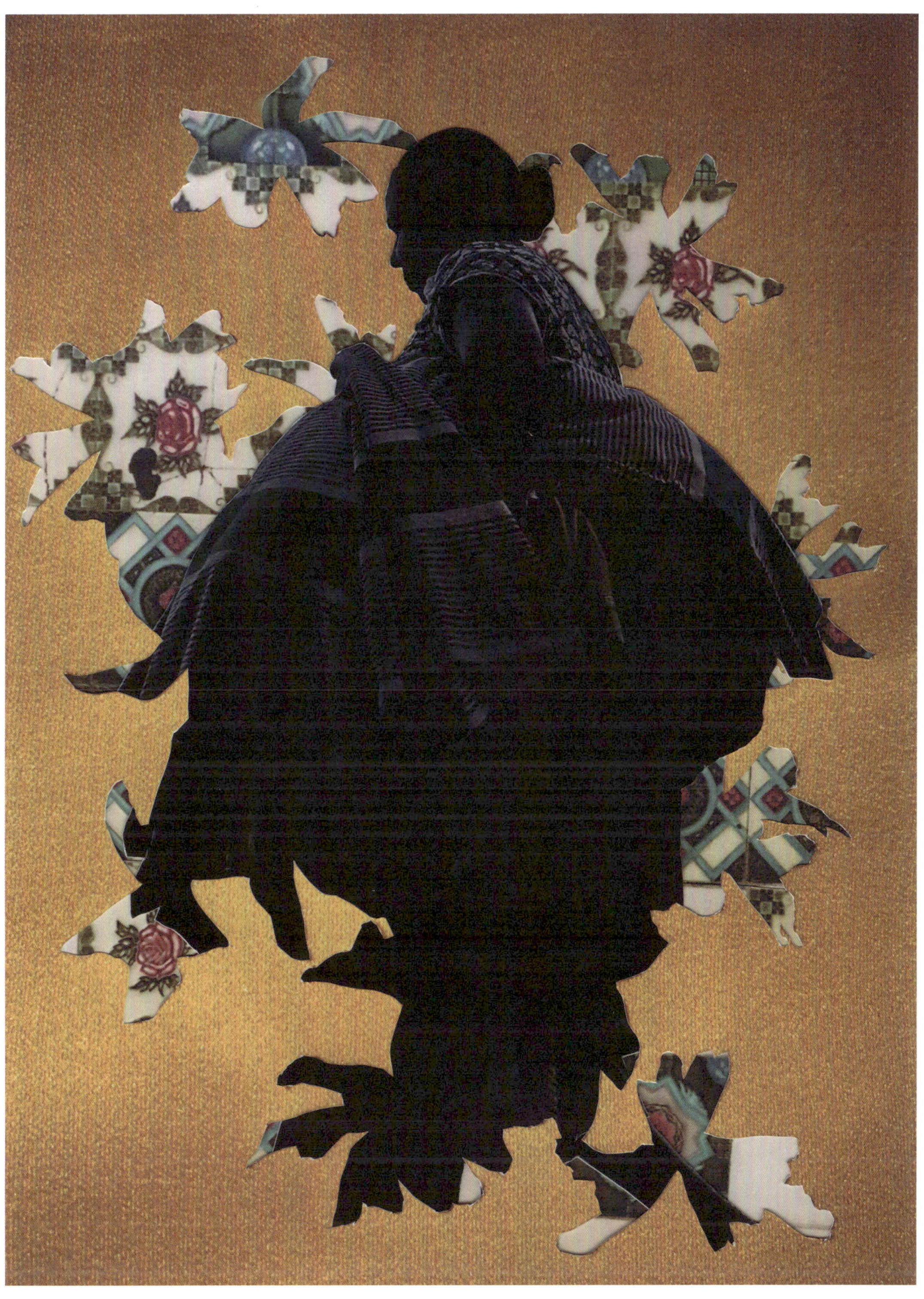

TITLE

# REVUE NOIRE

COVER

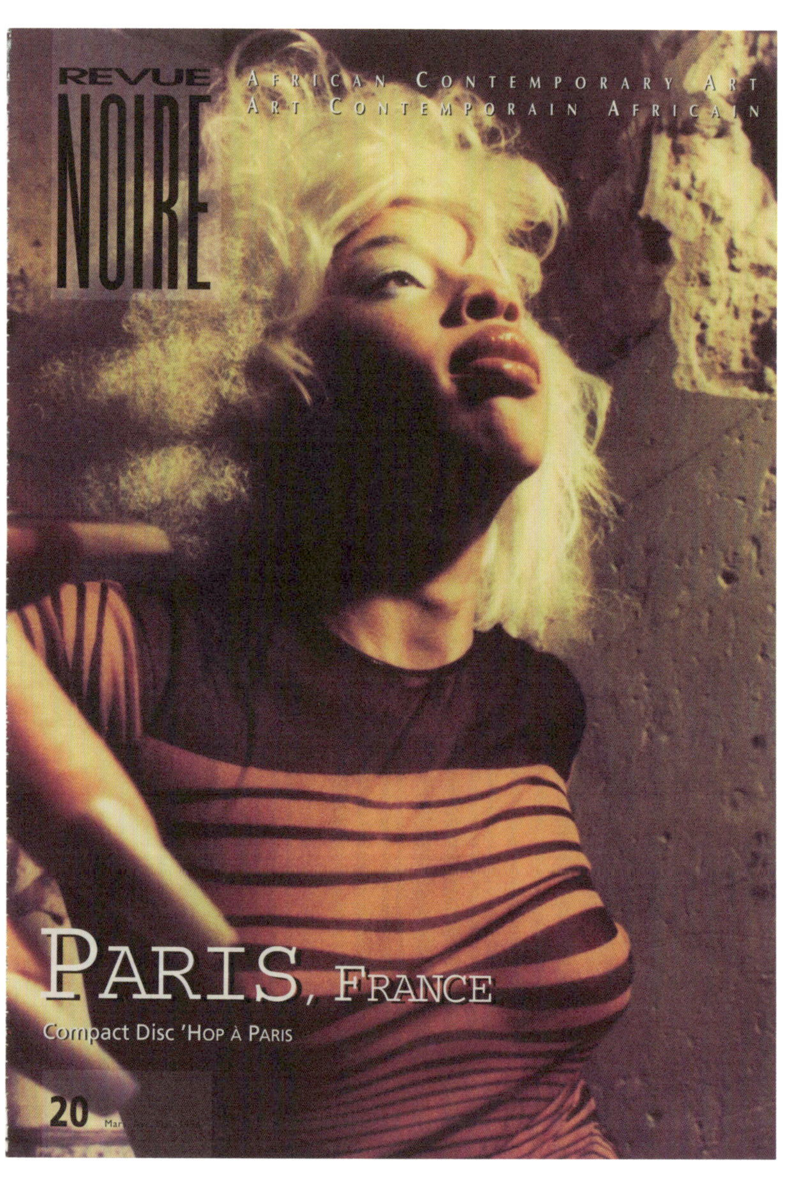

| | |
|---|---|
| PUBLISHER | Revue Noire |
| SPECIFICATIONS | REVUE NOIRE 01 // OUSMANE SOW<br><br>— 60 pages<br>— first published in 1991<br>— size: 40 × 28 cm<br><br>REVUE NOIRE 12 // MEDITERRANEAN AFRICA – BLACK AFRICA<br><br>— 68 pages<br>— first published in 1994<br>— size: 40 × 28 cm<br><br>REVUE NOIRE 20 // PARIS NOIR<br><br>— 100 pages<br>— first published in 1996<br>— size: 33 × 23 cm |
| SUMMARY | *Revue Noire* was the first bilingual investigative journal dedicated to contemporary creators from Africa and its diaspora. A quarterly, it was founded in Paris in 1990 by Jean-Loup Pivin, Simon Njami and Pascal Martin Saint Léon (later joined by N'Goné Fall) to "report on the urban modernity and creativity of the African continent and its diaspora". All forms of contemporary creation in Africa are represented: visual arts, fashion, literature, cinema, photography, design, dance and music. The first issue came out on 1 May 1991. "The Nuba Wrestlers" by the Senegalese sculptor Ousmane Sow were chosen for the cover. Over 10 years and 35 issues, the editors carried out unprecedented research. They criss-crossed Africa and most of the continents linked to it, devoting issues to Senegal, Benin, Paris, the Caribbean and the Indian Ocean.<br><br>The magazine played a major role in revealing to the French and international public the dynamic cultures accross the African continent, in all artistic disciplines. By showing a modern and urban Africa that was constantly inventing and creating, it also changed the way Westerners looked at the continent.<br><br>© Patrice Félix-Tchicaya, *Revue Noire* N°20, Paris Noir<br>© Mohammed Kacimi, *Revue Noire* N°12, Black Africa<br>Design by © Mickael Kra, *Revue Noire* N°1 African London, *Revue Noire* N°20 Hip Hop à Paris<br>© Ousmane Sow, *Revue Noire* N°1<br>p. 19 © Touhami Ennadre |

REVUE
# NOIRE

## AFRIQUE MEDITERRANEENNE
## AFRIQUE NOIRE

MEDITERRANEAN AFRICA - BLACK AFRICA

ART & LITTERATURE

12 Mars-Avril-Mai/March-April-May 1994

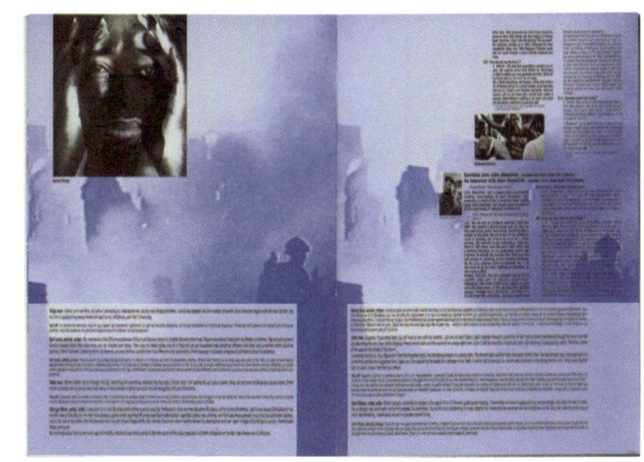

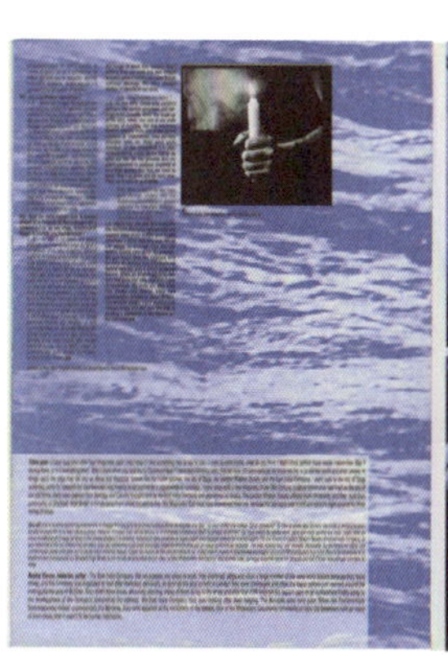

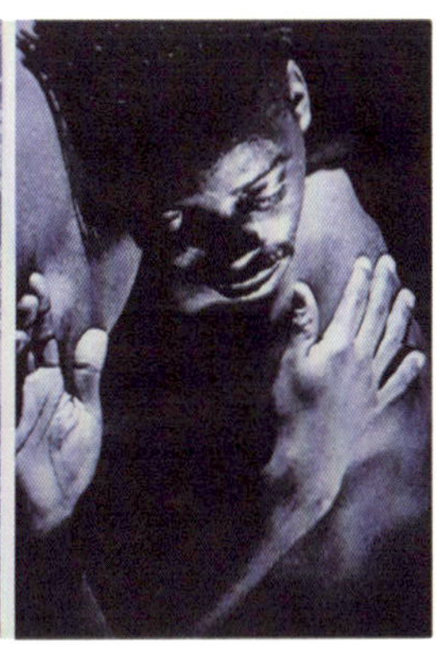

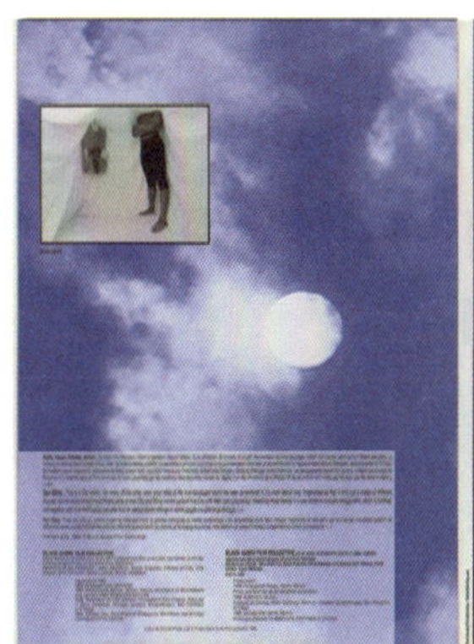

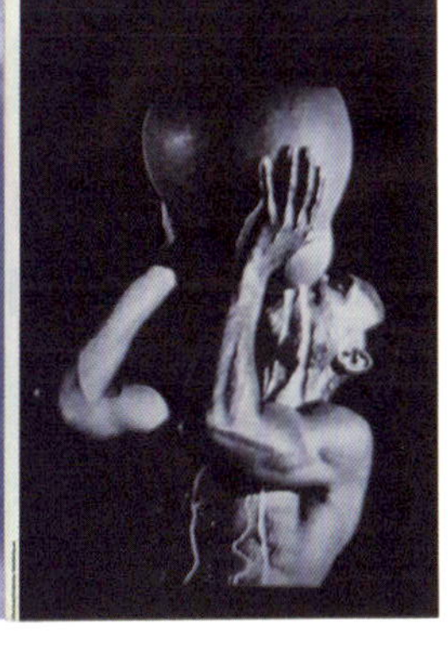

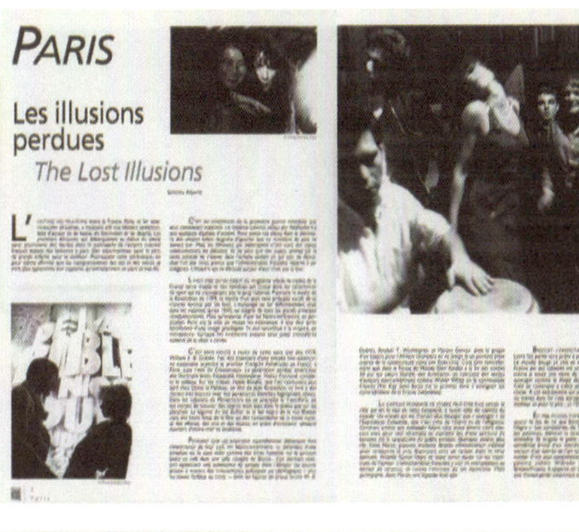

# PARIS

## Les illusions perdues

*The Lost Illusions*

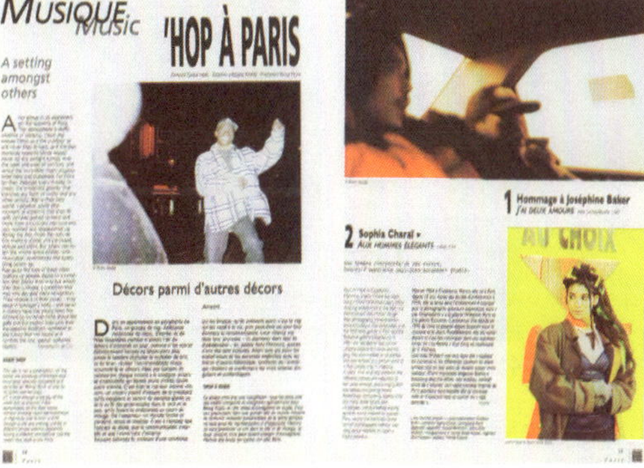

# MUSIQUE *Music*

## 'HOP À PARIS

*A setting amongst others*

### Décors parmi d'autres décors

1 Hommage à Joséphine Baker

*J'AI DEUX AMOURS*

2 Sophia Charaï »

*AUX HOMMES ÉLÉGANTS*

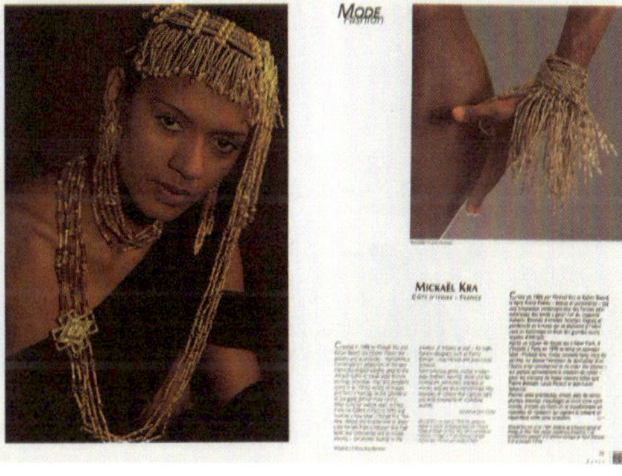

# MODE *Fashion*

## MICKAËL KRA

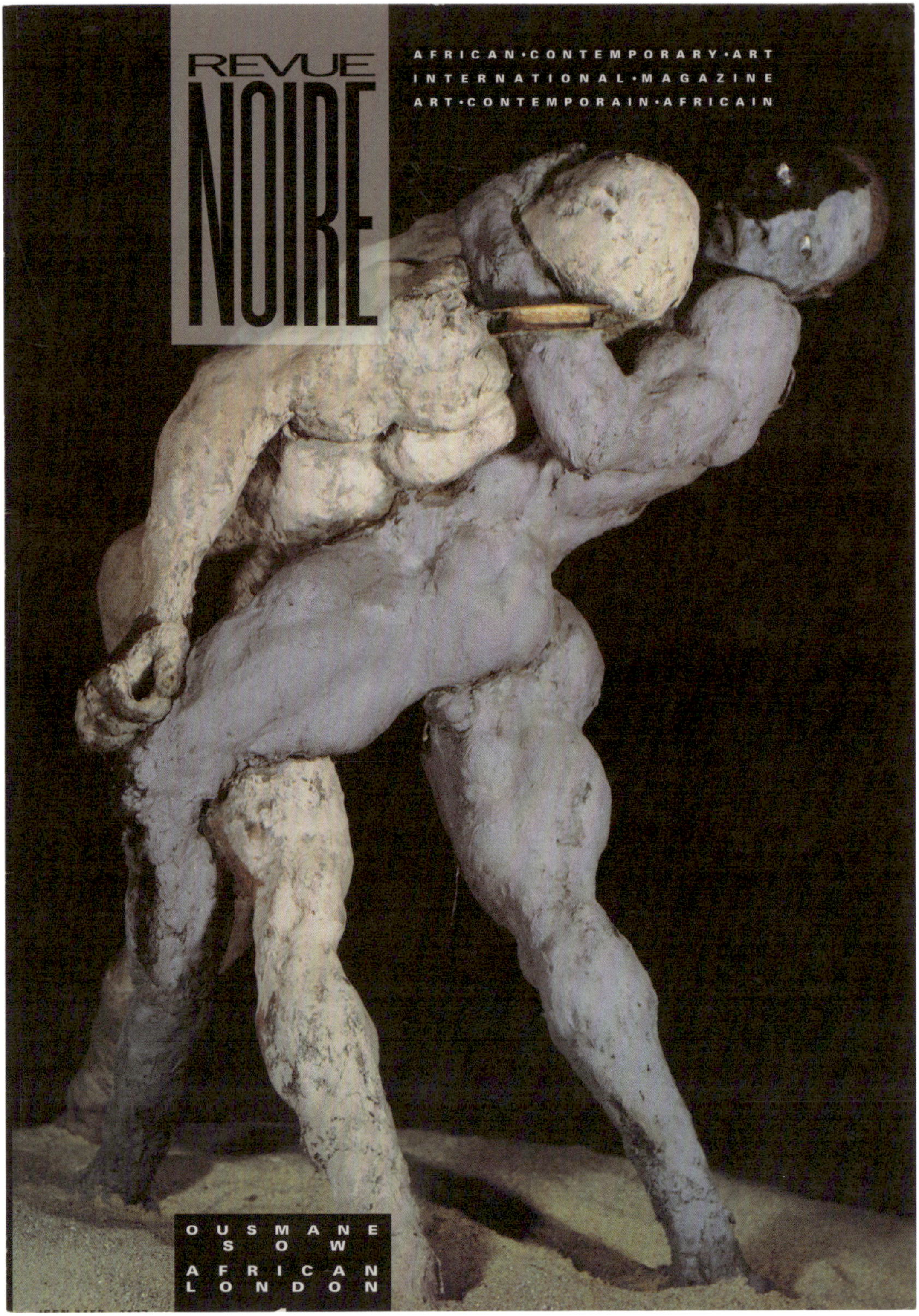

REVUE
# NOIRE

AFRICAN • CONTEMPORARY • ART
INTERNATIONAL • MAGAZINE
ART • CONTEMPORAIN • AFRICAIN

OUSMANE
SOW
AFRICAN
LONDON

1

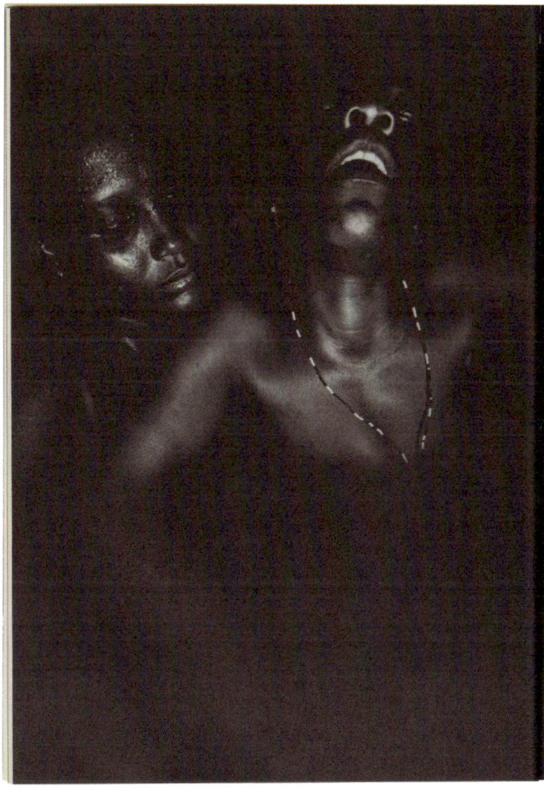

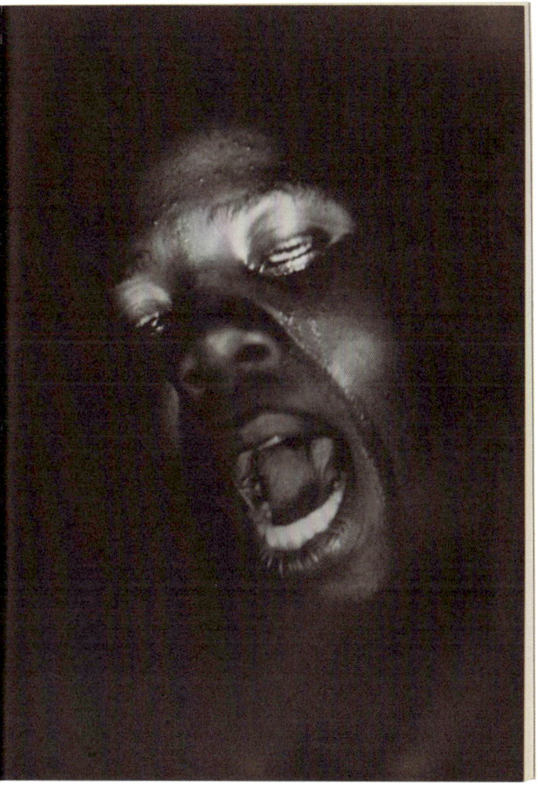

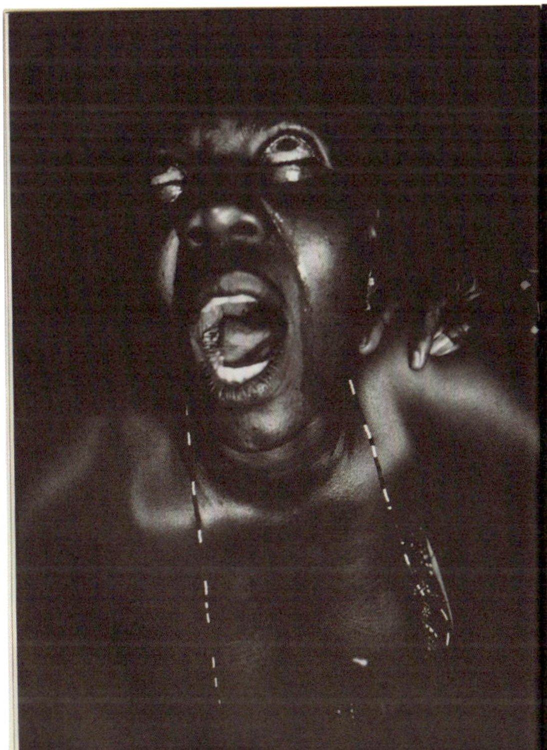

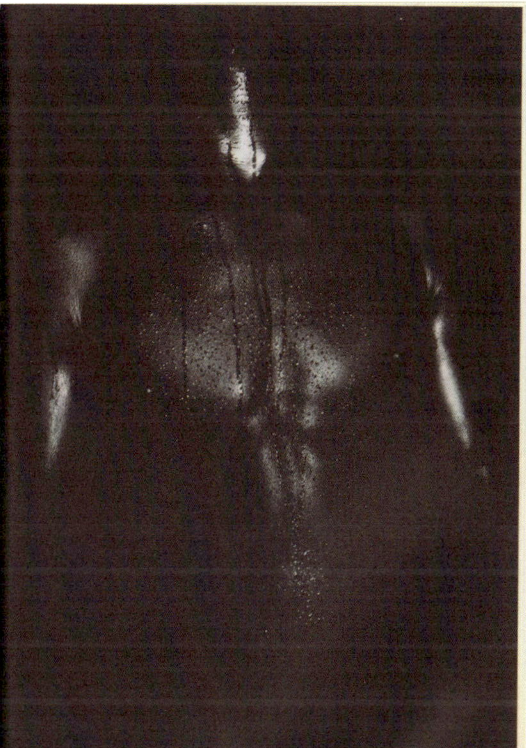

# MOHAMED BOUROUISSA

## NOUS SOMMES HALLES & PÉRIPHÉRIQUE

Mohamed Bourouissa was born in 1978 in Blida, Algeria. He studied in Paris, obtaining a DEA (master's degree) in visual arts from the University of Paris 1 Panthéon-Sorbonne and a diploma from the École Nationale Supérieure des Arts Décoratifs, specializing in photography. Today, he lives and works in Paris. His first works illustrate the tensions and issues that young people in the French suburbs are confronted with daily. Inspired by classical painting, Mohamed Bourouissa constructs his photographs like paintings. After a long immersion phase, he poses the subjects in carefully designed settings. This combination of documentary-style content and formal composition produces striking images. Mohamed Bourouissa is represented by Kamel Mennour Gallery.

"Nous sommes Halles" is Mohamed Bourouissa's first photographic series. It brings together portraits of young people from the suburbs who met in the Châtelet–Les Halles district between 2002 and 2003. The photographer made this series with a second-hand Pentax 35 mm camera, after discovering Jamel Shabazz's photographs, particularly those in the book *Back in the Days* about the emergence of hip-hop culture in New York in the 1980s. The work was produced in collaboration with anoushkashoot.

The "Périphérique" series was produced between 2005 and 2008. The book brings together photographs taken in the French suburbs of La Courneuve, Pantin, Clichy-Montfermeil, Argenteuil and Le Mirail, intending to bring in the "missing images": those that are not in the newspapers or on gallery walls. The artist plays with the stereotypical representations of the mass media and tries to deconstruct prejudices.

"Nous sommes Halles" with *anoushkashoot* (2003–2005)
© Mohamed Bourouissa in collaboration with anoushkashoot, courtesy Kamel Mennour Paris and London

"Périphérique" (2005–2008)
© Mohamed Bourouissa, courtesy Kamel Mennour Paris and London and Blum & Poe Los Angeles
*La république*, 2006
*L'impasse*, 2007
*Le reflet*, 2007
*Périphérique*, 2007
*Le cercle imaginaire*, 2008
*La fenêtre*, 2005

*Périphérique*
Texts by Clément Chéroux et Taous Dahmani
Loose Joints Publishing, 2021

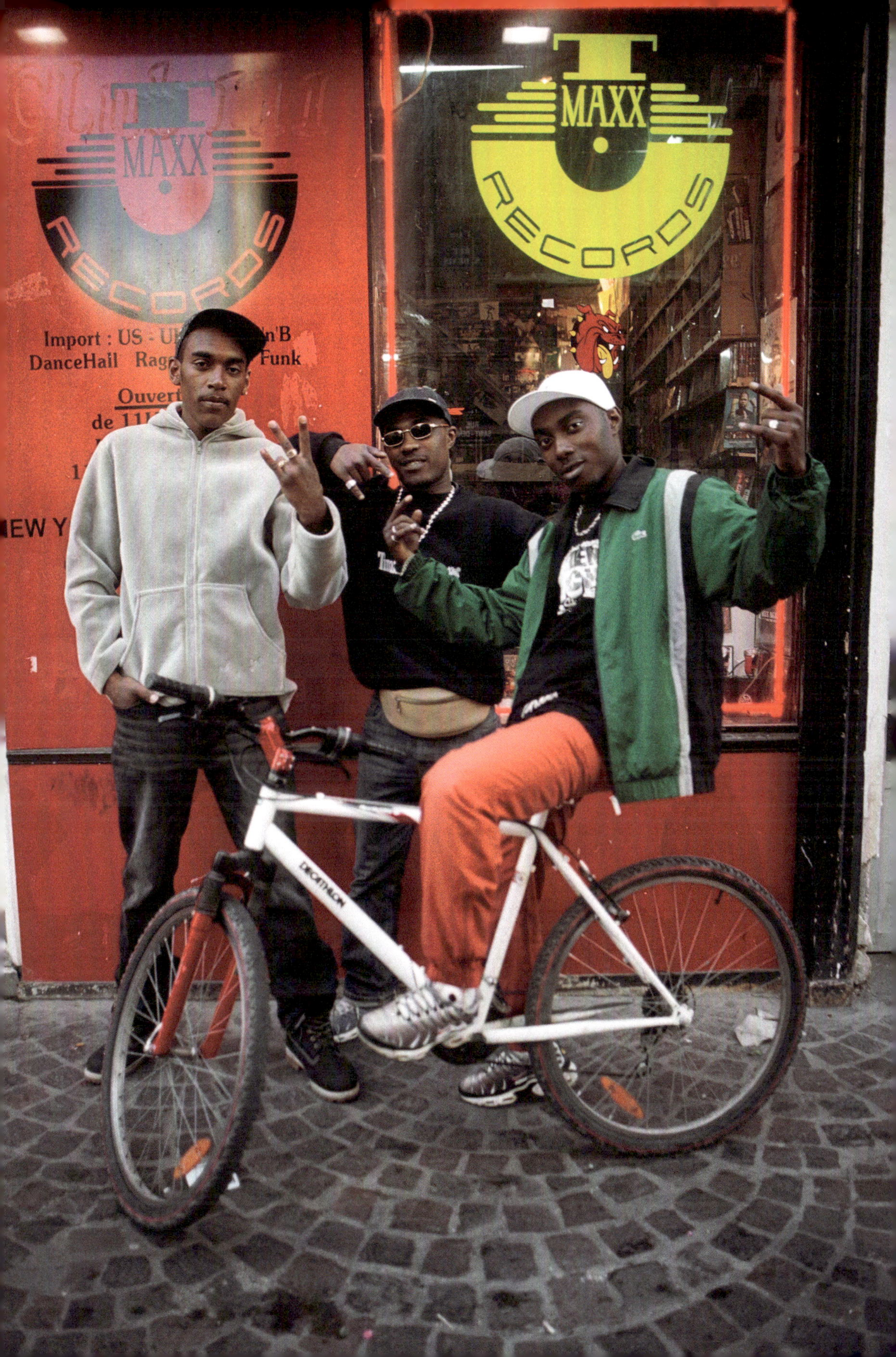
MAXX
RECORDS
Import : US -
DanceHail
Funk
Ouvert
MAXX
RECORDS
DECATHLON

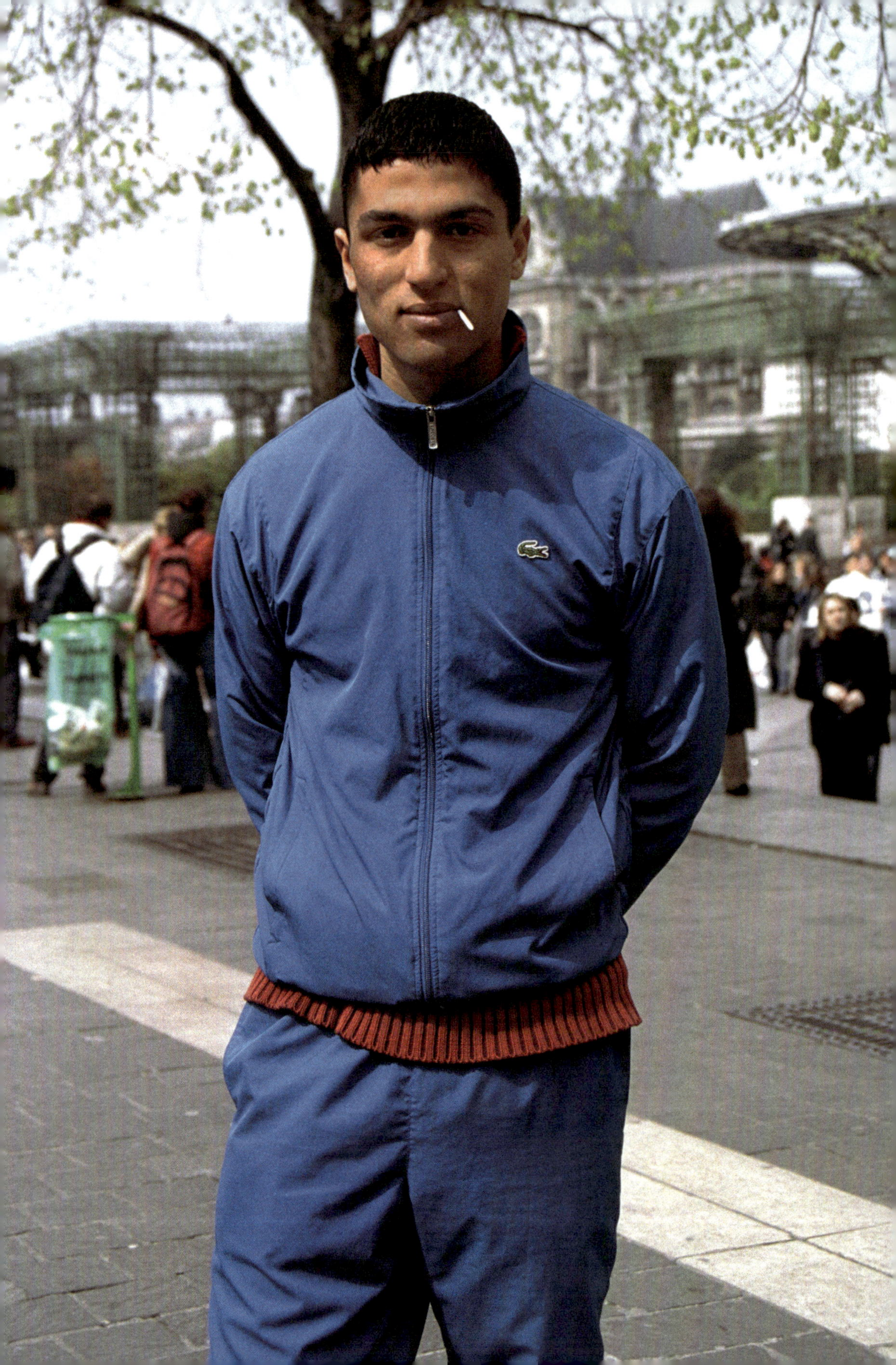

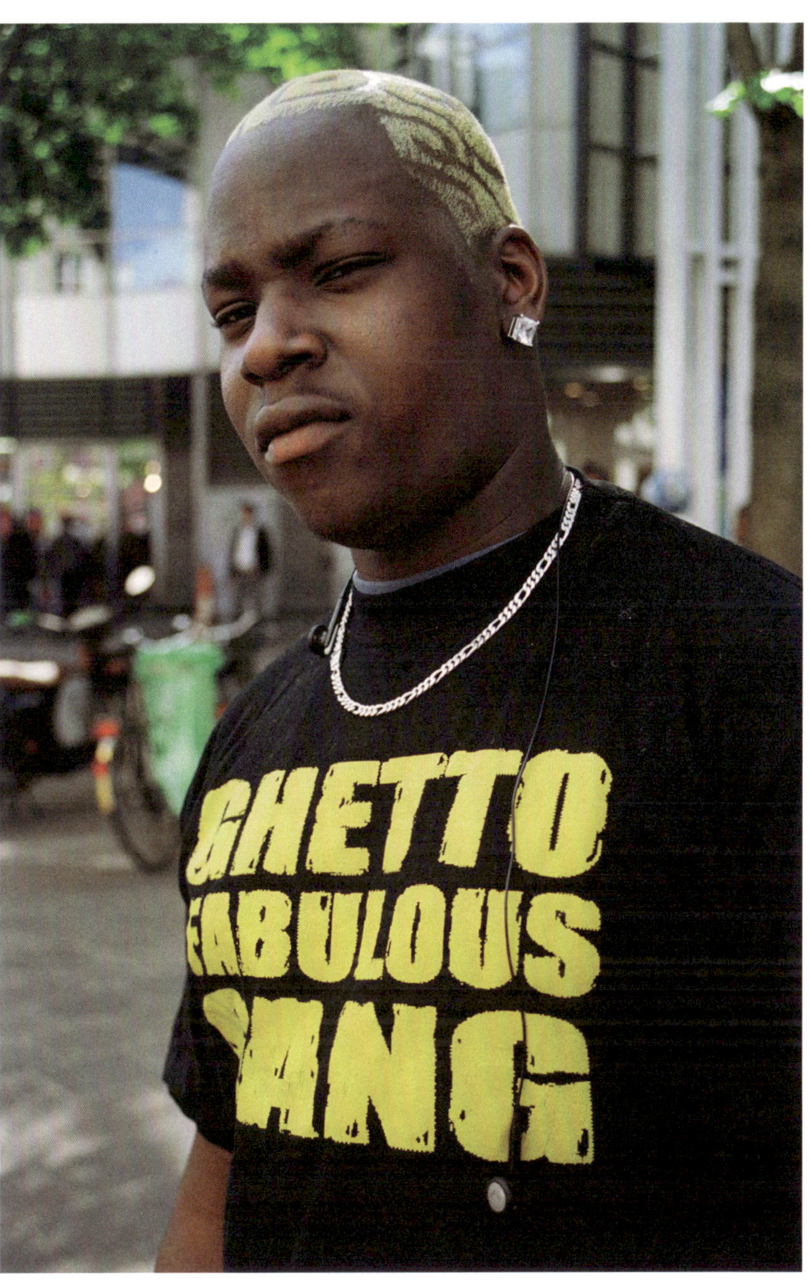
GHETTO
FABULOUS
GANG

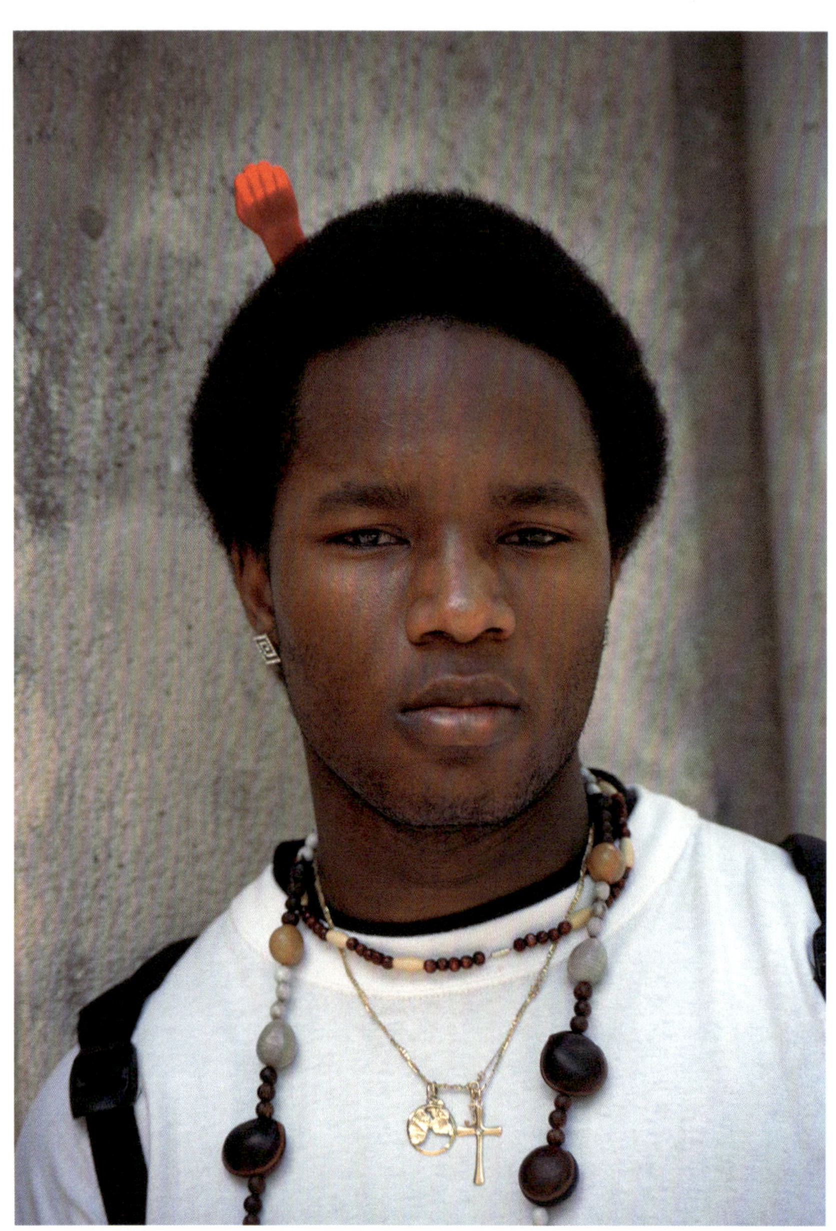

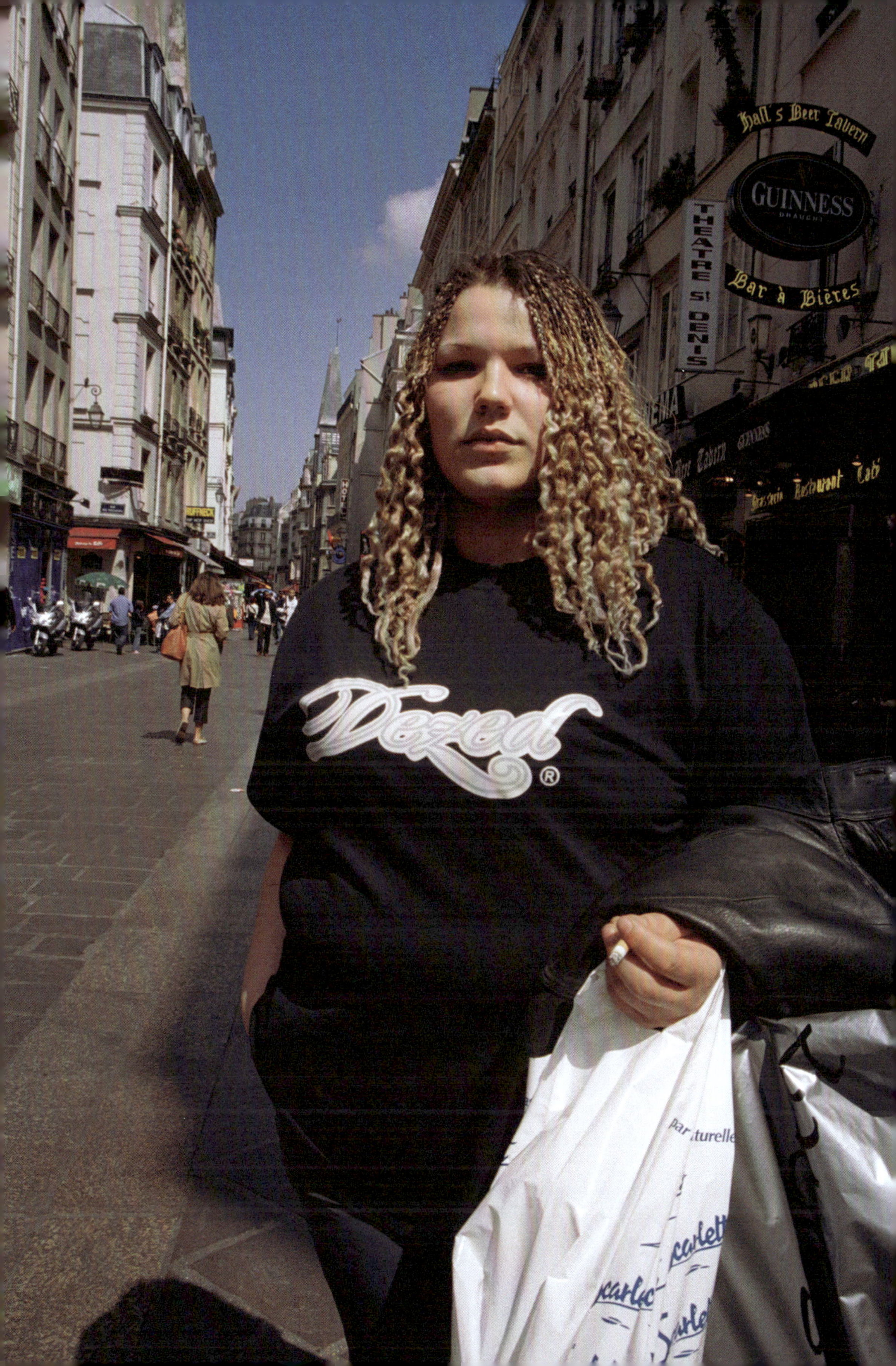
Hall's Beer Tavern
GUINNESS
THEATRE St DENIS
Bar à Bières
Dezed®
Restaurant Café

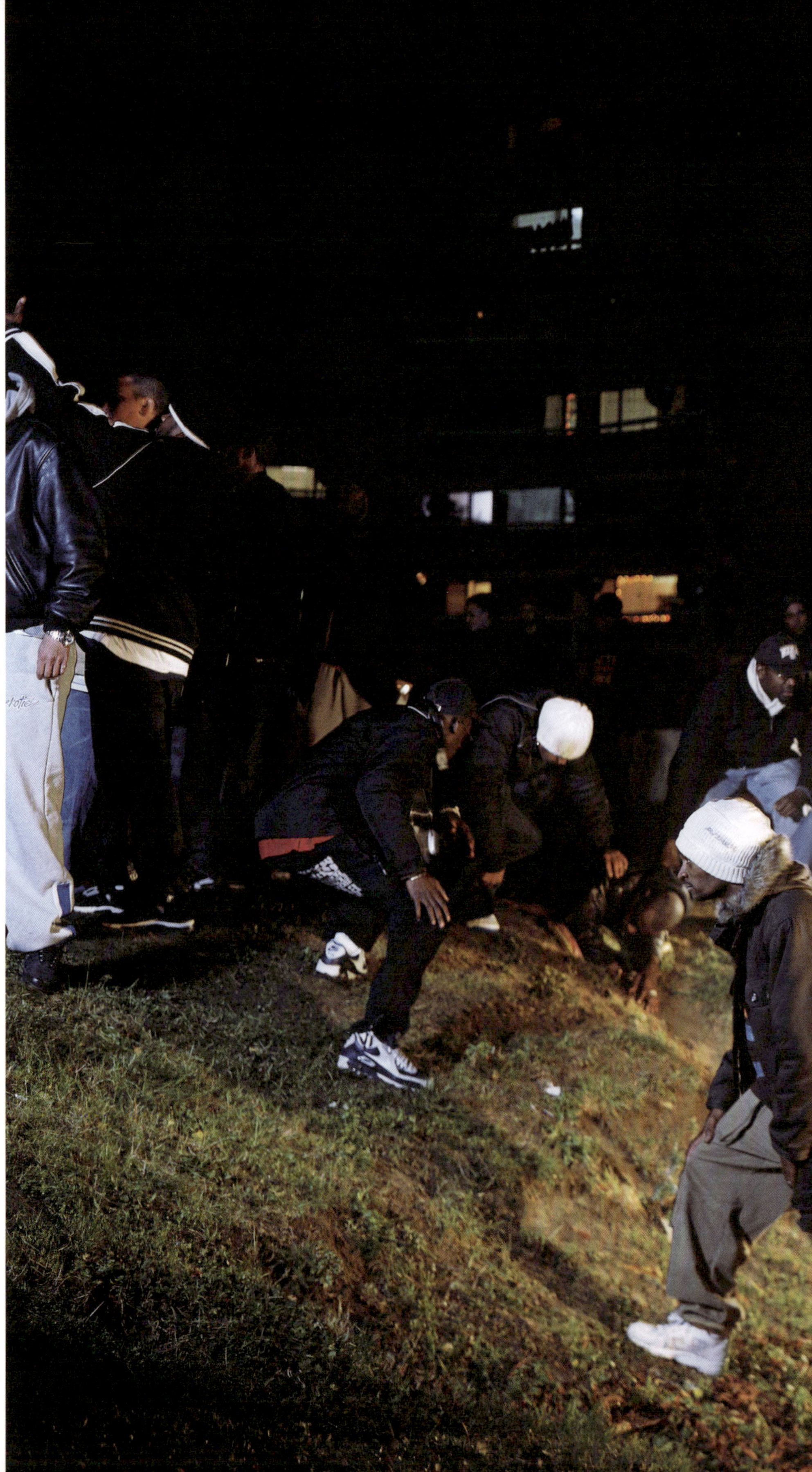

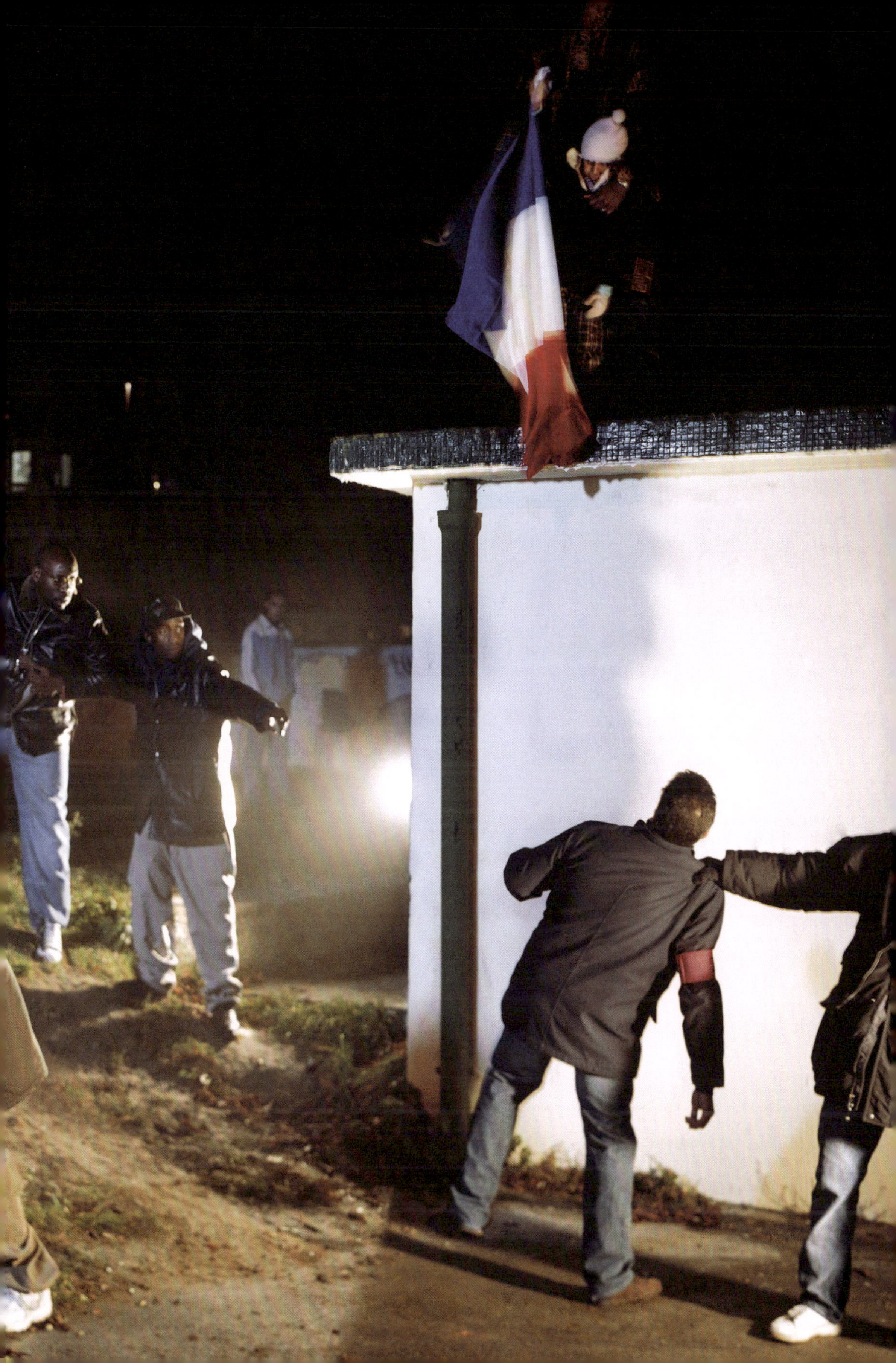

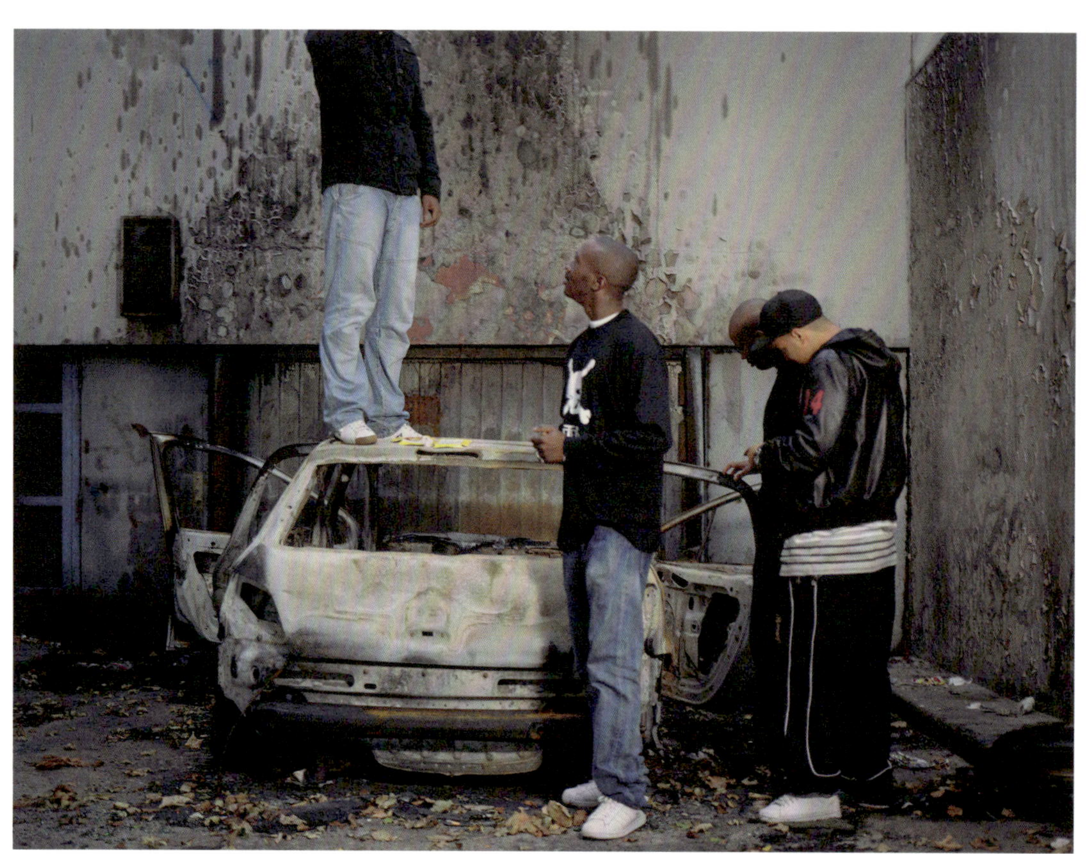

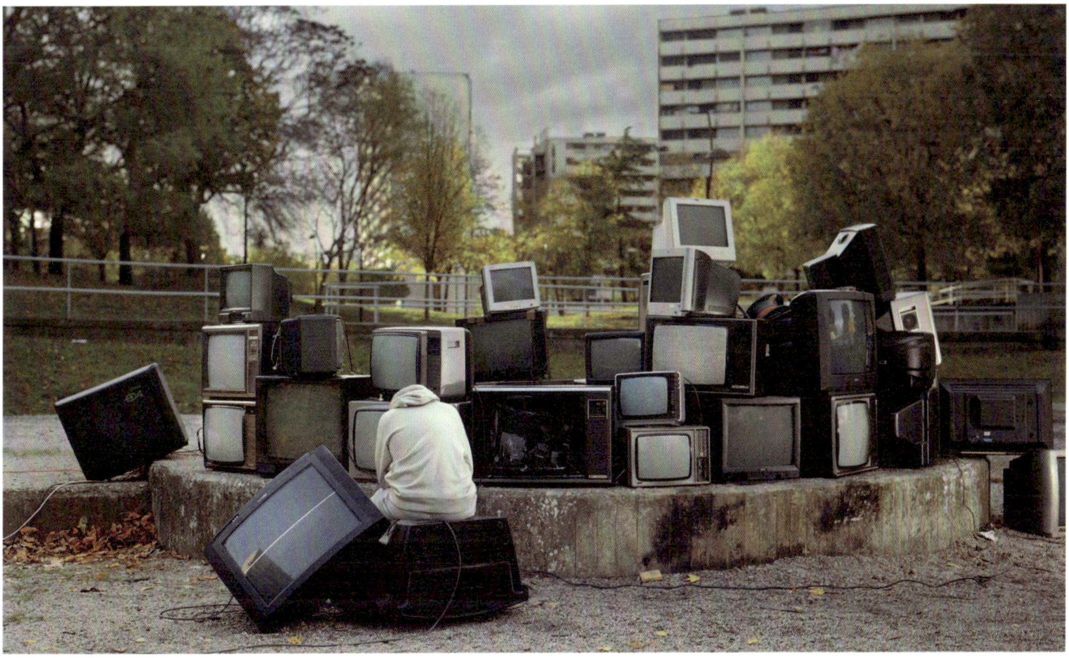

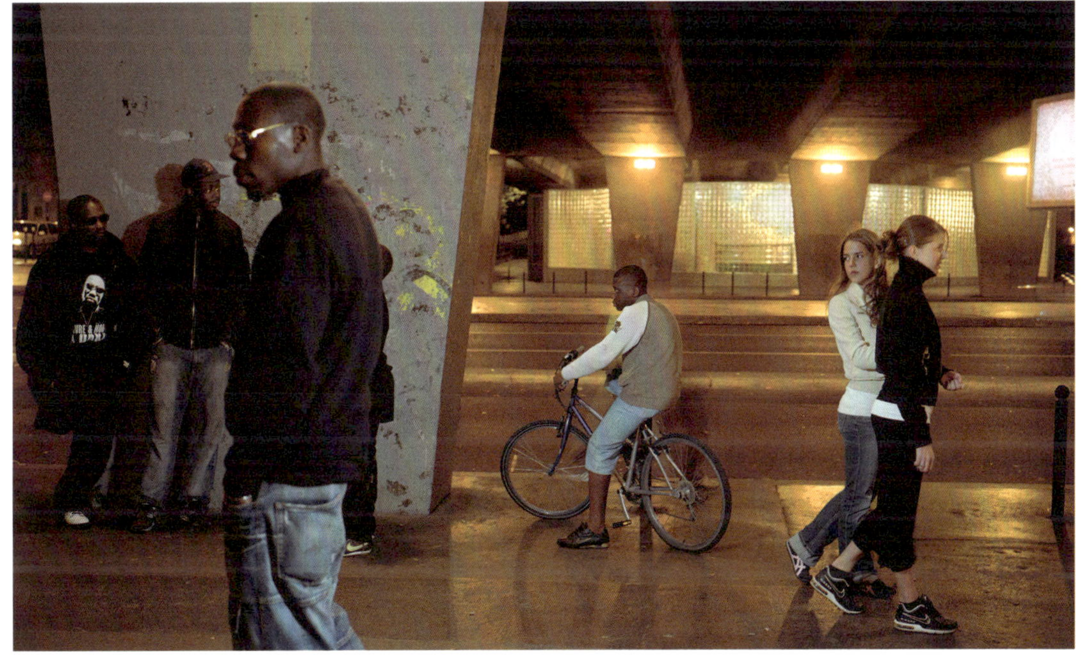

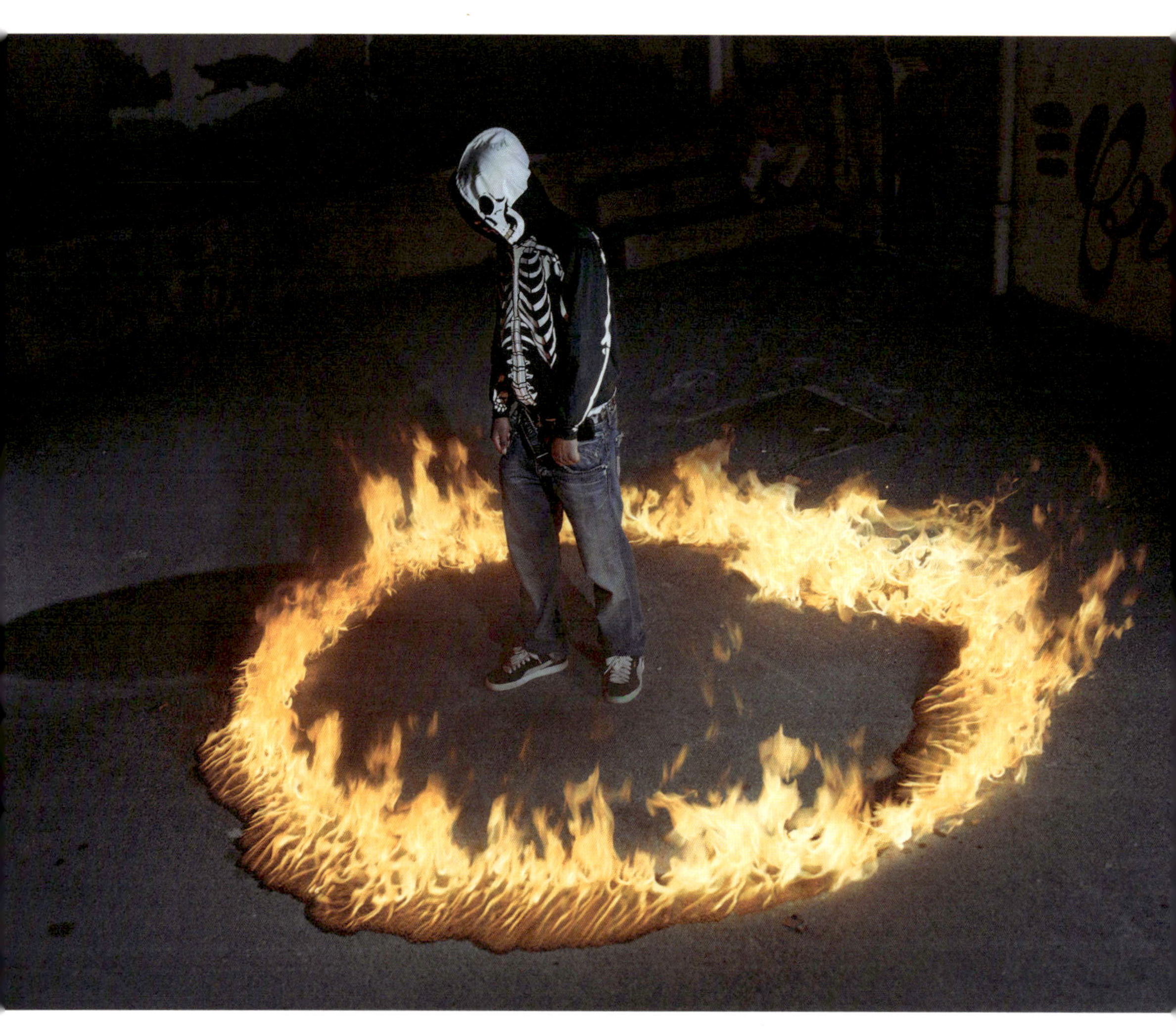

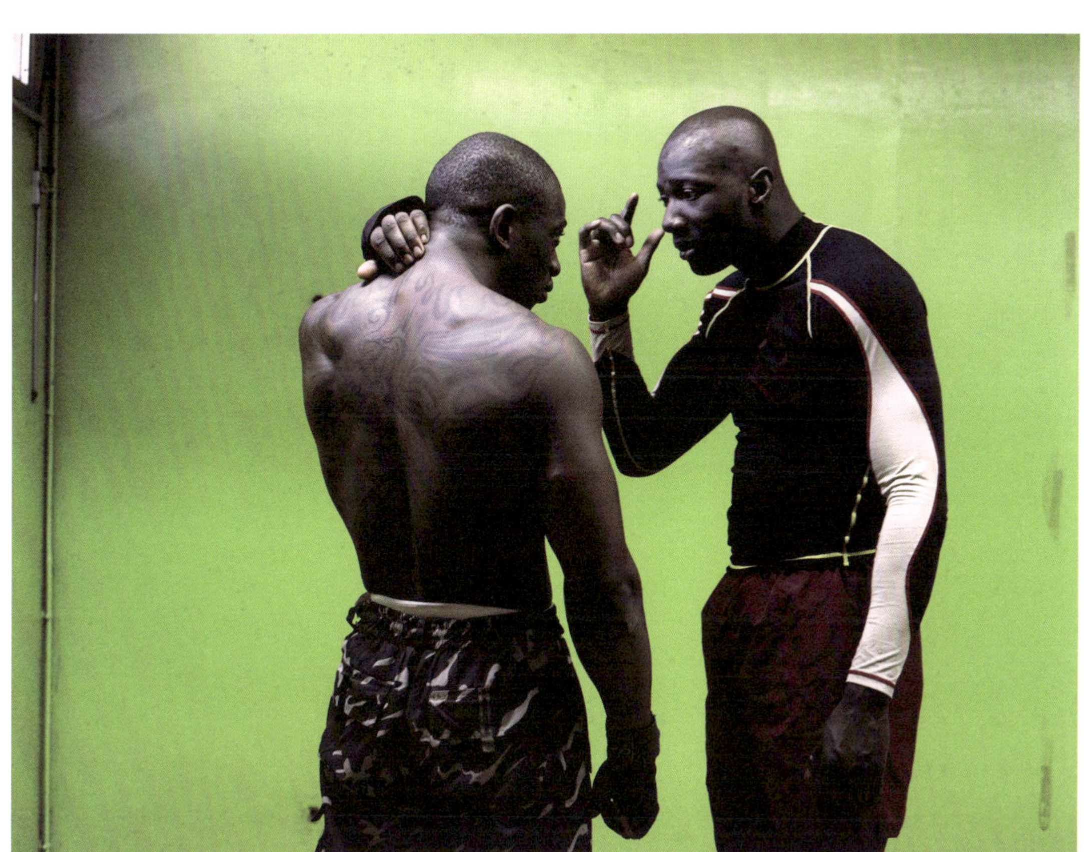

# SPECTRES AND TEXTURES: THE B—SIDE WINS AGAIN

Text and images
by Johny Pitts
Guest curator

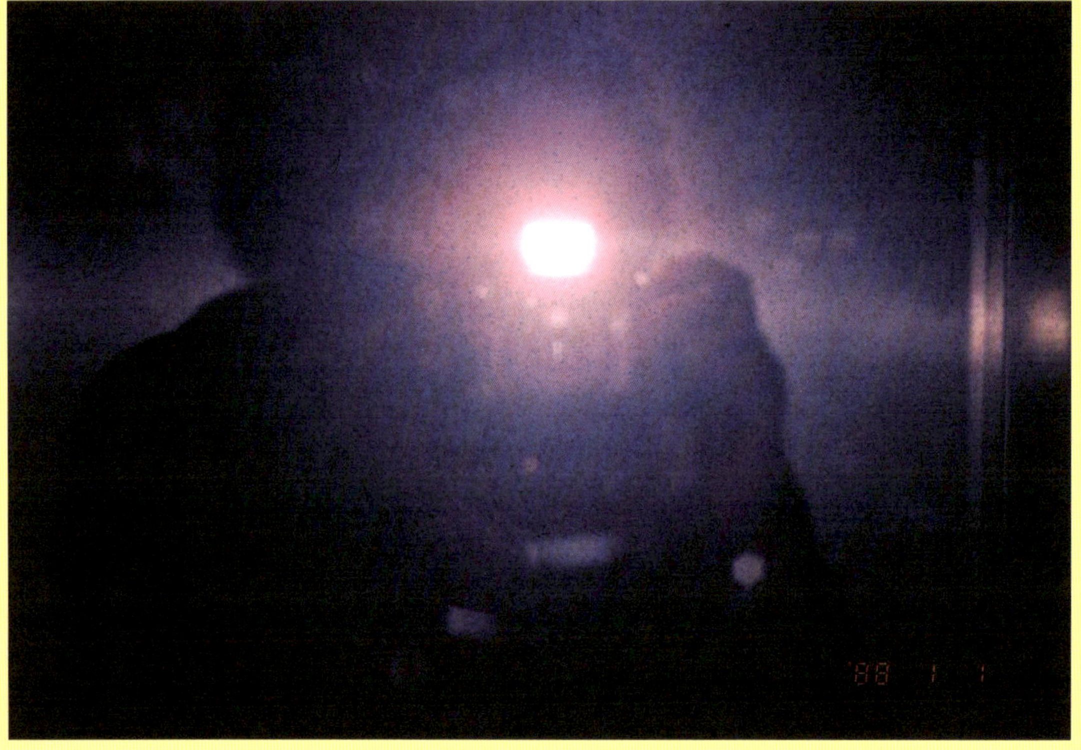

*Self Portrait*, 2017

Like the best photography, the power of a portmanteau often lies in its ability to be succinct yet plural. As somebody with brown skin growing up in Europe, "Afropean", a neologism that emerged in the 1990s, seemed to celebrate multiple cultural allegiances, but also suggested a way of thinking about myself and my community that was whole and unhyphenated. There was something wonderful about its neatness and compactness and its ability to conjure, in just four syllables, a thousand possibilities and configurations. A confounded white Portuguese man born in Mozambique once asked me, "Am I an Afropean?" An Algerian woman wondered about the place of the Maghreb in the term, reminding me that Algeria is the biggest country in Africa, and a British Jamaican friend said the term was diasporic, and in English the 'ean' in Afropean didn't just stand for European, but also for Caribbean.

Initially, I wanted Afropean to suggest something entirely aspirational. The term emerged out of what came to be known as the "world music" scene, and was coined by David Byrne and Marie Daulne from Zap Mama in 1991 – Byrne of course influential in developing "world" and "ambient" music with Brian Eno and Ryuichi Sakamoto during the preceding decade. Often, music from the US or Britain was known simply as music, whereas anything outside the States or Europe was labelled world music, and so the term is guilty of centring hegemonic powers – "the West and the rest" – which is why there is sometimes a cynical response to it. I think, however, that it was a real attempt to look at shared experiences and commonalities across cultures, which is ultimately what I wanted to achieve with Afropean; to piece this "world" scene back together somehow, using Afropean as a success story of multiculturalism.

As I tried to apply it to the everyday reality of the Black community, outside of the music and fashion industry from where it originally emerged, the term was challenged and ultimately fell apart. I couldn't be quite as oblivious to the dark side of the postcolonial state of play as world music was, couldn't exclude working-class multicultural communities like the one I was born and raised in in Sheffield, England. I realized that if I was going to use this term, Afropean had to function outside the demands of a global market place, connecting Black radical politics with the forgotten notion of internationalism, which over time was swamped up by globalization in neoliberal capitalist terms.

Afropean felt like something I could anchor myself to, but that didn't mean it should signify something monolithic – it needed to be allowed to shift and move as a term, functioning in antithesis to the way nationalism does, with its ethnic absolutism and blood and soil narrative. It needed to be a site of fusion and blurring.

I began searching for stories lurking beneath the surface of Europe and the shadows under the corporate gleam of globalization. To use a musical analogy, Europe was promoting its A-side, but I was more interested to hear its B-side. From my starting point – somebody with brown skin living in Europe – it was important to think of Afropean as belonging to a long lineage of traditions from across the globe that have sought to offer counter-narratives of togetherness; things and people connecting and moving outside or beyond the realms of officialdom.

I WANTED TO PIECE THIS "WORLD" SCENE BACK TOGETHER SOMEHOW, USING AFROPEAN AS A SUCCESS STORY OF MULTICULTURALISM

# THE B-SIDE IS A CULTURE THAT IS CONSTANTLY IN DANGER OF BEING CANCELLED BY PLACES OF OFFICIALDOM

Towards a B-side aesthetic

When a series of Wong Kar-Wai films from the 1980s and 1990s were digitally remastered recently, the Hong Kong auteur was a little tentative, because he knew something important about the way in which his films had often reached an audience when they first came out – as bootleg VHS tapes smuggled out of Hong Kong, which is certainly how I first discovered his work in my teens back in Sheffield. I have beautiful neon-drenched memories of a pirated copy of *Chungking Express*, with its glitches and inconsistent audio, rolling tape lines and bad tracking mixed with the street scenes shot by Wong Kar-Wai's cinematographer Christopher Doyle; murky yet glowing all at the same time. The original reels – captured on the fly on Agfa film, using the natural ambience of Hong Kong in addition to the atmosphere added by poor-quality dubbing and tracking – created an intoxicating brew.

At play here is, of course, a certain nostalgia for another period that VHS tapes – and old formats in general – embody, but there is also the feeling-tone encoded by a process and a path. The bad quality of these videotapes involved subaltern, clandestine manoeuvres. Who was involved? Which authorities had to be circumnavigated? Which scene did you need to be part of to get your hands on a copy (I got mine from a Chinese man who would sell them at my Caribbean barbershop)?

If it isn't simply about nostalgia, neither is it merely a valorization of the "underground" or the black market as a big fuck-you to "the system". No, it is something simpler. The quality of these pirated videos made you feel that the work wasn't just filmed in the Chungking Mansions (a Hong Kong high-rise filled with migrants from all over Africa and Asia, and commerce that is both over and under the counter), but was *of* the Chungking Mansions – made from the same stuff, passed through the same channels; was, in its path through commerce and its materiality, part of the thing being documented. I have no doubt that many bootleg versions of *Chungking Express* actually did pass through the Chungking Mansions at some point, which leads me to the conclusion that *Chungking Express* on a pirated VHS is a more evocative document of Chungking in 1994 than it is on a restored DVD; that there are stories outside the stories, unofficial narratives not overtly present in the sanctioned version, not necessarily even authored or desired by their creator – weird, hard-to-pin-down embodied energies housed in objects with alternative histories, thus suggesting alternative futures. Let's call these hidden stories, these spectral energies,[1] capable of conjuring up a kind of dark magic, the "B-side".

To continue with Wong Kar-Wai for a moment: through the bootlegging, his films acquired a certain patina, an unintended after-effect that has reverberated through the years without his consent and adopted a life and beauty of its own. In the African American tradition this notion surfaces in the form of the "concrete rose". Everyone from Ben E. King ("[A Rose in] Spanish Harlem") to Aretha Franklin ("A Rose is Still a Rose") and Tupac Shakur (his recurring theme of "The Concrete Rose") has asked us to admire the rose that hasn't been nurtured, the rose that is dishevelled and dirty, with a crooked stem and tatty petals. No one asked this rose to grow; its home is a crack in the sidewalk, yet it miraculously emerges anyway. The aforementioned artists want us to see beauty in this rose. In fact, they suggest that this rose may even be more beautiful than the prettiest, most perfect rose you might find in a well-tended garden. What is this alternative beauty of the concrete rose? It is the beauty of the B-side.

Though this certainly isn't an exclusively Black idea or aesthetic, Black practitioners have often championed the B-side because of their enforced proximity to it, and have

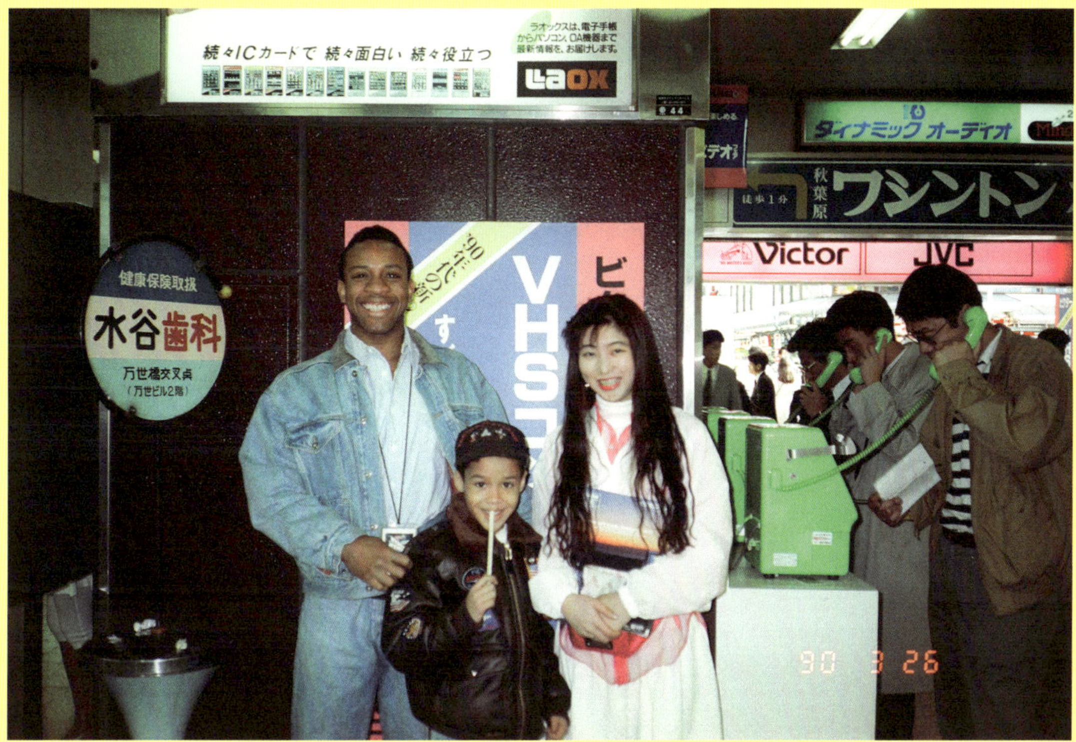


*VHS, Tokyo*, 1990 (From "The Bubble Era Archive")

produced much work across all creative fields that has invoked its ambiguous, sometimes contradictory qualities. The British sociologist Paul Gilroy has argued that, serving as a counterculture to modernity, Black Atlantic cultures with one foot in and one foot out of Western capitalism (kept at a certain proximity to it by way of subjugation) have documented and channelled the injustices, tragedies and narratives of disenfranchised experiences through indirect methods using what he calls "vernacular culture". Encoded within a James Brown yell, for instance, is the acknowledgement of the impossibility of words to express the horrors of pain and injustice lurking within the Black experience. When he shouts "get up!" more is going on than might first appear: it is an expression of the inexpressible; the struggle of being Black in a white man's world. John Akomfrah, formerly of the Black Audio Film Collective, one of the most important visual interventions in Black British history, corroborated this notion when speaking about a song by the blues musician Howlin' Wolf, entitled "Forty Four", after the .44 Magnum pistol. Akomfrah remembers listening to it, ruminating, " 'What the hell is he angry about?' Because what is animating the song is actually not present in the song itself."[2] Akomfrah came to an understanding that the *vibe* of the music served as a mysterious entry point to discover the issues behind the anger, preserving information in a way that expressed the inability to truly convey it but nonetheless carried with it the spectre of a journey, of a people a place and a time – a haunting that lurks somewhere in the recorded material, even if only in abstract terms. To make my point again: stories outside the stories, unofficial narratives not overtly present in the official narrative, not necessarily even authored or desired by their creator. Hidden, spectral stories. The B-side.

This is an important, subversive way of transferring information and is very often the way Black communities have managed to keep a culture alive despite continuous attempts by the West – from the transatlantic slave trade to colonialism (and perhaps

## WHAT MAKES ART BEAUTIFUL IS ABOUT MUCH MORE THAN TECHNIQUE, BUT ABOUT STRUGGLE, SOUL, LIFE; A DANCE WITH THE WORLD

now neoliberal algorithms) to cancel it. It always amuses me when people – usually middle-aged, middle-class white men who've benefited from these systems – have the temerity to warn young Black kids of the dangers of "cancel culture": who, really, has historically been cancelling who?! The B-side is a culture that is constantly in danger of being cancelled by places of officialdom – the working-class photographer not taken seriously by recipients of hedge funds controlling the arts sector, the musician who won't get played on the radio ... this rejection either destroys subaltern creativity or inspires practitioners to forge alternative routes to production and distribution.

When I spoke to my friend and collaborator the poet Roger Robinson, he mentioned that what sustained Black art was the conversation it had with God – a belief that sustains a practitioner when no one else is watching or listening. God in this case could mean being connected to a religion, or simply mean being in tune with the spiritual world, a faith that things will work out despite being faced with overwhelming evidence to the contrary. A faith that is transmittable. The singer D'Angelo spoke of this in connection with his Baptist church: "They used to say: 'Don't go up there [to perform on stage] for no form or fashion.' So I guess what that means is: listen, we're up here singing for the Lord, so don't be up here trying be cute, 'cause we don't care about all that, we just want to feel what the spirit is moving through you."[3] David Byrne echoed this when he said, in the recording of the Talking Heads' tour "Stop Making Sense": "The better a singer's voice, the harder it is to believe what they're saying, so I use my faults to an advantage." It may not be quite that simple (Donny Hathaway had a "better" voice, yet I believe every word he sang), but what D'Angelo and Byrne are getting at is that "perfection" when used in its most banal sense is often merely a veneer that robs us of a deeper truth. As it pertains to photography, this notion is especially true in an era of filtered Instagram selfies and perhaps also in so much street photography that captures a "decisive moment". I often feel that street photographers become so infatuated with their mastery of geometry and technique, so amused by their sense of surrealism and juxtaposition, that they forget to document anything at all, aside from the evidence of their own egos. There is no "God" in their images.

I won't dwell too much on photography's direct relationship to the B-side in this essay, because this entire issue of *The Eyes* will speak of it in the most important terms known to photography, which are visual. Let's instead think of how the B-side has been expressed through other mediums, then allow that to soak into our photographic practice, if we wish, and also inform the way we experience the images included here. I will say, though, that perhaps more than anyone, Roy DeCarava championed the B-side, not only with his insistence on playing in shadows rather than light and his interest in blurs, but also through the Kamoinge Workshop for Black photographers (which he co-founded), bringing us people such as Ming Smith, and creating a crucible for what I call B-side photography: shadows and shakes and imperfection. In his first book, *Somnambule*, documenting Paris nightlife in the 1980s, African American photographer Stanley Greene called DeCarava's lineage "photographing at the edge of failure".

The most obvious mainstream reference for this kind of B-side beauty is the Japanese aesthetic principle of *wabi-sabi*, which in simple terms suggests that there is beauty in imperfection. The imperfection is beautiful because it reminds us of something organic; deeper truths about the liminal, ephemeral nature of our existence. This sentiment can also be found in an ancient Japanese folk tale about a student trying to master a new flute, shared by Stephen Nachmanovitch in his book *Free Play:*

*Improvisation in Life and Art.*[4] When an old master arrives at a small village and plays it, after the performance a village elder exclaims: "Like a God!" and sends a young protégé into the woods with the master to learn. The protégé quickly and easily picks up the technique, but every day the master, upon hearing him, says: "Something lacking." This goes on for months and, with the student eventually growing despondent and too ashamed to return to his village having not mastered the flute, he becomes a recluse in the woods. Years later, the student is now an old man, and one of the village elders remembers him, and asks him to come to the village to perform for the children. Now, having lost everything, with nothing to lose, he picks up the flute he hasn't played since his younger days, when he failed to master it. When he finishes playing for the village there is silence, and an elder exclaims: "Like a God!" The student is now a master.

The moral of this story is that what makes art beautiful is about much more than technique, but about struggle, soul, life; a dance with the world. No amount of perfect technique could make the musician play the flute like a God; it was only the journey of life – with all its surprises and setbacks, struggles and synchronicities – that could. At the heart of the Japanese fable, and this notion of the B-side, then, there is a Sartrean "loser wins" logic that makes me think of an Erykah Badu lyric: "My dress ain't cost nothin' but seven dollars / But I made it fly" – being able to buy a more expensive dress would not have encouraged such creativity. This is also echoed in the immortal words of Public Enemy, who describe how the streets reject the A-side for the more political, raw and revolutionary B-side: " 'Cause the B-side / Wins again, again, again."

But we must not get too romantic about the B-side. Channelling the struggle through your flute playing may be beautiful, but I wouldn't necessarily want my daughter to grow up to become a hermit in the woods, feeling full of shame, to get there, like the protagonist in the folk story. And *Chungking Express* on pirated VHS may be evocative, but who would want their work to get bootlegged? This is why the B-side is so powerful; you can't fake it (even though something that invokes the B-side can, in fact, *be a fake*). What I mean is that shooting a film and then putting Adobe VHS effects on it will never be the same thing as a 1994 Wong Kar-Wai bootleg VHS from Hong Kong. The B-side is early hip-hop, built out of the socioeconomic ruins of 1970s New York that encouraged poor inner-city kids to make music without instruments; is various

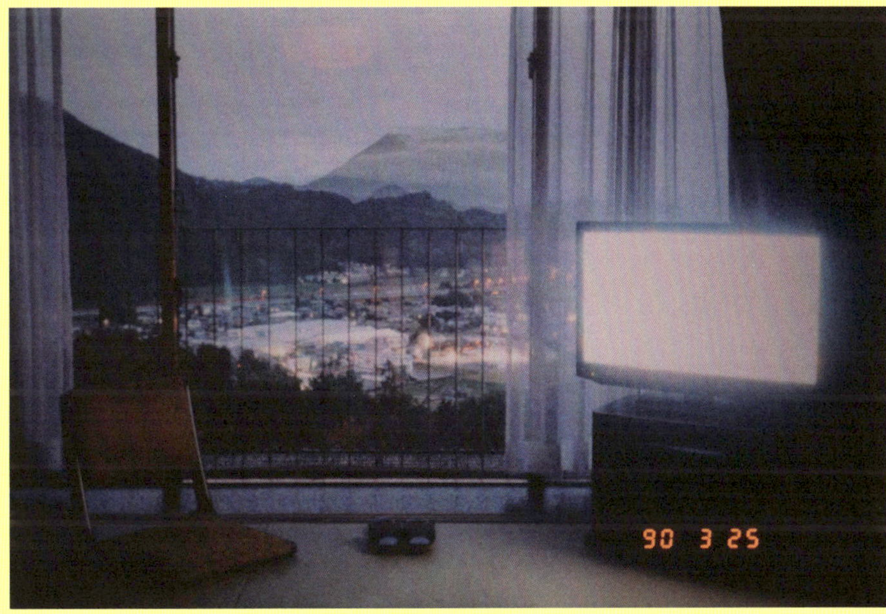


*View from Ohito Hotel,* 2019

incarnations of "soul food" from across the African diaspora, conjured out of the leftover pieces of meat that the master didn't want, yet made into something delicious. We can invoke and get inspired by the B-side, but we can't pretend something is B-side when it isn't. This beautifully produced issue of *The Eyes*, for instance, is examining the B-side, is channelling it, but isn't the B-side. A B-side photography book would be something like what broke Japanese photographers in the 1970s were doing during the Provoke era, using Xerox prints to challenge glossy magazines with frenzied black-and-white images.

All that we can do is try to create the right environment for the B-side to thrive in. Wong Kar-Wai, for instance, has described his filmmaking style as "jam sessions" – that is, getting a bunch of creatives to gather around a loose structure to see what happens. Already in his work is an otherness, an energy outside of his control, the opening up of a space in which others can participate. We will hear more about how the B-side is a site that opens up space later in this issue (in the conversation between myself, journalist Melissa Chemam,[5] award-winning poet Roger Robinson and the legendary dub producer Mad Professor, who did much to popularize the B-side and "version" in British music), but for now it is enough to say that the B-side is a bricolage. That is, an art constructed by whatever is at hand, and because of this, the B-side can be kitsch and counter-intuitive, and often exists in that wonderful world outside of hashtags and algorithms. It can offer a challenge to heteronormativity, middle-class etiquette, "good taste" and bourgeois values, functioning in the way Jean Genet had in mind when he wrote that "to achieve harmony in bad taste is the height of elegance"; for the B-side is built from the rubble of empires, the backwash of capitalism, multiple allegiances and hybrid cultures. This quality is what makes the B-side so resilient, despite the worst odds. Here I am, writing about Japanese folk tales, Sartre's philosophy and Hong Kong cinema, and not only claiming it all as B-side but also claiming it under the banner of the Black experience in Europe. An experience "rooted in, but not restricted by, Blackness", to quote Michael Eric Dyson.[6] And of course I'm in a long lineage of practitioners working in this tradition (especially after the advent of postmodernism): the Wu-Tang Clan using samples of Hong Kong movies in their classic *36 Chambers* album (perhaps the ultimate sonic invocation of the B-side); Marseille's IAM taking ownership of ancient Egypt; impoverished African American drag queens claiming high European couture as their own in *Paris is Burning*; kuduro music fusing Angolan rhythms with electronica; *sapeurs* strolling in Kinshasa dressed in three-piece suits that look as if they were tailor-made on Saville Row; or early UK grime artists making music using their PlayStation 1s.

And here we have a paradox: cultural appropriation as a two-way stream, the A-side turned into the B-side, transfigured so that it functions in antithesis to the way cultural appropriation usually works when it is top-down. Instead of aping another culture solely for the purposes of commodifying it for one's own ends, the B-side can take mainstream artefacts and make them weirder, less cookie-cutter, more inclusive of poor people. At an after-party for a D'Angelo tour, for instance, I once watched Questlove sandwich Britney Spears' "Toxic" between J Dilla and Outkast in a way that completely changed the way I experienced Britney Spears (Questlove has called his style of DJing "my version of a bouillabaisse"). I've witnessed respected Rastas listening to Celine Dion, and on page 65, check out how Mad Professor casually speaks of his admiration for The Bangles' most mainstream hit "Eternal Flame", and inspires us to see in it the essence of reggae and trip hop. As Jonathan Meades put it, "there is no worthwhile art without mongrelism".[7]

This is where Afropean and the B-side meet. For me, Afropean has always been about finding a way to celebrate Blackness in Europe, but only as part of a trajectory that ultimately ends with human connection across cultures and boundaries. For this issue of *The Eyes*, I wanted to begin at Black photographers in Europe and at the same time try not to cordon them off. Rather, I wanted to show them living in, taking part in, being influenced by and interacting with the world around them, to open up a broader conversation about different ways of seeing and documenting the world. And though

I can't speak for the artists involved, here I offer their work like I offer my own work with Afropean: as a site of fusion and possibility. The photographers we have chosen are all highly skilled, and of various degrees of education; some grew up with access to money and resources, some didn't. But in all of their work I feel a kind of struggle; what Martin Luther King and later Talib Kweli called "the beautiful struggle". A struggle to keep the B-side alive, during a time when it has never been more under threat. The notion of music as a physical object is dying, so the B-side as a framework is at first glance somewhat anachronistic. More worrying than this, however, is the disappearance of B-side topographies — the spaces that gave birth to the B-side in the first place: high-rise estates, youth clubs, entire communities displaced by privatization and middle-class gentrification. I would therefore like readers to experience this issue as an echo of the recent past; the music [on page 72] and the spread of items on the opening pages, taken from my own journey through the B-side, is an invitation to look at the relics of 1980s and 1990s B-side culture, and think of how we might carry their energies into new forms and expressions, ensuring they survive into/despite the Digital Age. The photographers included here are doing just that. The B-side often wants to be a part of the A-side, and may incorporate the A-side in its work, but its failure to truly become the A-side can also become its strength, creating something new. The B-side is found at the periphery, and despite the challenges it faces, this is where I believe the future is being incubated.

*A note on the photographs: Johny's father landed a role in a musical that toured Japan on and off between 1987 and 1990. When Johny returned to Japan for the first time as an adult, in 2013, he witnessed what he describes as a "postmodern landscape in stasis" – a 1980s future that never arrived. He returned from that first trip with bland images from a digital camera. It was only when he began to look at his family's Japan albums that he realized what he must do: dig out the two cameras his parents used and shoot Japan on Konica film that expired during the "bubble era", mixing them with the family archive. In the ongoing series "The Sequel to a Dream: Ghosts of 1980s Japan", he deals with mourning – for his late father, Richie Pitts, but also for the death of a future proposed by Japan in the late 1980s "bubble economy" and the problematic energies of the late 20th century. In these old family cameras a séance begins to take place, where the ghosts of the past haunt the simulacra of the present, revealing the B-side of Japan that Johny was shielded from when he was a child.*

JOHNY PITTS
Johny Pitts is the curator of the ENAR (European Network Against Racism) award-winning online journal Afropean.com and the author of Afropean: Notes from Black Europe (Penguin Random House). Translated into French, German, Italian and Spanish, it has been awarded the 2020 Jhalak Prize and the 2020 Bread & Roses Award for Radical Publishing and is the recipient of the 2021 Leipzig Book Award for European Understanding and the 2021 European Essay Prize. As the conferee of the inaugural Ampersand/ Photoworks Fellowship, he is currently creating a new body of work reflecting on Black Britishness through its myriad manifestations.

1 I use the word "spectral" here partly to conjure Derrida's reading of Marx's "a spectre is haunting Europe" and the concept of "hauntology": that the present is haunted by other possible futures that have never come to pass. *Specters of Marx*, by Jacques Derrida, Routledge, 1994.
2 *The Ghosts of Songs*, the film art of the Black Audio Film Collective, edited by Kodwo Eshun & Anjalika Sagar, p. 132, Liverpool University Press, 2007.
3 Red Bull Music Academy, "D'Angelo on Questlove, Neo-soul and Voodoo" [video], YouTube (uploaded 3 May 2014), 11:46.
4 Stephen Nachmanovich, *Freeplay, Improvisation in Life and Art*, Penguin/ Tarcher, 1990.
5 Author of *Massive Attack: Out of the Comfort Zone – The Story of a Sound, A City and a Group of Revolutionary Artists*, Tangent Books, Bristol, 2019.
6 Touré, *Who's Afraid of Post-Blackness?: What It Means to Be Black Now*, foreword by Michael Eric Dyson, Atria Books, 2011.
7- https://thequietus.com/articles/29856-jonathan-meades-pedro-and-ricky-come-again-owen-hatherley-interview

# JAMES BARNOR

James Barnor was born in 1929 in Accra, Ghana. He is now retired and living in the UK. He began his career as a portrait photographer in his home town and in the early 1950s opened a studio called Ever Young, where a diverse clientele of young brides, civil servants and dignitaries, teachers and students, and street performers flocked. In parallel, he worked as a photojournalist for the local and international press. In 1959, two years after Ghana gained independance, he moved to London and studied photography at Medway College of Art in Kent. During the 1960s, he photographed "Swinging London" and the daily life of the African diaspora in the metropolis. Towards the end of the 1960s, he was recruited and trained by the Agfa-Gevaert group. Back in Ghana, in 1969, he founded the country's first colour laboratory and Studio X 23 in Accra. He then worked as a freelance photographer and for some state agencies in Accra.

On both continents, his portraits bear witness to a society in transition: Ghana moving towards independence, London becoming a multicultural metropolis. In his photographs taken in Europe, Barnor's gaze rests tenderly on many couples. These love duets embody personal journeys and family narratives woven together with stories of postcolonial immigration.


*James Barnor with a model at the special Agfa-Gevaert studio*, Mortsel, Belgium, 1969
*The wedding of Mr and Mrs Sackey*, London, c.1966
*John Martey Allotey and his wife at the wedding of Mr and Mrs Sackey*, London, c.1966
*A group of friends taken during the wedding of Mr and Mrs Sackey*, London, c.1966
*At the wedding of Mr and Mrs Sackey*, London, c.1966
*A Ghanaian family gathering after the baptism of James, the newest member of the Vanderpuye family, held by his godmother*, London, early 1960s
*A Ghanaian family gathering after the baptism of James, the newest member of the Vanderpuye family*, London, early 1960s

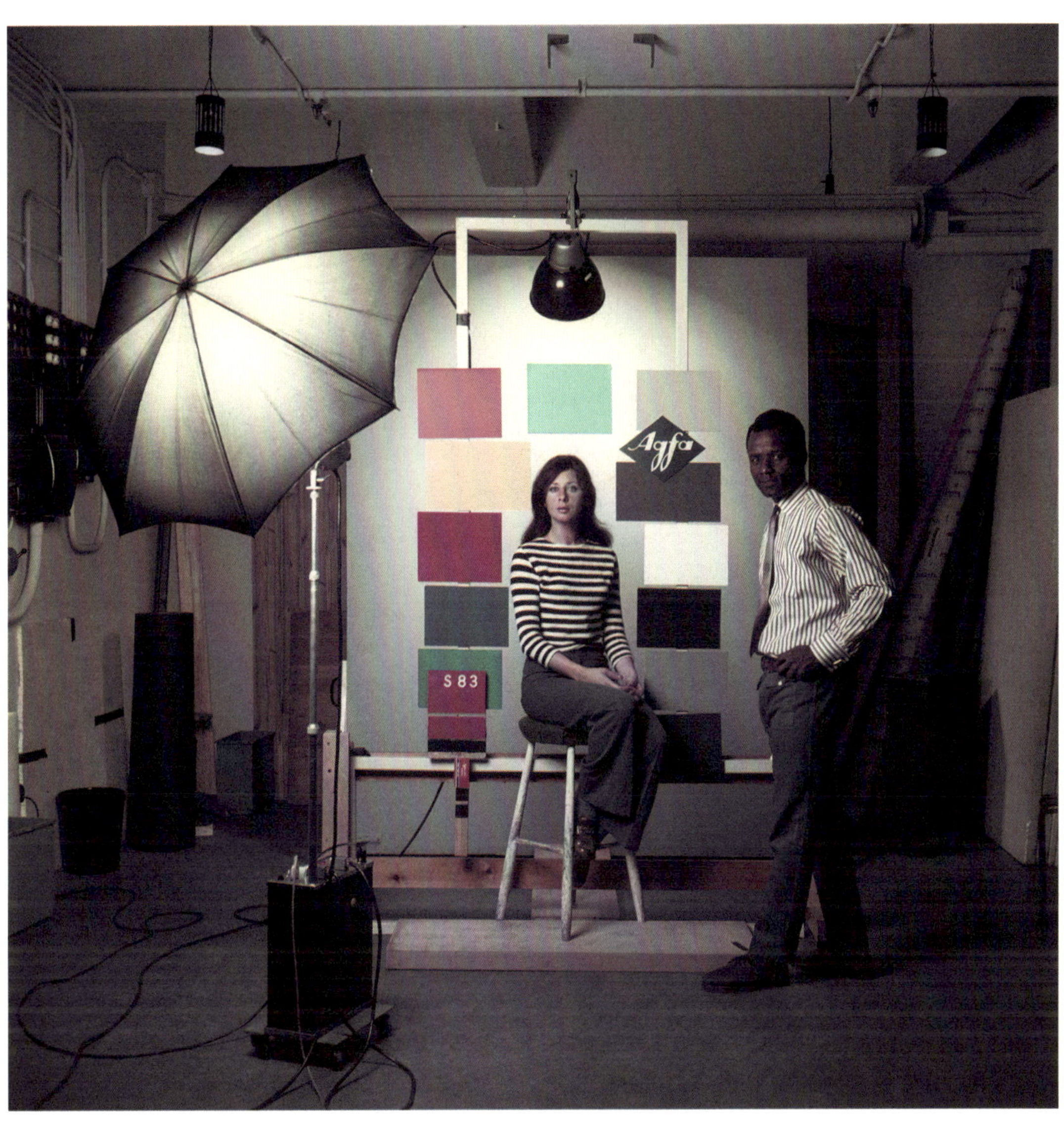
Agfa
S 83

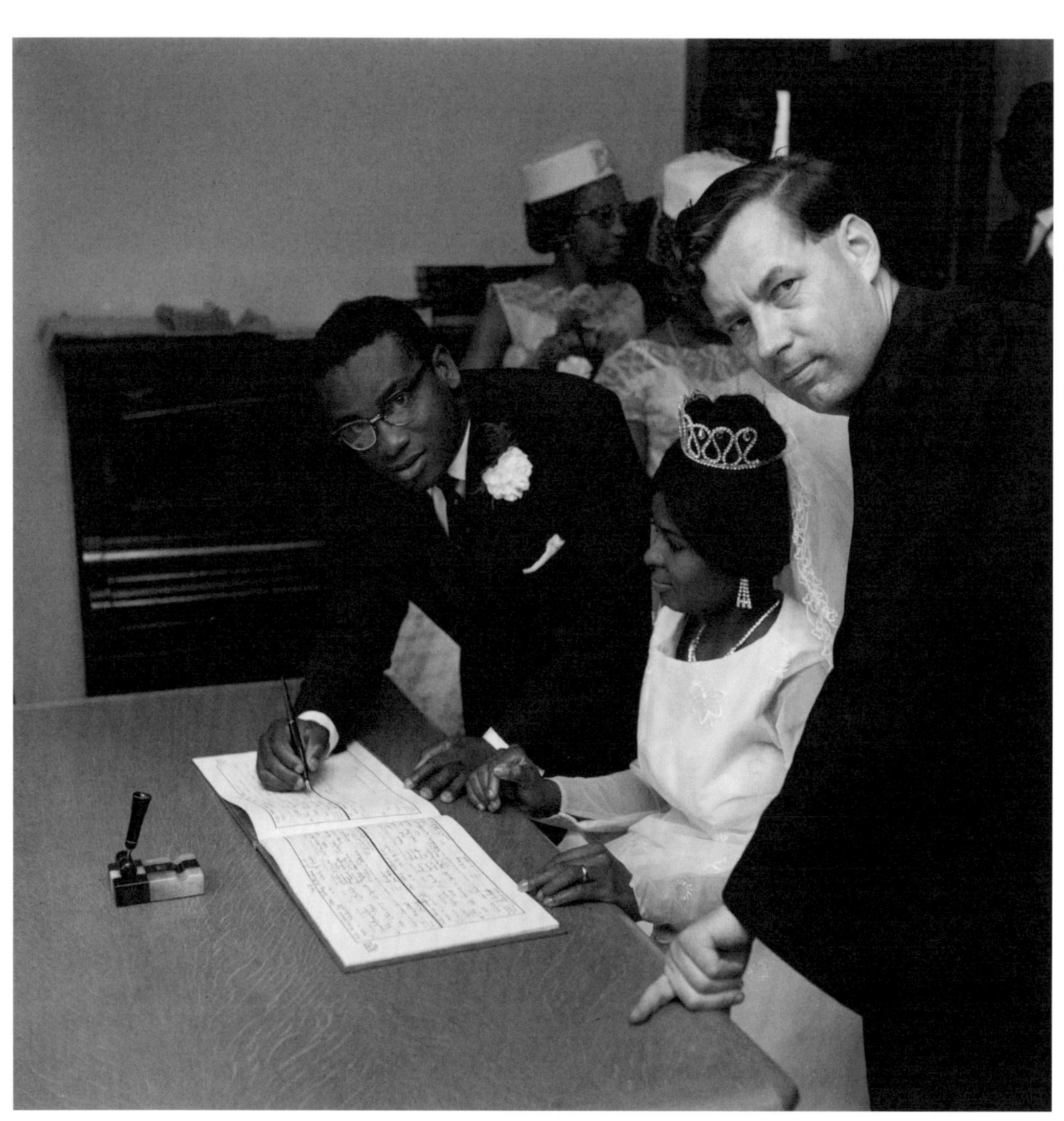

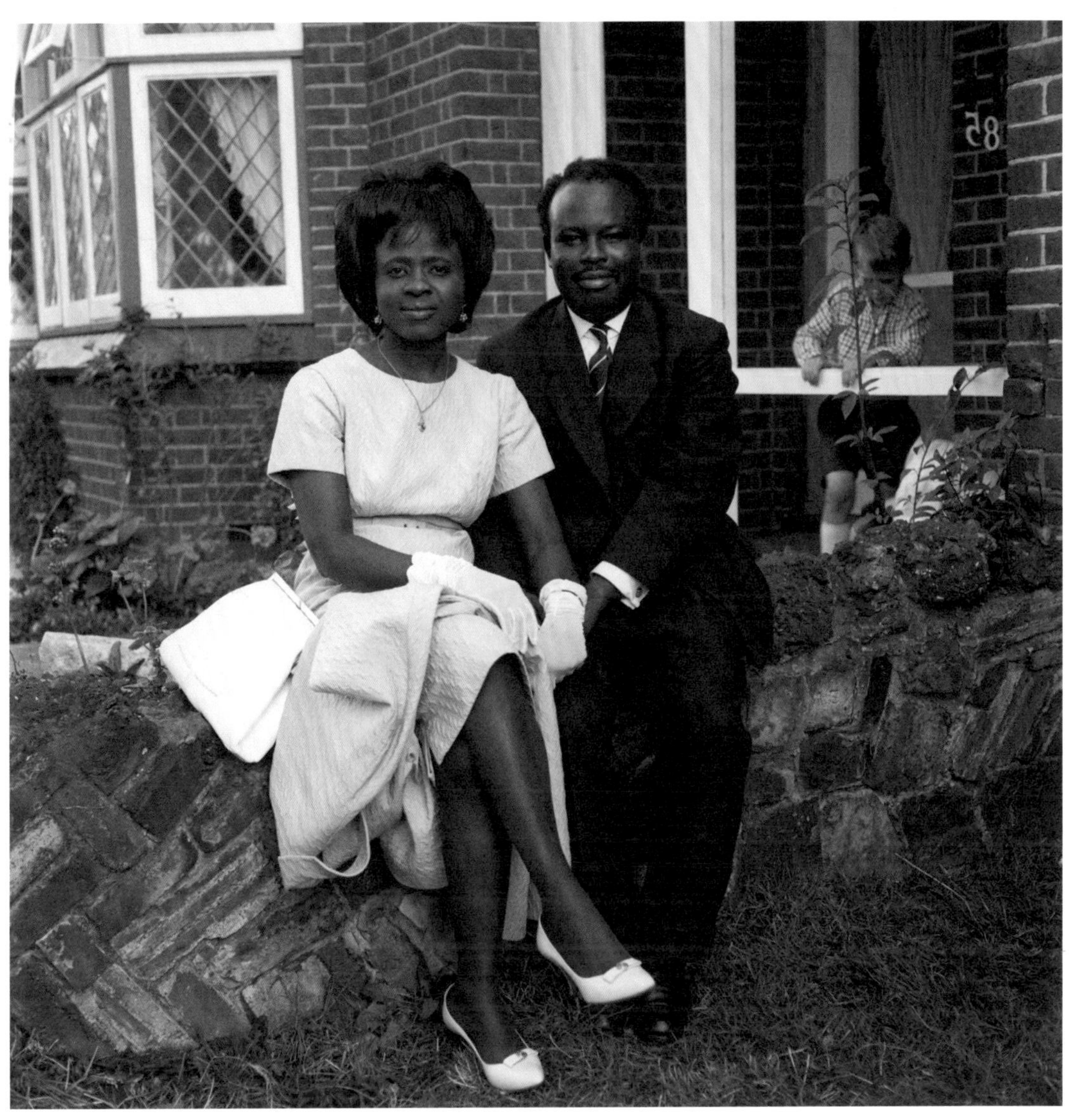

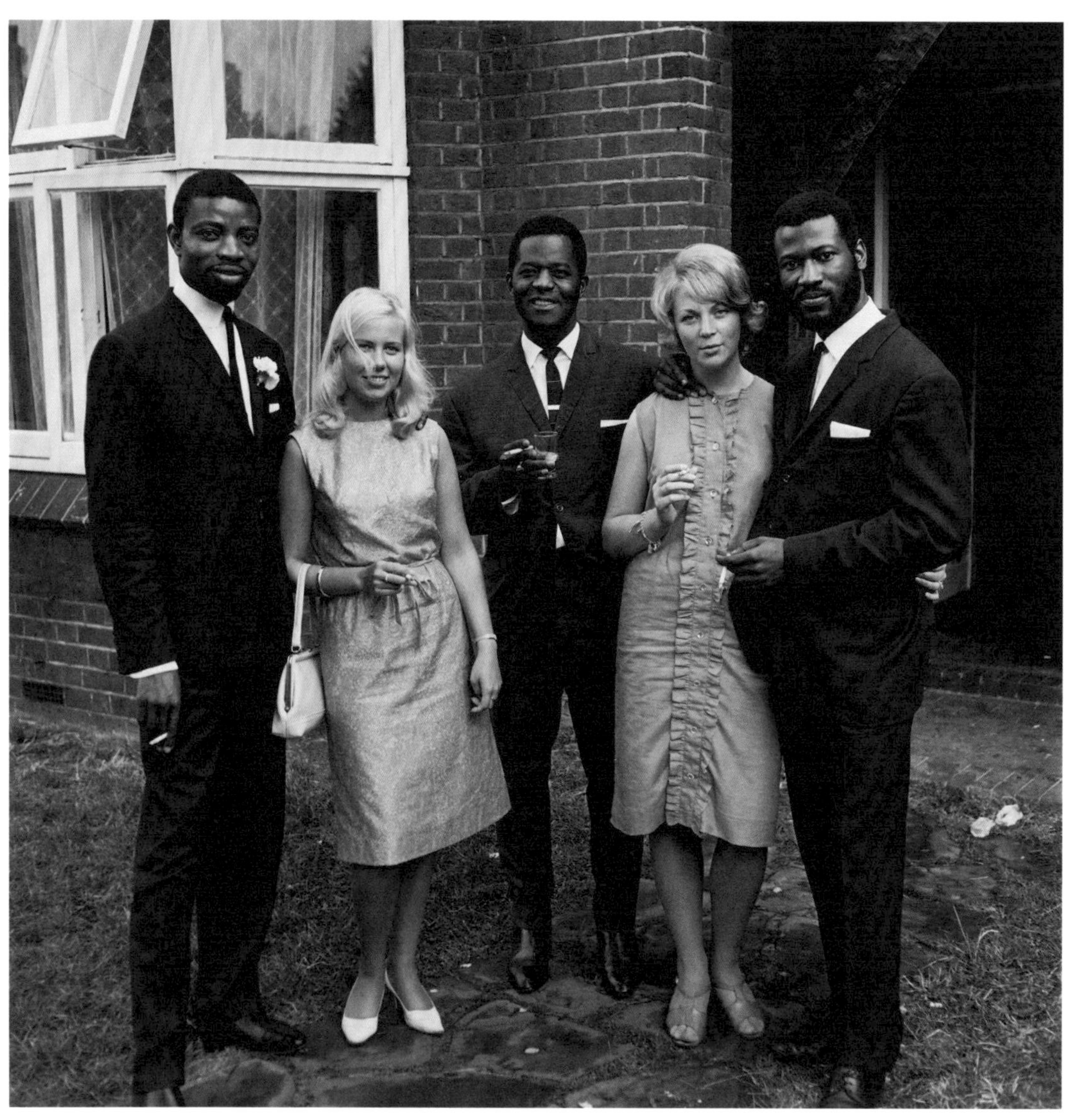

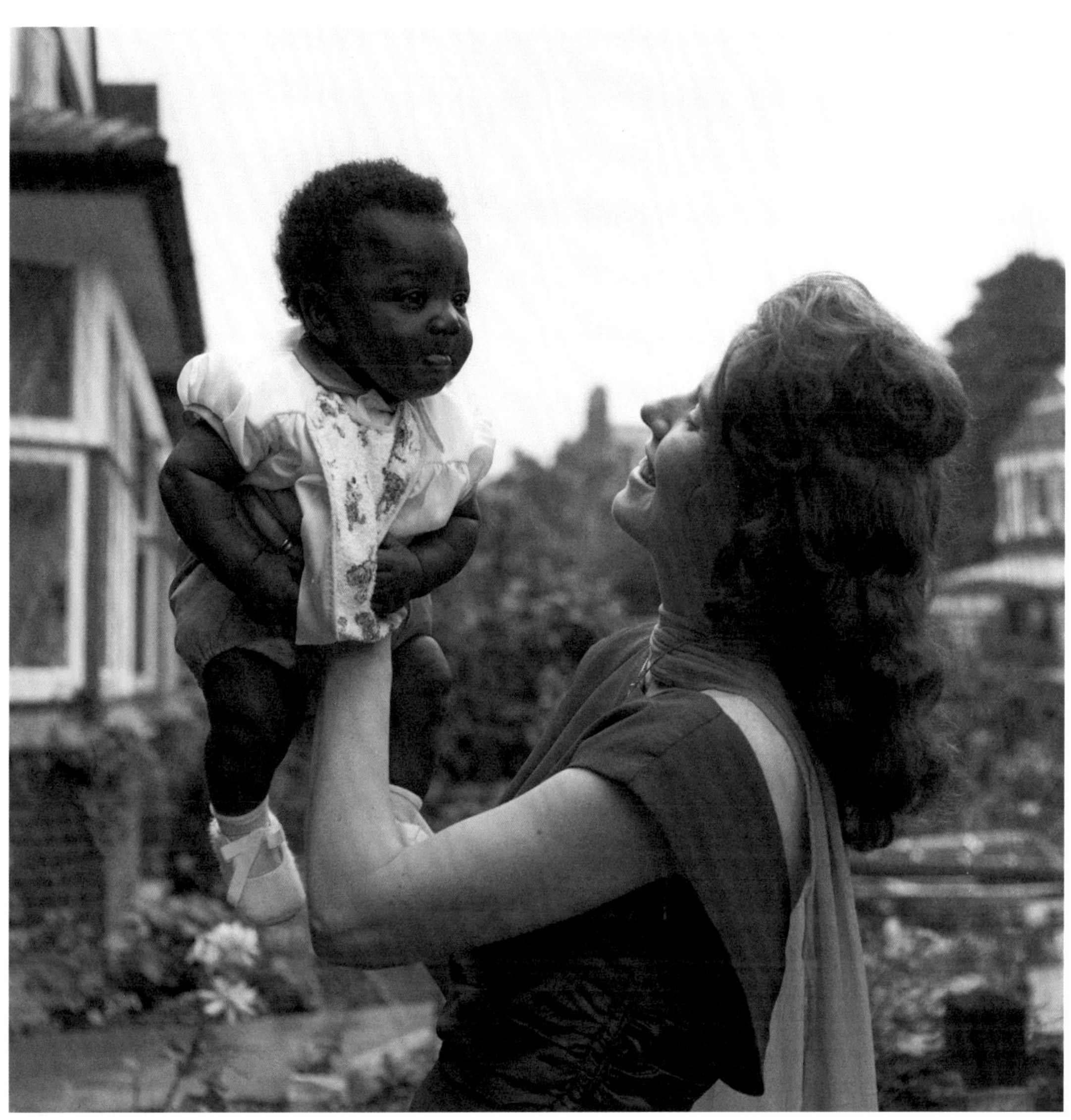

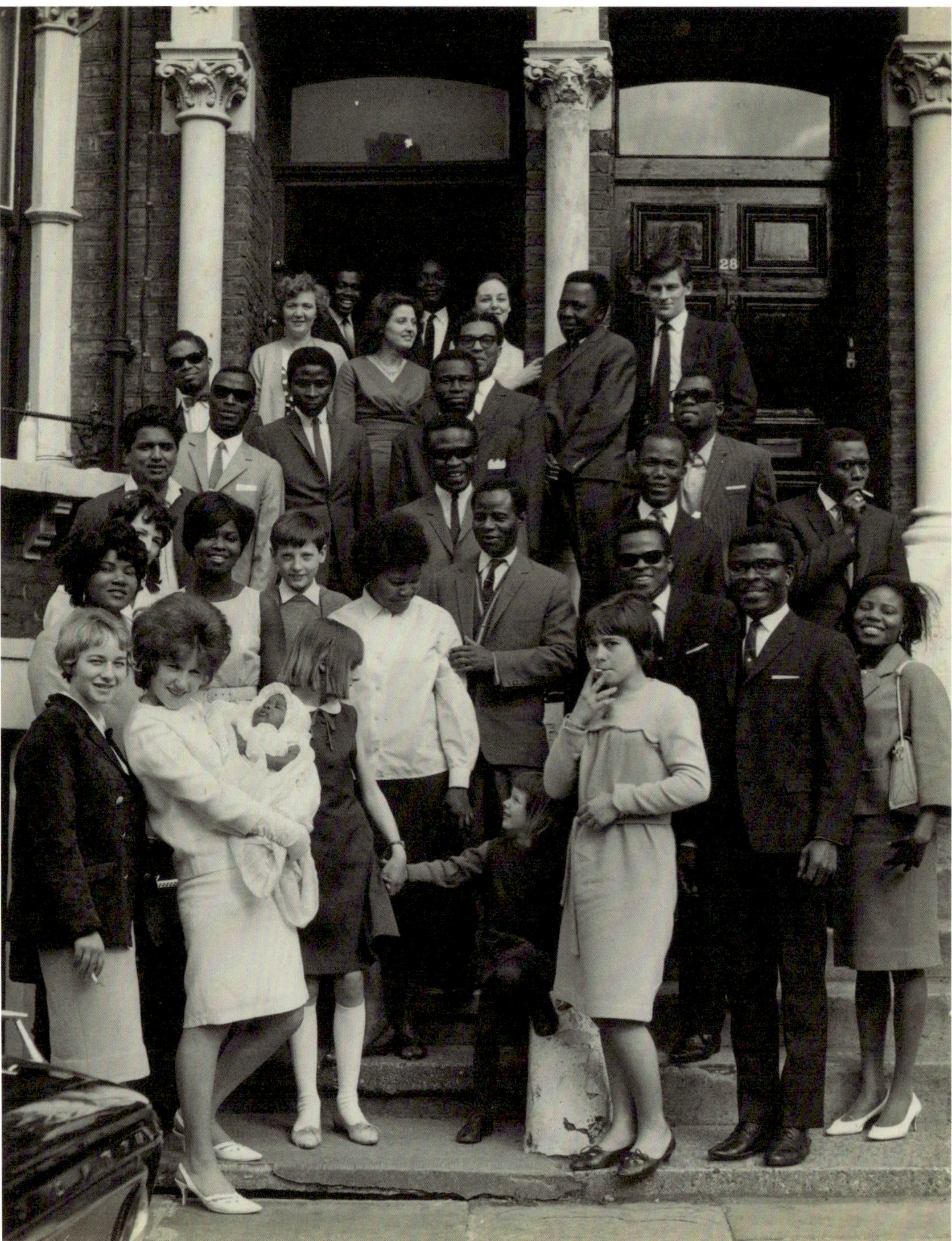
28

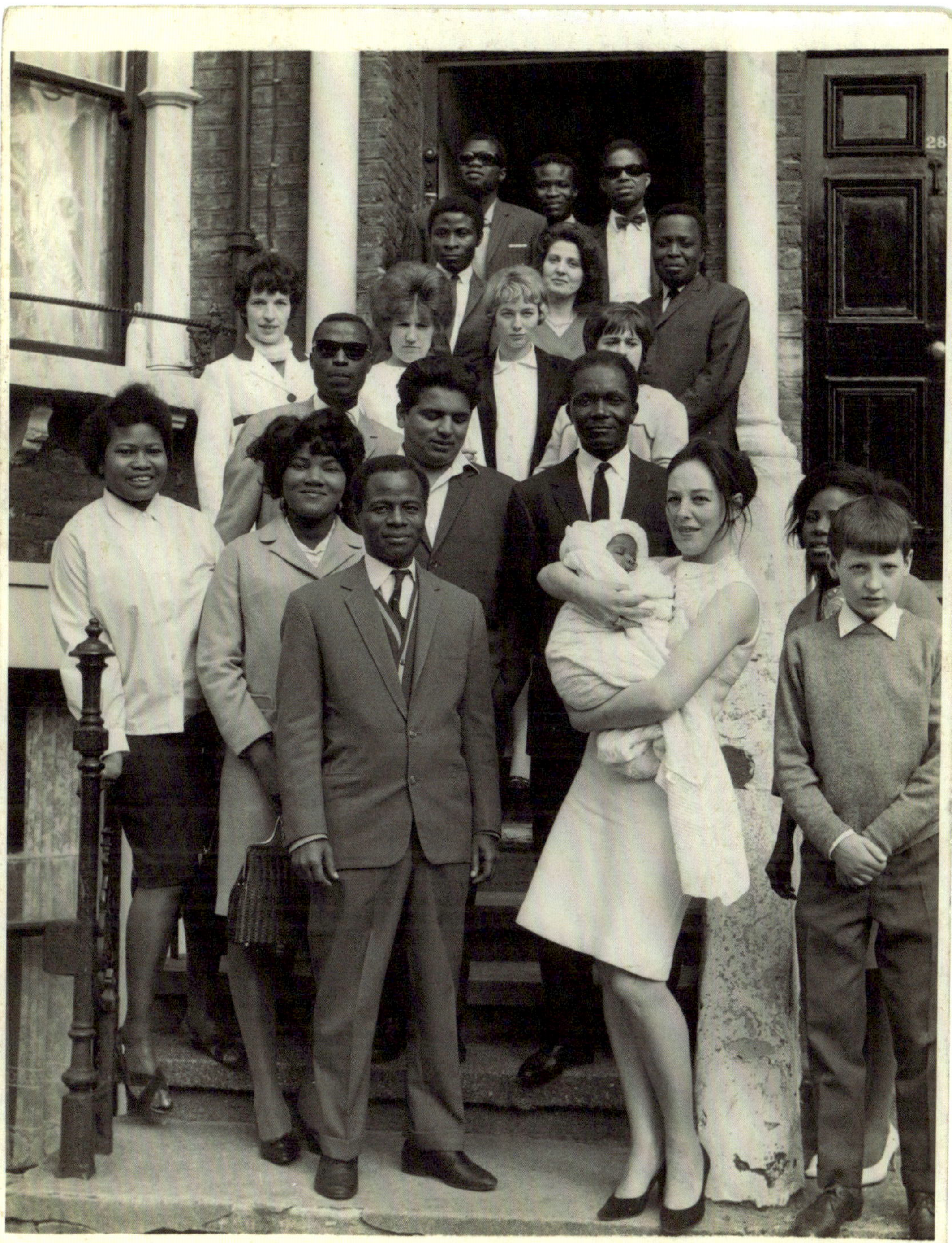
28

TITLE

# 10 YEARS OF TRACE

COVER

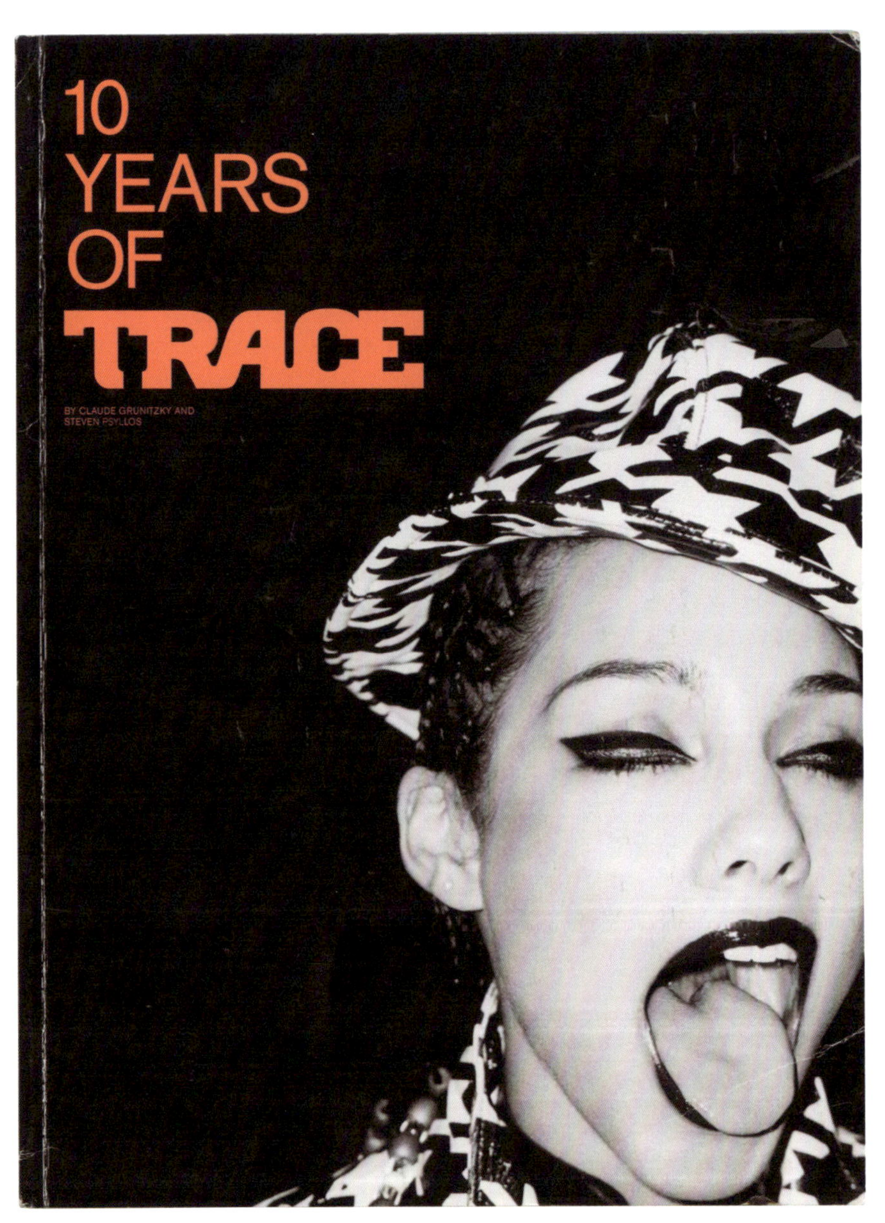

| ARTIST | Claude Grunitzky |
|---|---|
| PUBLISHER | Booth-Clibborn Editions |
| SPECIFICATIONS | — 296 pages<br>— first published in 2007<br>— size: 19.37 × 26.04 cm |
| SUMMARY | *TRACE* magazine was created in 1997 by Claude Grunitzky, following the magazine *True* created two years earlier in London. It was dedicated to the fashion, music and lifestyles of a new urban generation. For 10 years, the monthly magazine was the leading source of information on cross-cultural ideas and fashions. A strong advocate and representative of transculturalism, Claude Grunitzky published *Transculturalism: How the World Is Coming Together* (PowerHouse Books, 2004, translated in French by Éditions Grasset, 2008) – a collective work of images, stories and analyses that broke free from the idea of fixed idendities and described belonging to several cultures.<br><br>For its 10th anniversary issue, *TRACE* looked back at the previous decade in terms of style. The magazine compiles articles, essays and emblematic covers of the artistic and musical trends of this period. It also presents the work of the photographers, stylists and designers who forged the magazine's identity. |
| BIOGRAPHY | Claude Grunitzky is a French American Togolese journalist, publisher and entrepreneur who was born in 1971. He is the founder of the investment fund the Equity Alliance and media companies such as the media platform True Africa and the magazine *TRACE*. Claude Grunitzky is also the co-founder of the television channel TRACE TV (now Trace Urban), dedicated to urban music and culture. |

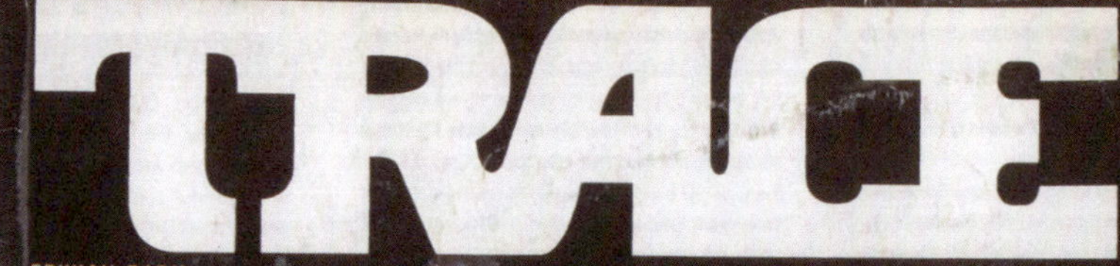
TRACE
ERYKAH BADU
BOOTCAMP CLIK
WU-WEAR
NEW JUNGLISTS
URBANMAGAZINE
APRIL 1997 / £2.50
NOTORIOUS
B.I.G
1972-1997
THE LAST INTERVIEW
ISSN 1366-1752
ISSUE#04TRACEURBANMAGAZINE

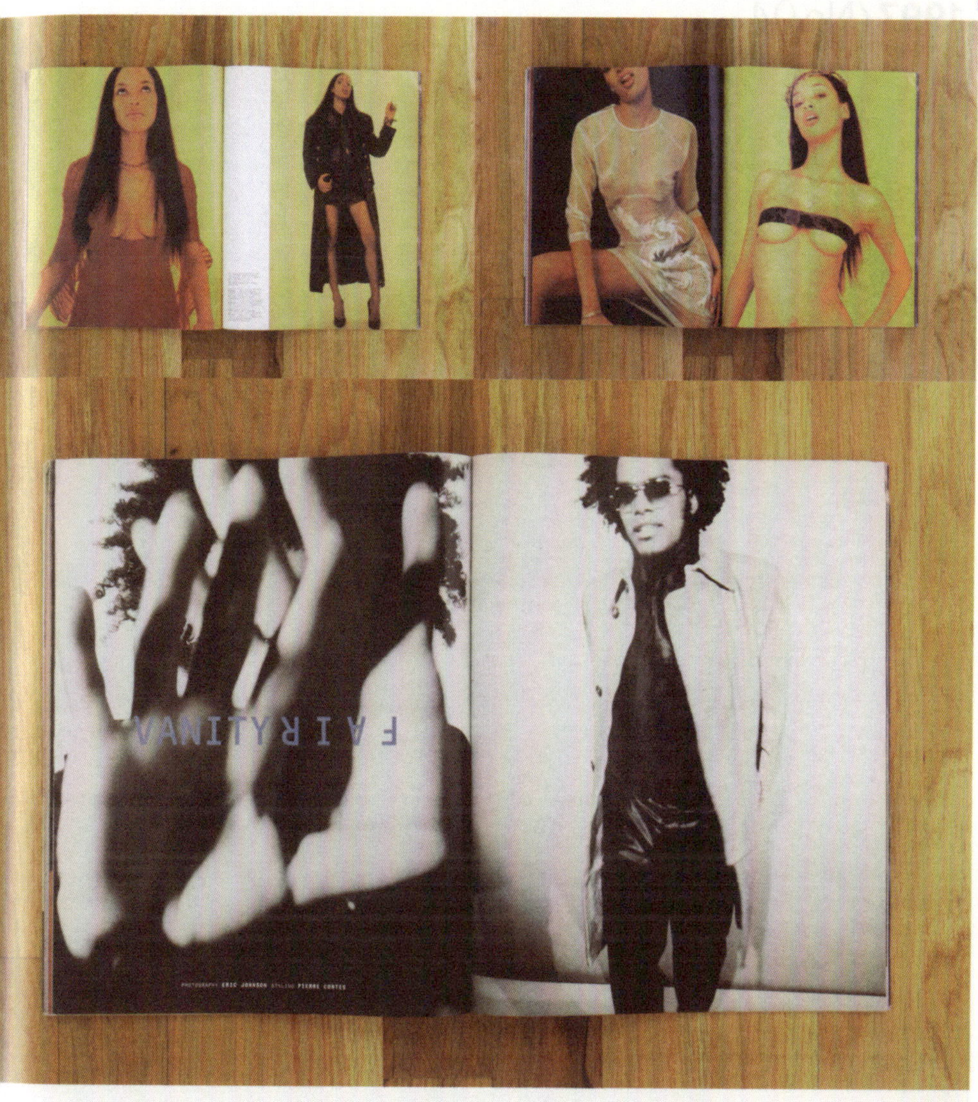


TAR(S)
OTORIOUS B.I.G.

PHOTOGRAPHY
MARTINA HOOGLAND-IVANOW

TRIM SIZE
9 X 11.25"

ART DIRECTOR
GRAHAM ROUNTHWAITE

ISSUE DATE
APRIL 1997

ISSUE NO. 04

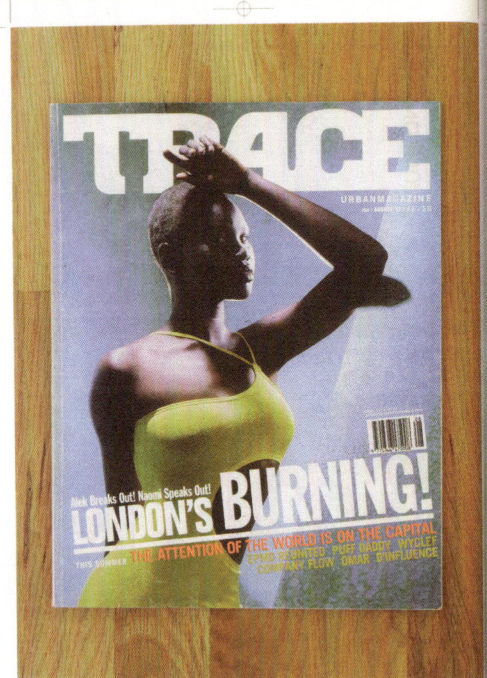


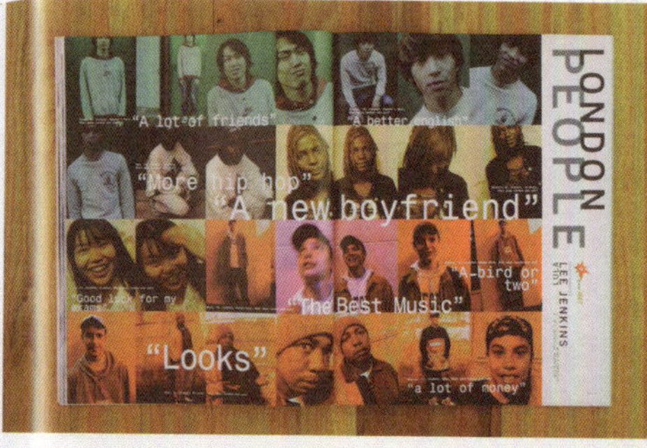


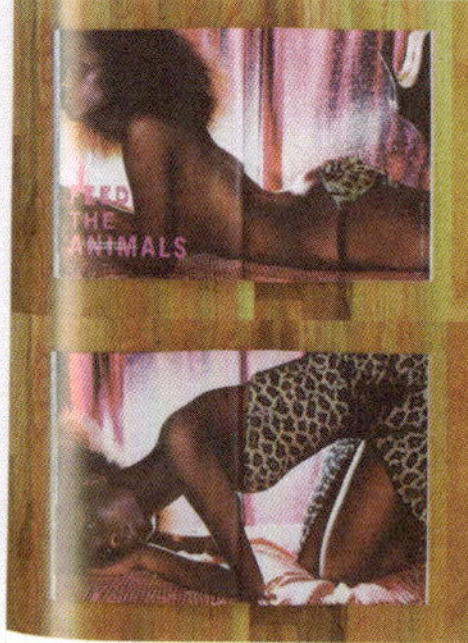


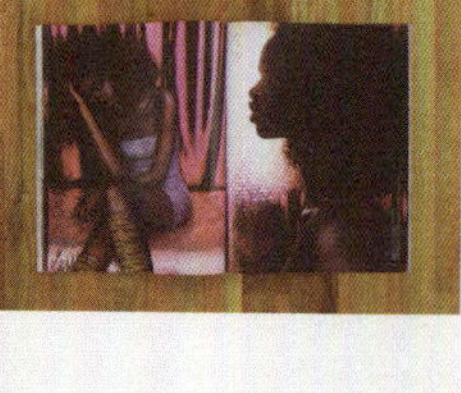

ISSUE NO. 07, PREVIOUS SPREAD: P. 32-39, PHOTOGRAPHY_LEE JENKINS, FASHION_PIERRE CORTES. THIS PAGE: P. 42-45, PHOTOGRAPHY_LEE JENKINS, ASSISTED BY LULA; P. 74-79, PHOTOGRAPHY_KIM ANDREOLLI, FASHION_JOAN CAMPBELL

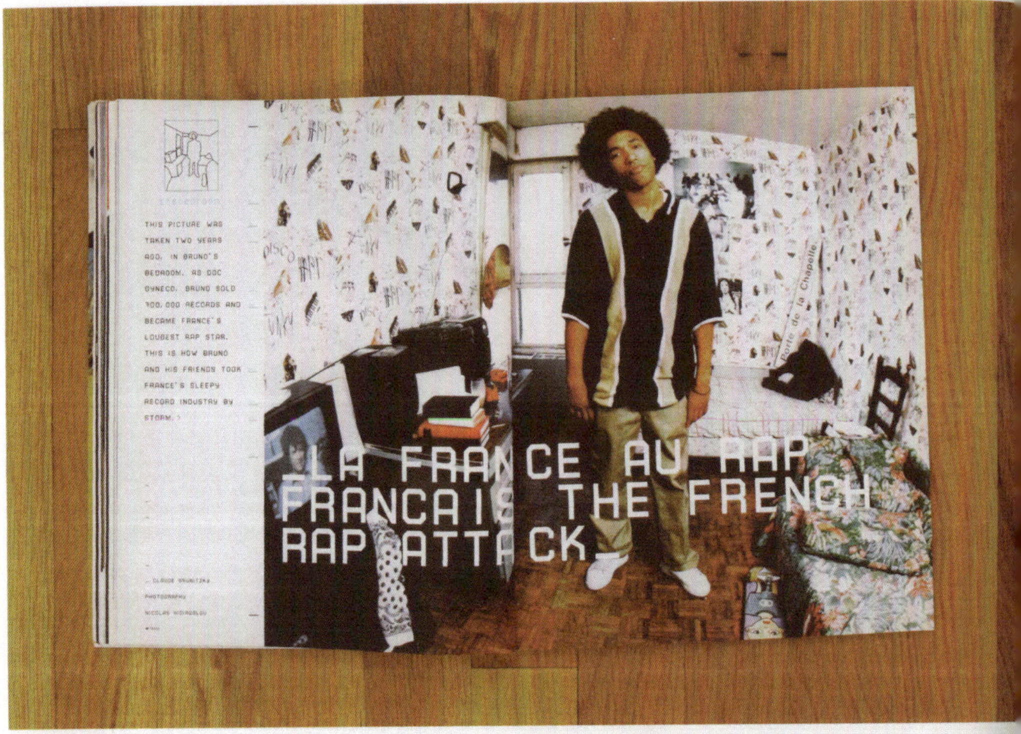

THIS PICTURE WAS TAKEN TWO YEARS AGO, IN BRUNO'S BEDROOM. AS DOC GYNECO, BRUNO SOLD 700,000 RECORDS AND BECAME FRANCE'S LOUDEST RAP STAR. THIS IS HOW BRUNO AND HIS FRIENDS TOOK FRANCE'S SLEEPY RECORD INDUSTRY BY STORM.

_LA FRANCE AU RAP FRANCAIS THE FRENCH RAP ATTACK_

Porte de la Chapelle

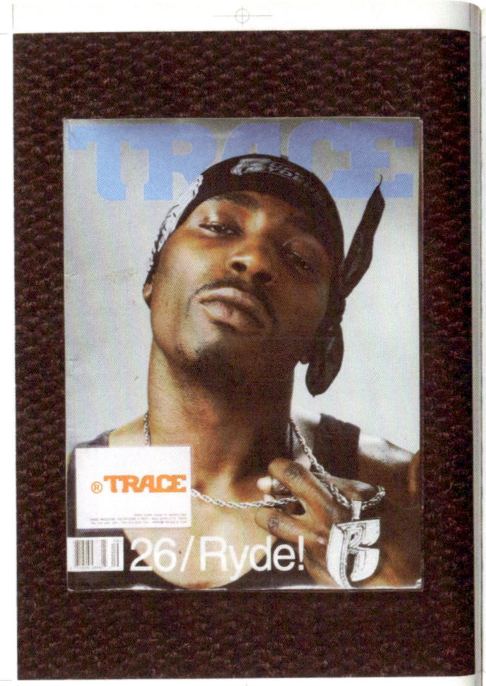


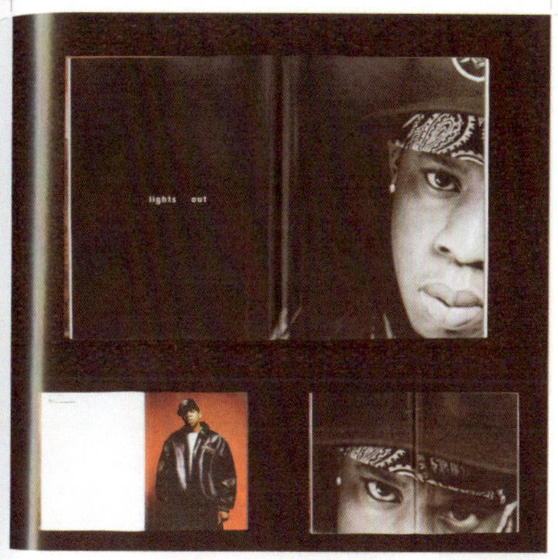


NO. 26, PREVIOUS SPREAD: P. 72-75, PHOTOGRAPHY_MAX LUCAS; THIS PAGE: P. 58-63, PHOTOGRAPHY_JONATHAN MANNION

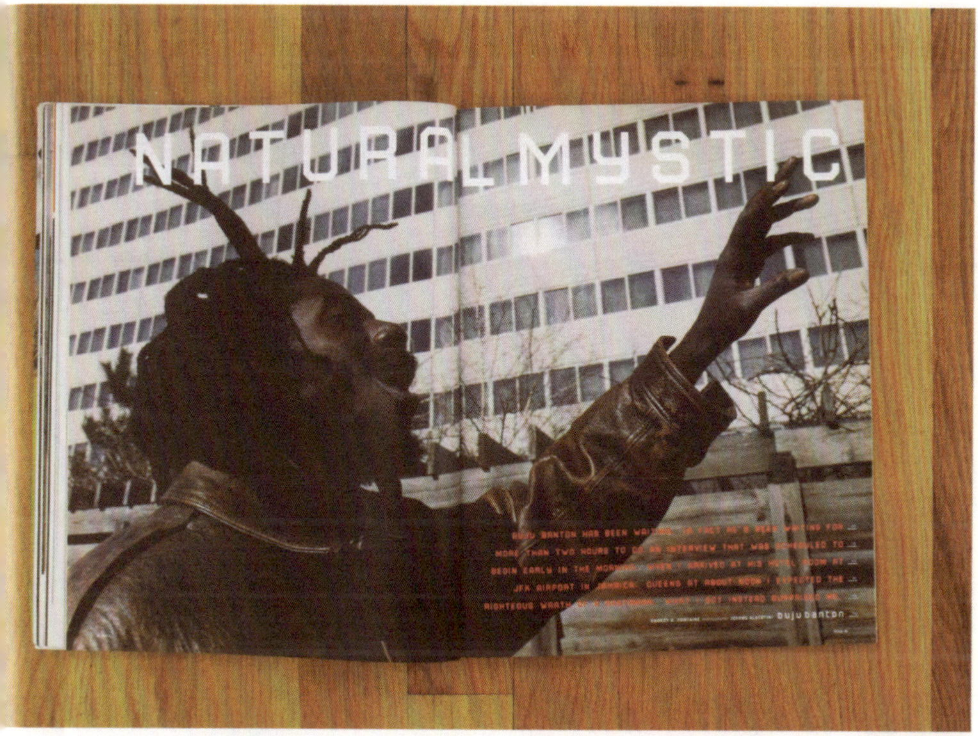

NATURAL MYSTIC

buju banton

# EDDIE OTCHERE RÉMY BOURDEAU

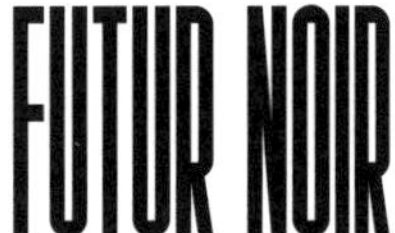


Eddie Otchere, born in 1974, is a Black British photographer and exhibition curator whose projects use photography and sound to tell the story of the Black British experience. He exhibits his photographs and makes soundtracks in the UK and abroad. Between 1994 and 1996 he was the official photographer for Metalheadz – Blue Note Sessions.

“I took photographs to capture our culture, the spirit of the dance and the amazing producers who created hard-hitting songs,” said Otchere, explaining why he got into photography. London-based photographer Eddie Otchere has taken portraits of some of the biggest rappers and DJs of the 1990s including Jay Z, Aaliyah and Wu-Tang Clan. His photographs have helped shape the visual history of hip-hop.

At the same time, on the other side of the Channel, French photographer Rémy Bourdeau, a graduate of the Lycée Brassaï in Paris and specializing in urban cultures, was immortalizing the tours of Erykah Badu, Sampha, Dizzee Rascal and many others.

Gathered in the collaborative exhibition “Futur NOIR” by Eddie Otchere, Rémy Bourdeau and Ludovica Bulciolu, at the San Mei Gallery in London during the summer of 2020, their photographs pay tribute to hip-hop and its legendary figures. The result of a series of conversations, the exhibition explores their musical, graphic and photographic influences.


*Blackstar*, Eddie Otchere, New York, 1998
*Coolio*, Eddie Otchere, London, 1995
*Coolio*, Eddie Otchere, London, 1995
*Junglists*, Eddie Otchere, East London, 1994
*Junglists*, Eddie Otchere, East London, 1994
*Artists*, Rémy Bourdeau, Boiler Room Peckham Festival, 2019
*Artists*, Rémy Bourdeau, Boiler Room Peckham Festival, 2019
*Erykah Badu*, Rémy Bourdeau, Field Day Festival, 2018
*Erykah Badu*, Rémy Bourdeau, Field Day Festival, 2018

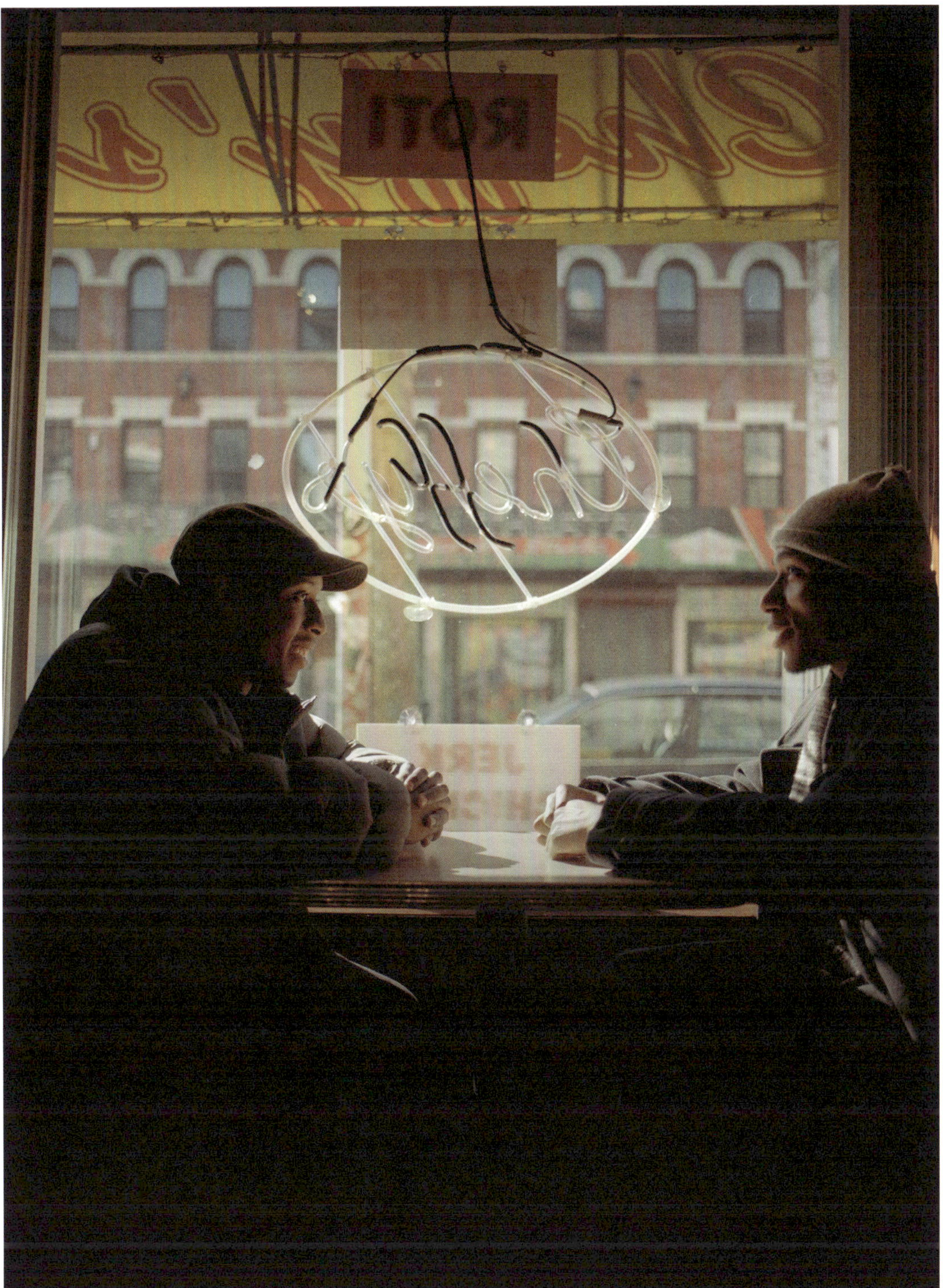
ROTI

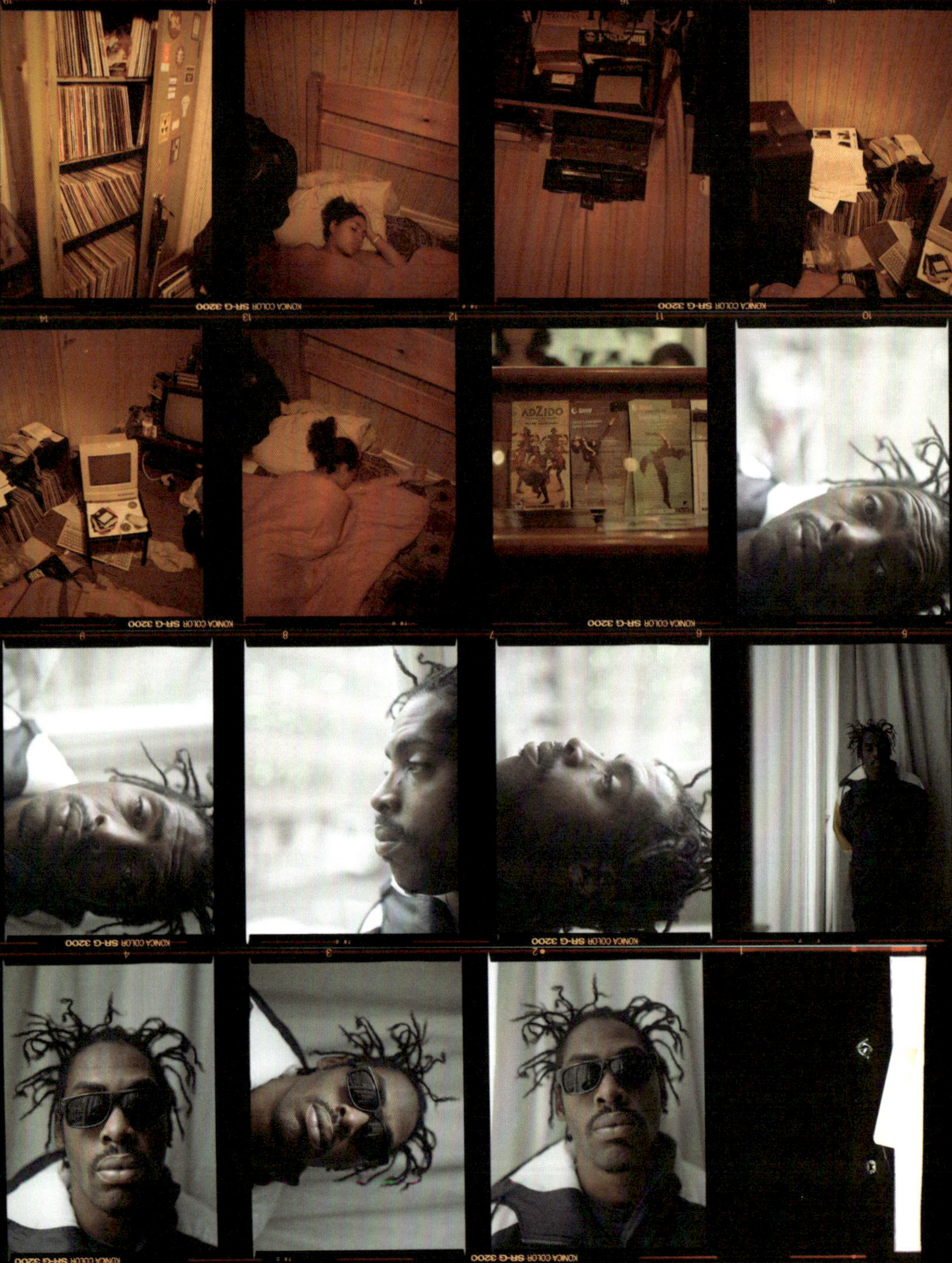
KONICA COLOR SR-G 3200
ADZIDO

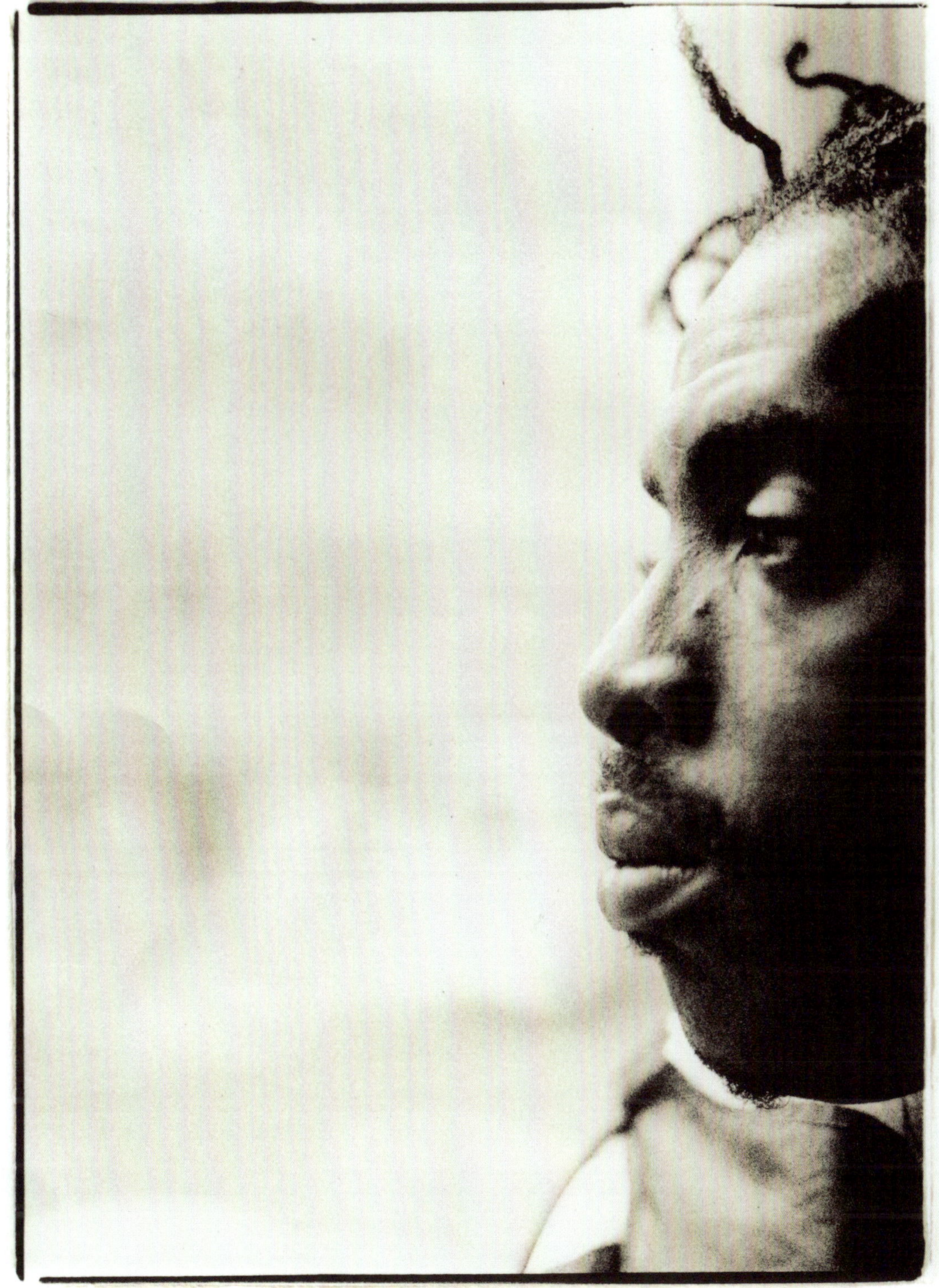

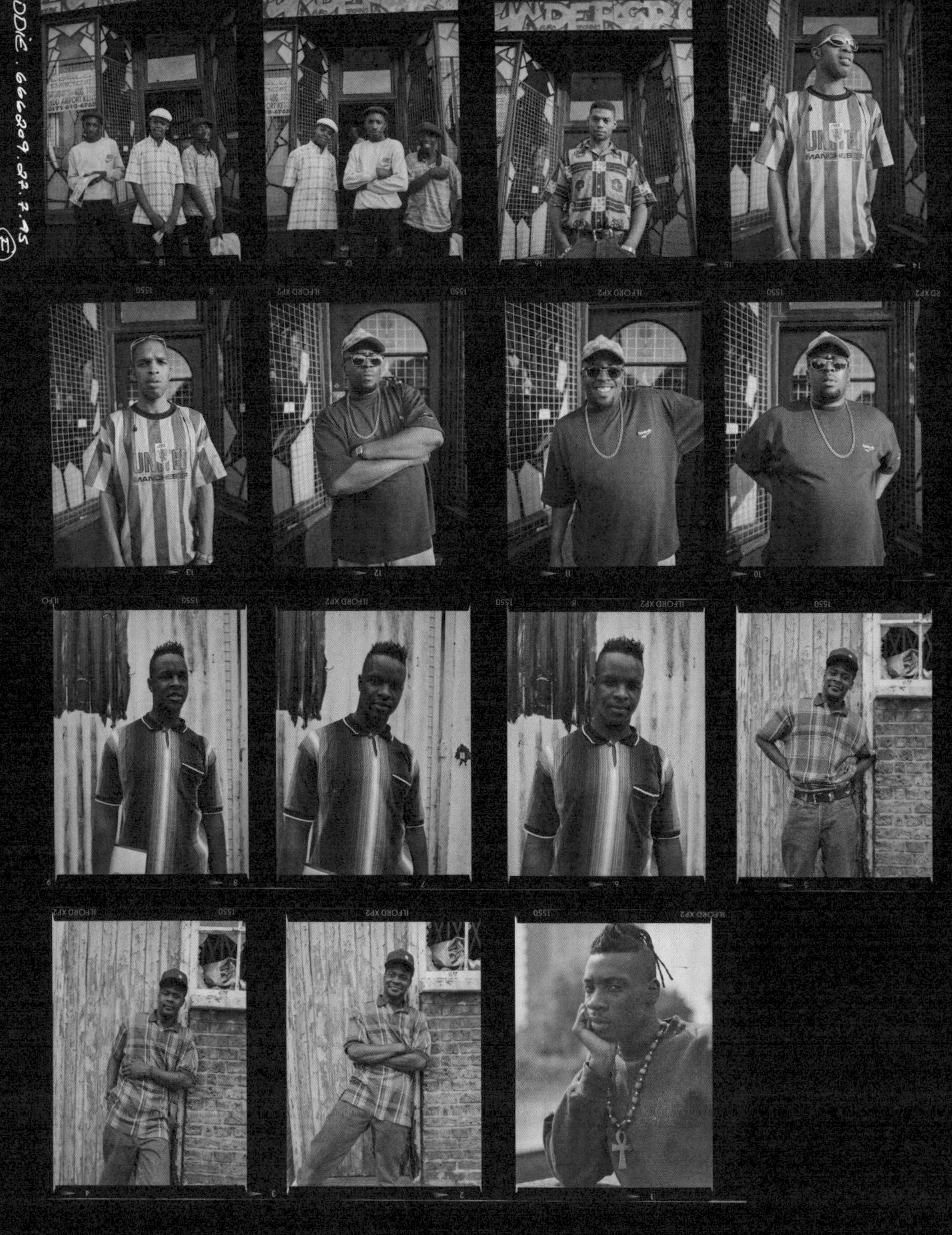
EDDIE . 666809 . 27.7.95
F
ILFORD XP2

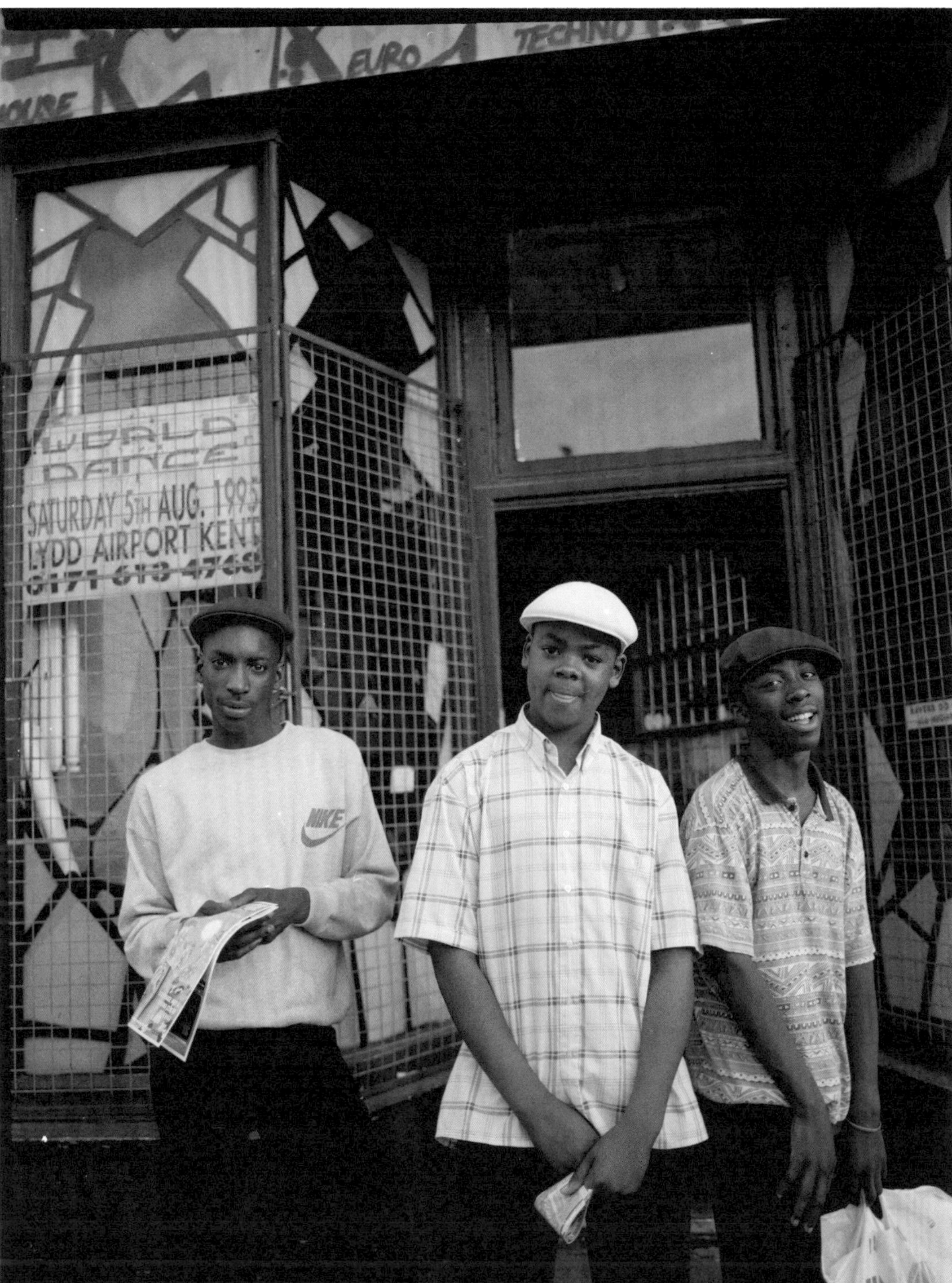
HOUSE
EURO
TECHNO
WORLD DANCE
SATURDAY 5TH AUG. 1995
LYDD AIRPORT KENT
NIKE

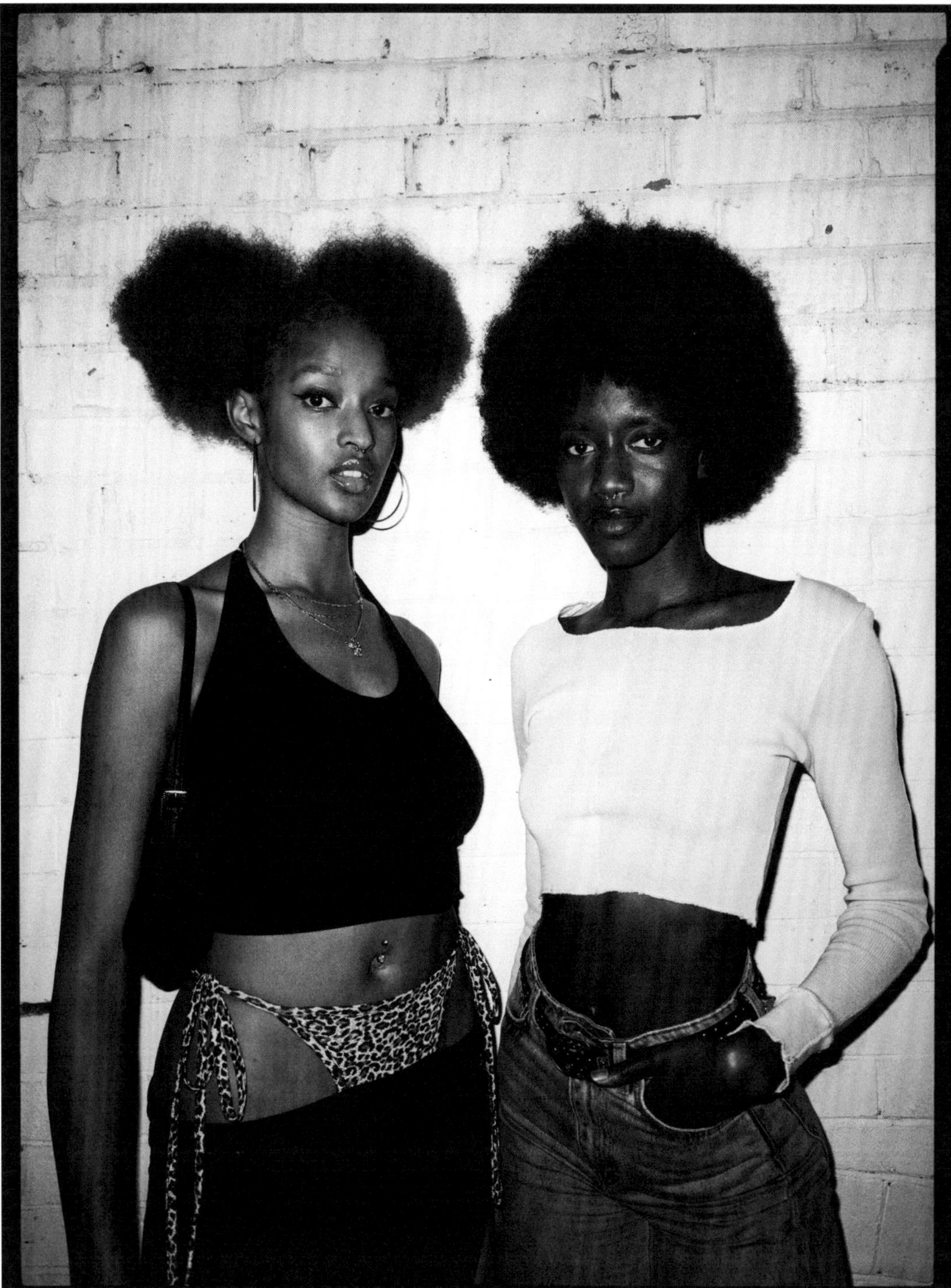

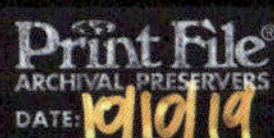

Print File
ARCHIVAL PRESERVERS
DATE: 10/10/19



BOILER ROOM DAY 2
EMULSION SIDE DOWN
STYLE NO. 120-4UB
ASSIGNMENT:
FILE NO:


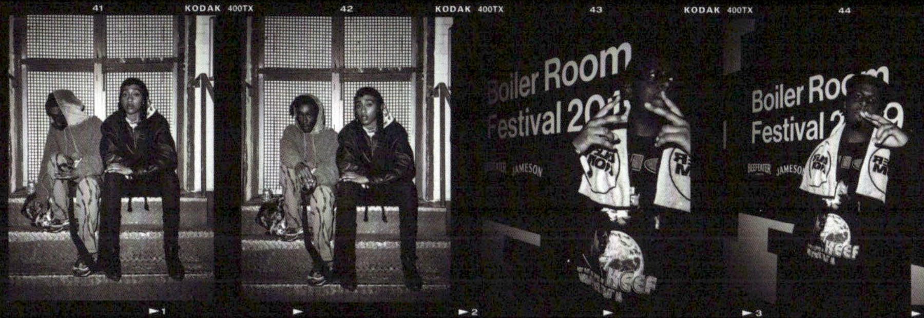

KODAK 400TX
Boiler Room
Festival
JAMESON


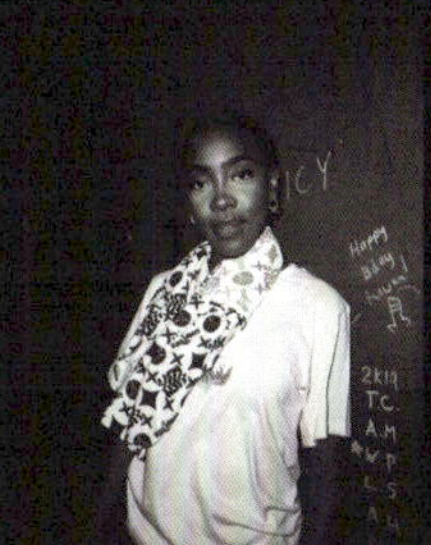

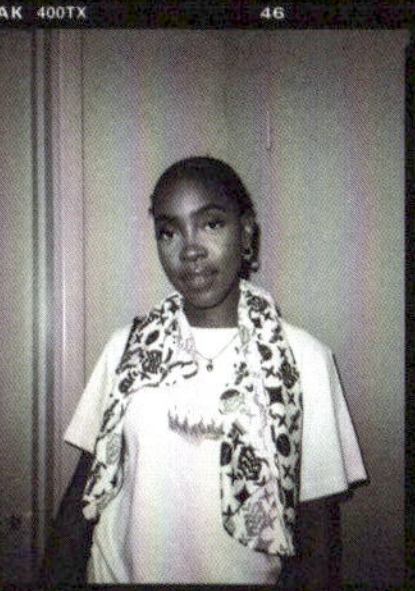

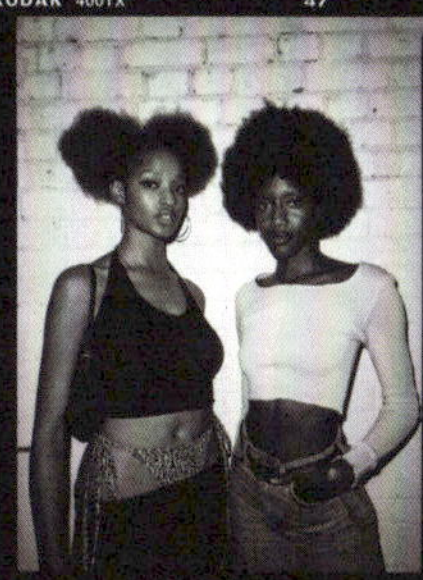

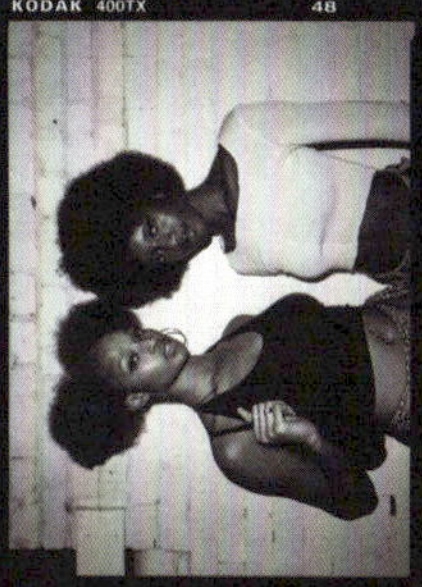

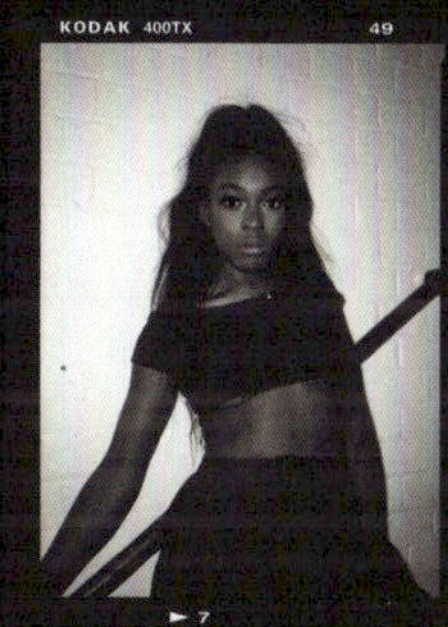

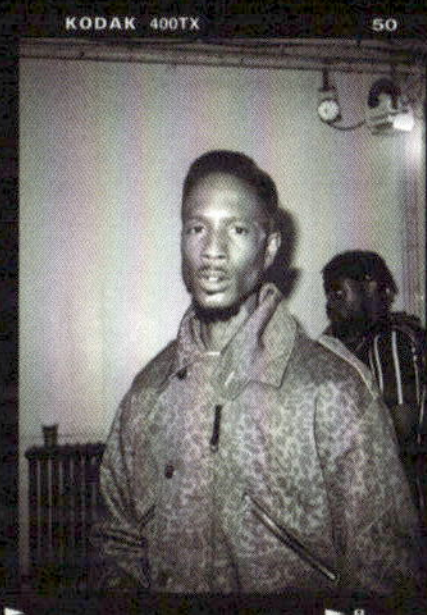

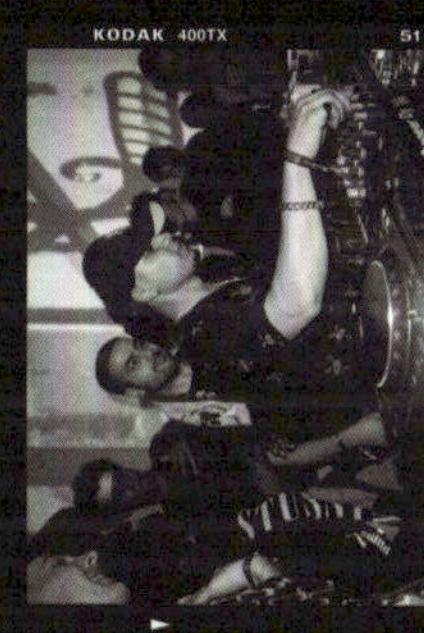

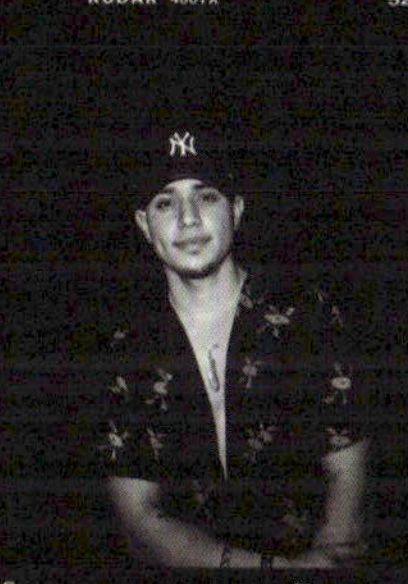

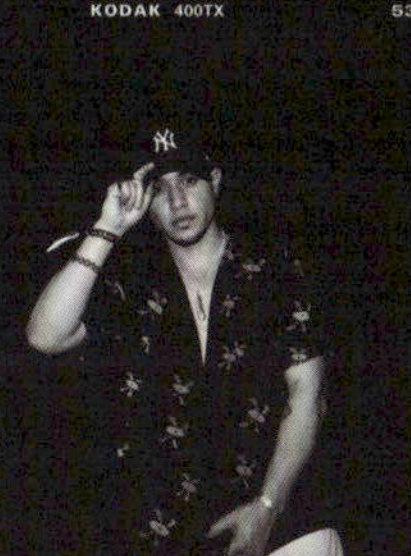

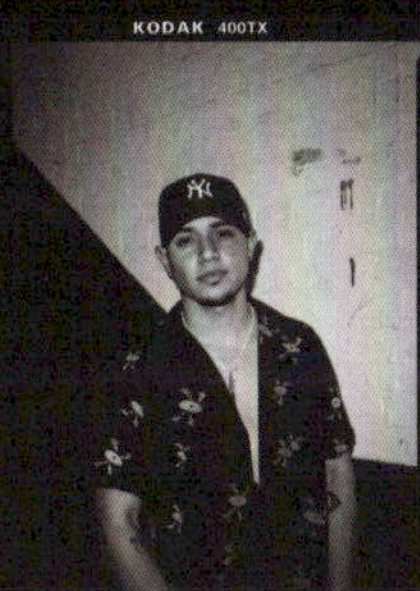

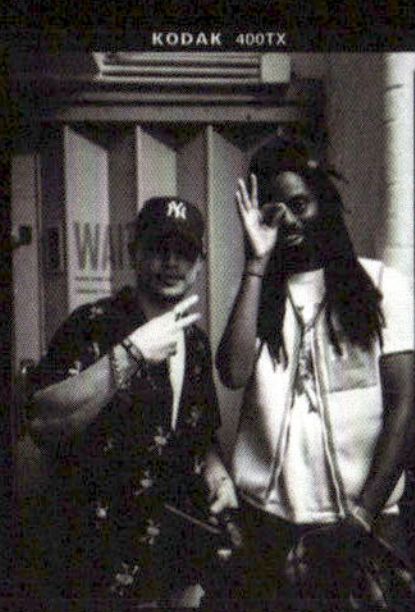

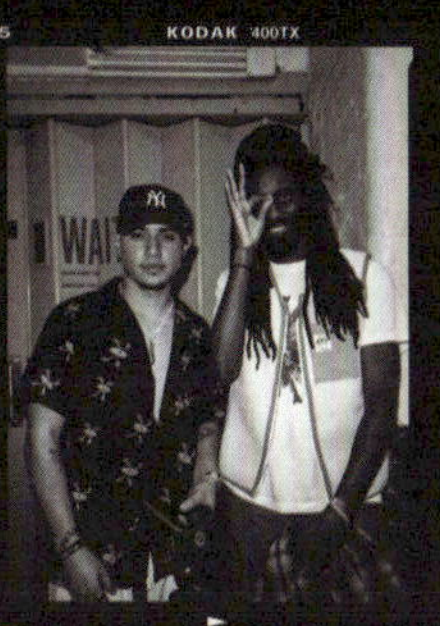

Print File ARCHIVAL PRESERVERS WWW.PRINTFILE.COM INSERT EMULSION SIDE DOWN STYLE NO. 120-4UB

DATE 02/06/18 ASSIGNMENT Field Days: Badu/thundercat + FILE NO:

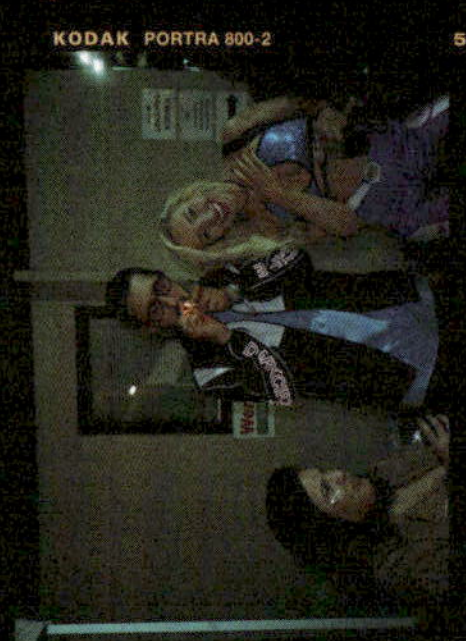
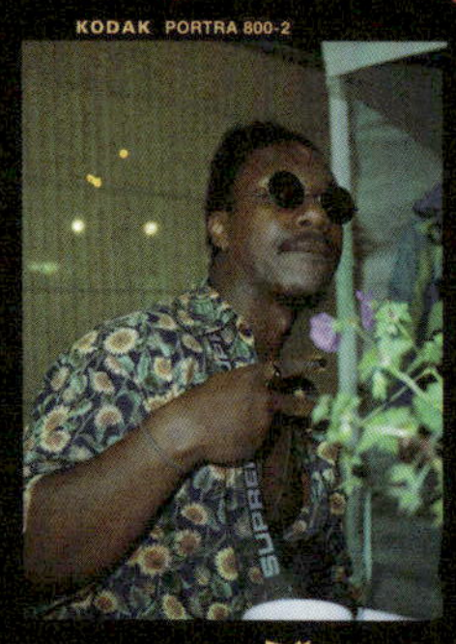
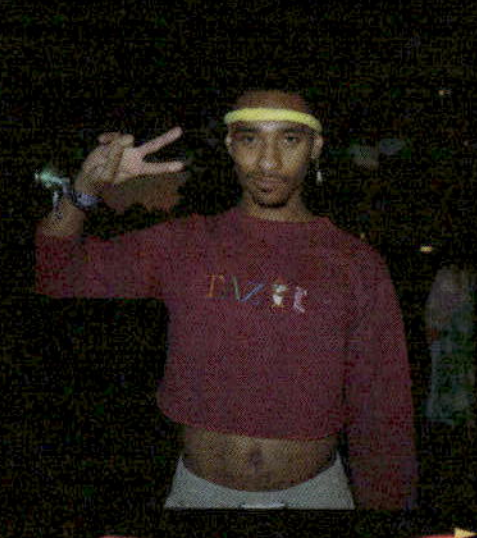
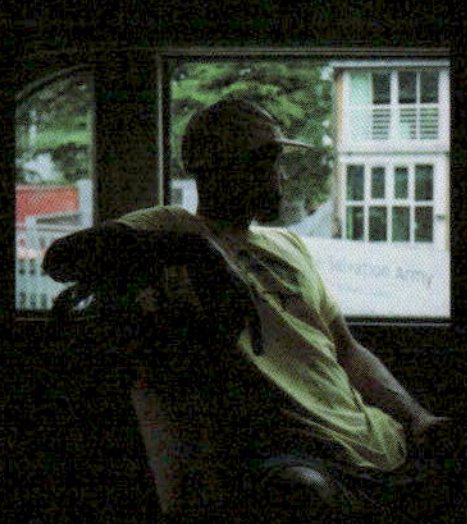
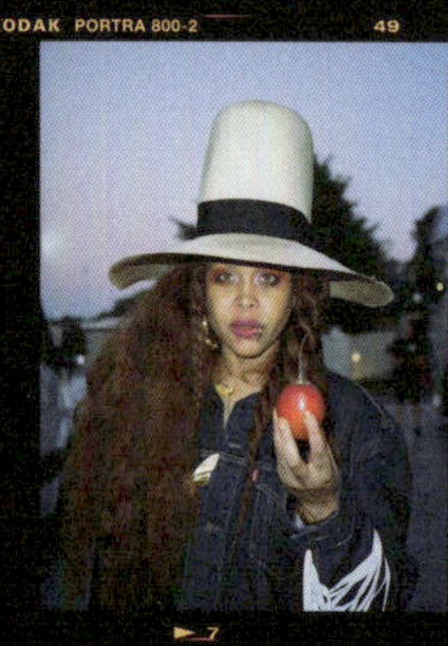
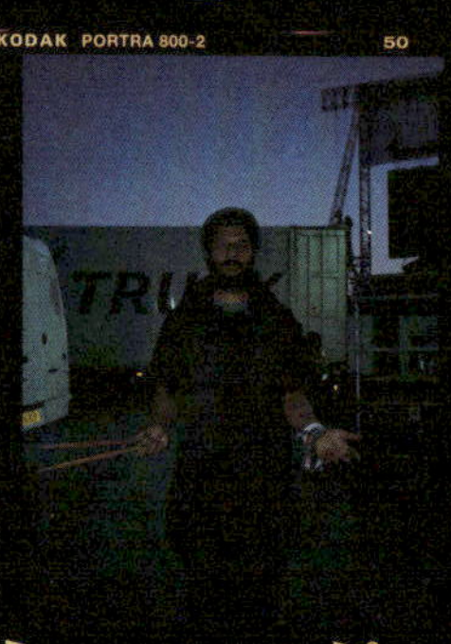
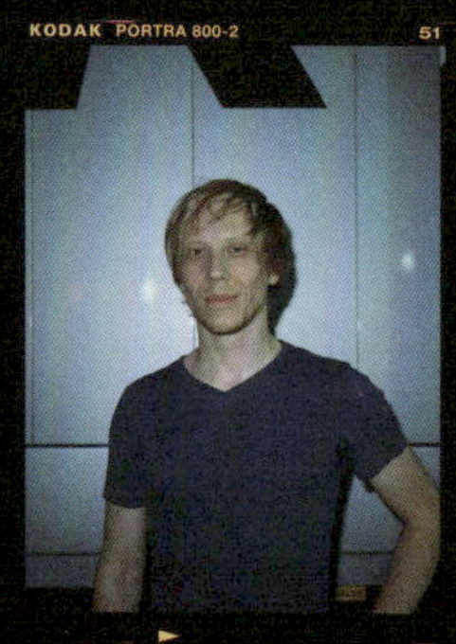
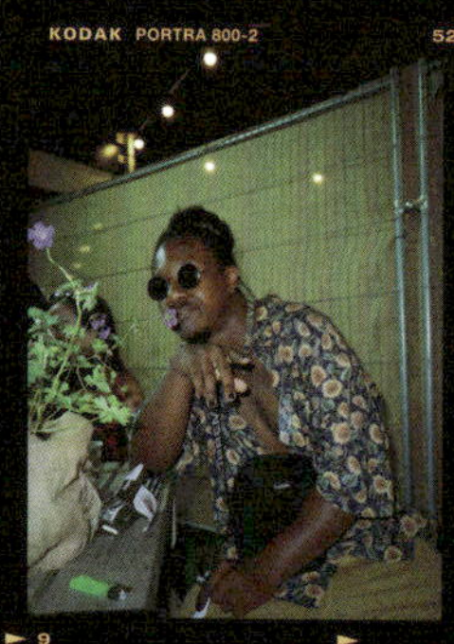
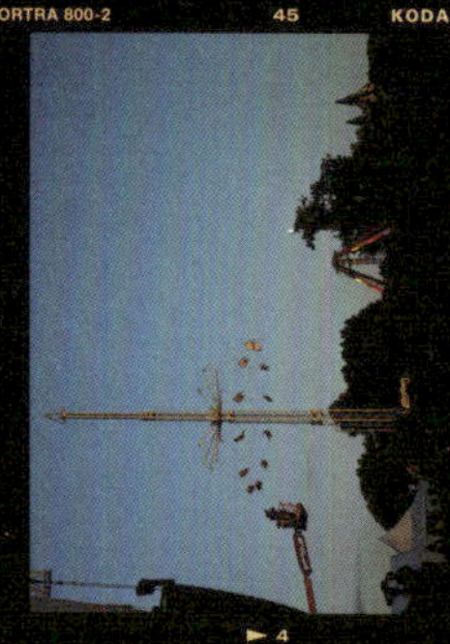
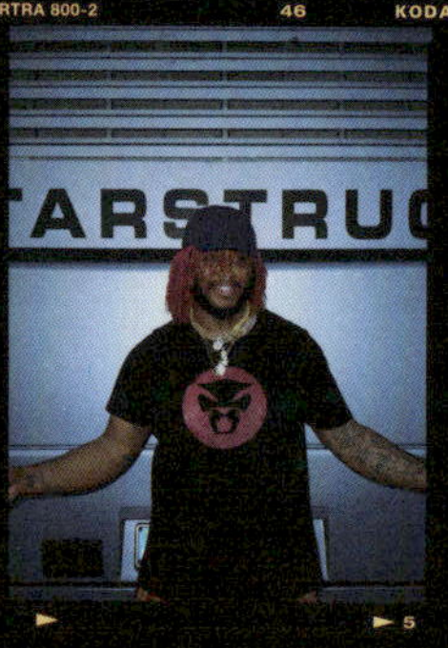

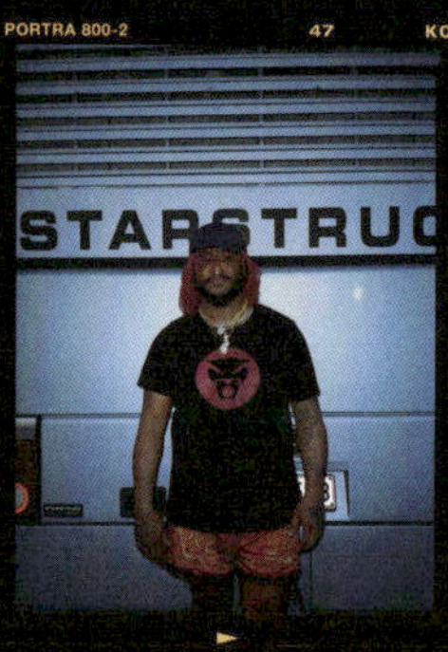

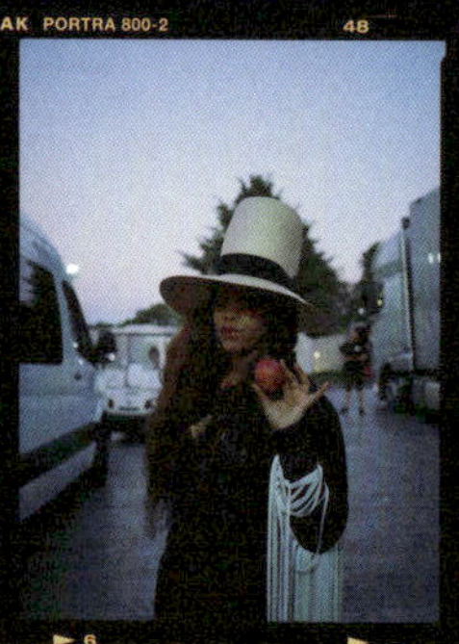
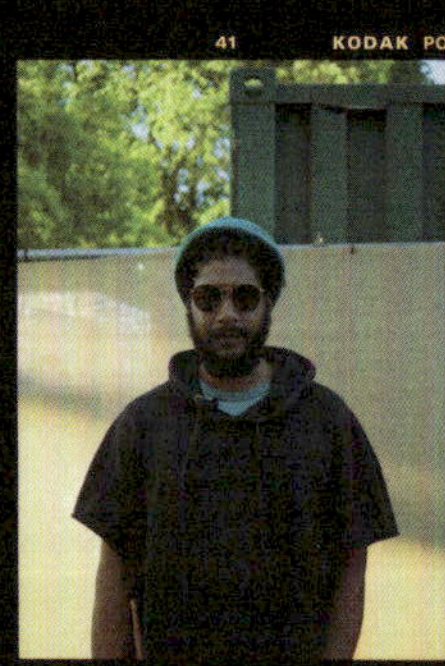
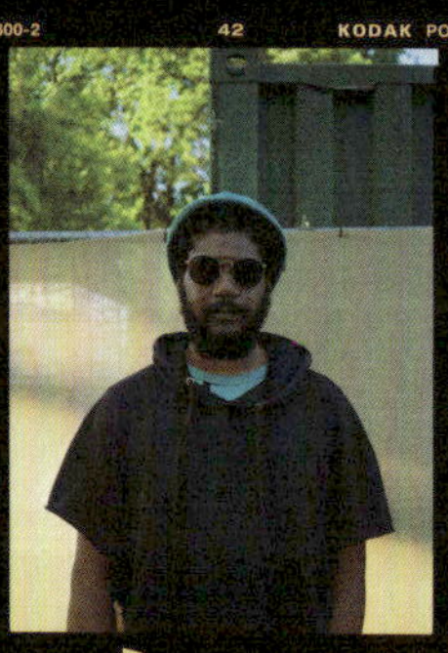
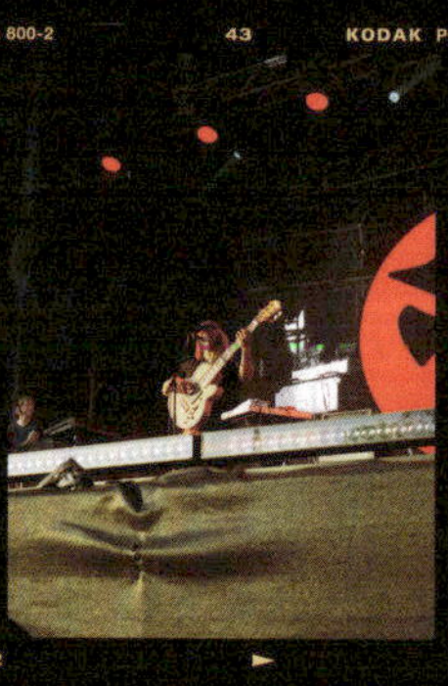
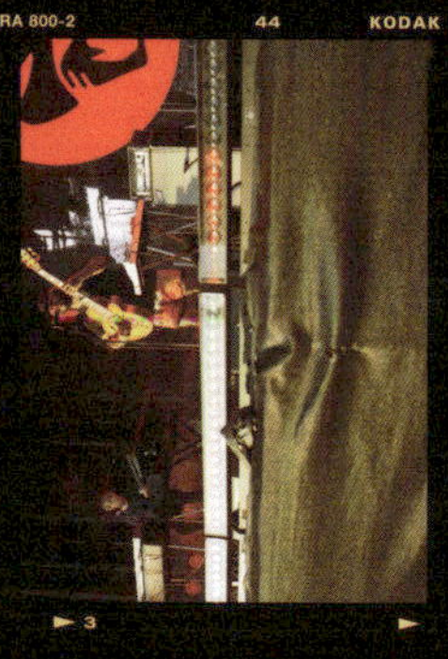

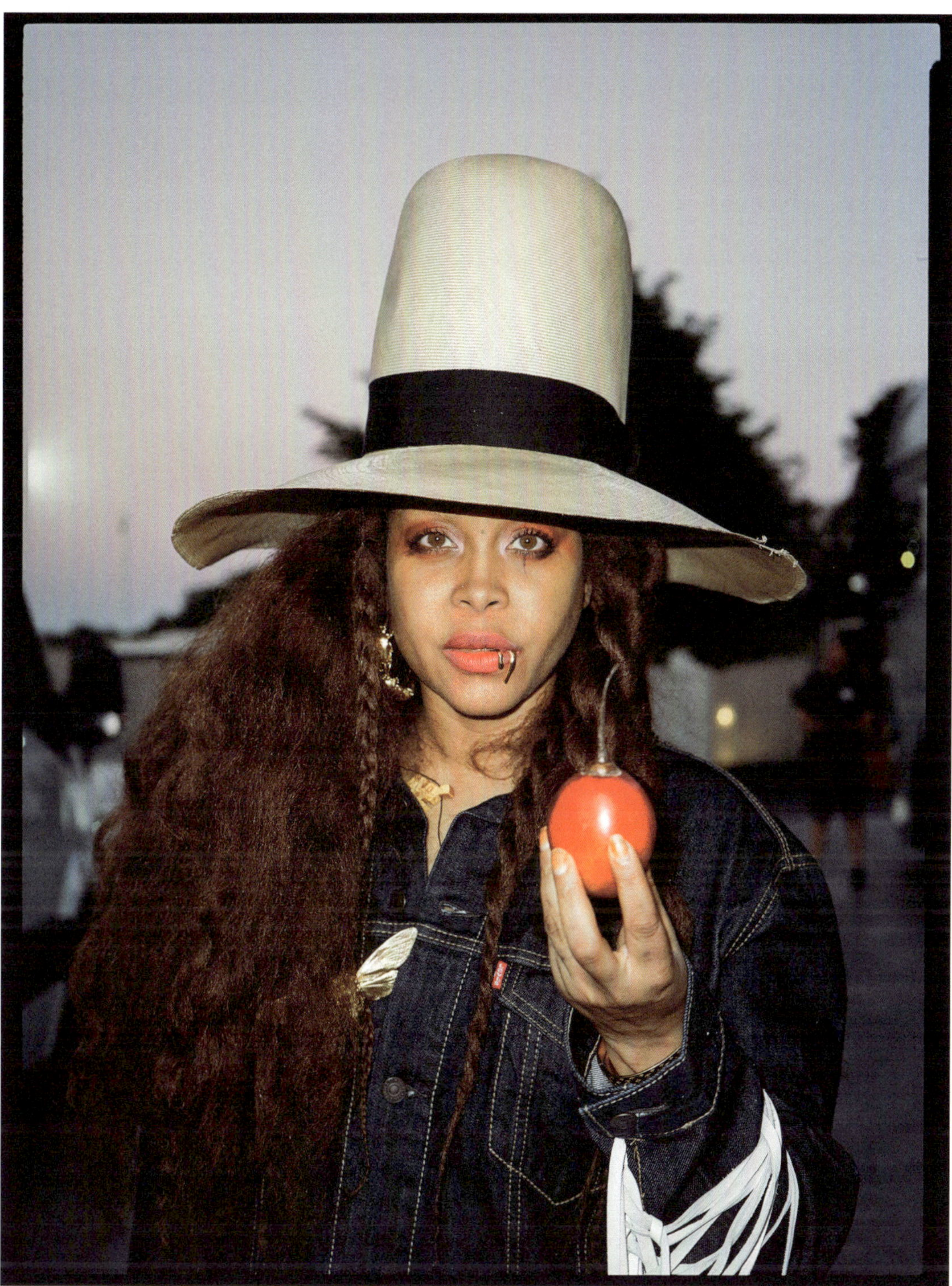

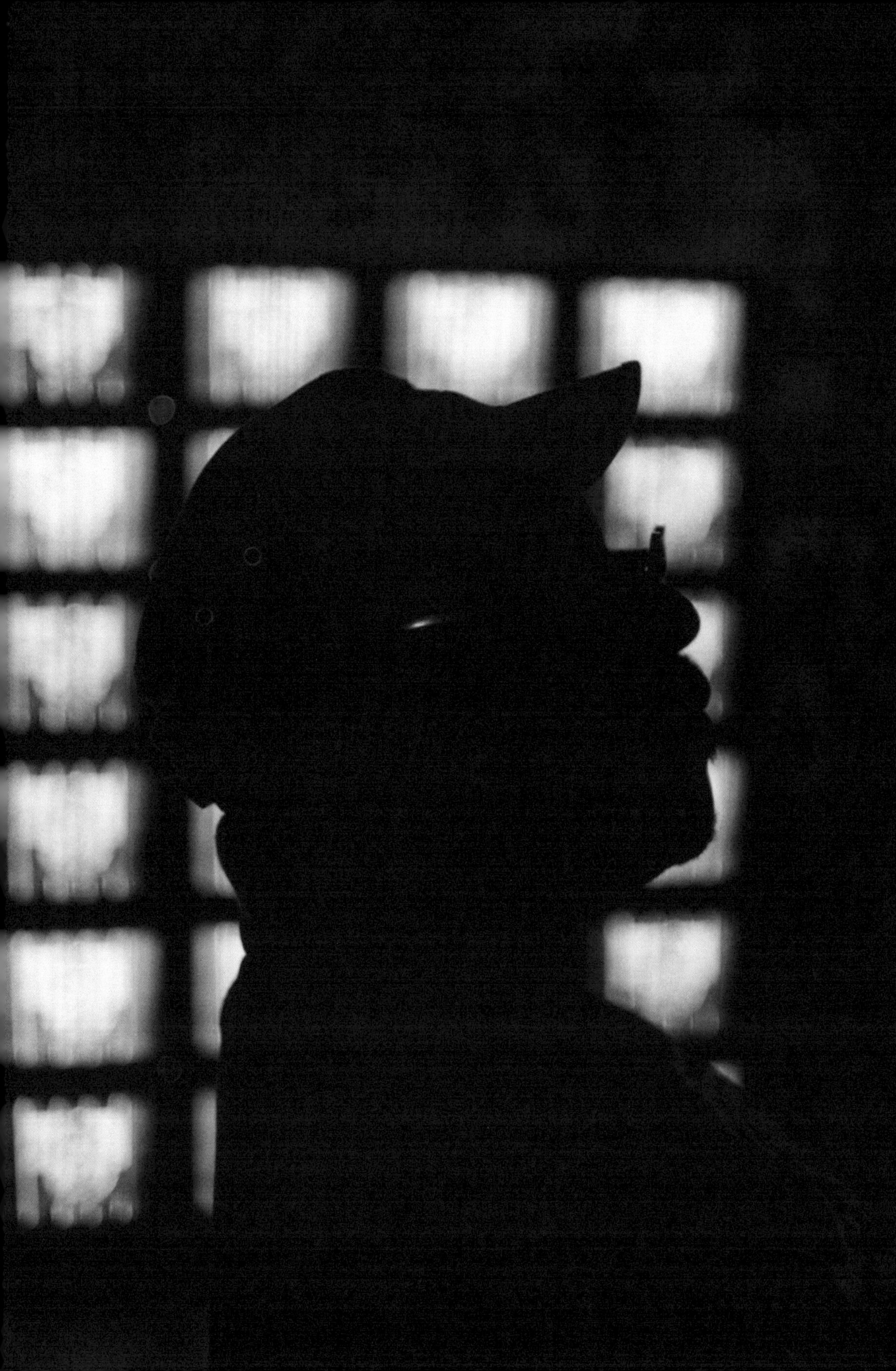

# CONVERSATION WITH MAD PROFESSOR

Melissa Chemam, Johny Pitts and Roger Robinson met with Mad Professor, born Neil Fraser in British Guyana, to discuss the notion of creativity and the "B-side" in his music and Black culture. They sat in Bristol, ahead of his show at Strange Brew, on Sunday 27 June 2021, at the beer garden of the Attic Bar, in Stokes Croft.

JOHNY PITTS Neil, from the day I heard you at Melissa's book talk at the British Library, I've thought about what you and Mark Stewart (of the Bristol pioneering post-punk band The Pop Group) said about the importance of the "B-side" in music – how a culture surrounded the B-side of an official release, and in many ways was only a manifestation of larger B-side culture born of mainstream rejection: pirate radio stations, illegal blues parties and so on. When you look at all the work Black photographers have done over the years, from Vanley Burke to more recently Liz Johnson Artur, they are searching for different ways of looking at the world. Sometimes for economic reasons, sometimes due to different cultural perspectives. And so they produced work that was very different from most mainstream documentary photographers. I wanted to come back to this discussion between you and Melissa on this notion for our issue.

MELISSA CHEMAM Yes, Neil, I've interviewed you many times since 2018, for my book on Bristol's music, and for the 40 years of your label, Ariwa, created in 1980. We discussed many of the events of your music history. If we go back to that idea of the B-side, 2020 was an interesting year to reflect on the type of music you produced, and think about this notion. For me, as I didn't grow up in Britain, what struck me in the story of reggae and dub is how much it was produced

© Johny Pitts, *Mad Professor*, Bristol, 2021

on the side of the mainstream, with very little money and very little support. I visited your studio in South London and most of the space was literally made by you, started as a home studio. Were you always aware of this notion of producing for the "B-side"?

NEIL FRASER You know, when you always work for the love of it, it's a different spirit than when you work to make £1,000 or £10,000. When you work for the love of music, you want to get to that point, in your head, in your soul, where you achieve something. So it's different. And most of the time, people around you don't have the same vision. What you got, you got it in your own head and you have to get it to that stage where it's out. And even then it could even be refused, abused or dismissed. If you're lucky it could be accepted, but most of the time, if it's coming from you only, it's hard to get it to be accepted. So the B-side, it really started like a fiction, like a feeling thing. It hasn't started with us, obviously. Think of proverbs and stories like the "ugly duckling that becomes the swan" or "the stone that the builder rejected" ... In other words, when you're creative and you may be ahead of your time, it can take time for people to catch up with you, but you have to go on.

JOHNY PITTS Do you think it has something to do with what J. G. Ballard once wrote, about the periphery being the place where the future reveals itself?

NEIL FRASER Yes, there is that, but also, you know, creative people sometimes see things that others don't see, and entrepreneurs as well, and visionaries. Like Marcus Garvey for instance. He was at a place when Black people came out of slavery, but the way forward was to be part of the system. And he saw his people as something other than a Black version of white people; he wanted to look to Africa. He ran away from the idea that "Black is ugly". He was received as out of place, or even mad. But a few years later, other people like Malcolm X and artists like Bob Marley and Burning Spear saw it in the same way and took it further.

ROGER ROBINSON Is it part of the vision that said that if you're doing work but not getting paid, you're actually creating culture? Did you have a vision that you were part of a scene that was creating culture?

NEIL FRASER Well, I had no such big idea. It was more humble than that. You know, as a little boy, I wanted to do some form of electronic music; that was my passion. And I heard a lot of things that inspired me. When I started to make music, you had to play an instrument. Electronic music came to give us the power to create music without instruments. Technology could take over. You could record sound, noise, or just knock on some wood and create something.

MELISSA CHEMAM And create rhythm, right? Which in itself is embedded in the African tradition? As in seeing music as part of your daily life, your spiritual life, and not as an industry. That is also related to the idea of the B-side, isn't it? It's not about business or career; it's a way to express yourself.

NEIL FRASER Yeah, you just do it with love and for the love of it. It's just important to you. It may be dismissed when it comes out, but later on, somebody else might get it.

ROGER ROBINSON Did you see examples of other people doing that as well?

NEIL FRASER Yeah, probably Tubby, King Tubby. I thought he was amazing; he was making music from effects, echoes, reverbs, etc. Creating different landscapes and moods. The sound of that siren we hear now, even [the sound of a siren whirrs in the background as we conduct the interview], we can take it, record it and make something creative out of it.

JOHNY PITTS And where do you think that interest for the atmosphere and the texture comes from?

NEIL FRASER I guess, the thing about atmosphere is about caring about the moment of the recording, its uniqueness. Recording is to capture the sound of a specific time. Even 10 minutes later, you'd get a different sound and a different atmosphere. And it's the beauty of recording; it's like photography again; it documents a moment.

MELISSA CHEMAM It's interesting because it gives us something that is the opposite of a product, of the reproduction of the same format, just like you said before about being organic, and it's again creating something that is unique to an artist or a group, isn't it?

NEIL FRASER Yes, and this way it's got its own life.

JOHNY PITTS Was it also a means to document an era that no one else was documenting?

NEIL FRASER Well, it's about giving other people the opportunity to relive that moment that we, musicians and producers, witnessed. That's what production is about: using all the tools you have to make it the best moment to later be shared for people to relive that time.

ROGER ROBINSON Going back to Tubby, he would use the studio as almost an instrument; is it something that you saw for yourself?

NEIL FRASER Yes, well, it *is* an instrument. It becomes part of you. And then you create your technique, and your texture, your way of capturing that moment, so then people can recognize "Oh, that's Mad Professor!"

JOHNY PITTS That is how the photographer Eddie Otchere [included in this issue] thinks of the darkroom – that the energy you take there as you process and develop informs the image as much as pressing the shutter. He said that he noticed when he was angry his prints had more contrast! With your studio, were you conscious of the space itself, and what it felt like? You started recording in your kitchen or your front room, right?

NEIL FRASER I did, but I wasn't conscious of the potential of this space, it was just budget limitations. I started the studio in 1979 when I could soundproof a place. At the time, it cost money, and money you didn't have.

MELISSA CHEMAM And I remember you telling me that you had to keep on working other jobs from Monday to Friday, while recording music on Saturdays, then most of your weekends, then even in the evenings ...

NEIL FRASER Oh yeah, and for that you need money; it was always costly, not bringing in much money at first.

ROGER ROBINSON Is there anything that you learned from these restrictions?

NEIL FRASER Well, yeah, I mean, things like reverbs, for instance. At the time, you could build a cheap spring reverb. We used spring reverbs out of necessity, then people wanted to recreate the imperfect sounds we made so they became really expensive. And some other years later, people started to collect the old ones. Later, I moved onto other things, other technology.

MELISSA CHEMAM You still have a lot of analogue machines in your studio though, tape recorders, master recordings, etc.

NEIL FRASER Yeah, that's it, because some of them really cannot be reproduced by a computer. Apple cannot give you the sound of a studio tape machine. It's warmer, and even though it now looks old, it sounds futuristic in some way.

ROGER ROBINSON Technology kind of failed the quality of music.

MELISSA CHEMAM And there is also the idea that the limitations create the unique music. And that's how Massive Attack's *Blue Lines* came about, with one sampler for a weekend, a unique day at the studio when the singer could come in to record; the best ideas had to be recorded and only the greatest made it ... It was uniquely recorded when all people could come together in a specific moment. And all the music that nourished you, especially for Black music, the knowledge of all the singers and songwriters you know but didn't become famous, inform you in that moment. It's about not missing the chance to make something new and special. So you pour all your soul into the few minutes of recording. Then all the accidents become unique, right?

JOHNY PITTS And also there is the same effect for photographers. The analogue instruments allowed some mistakes, and sometimes they become the most beautiful parts – what Barthes calls *punctum*: the inexplicable thing that pierces your heart. Which is why people are going back to film; because current technology is too clean ... Do you ever look back to that?

NEIL FRASER Yeah, if we think of my first albums, my first dubs, those tracks, I wasn't even going to use them. I had done them when

I started and they remained a stepping stone to where I wanted to be. But once, while playing old tapes, listening back, I thought even though they're from 40 years ago, I want to put them together and create a series. They were the first dubs, and they're really special. I can't put my finger on what it is, but it's rough, the spring reverbs sound so metallic, they have something, and it's deep. As I went along, some of them were really actually B-sides. And they're special, because at the time, nobody wanted them. But we ended up getting back to them. And some people, years later, bought the singles just for the B-side, for instance with 'One Million Man Dub'. And even later some became hits when re-released.

ROGER ROBINSON For me, the B-side is also an invitation for people to take part, to add the voice of the MC for instance on a dance floor, as often they have minimal vocals, or they might mix a different sound on it. It can open a space.

NEIL FRASER Yeah, man. Interesting.

ROGER ROBINSON I kind of know you for your mixes. What do you enjoy most, the remix or the straight-up tracks?

NEIL FRASER It depends if I'm the producer or not. As a producer, I like to get to a special place. If you mix 10 versions, the artist might not even know the difference, but I would. I can hear and spot all the tiniest differences.

MELISSA CHEMAM There is a saying in the music industry that claims that only producers know when a song is actually ready, that musicians or DJs get lost in the creative process ... So it takes a producer with a very special ear to finish a track. It sounds even truer for dub music. The production could turn even the worst piece of music into something completely different ...

JOHNY PITTS Like the role of a good photo editor!

NEIL FRASER There are a lot of vocals for instance, especially in pop music, that you could entirely save. I remember hearing a song by The Bangles one day, normally not my type of music, but the work of the engineer captured my attention. It was about the texture. It was 'Eternal Flame'. The vocals were really special.

ROGER ROBINSON There is actually kind of a reggae thing in it, a lovers' rock tone!

JOHNY PITTS And it reminds me of Massive Attack's 'Teardrop' now that you mention it. Going back to the B-side, I think about people who told me recently that they loved the VHS version of a film more than the digitally remastered version. When I think of your beginnings [Mad Professor], I think the same thing. And for you, even on the radio, you first listened to your favourite songs on the lower-quality medium-wave frequency ...

NEIL FRASER True, when I was in the Caribbean, we would search for these medium waves to hear the best songs. And they had that sort of slightly distorted sound, almost on the verge of disappearing. They were hard to catch. Then FM came later and was a lot cleaner. A lot of the soul music was hard to find. Most of us, from that era, we experienced the trials and tribulations of the medium waves.

MELISSA CHEMAM That's how you started, by making the electronics, being in charge of the technical side and building things, right?

NEIL FRASER Yeah, I just taught myself about the machines and the sound, putting the wires together to get some sound, and I analysed how everything worked. I broke it down and built my own. Then I started to get an understanding of how to get it. You get a piece of wood and you carve it to make a guitar, get some strings and add them! In the same way, in the studio, I had no money to get the things, so I had to build my own. Even now the technical side of the studio is important to me and my other engineers.

MELISSA CHEMAM And also the radio, once you produced music, remained a two-way path for you. You often said that the BBC wouldn't play reggae or dub, so you had to find your own channels to play your music, didn't you?

NEIL FRASER Absolutely. Radio became such an important medium for artists in the 1980s, so if not played we had to find our own ways. Always.

JOHNY PITTS To conclude on the B-sides, were they a way to be more creative, less concerned with being "popular"?

NEIL FRASER The B-side was basically used to fill in space. But if I produce a track for someone, as a remix, for instance, then yes, it will end up on the B-side, so then it's my own territory.

MELISSA CHEMAM And a generation later, in the 1990s, the B-side became the real side too, when the A-side had to be a "radio edit" version, no more than four minutes. So the artists would put the longer, original version of the track on the B-sides. And these versions and remixes became a new reason to collect singles ...

NEIL FRASER Exactly.

NEIL FRASER AKA MAD PROFESSOR

Mad Professor is a Guyana-born, London-based music producer and DJ. He celebrated the 40 years of his record label, Ariwa, in 2020. The label has produced some of the best British reggae and dub records and remixes since 1980. Neil Fraser (the Professor's real name) has worked with the likes of Lee "Scratch" Perry, Horace Andy, Sade, the KLF and Massive Attack.

MELISSA CHEMAM

Melissa Chemam is a Paris-born, Bristol-based journalist, writer, broadcaster and lecturer. After a decade as a reporter in America, Europe and Africa, from 2015 she started researching the cultural history of Bristol, interviewing artists, historians, musicians, rappers and engaged Bristolians. Her book, *Massive Attack: Out of the Comfort Zone*, was first published in France in 2016, and came out in the UK in 2019. She regularly writes about multiculturalism, anti-racism and social change.

ROGER ROBINSON

Roger is a writer and educator who has taught and performed worldwide and is an experienced workshop leader and lecturer on poetry. He was chosen by the Arts Council's Decibel showcase as one of 50 writers who have influenced the Black British writing canon. He received commissions from the National Trust, Open House London, the BBC, the National Portrait Gallery, the V&A, Iniva, MK Gallery and the Theatre Royal Stratford East, where he also was associate artist. He is an alumnus of The Complete Works.

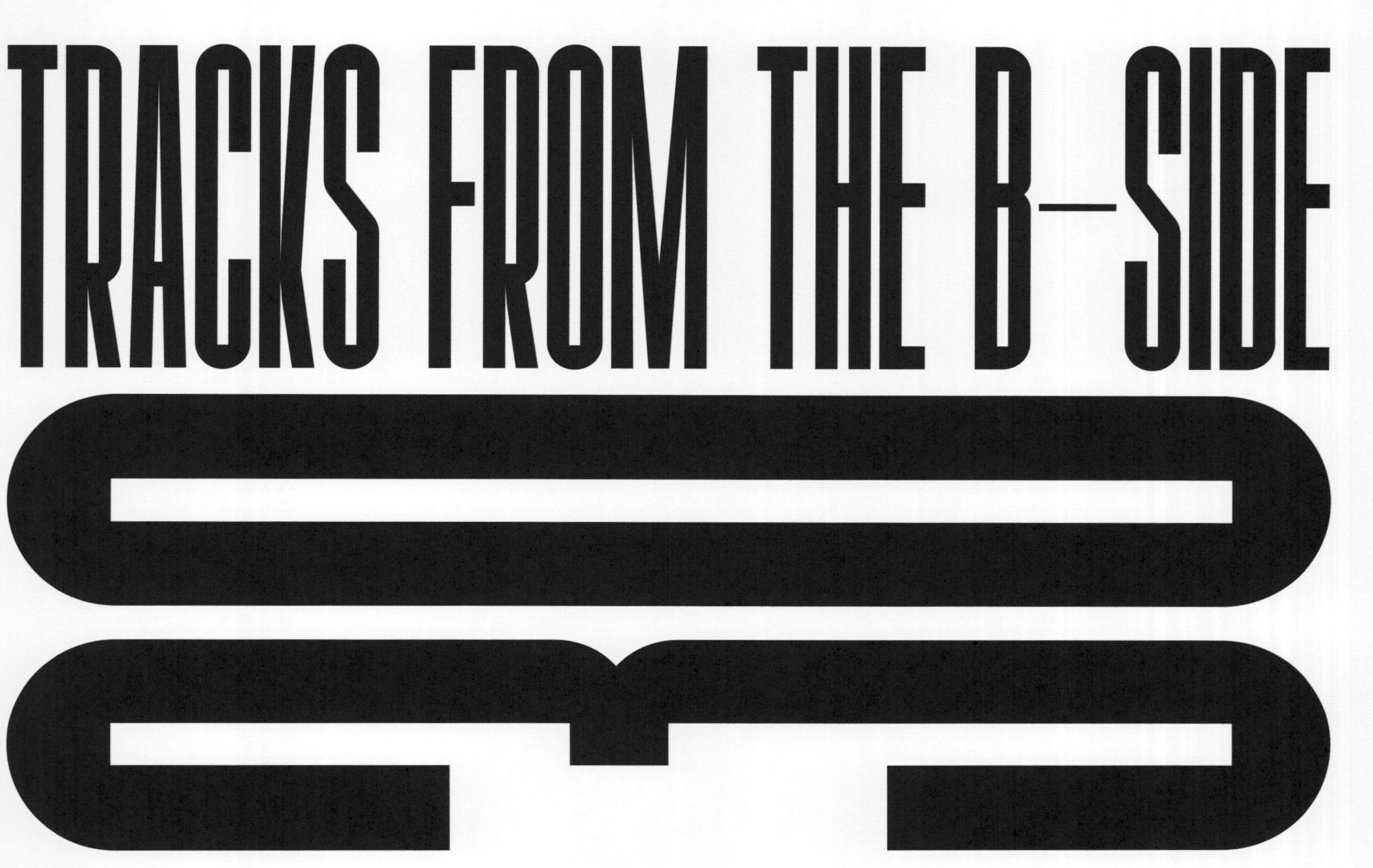
30
TRACKS FROM THE B-SIDE

Johny Pitts'
Afropean playlist

| | | |
|---|---|---|
| 1 | Lee Scott | "Bootl£gliving" |
| 2 | 2814 | "新宿ゴールデン街 / Shinjuku Golden Street" |
| 3 | Vivien Goldman | "Launderette" |
| 4 | U-NIQ ft. Sticks, Rico and Shyrock | "Politiek" |
| 5 | Ken Ring | "Du & Jag" |
| 6 | Stephen Simmonds (ft. Big L & Marquee) | "Alone (Lord Finesse Remix)" |
| 7 | Davina ft. Raekwon | "So Good (Remix)" |
| 8 | Akhenaton | "Lyrix Files" |
| 9 | Neneh Cherry ft. Notorious B.I.G. | "Buddy X (Falcon & Fabian Remix)" |
| 10 | Yellowman | "Yellowman Wise" |
| 11 | Massive Attack | "Teardrop (Mad Professor Mazaruni Vocal Mix)" |
| 12 | The Pharcyde | "Emerald Butterfly" |
| 13 | D'Angelo | "Me & Those Dreaming Eyes Of Mine (Jay Dee Remix)" |
| 14 | The Pharcyde | "She Said (Jay Dee Remix)" |
| 15 | Zap Mama | "Nostalgie Amoureuse (Bootleg Mix)" |
| 16 | Herbie Hancock ft. Chaka Khan | "The Essence" |
| 17 | Faye Wong | "Dreams" |
| 18 | Sade | "Love is Stronger Than Pride (Mad Professor Remix)" |
| 19 | 2Pac | "I Ain't Mad Atcha" [video version] |
| 20 | Klashnekoff | "Parrowdice" |
| 21 | Les Nubians | "Makeda (DJ Spinna Remix)" |
| 22 | Taiyo & Ciscomoon | "Be Cool Down" |
| 23 | Ryuichi Sakamoto | "We Love You" [single version] |
| 24 | Donny Hathaway | "Yesterday" [live version] |
| 25 | Valete | "A Verdade Monogamia (Sam The Kid Remix)" |
| 26 | Bare Knuckle Soul | "Bare Knuckle Soul" |
| 27 | Grace Jones | "Libertango (Extended Dub Edit)" |
| 28 | Ibeyi | "Stranger / Lover (Mura Masa Remix)" |
| 29 | Level 42 ft. Omar | "The Sun Goes Down 98 Mix" |
| 30 | Waxolutionists | "Slangdunk" |

# SILVIA ROSI

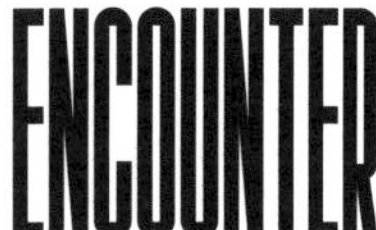


Silvia Rosi was born in 1992 in Scandiano, Italy. She studied photography at the University of the Arts in London and is now based in England. Her work as a photographer and video-maker focuses on her family history, her Togolese heritage and the notion of origin. She draws some of her inspiration from the tradition of mid-20th century West African studio portraitists such as Mama Casset in Senegal, Joseph Moïse Agbojelou in Benin, Cornélius Augustt Azaglo in Côte d'Ivoire, and Felix Diallo and Seydou Keïta in Mali.

In the series "Encounter", Silvia Rosi presents her family history. This series was born from the discovery of a photograph of her mother as a young vendor in the market of Lomé, Togo.

Playing, in turn, her father and her mother, she retraced the migratory journey of her parents from Togo to Italy. She recreated visual and oral stories through photography, text and video. The reference to the aesthetics of West African studio portraits is perceptible through the use of a backdrop and the presence of accessories. Carrying loads on the head, a skill traditionally passed down from mother to daughter, is at the heart of this work. Silvia Rosi learned this skill to recover a tradition that was lost due to her parents' migration and her status as a European.


*Self Portrait as my Mother in School Uniform*, 2019
*Self Portrait as my Father*, 2019
*Self Portrait as my Mother*, 2019
Originally commissioned through Jerwood/ Photoworks Awards
*La sconosciuta*, 2019, stills
*Mother and Grandmother, Sihin*, 2019, stills
*Sihin*, 2019, stills

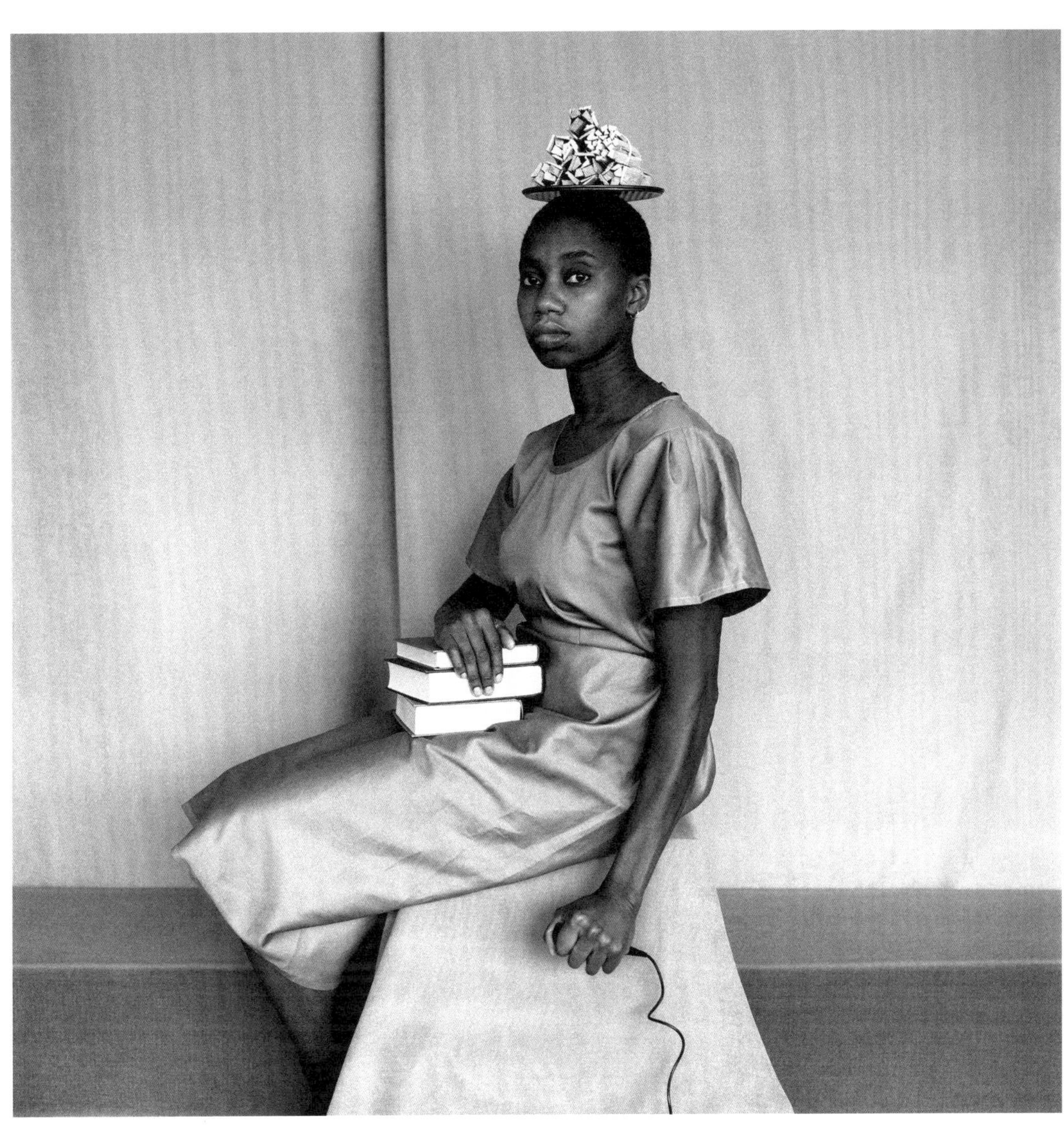

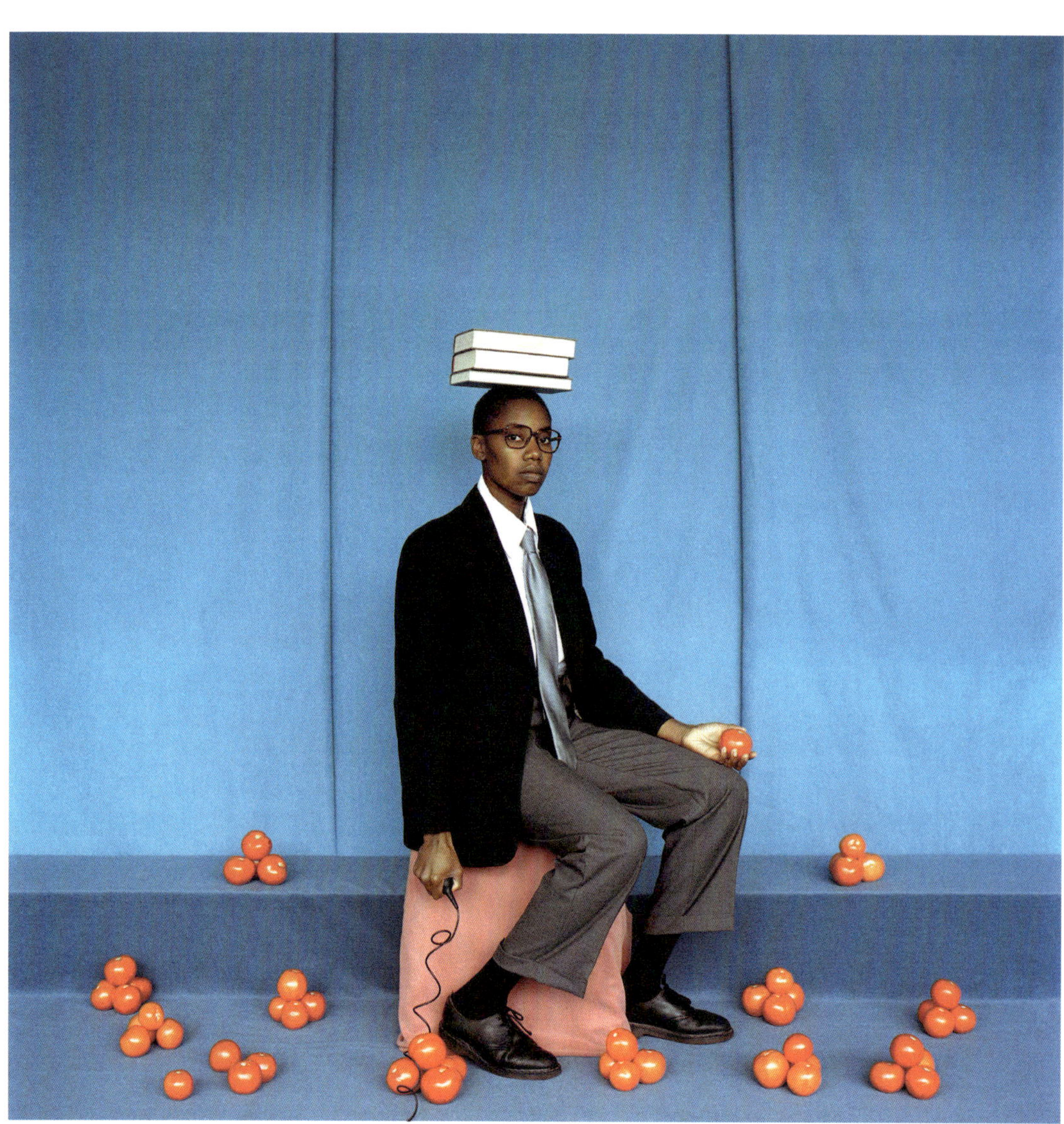

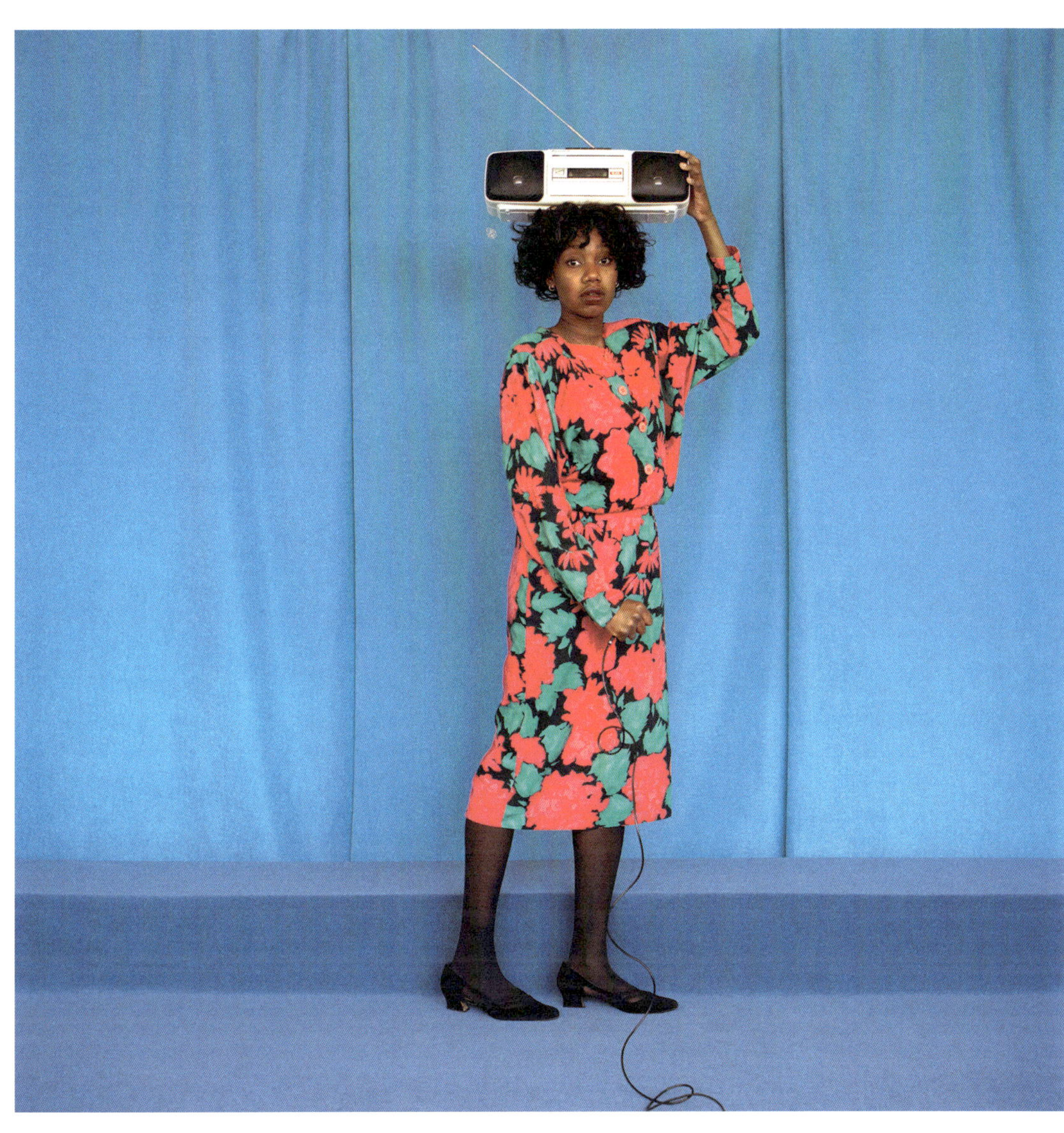

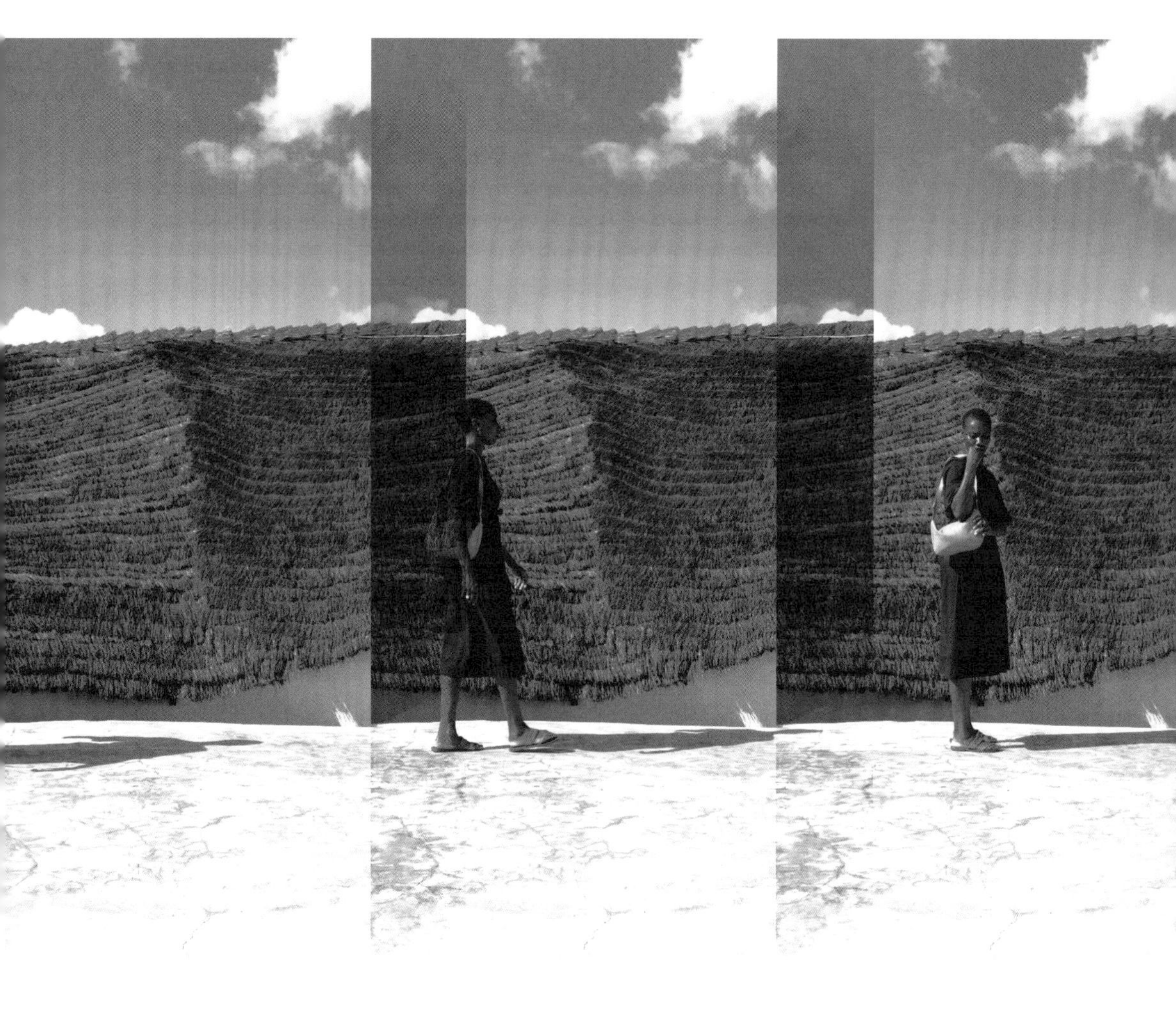

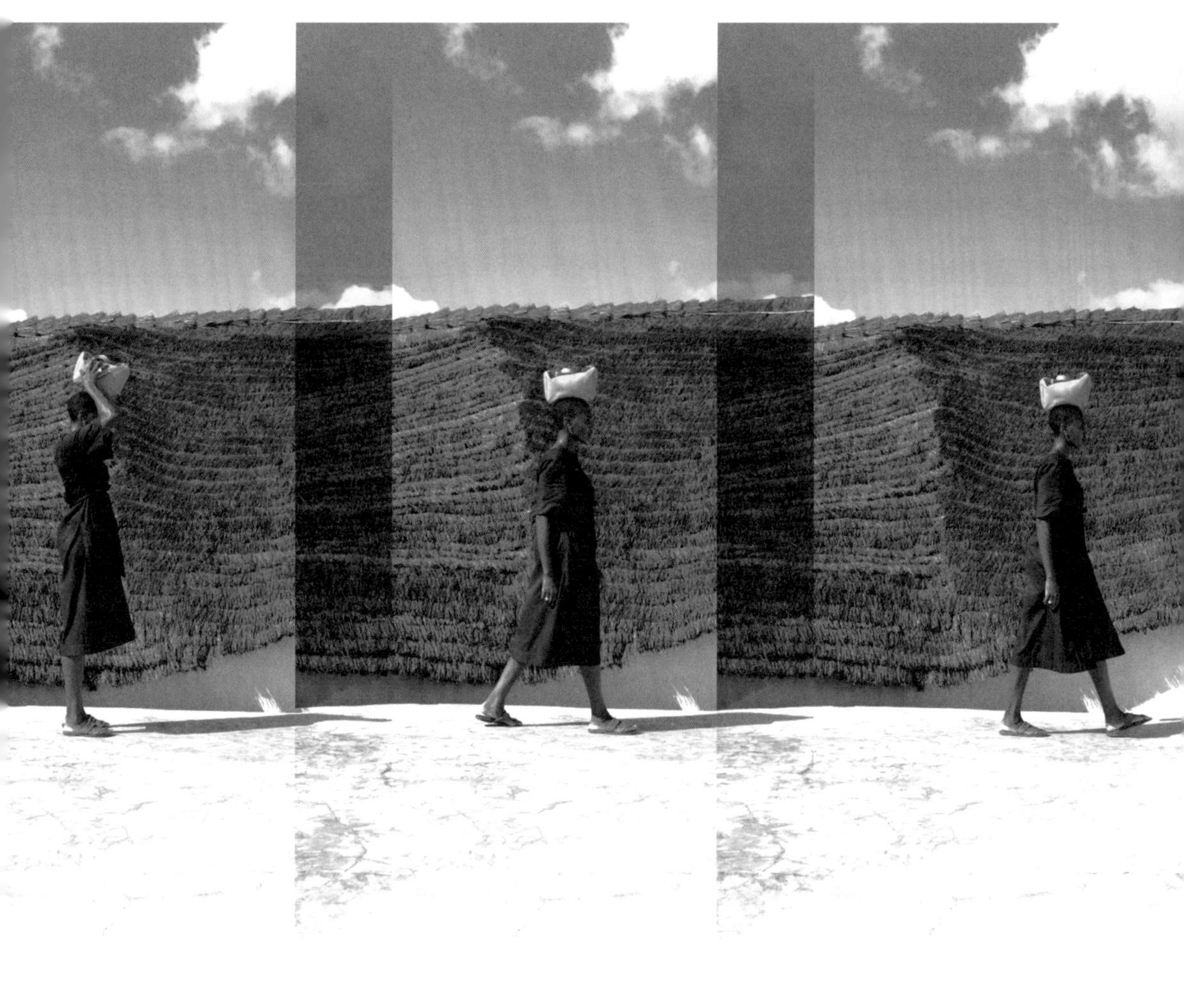

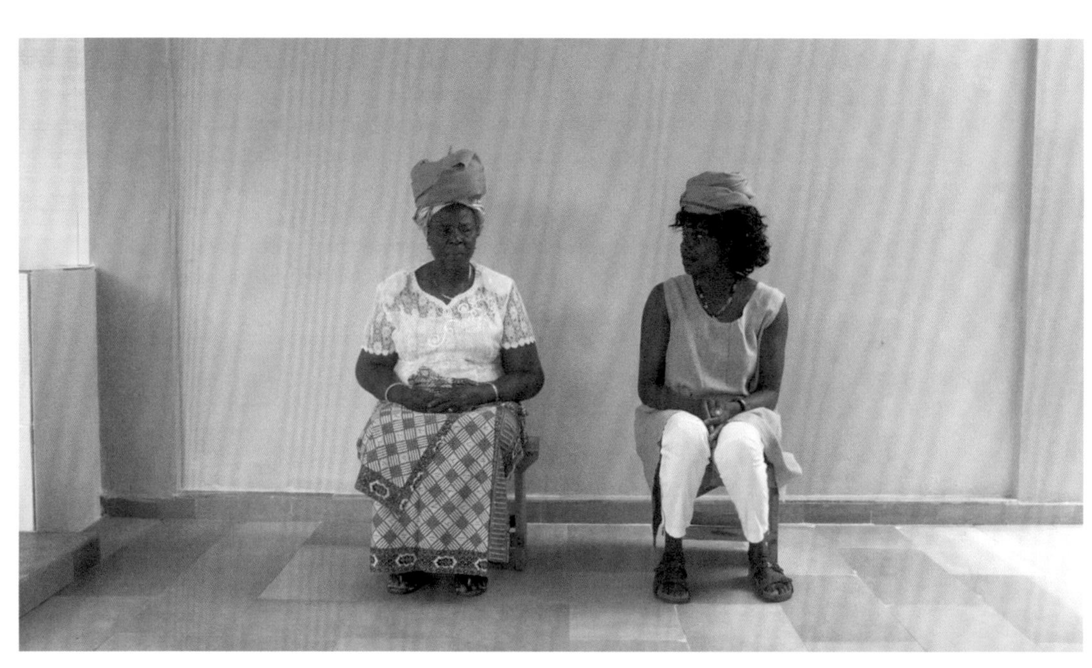

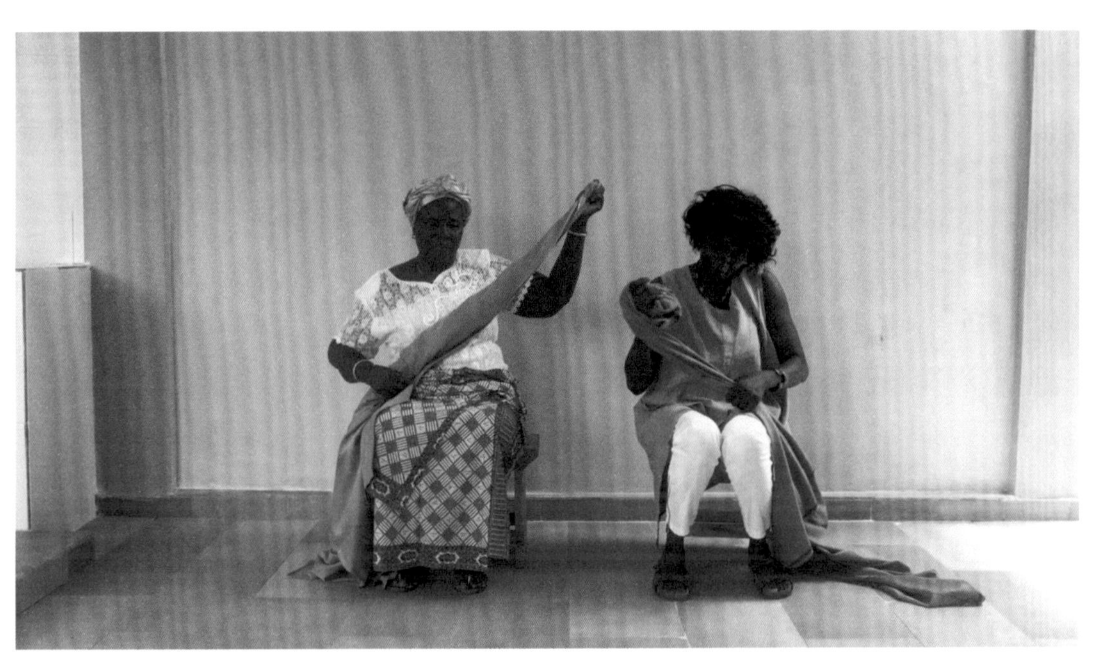

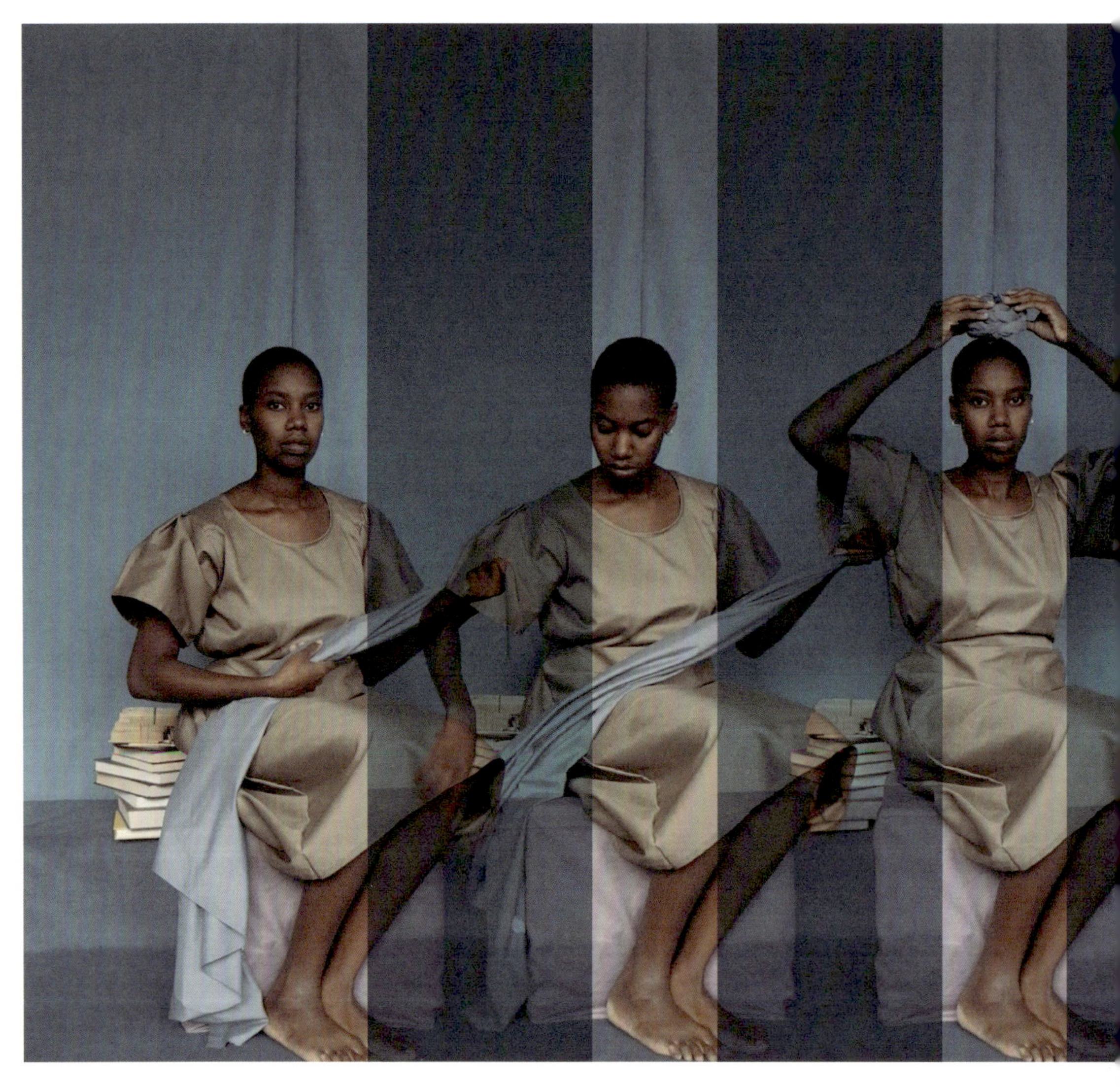

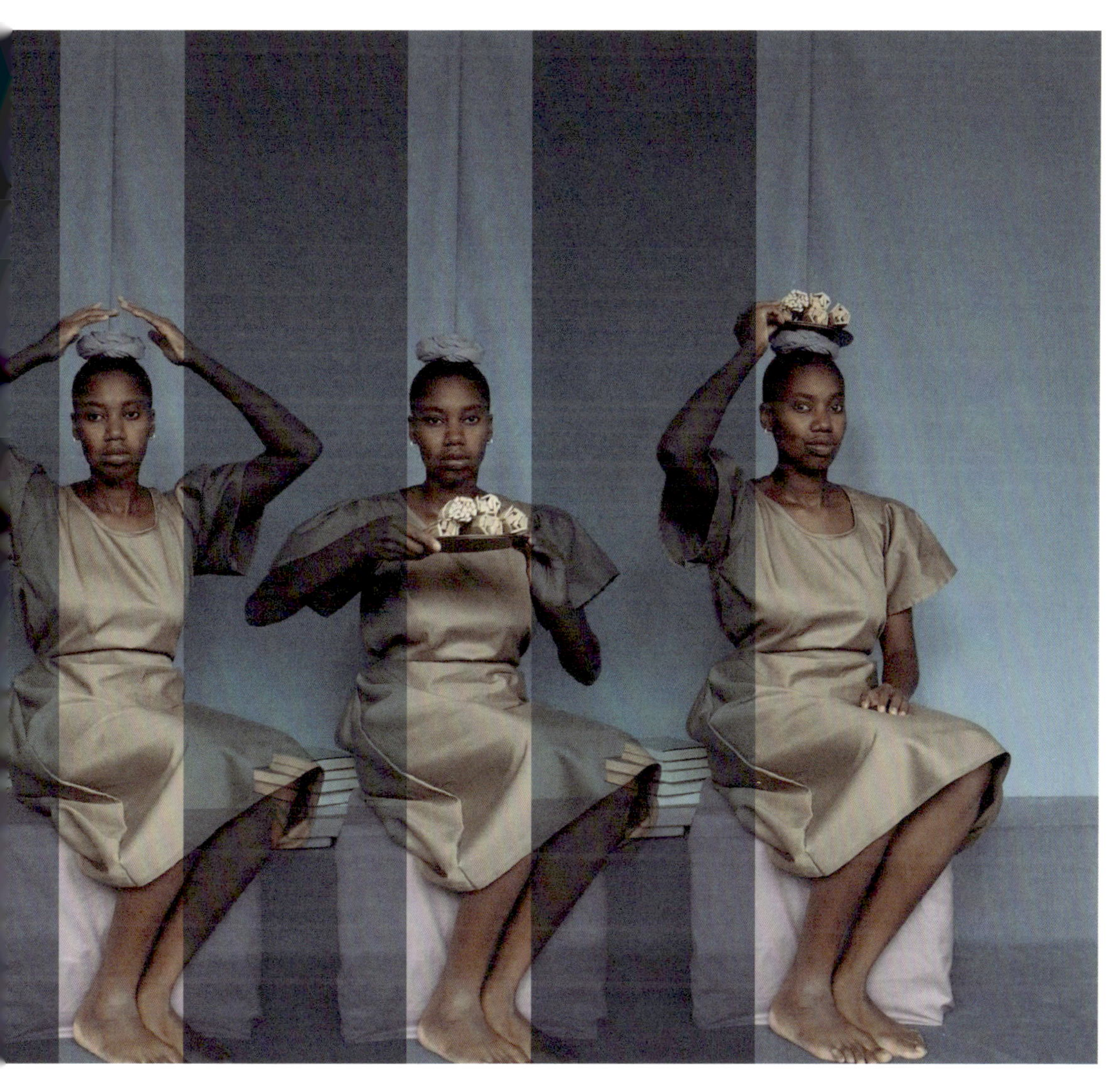

| TITLE | LIZ JOHNSON ARTUR |
|---|---|

COVER

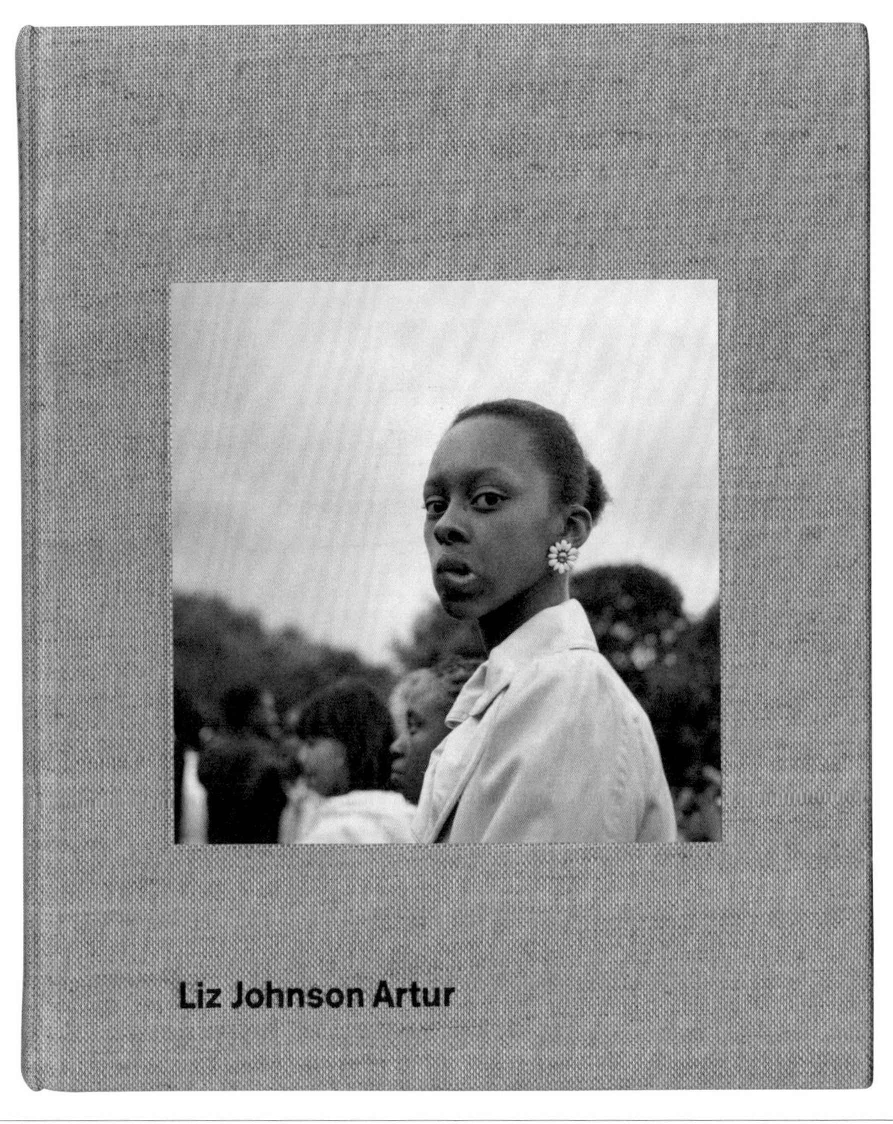

| ARTIST | Liz Johnson Artur |
|---|---|
| PUBLISHER | Bierke Verlag |
| SPECIFICATIONS | — 136 pages<br>— first published in 2016<br>— size: 27.5 × 22.3 cm |
| SUMMARY | Published in 2016, this book is the first monograph devoted to Liz Johnson Artur. It offers a retrospective of her work. The black-and-white and colour portraits come from different parts of the world, from Peckham in South London to Russia, from the United States to Africa, from the Caribbean to Europe. The book was included in the *New York Times* best photobooks selection in 2016. |
| BIOGRAPHY | Liz Johnson Artur was born in 1964 in Bulgaria to a Russian mother and a Ghanaian father. She grew up in Germany, raised by her mother. Her first trip to New York in 1985 proved decisive in her photography practice and her desire to represent Black identities in their diversity, far from the clichés of music, sports, ghettos, poverty and protest. Following this trip, she left to study photography in London. Since 1991, she has been building up the Black Balloon Archive, a body of documentary photographs, in colour and black and white, dedicated to the African diaspora around the world. Its name underlines the permanent growth of this corpus. "I'm interested in people," she says, "people I don't see represented anywhere." Liz Johnson Artur is the recipient of the 2020 Turner Prize and the 2021 Women in Motion Award for photography. She lives and works in London. |

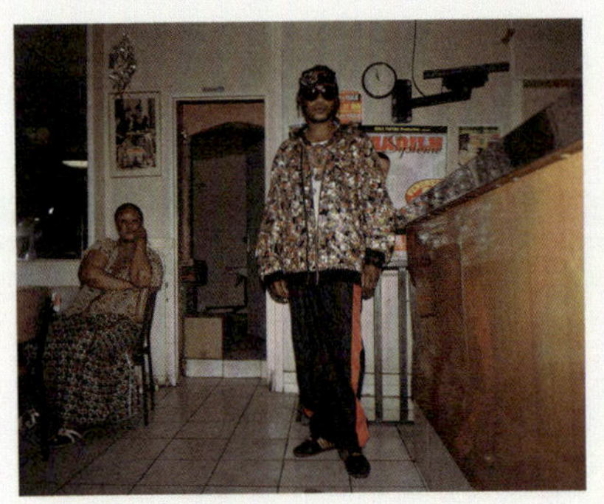

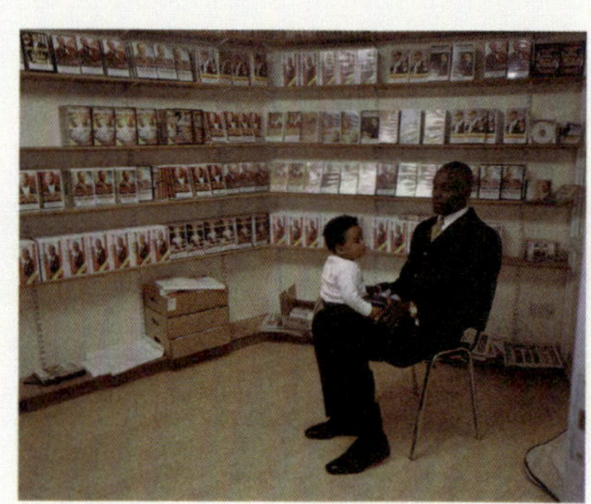

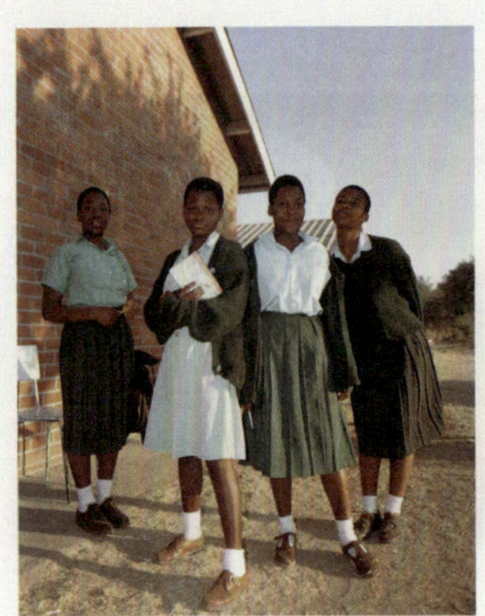

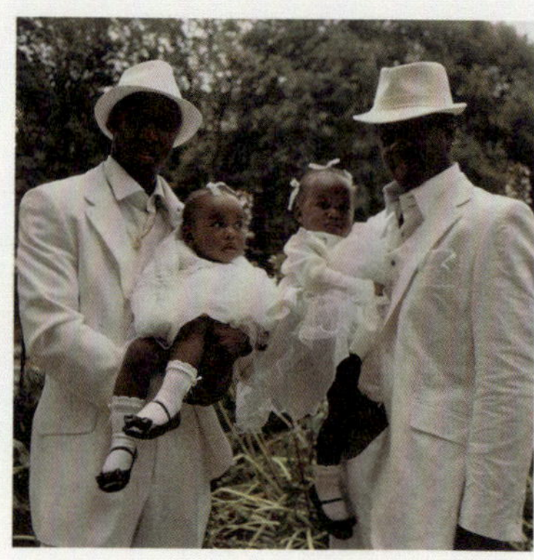

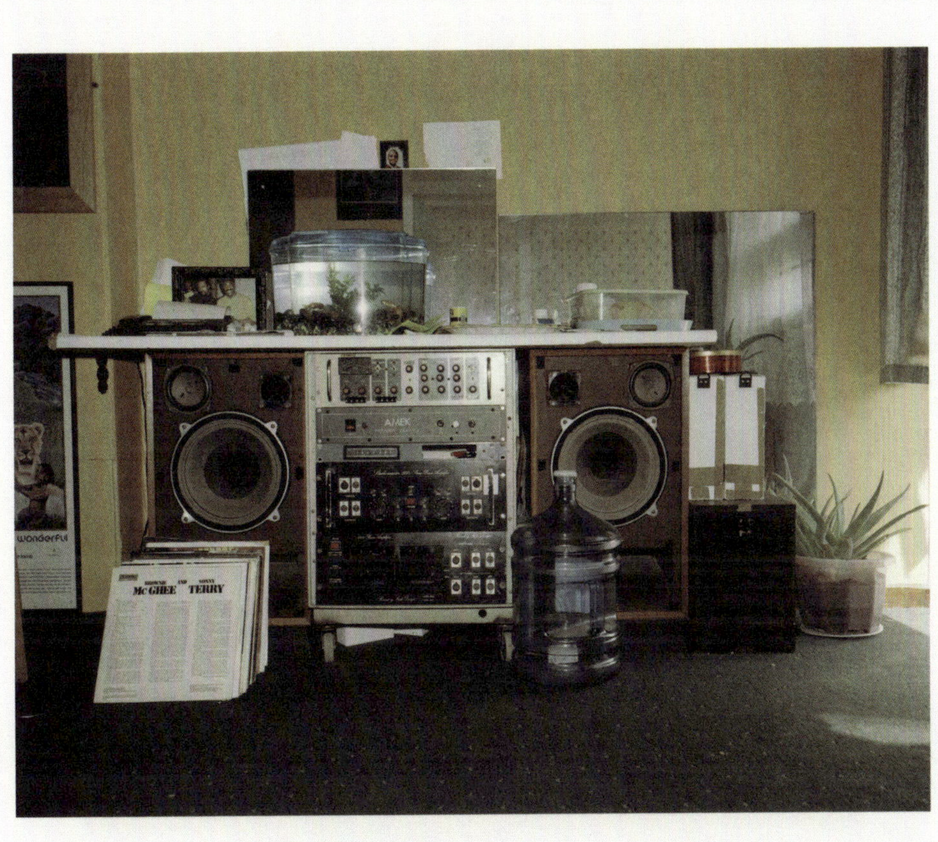
wonderful
AMEK
McGHEE TERRY

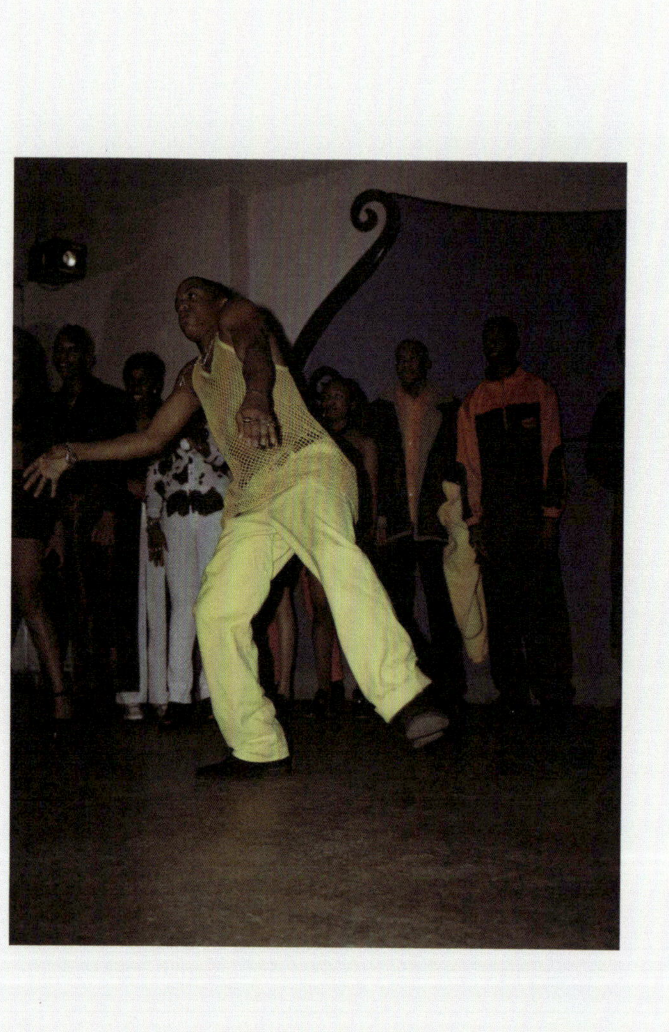

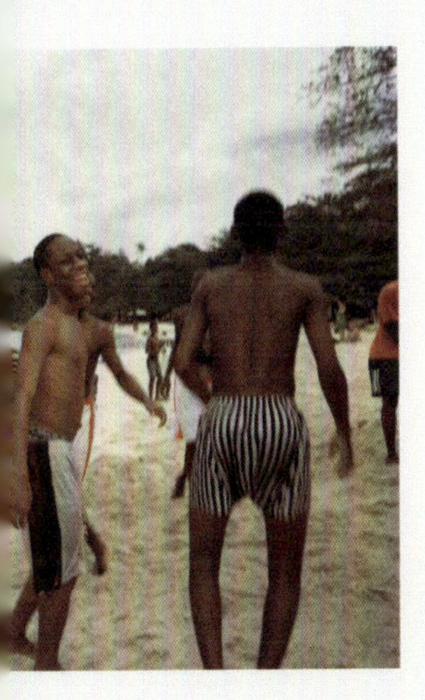

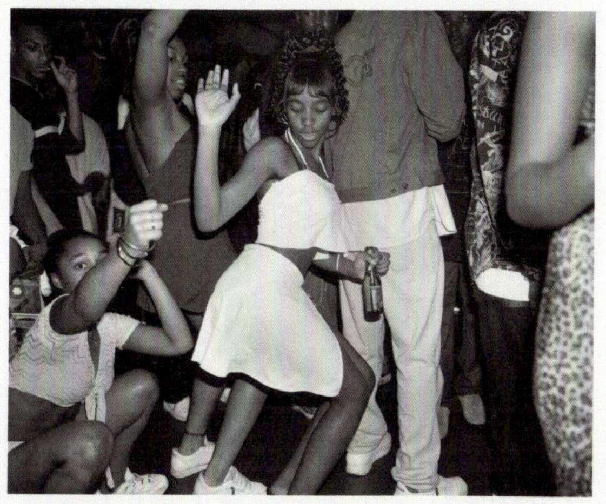

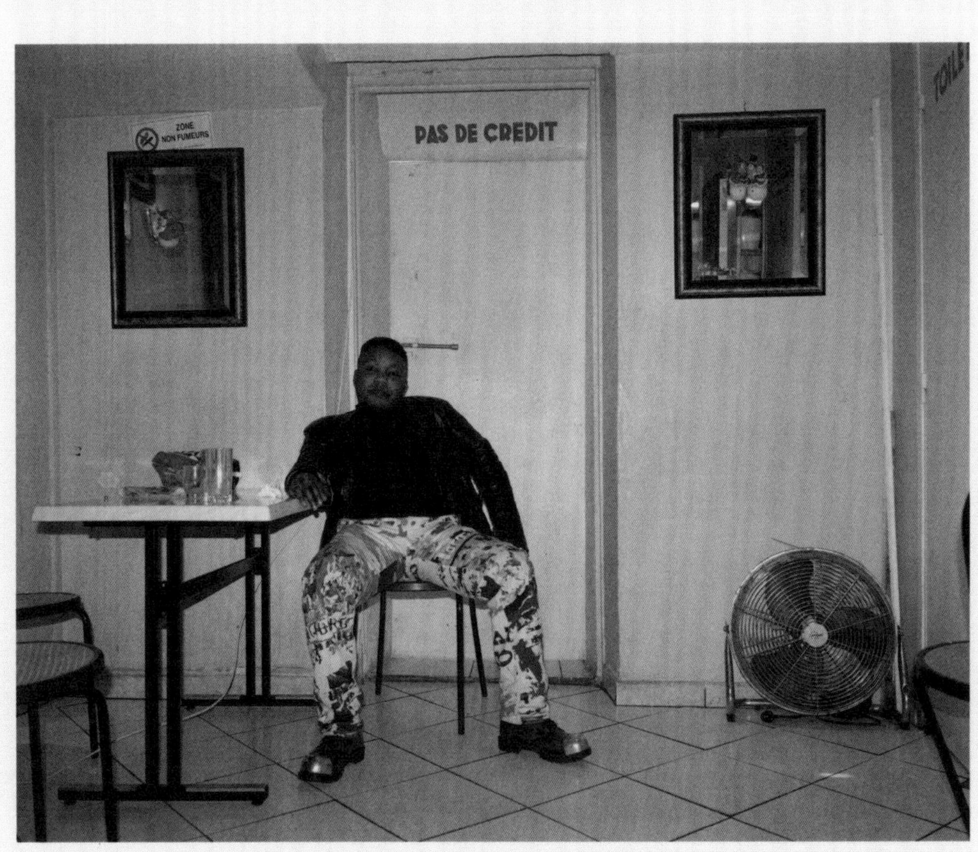
ZONE
NON FUMEURS
PAS DE CREDIT

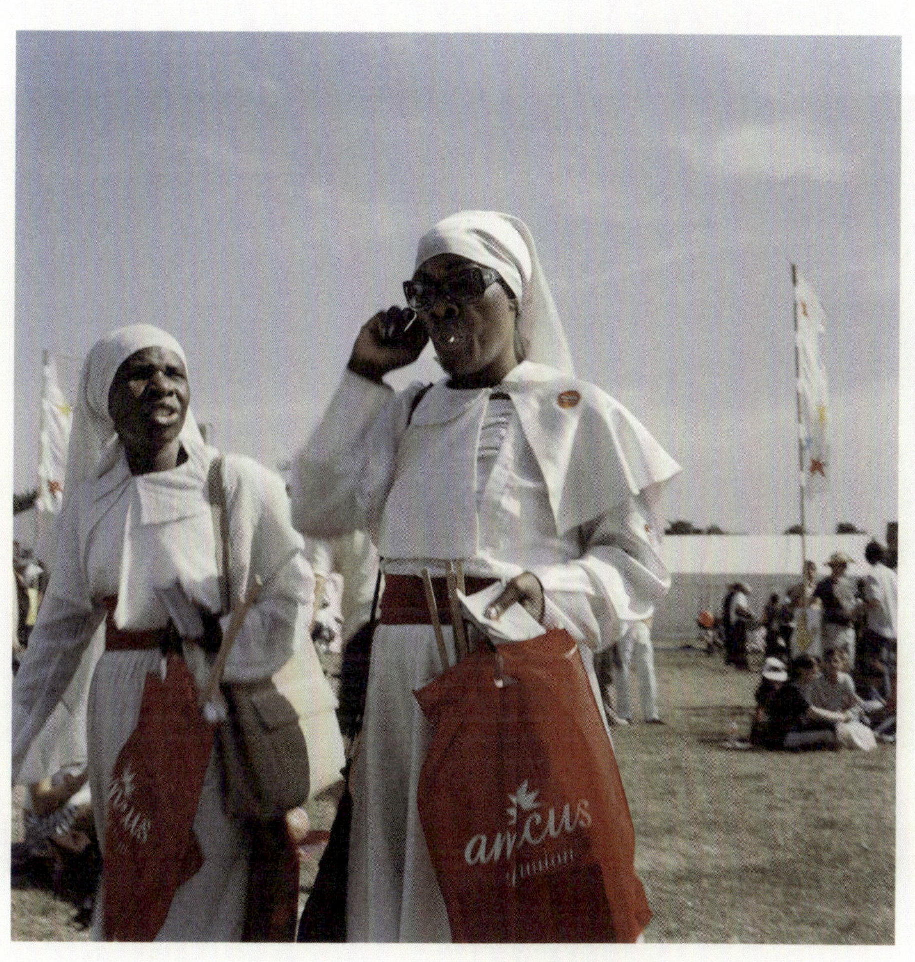
amicus

# CÉDRINE SCHEIDIG

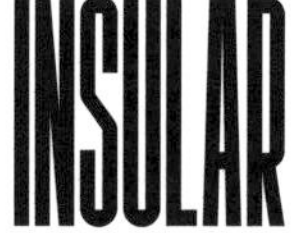


Cédrine Scheidig, born in 1994 in Bobigny, Île-de-France, is a French Carribbean photographer. She graduated from the École Nationale Supérieure de la Photographie in Arles. Her photographic work, inspired by the poet and philosopher Édouard Glissant, is based on the notions of insularity, diasporic imaginaries and cultural hybridization. Cédrine Scheidig won the Dior Prize for Photography and Visual Arts for Young Talents in July 2021.

The photographic project "INSULAR" documents the formation of an African diaspora in Malta. On the island opposite the North African coast of Libya, and in particular the city of Tripoli – the starting point for many economic, political and environmental refugees wishing to leave Africa and reach European shores – almost 30,000 people have arrived in the last 10 years. Cédrine Scheidig shares the daily lives of young men from West Africa and looks at how they experience the Maltese territory. Appropriating urban space while adapting to demographic challenges and social exclusion, they slowly create new visual histories of the city.

"INSULAR" aims to promote dialogue between different communities and cultures on the island of Malta to encourage understanding and inclusion and to give greater visibility to a population that is often excluded or misrepresented in the media and contemporary arts.

© Cédrine Scheidig
*Rich Homie Quan*, 2020
*In Zabbar*, 2020
*Terry*, 2020
*Hairdresser in Qwara*, 2020
*San Pawl Il Bahar*, 2020
*Anosike*, 2020
*Ta Fra Ben*, 2020

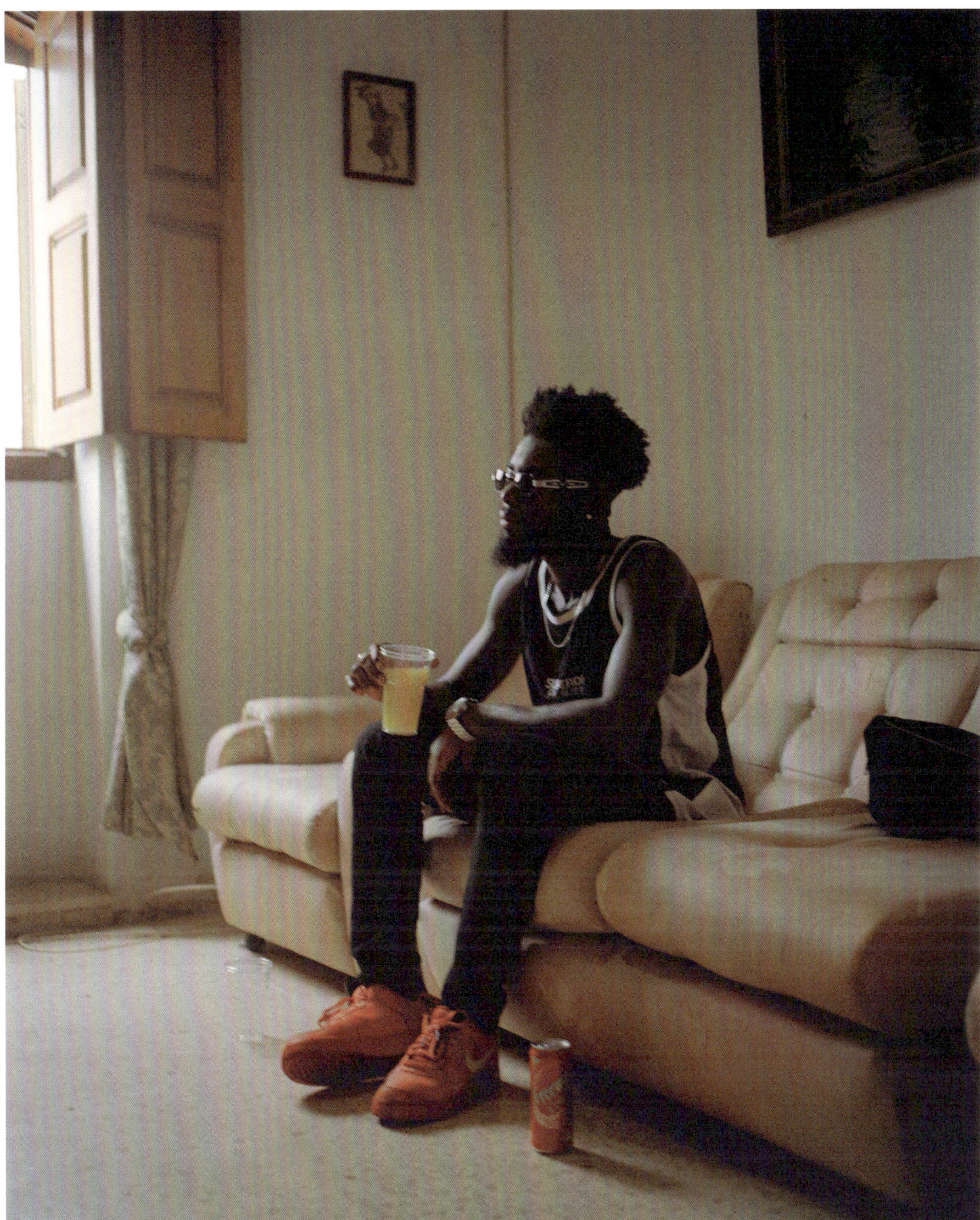

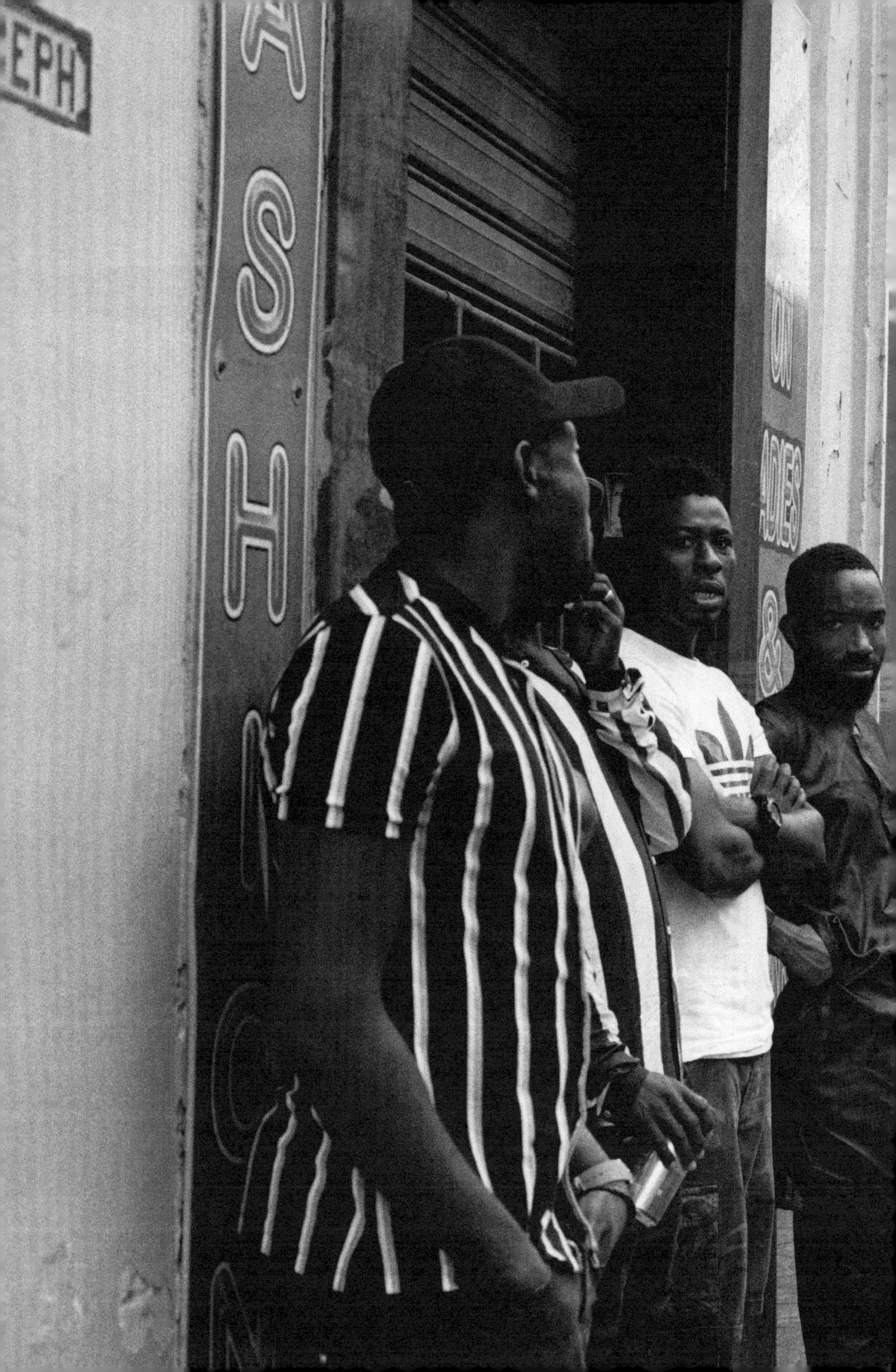
EPH
ASH
ON
ADIES
&

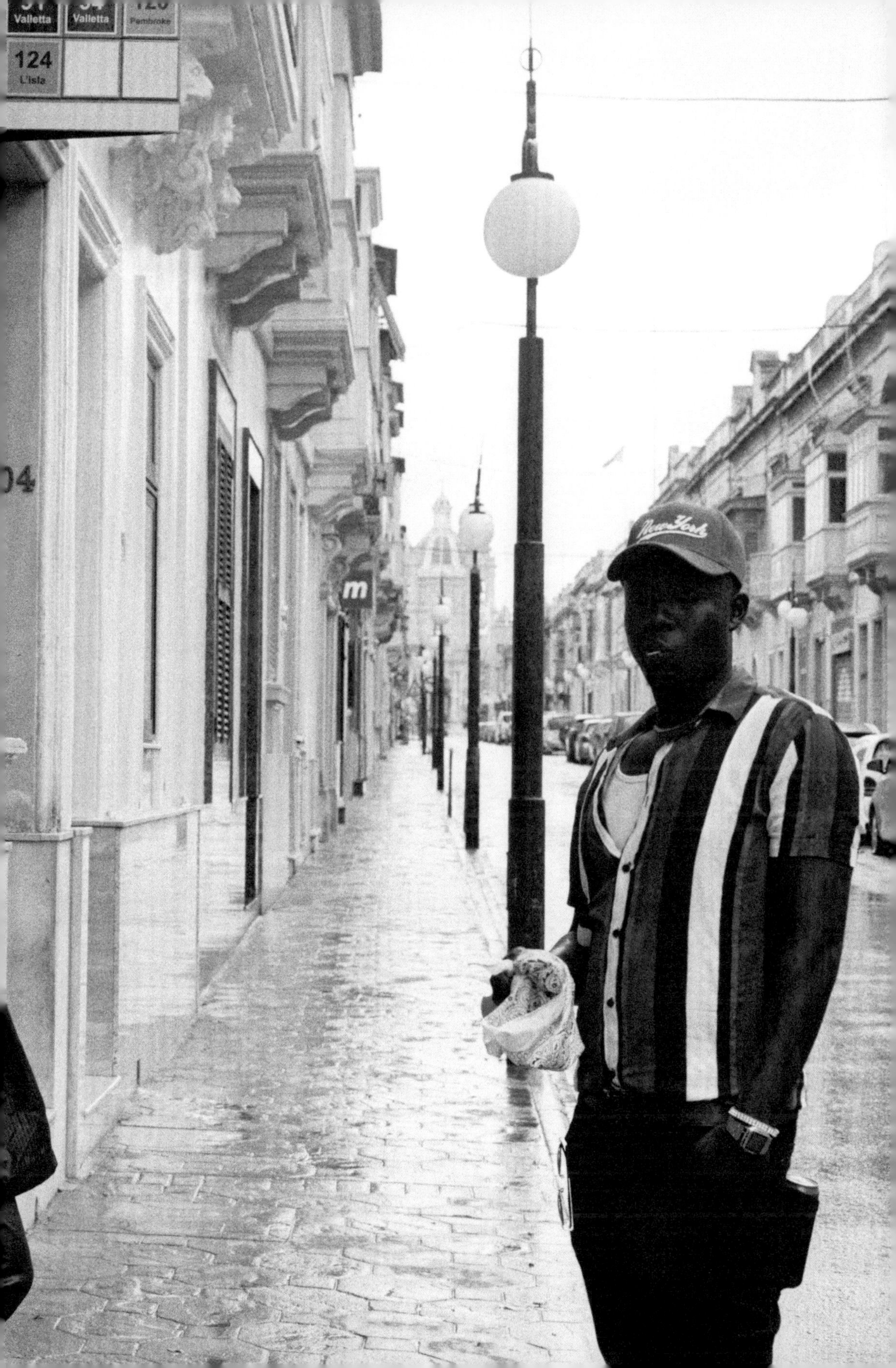
Valletta
Valletta
Pembroke
124
L'Isla
04
m
New York

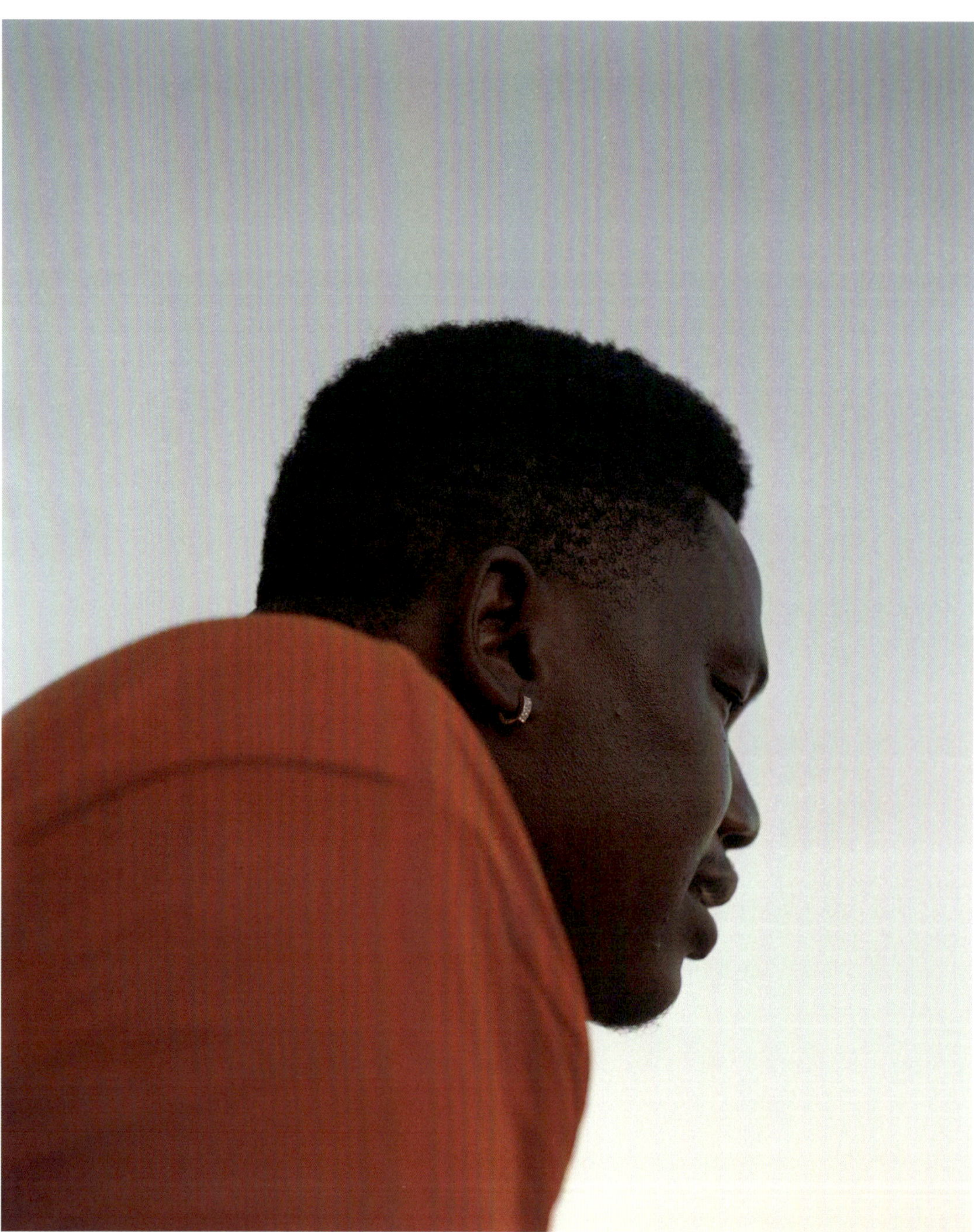

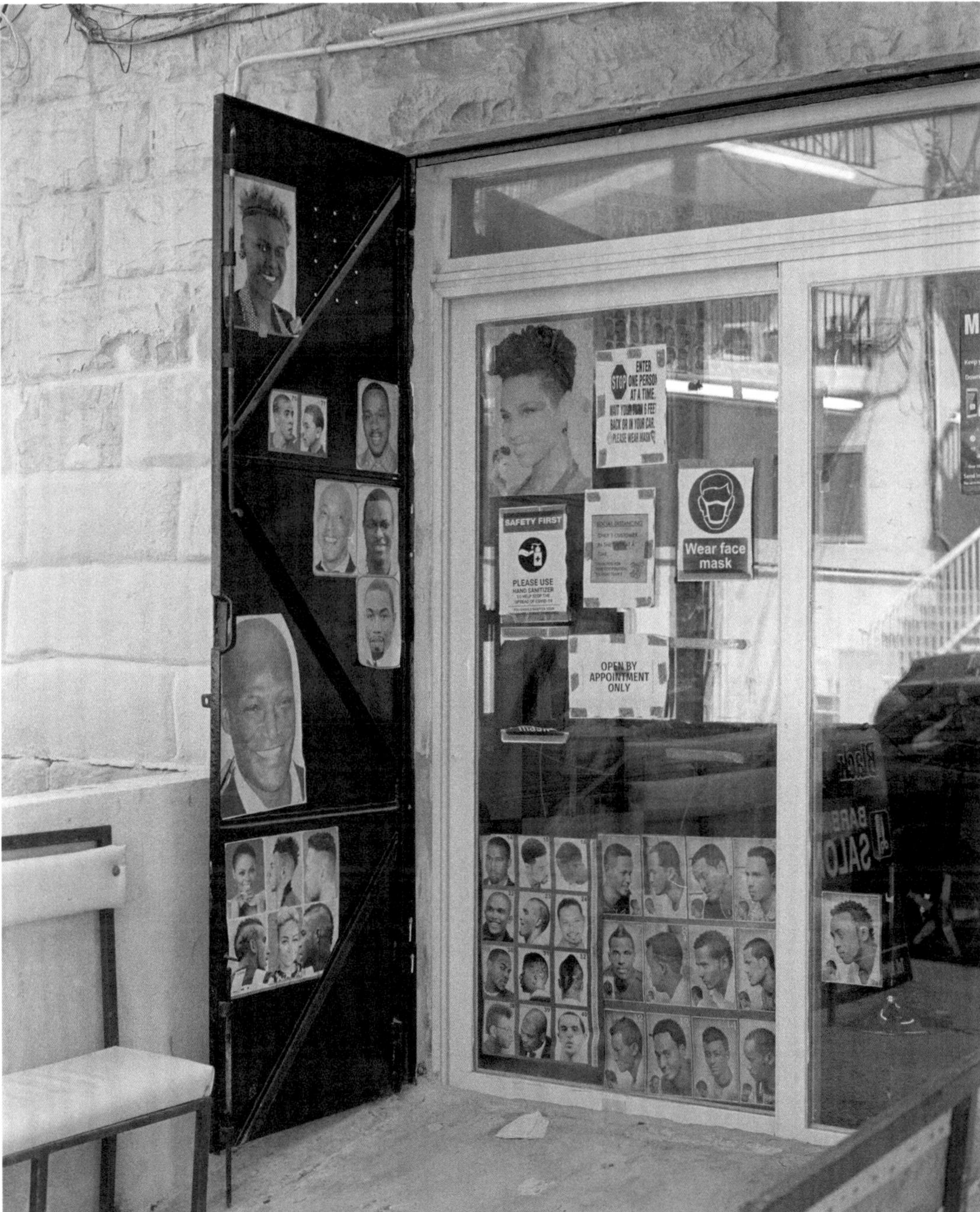
STOP
ENTER
ONE PERSON
AT A TIME.
SAFETY FIRST
PLEASE USE
HAND SANITIZER
Wear face
mask
OPEN BY
APPOINTMENT
ONLY

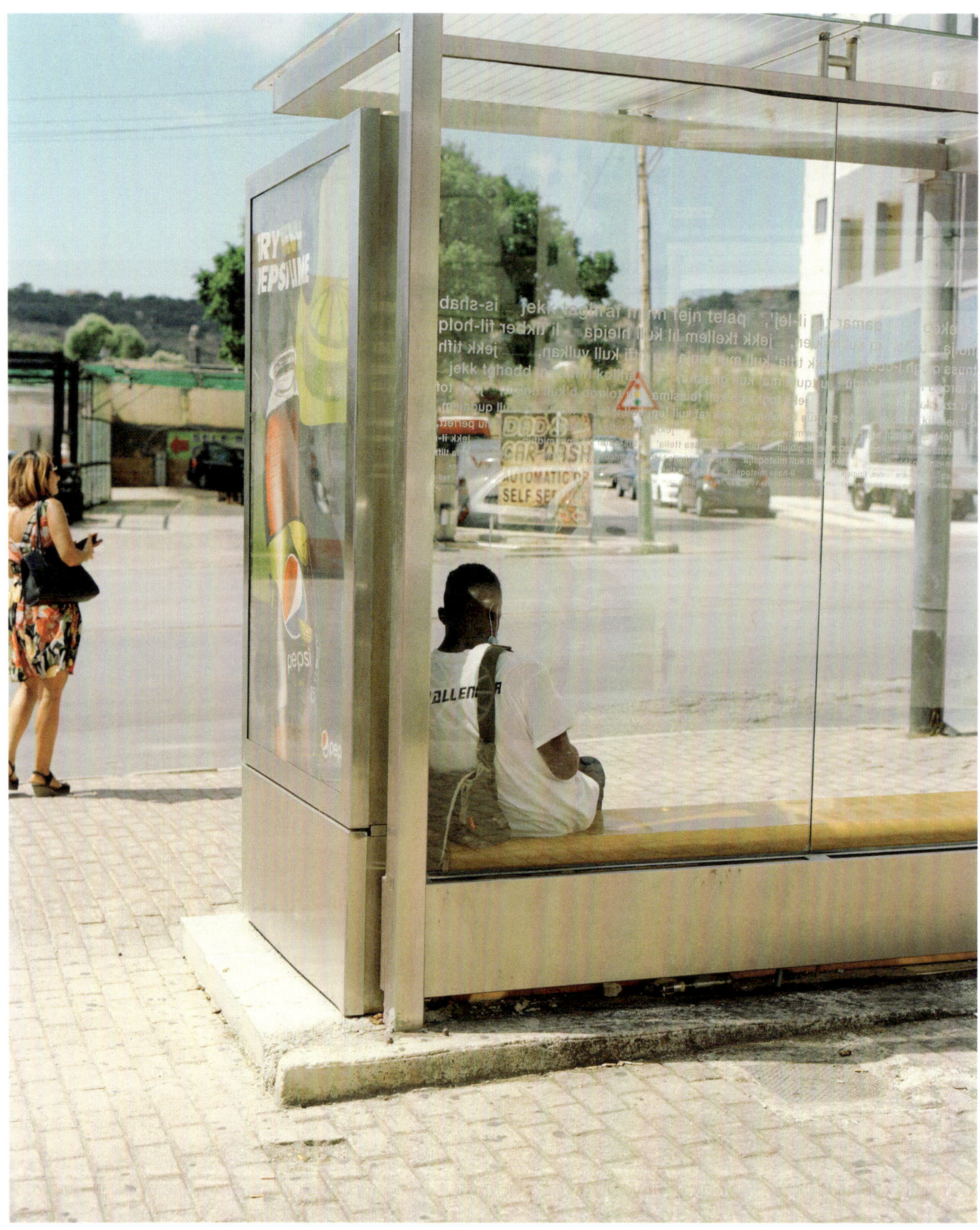
pepsi

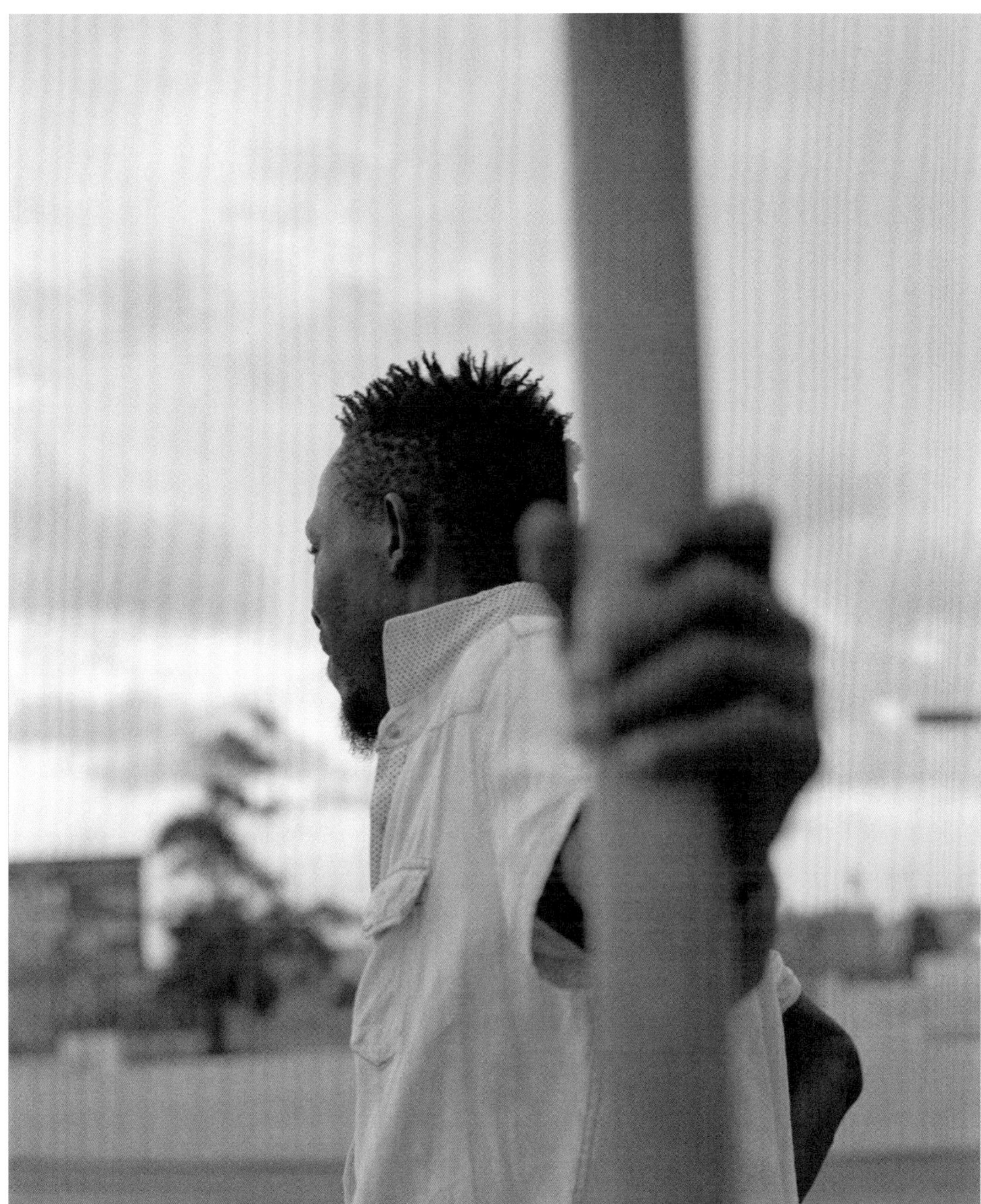

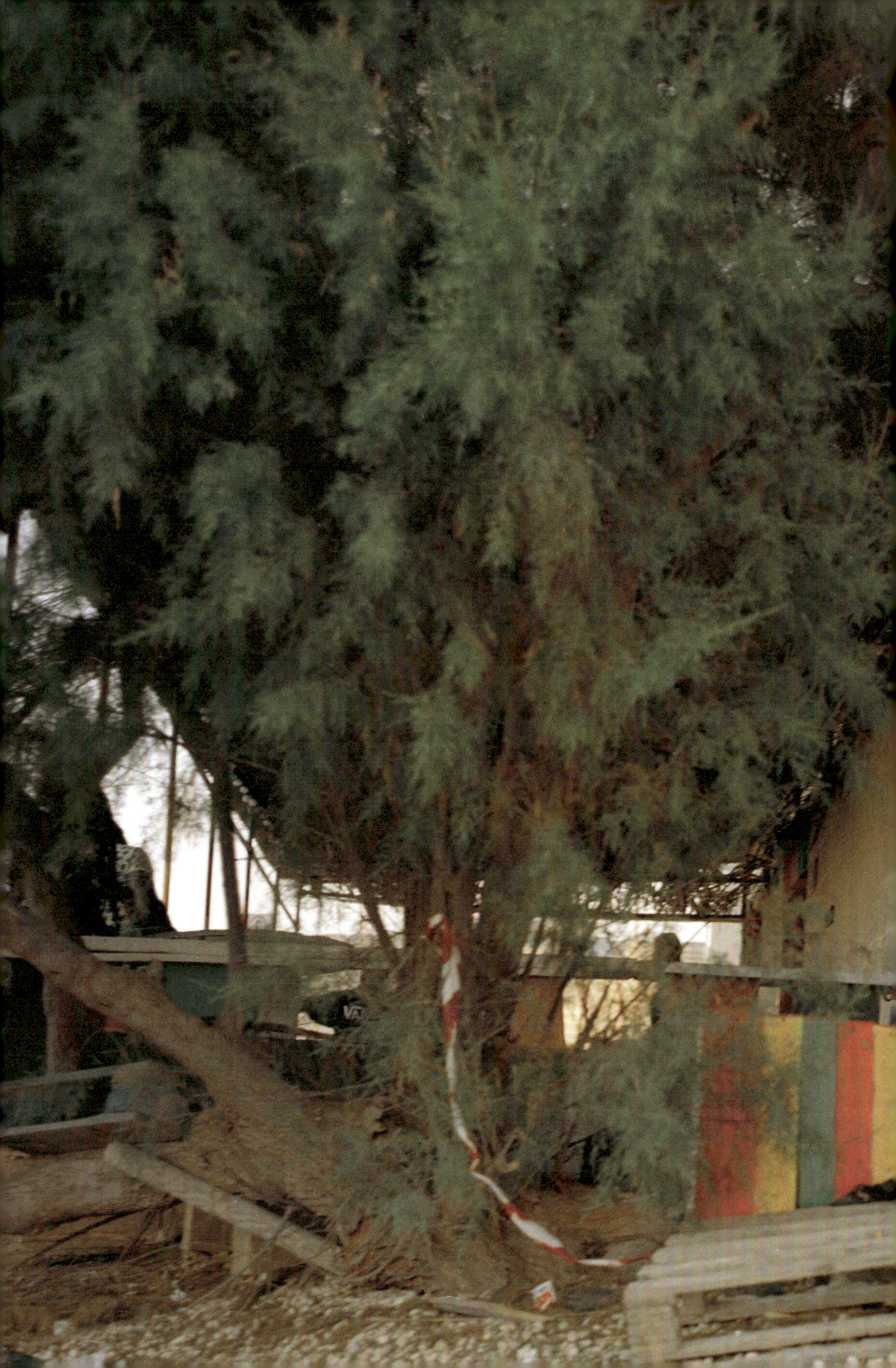

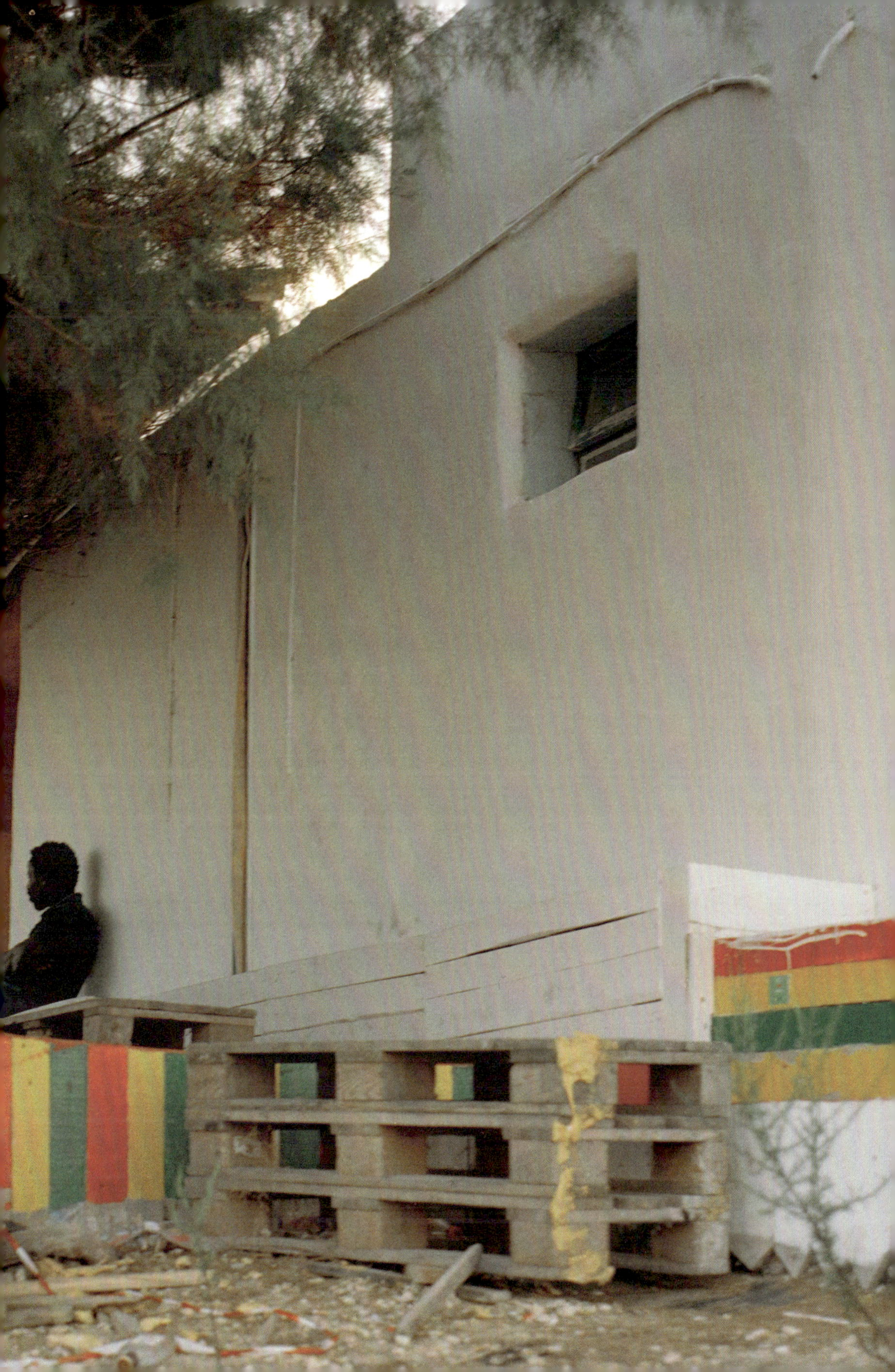

# ZINEB SEDIRA

## MOTHER, DAUGHTER AND I & MOTHER TONGUE

"*Mother, Daughter and I*" (2003)
*Mother, Daughter and I*, 2003 – Triptych I
*Mother, Daughter and I*, 2003 – Triptych II
© Zineb Sedira / DACS, London
Courtesy the artist and kamel mennour, Paris/London

Stills of the installation "*Mother Tongue*" (2002)
Installation. 3 videos (colour, sound)
"*Mother and I (France)*"
"*Daughter and I (England)*"
"*Grandmother and Granddaughter (Algeria)*"
© Zineb Sedira / DACS, London
© Photo. Zineb Sedira
Courtesy the artist and kamel mennour, Paris/London

Zineb Sedira was born in 1963 in Paris. Her parents had left Algeria for France two years earlier. After studying in London at the Central Saint Martins College of Art and Design and the Slade School of Fine Art, she began her career in the United Kingdom. Her personal and family history is the starting point for her artistic research, between photography, video and installation. She draws her inspiration from her quest for identity, that of a woman with a very particular origin and geography. Over the years, this autobiographical questioning has evolved towards more universal concerns: mobility, memory and transmission. Today, she carries out this work between Algiers, London and Paris. She is represented by Kamel Mennour Gallery.

In the video triptych "Mother Tongue", the artist, her mother and her daughter talk, two by two, on three screens. Each speaks in her mother tongue, respectively: French, Arabic and English. Through these informal exchanges, Zineb Sedira addresses the issues of multiculturalism and language as a link to a territory. She explores the fragility of memory and its transmission in a globalized world.

In the video triptych *Mother Tongue*, the artist examines the notion of preservation but also of loss of cultural identity. What emerges is the complexity and depth of family relations and the diculties inherent to any life in the diaspora. The triptych breaks the documentary framework and explores the fragility of memory and its transmission through language.

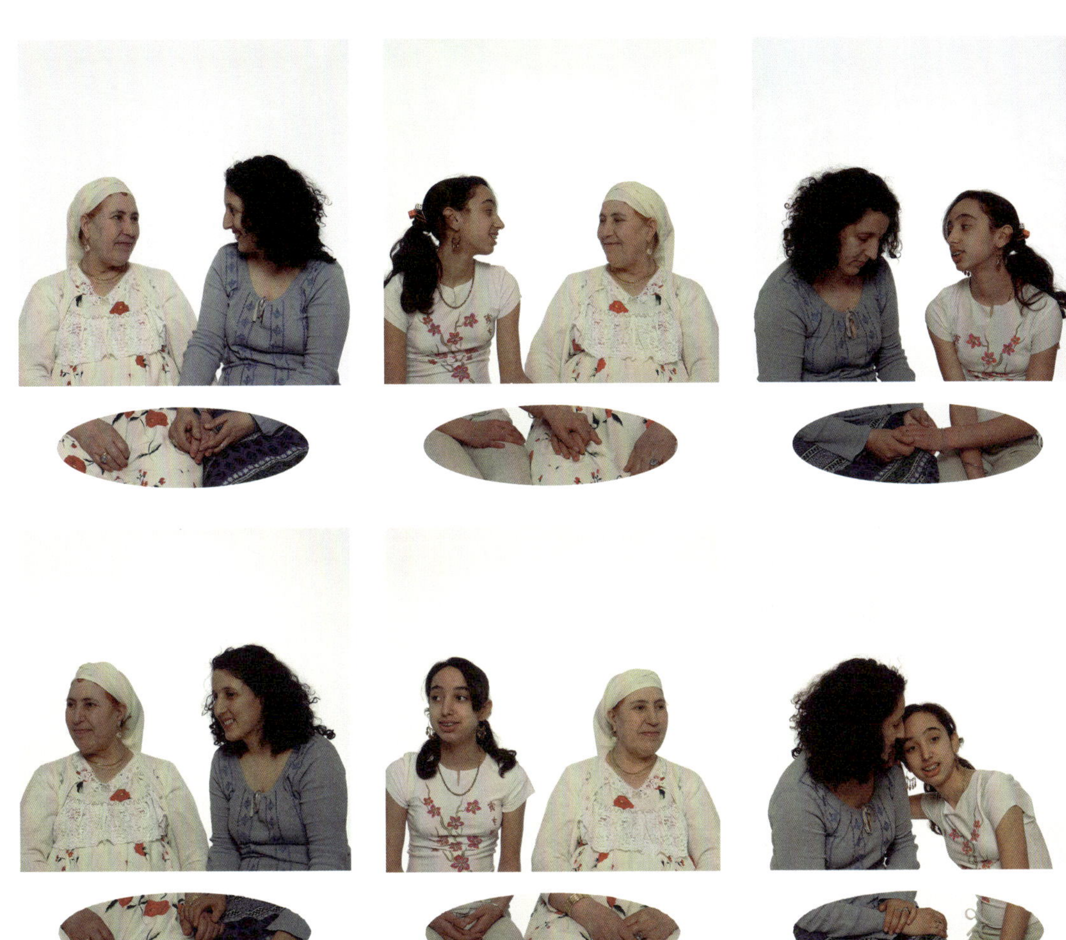

# MOTHER, DAUGHTER AND I

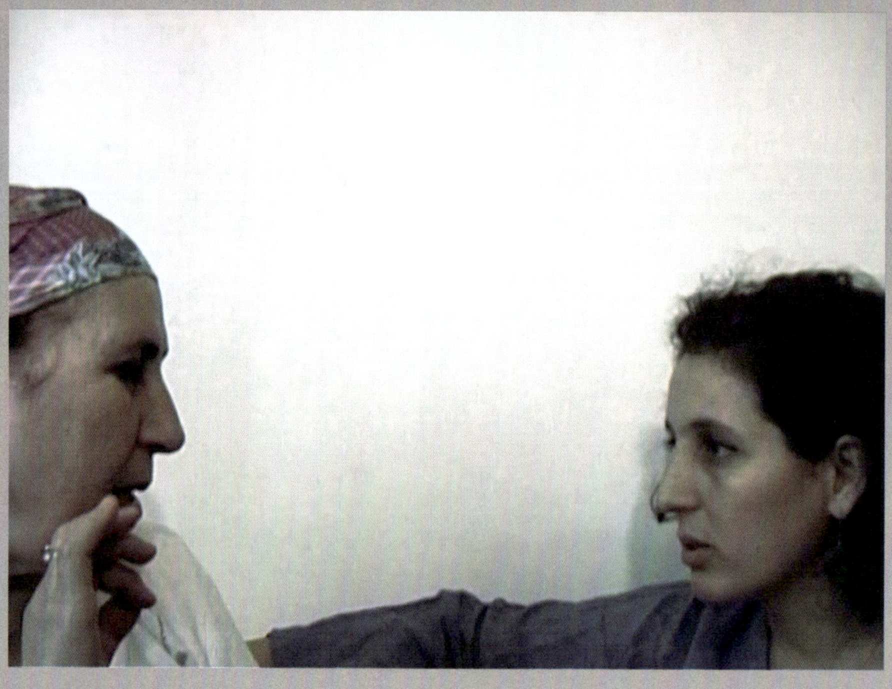

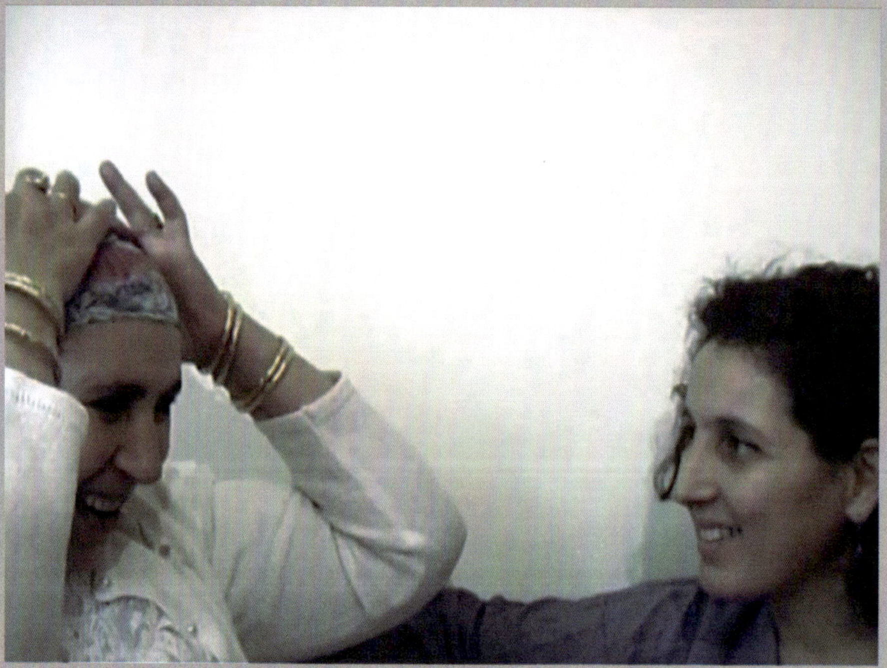

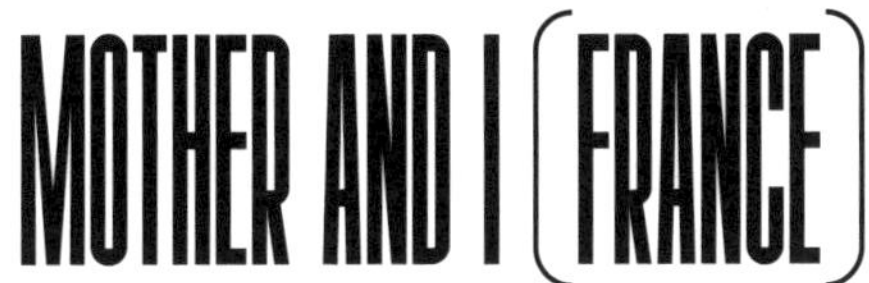


| | |
|---|---|
| Zineb Sedira | On commençait l'école à quelle heure le matin ? |
| Zineb Sedira's mother | على 8 س |
| Zineb Sedira | À 8 heures du matin si tôt que ça ? |
| Zineb Sedira's mother | نديكم على 8 سا و تدخلو على 8 س30 |
| Zineb Sedira | On rentrait à 8 heures et demi en classe. Tu venais nous chercher à quelle heure ? |
| Zineb Sedira's mother | À 4 heures |
| Zineb Sedira | À quand même ! Ça faisait une longue journée. Et on mangeait à la cantine ? |
| Zineb Sedira's mother | سويع تاكلو فلاكنتين و سويع نديكم لدار |
| Zineb Sedira | Pourquoi parfois on mangeait à la cantine et parfois on mangeait pas à la cantine ? |
| Zineb Sedira's mother | سويع جيني الكنتيلا غالية يمدوهالنا غالية تاكلو فالدار |
| Zineb Sedira's mother | سويع جيني الكنتيلا رخيصة تاكلو فليكول |
| Zineb Sedira | Et quand tu dis qu'on finissait l'école à 4 heures, on finissait vraiment l'école ou on allait à la garderie ? |
| Zineb Sedira's mother | نتوما ديجا تروحو للقردوري كنتو صغار متروحوش لكول نديكم للقاردور |

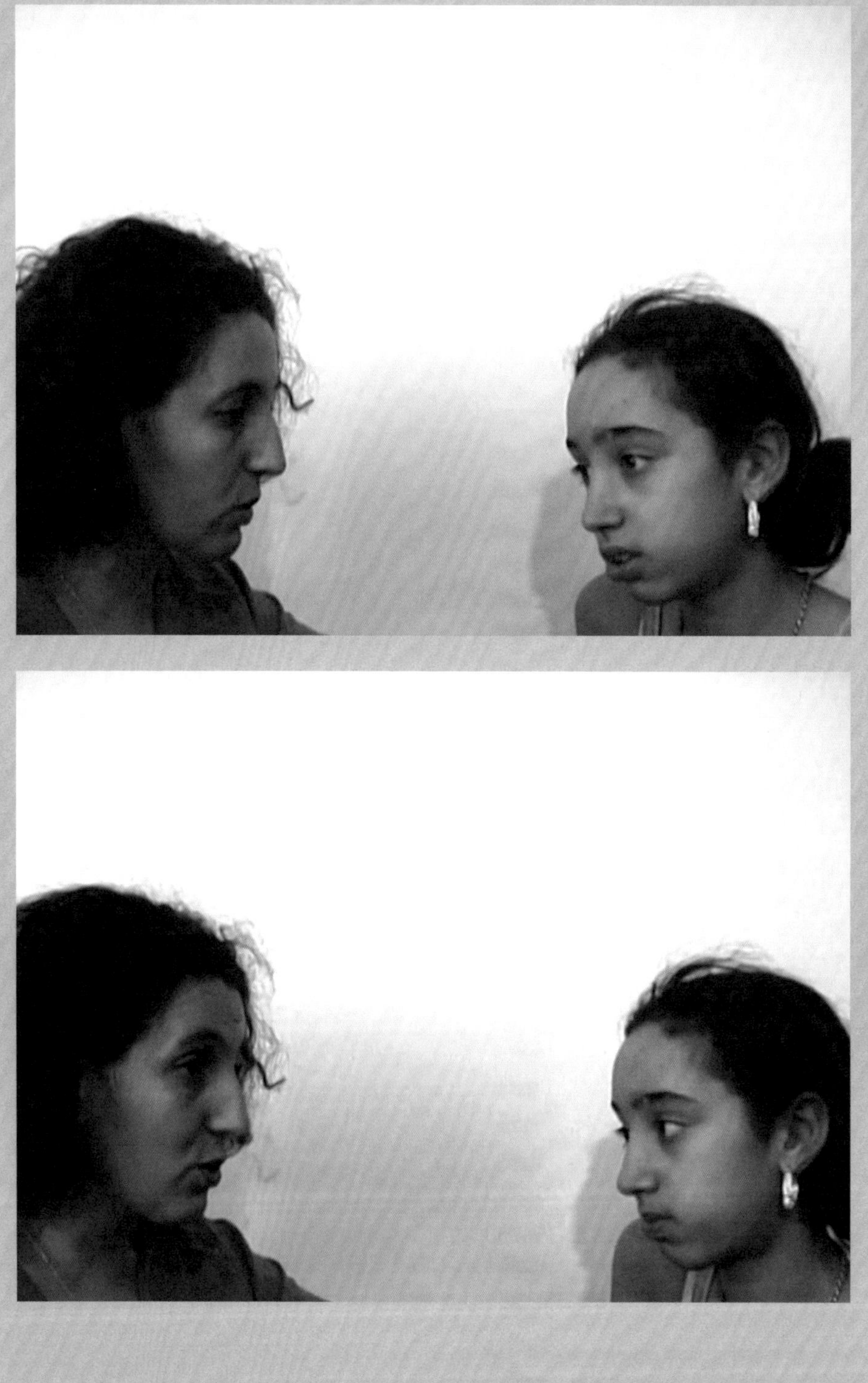

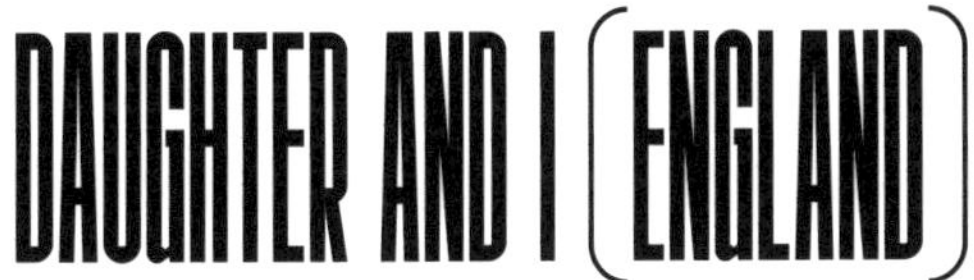


Zineb Sedira’s daughter

Did you play outside a lot?

Zineb Sedira

Tu veux dire pendant l’école ? Dans la récréation ?

Zineb Sedira’s daughter

After school!

Zineb Sedira

Après l’école, oui oui bah des fois, enfin quand il faisait beau en tout cas pas l’hiver. On sortait déposer nos cartables à la maison puis après je sortais avec mes copines et puis des fois avec mes frères, avec mes soeurs ça dépendait.

Zineb Sedira’s daughter

Did you have any friends around where you lived?

Zineb Sedira

Oui de toute manière j’habitais dans les HLM et l’école elle était dans les HLM. Donc après toutes les copines qu’il y avait à l’école c’était des voisines en fait, c’était toutes les copines qui habitaient aussi dans le quartier. Donc on se voyait le samedi, on se voyait le dimanche, on se voyait à l’école, on se voyait tout le temps en fait. Donc on était un groupe comme ça on se voyait beaucoup à l’école et en dehors de l’école.

Zineb Sedira’s daughter

Did you like your school dinners?

Zineb Sedira

J’aimais bien manger à la cantine parce que je trouvais que les repas étaient très bons. Ça me changeait aussi de ce que je mangeais à la maison. À la maison ma mère me cuisinait beaucoup de choses de cuisine algérienne.

# GRANDMOTHER AND GRANDDAUGHTER (ALGERIA)

| | |
|---|---|
| Zineb Sedira's daughter | Did you have family when you where child? |
| Zineb Sedira's mother | ... [silence] |
| Zineb Sedira's daughter | Did you have any animals around you!? |
| Zineb Sedira's mother | ... [silence] |
| Zineb Sedira's daughter | Did you enjoy yourself alone? |
| Zineb Sedira's mother | ... [silence] |
| Zineb Sedira's daughter | Did you ever got other people houses going around<br>by your self and see by yourself? |
| Zineb Sedira's mother | !مفهمتش يا بنيتي<br>مفهمتش واش راكي تقولي ! |
| Zineb Sedira's daughter | How old are you when you started doing things by youself?<br>And going to see other people? |

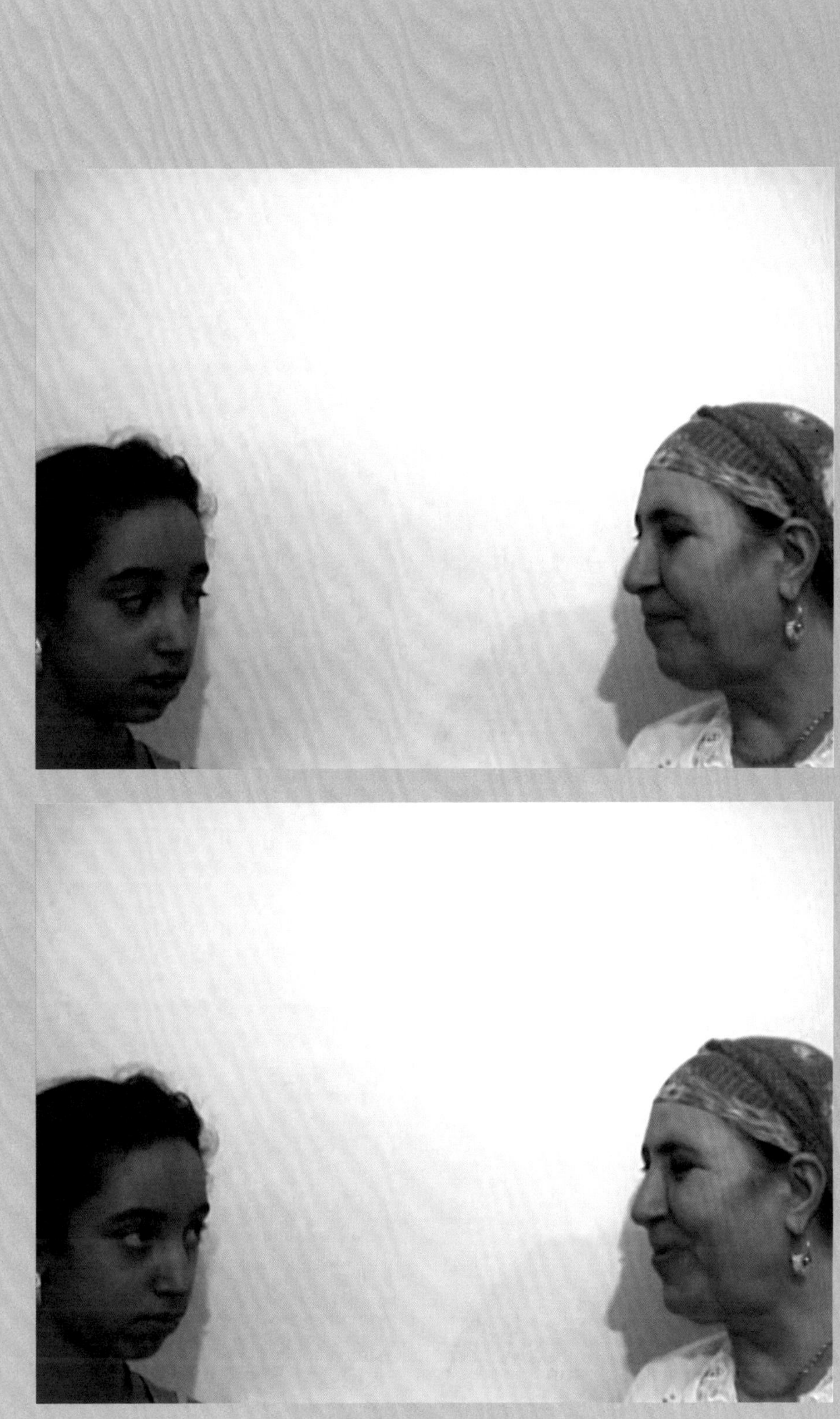

# BRUNO BOUDJELAL

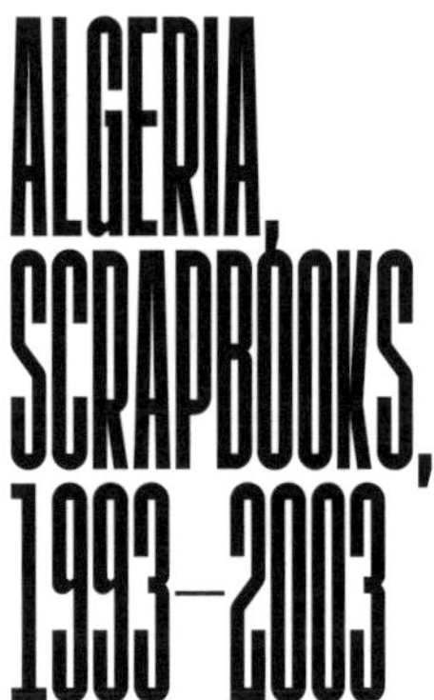


Bruno Boudjelal was born in 1961 in Montreuil, Île-de-France, to an Algerian father and a French mother. A self-taught photographer, he discovered photography during his first trip to Algeria. Over the years, he switched from black and white to colour. Since then, his photographic work has remained faithful to the principle of his first series. It is an engaged testimony, a "narrative in images that attempts to approach a complex reality". Bruno Boudjelal, a member of Agence VU', lives and works between France and Africa.

In 1993, Bruno Boudjelal left for Algiers in search of his identity. His father, who had left Algeria 45 years earlier, had never spoken to him about the country. This journey is the first of a long series of 10 years of explorations. Throughout his travels, Bruno Boudjelal collected impressions, thoughts, photographs (often stolen, due to the political context of the 1990s) and documents on the living conditions of the Algerians. Between a logbook and a diary, his scrapbooks bear witness to his personal experience and the reality of Algeria at the turn of the 21st century.

PEAU NOIRE, MASQUES BLANCS..
Cette pièce des scrapbooks algériens réalisée en 2008 représente mon père.
J'ai longtemps pensé qu'elle parlait de la colère que je ressentais
envers lui, de le voir disparaître de ma vie ! Mais c'est en relisant
FANON durant le confinement que j'ai compris que cela
parlait d'autre chose, de lui, de sa place en France.
" quand on est dans une société blanche ou
bien on porte un masque blanc
donc on se transforme en blanc ou bien
on garde sa couleur noire et on est assigné !
Mon père pendant plus de 40 ans s'est fait
appeler Claudio et tous ses amis pensaient
qu'il était originaire du sud de l'Italie. C'est
le jour où j'ai publié mon travail sur l'Algérie
que tout le monde a découvert la vérité ! D'avoir fait connaître
cela, mon père était si en colère qu'il ne m'a pas parlé pendant
dix ans !

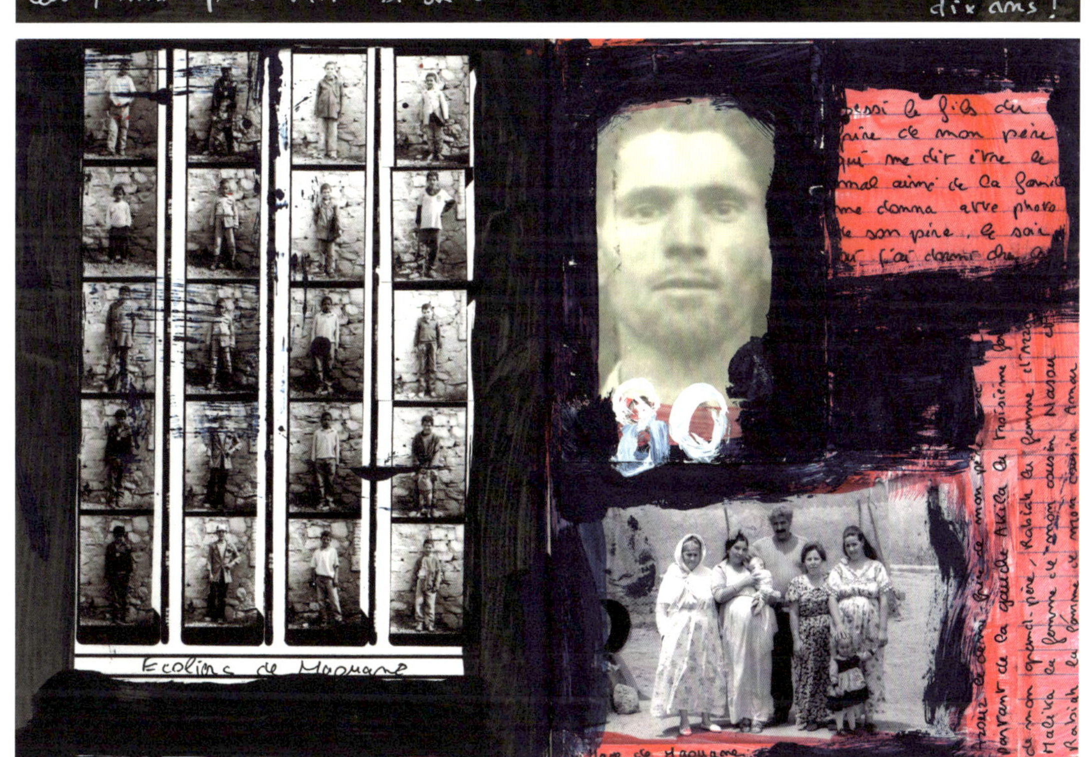

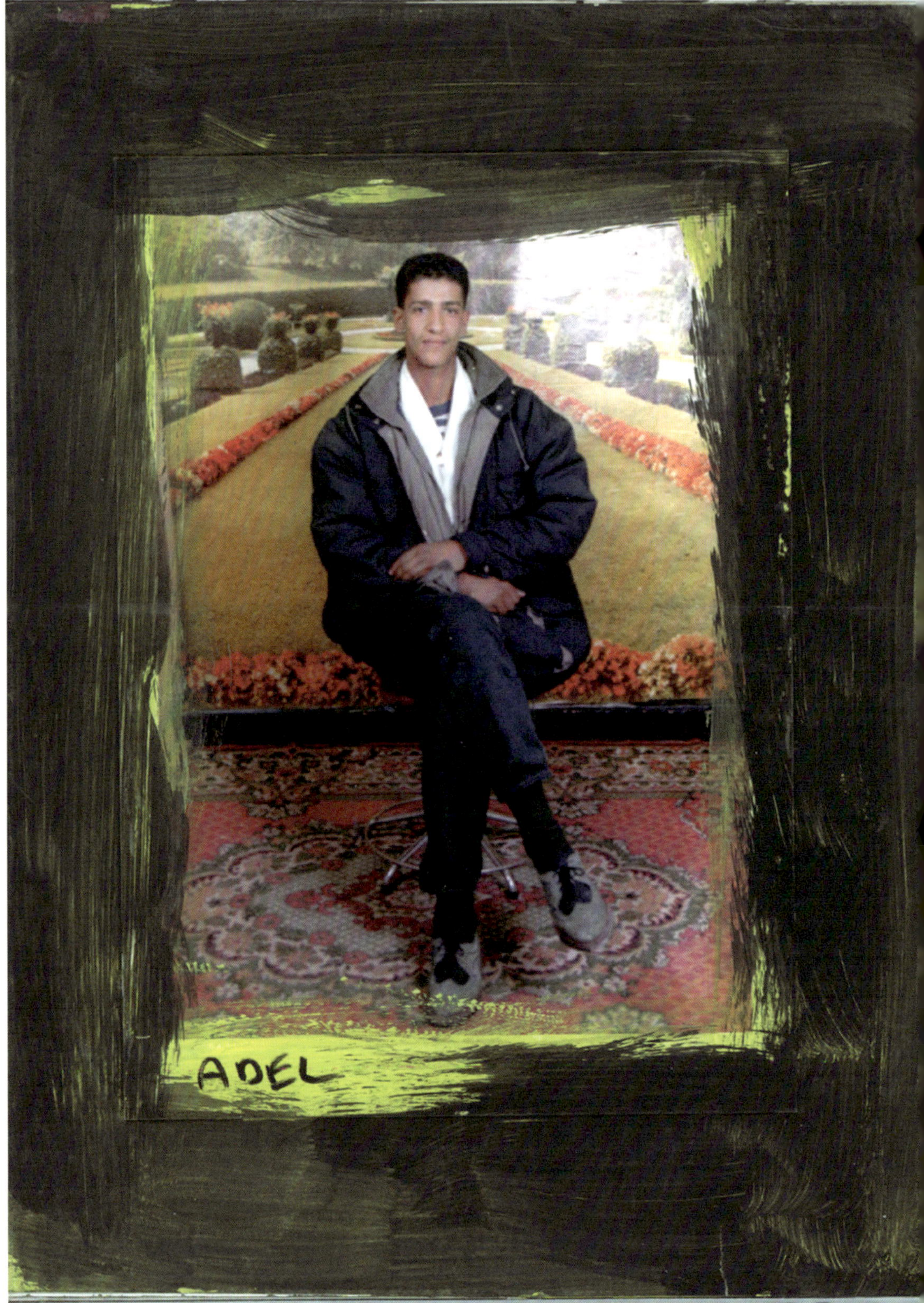
ADEL

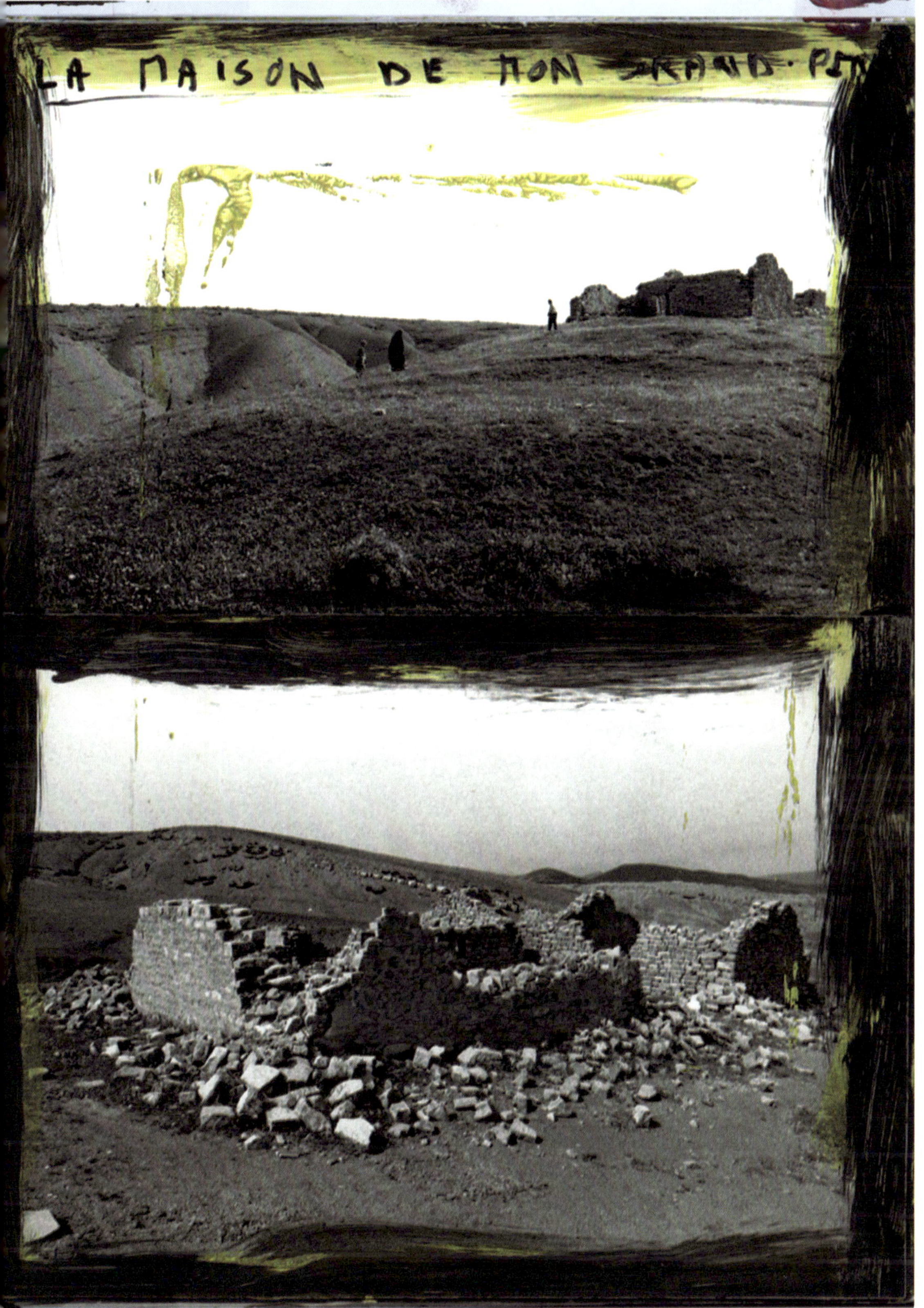
LA MAISON DE MON GRAND·PE

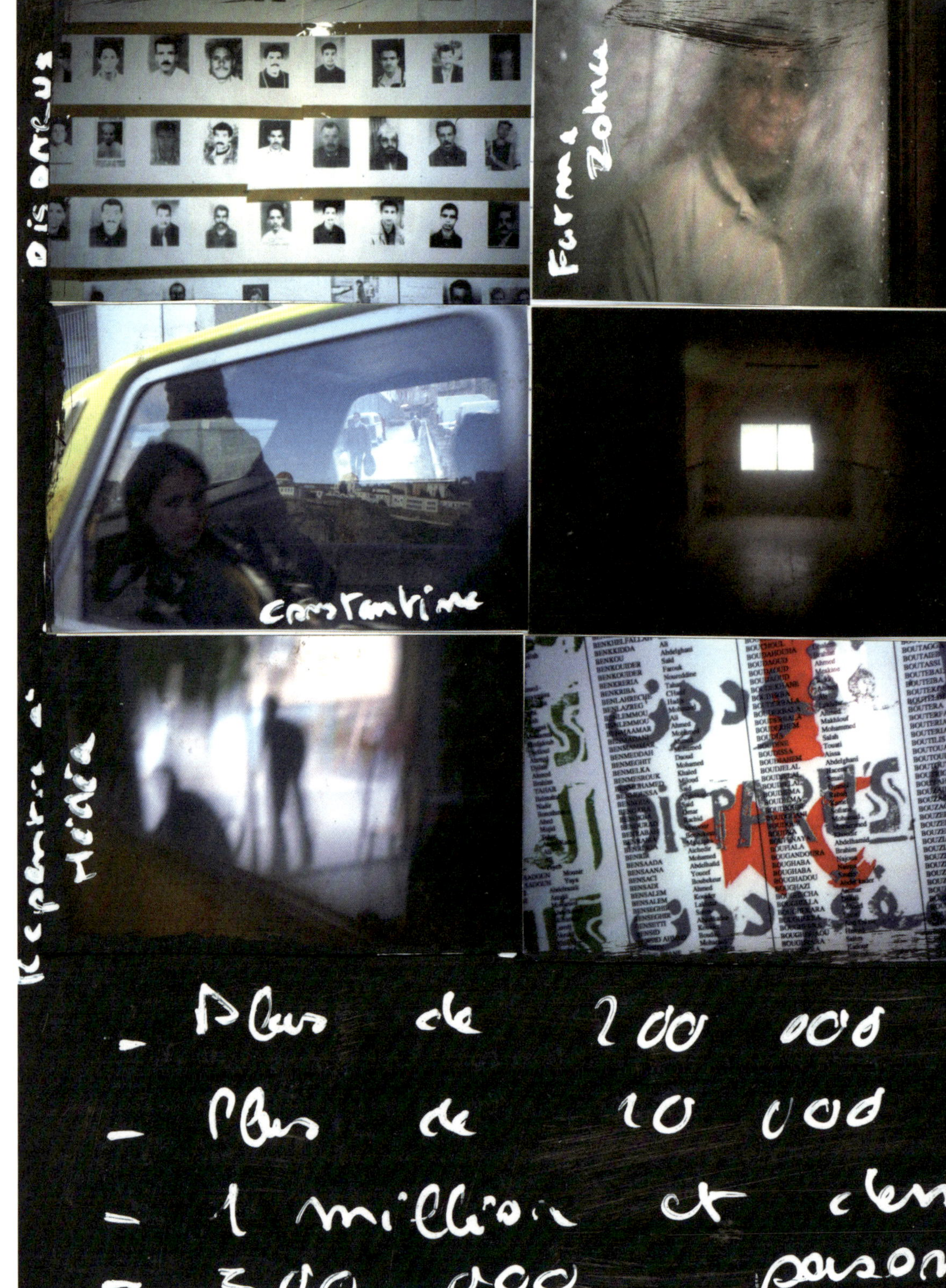
Constantine
DISPARUS
- Plus de 200 000
- Plus de 10 000
- 1 million et
- 300 000

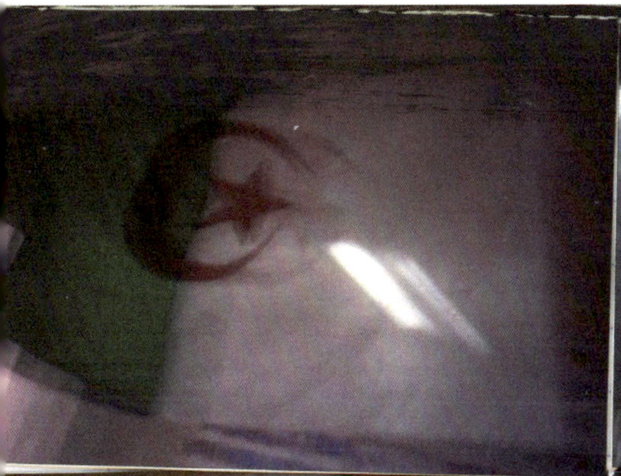

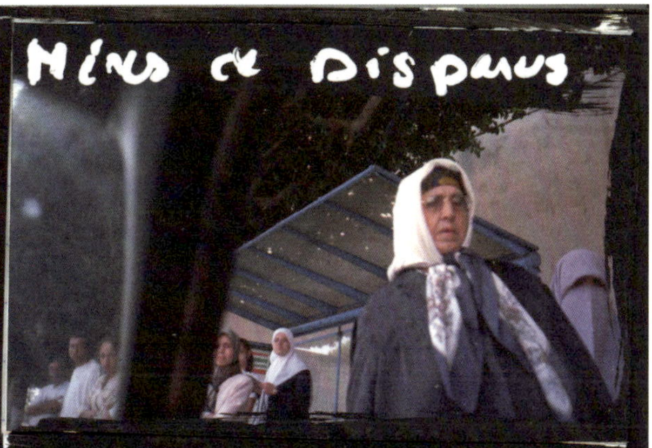

Mères de disparus

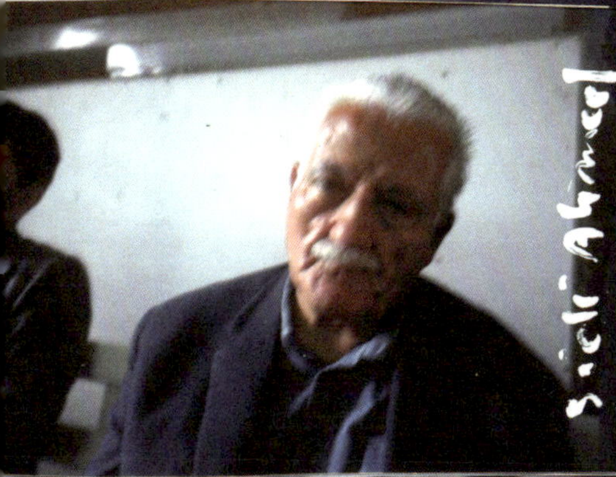

Toutes ces années de guerre le bilan est terrible

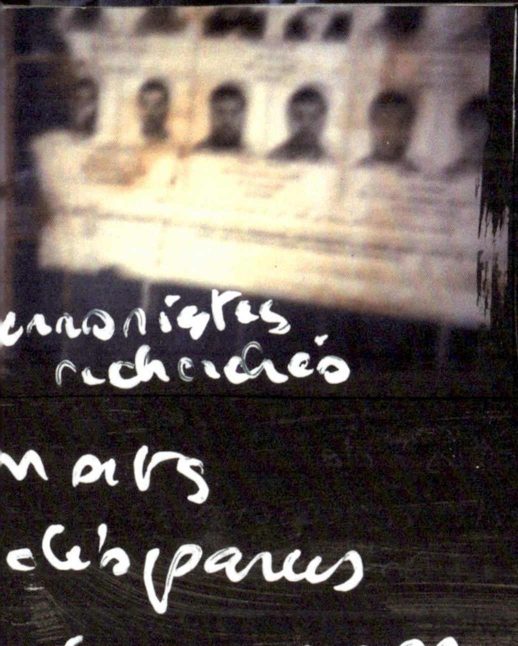

Sidi Ahmed

terroristes recherchés

morts disparus des personnes déplacées exilées

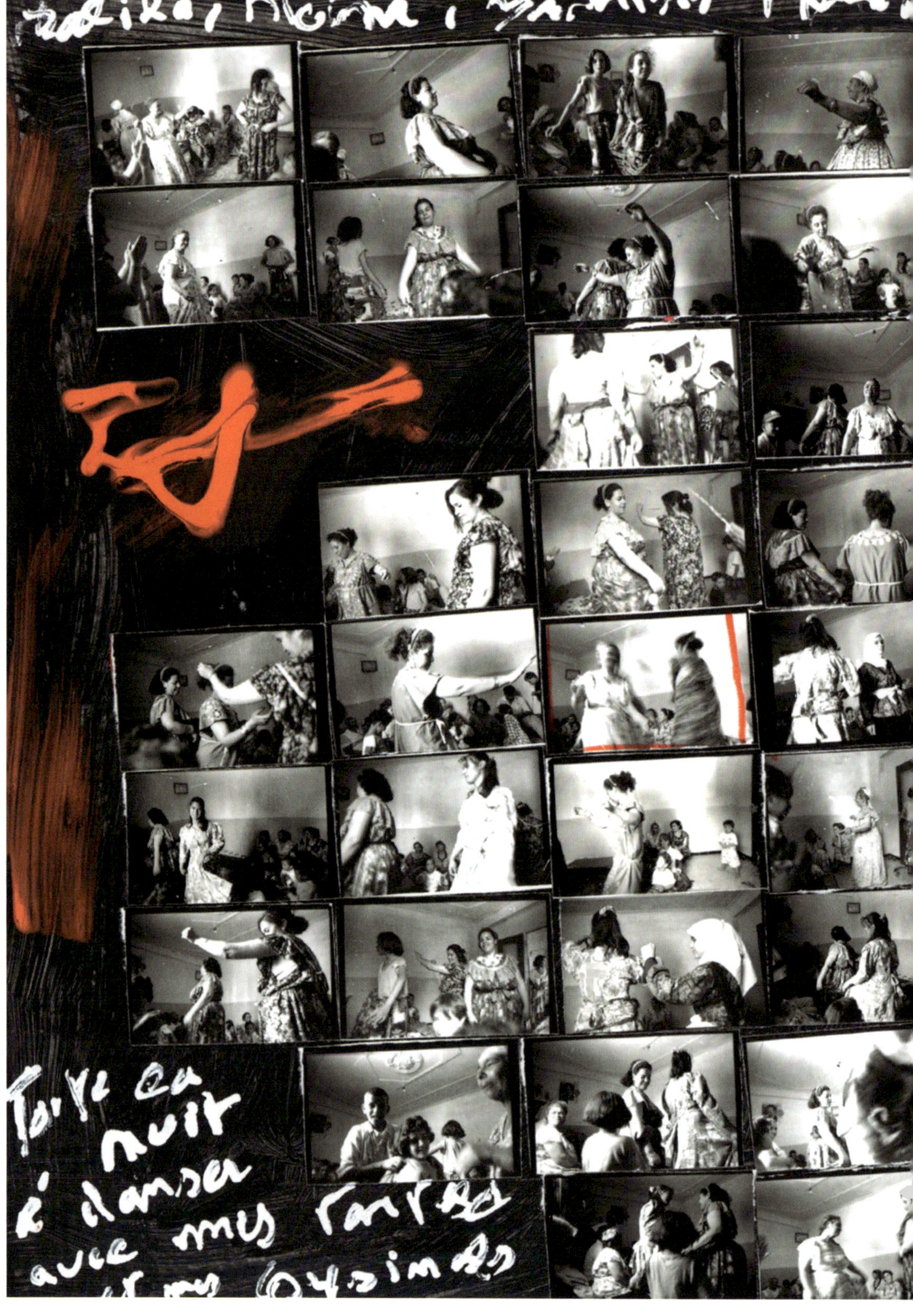
Toute la
nuit
à danser
avec mes tantes
et mes cousines

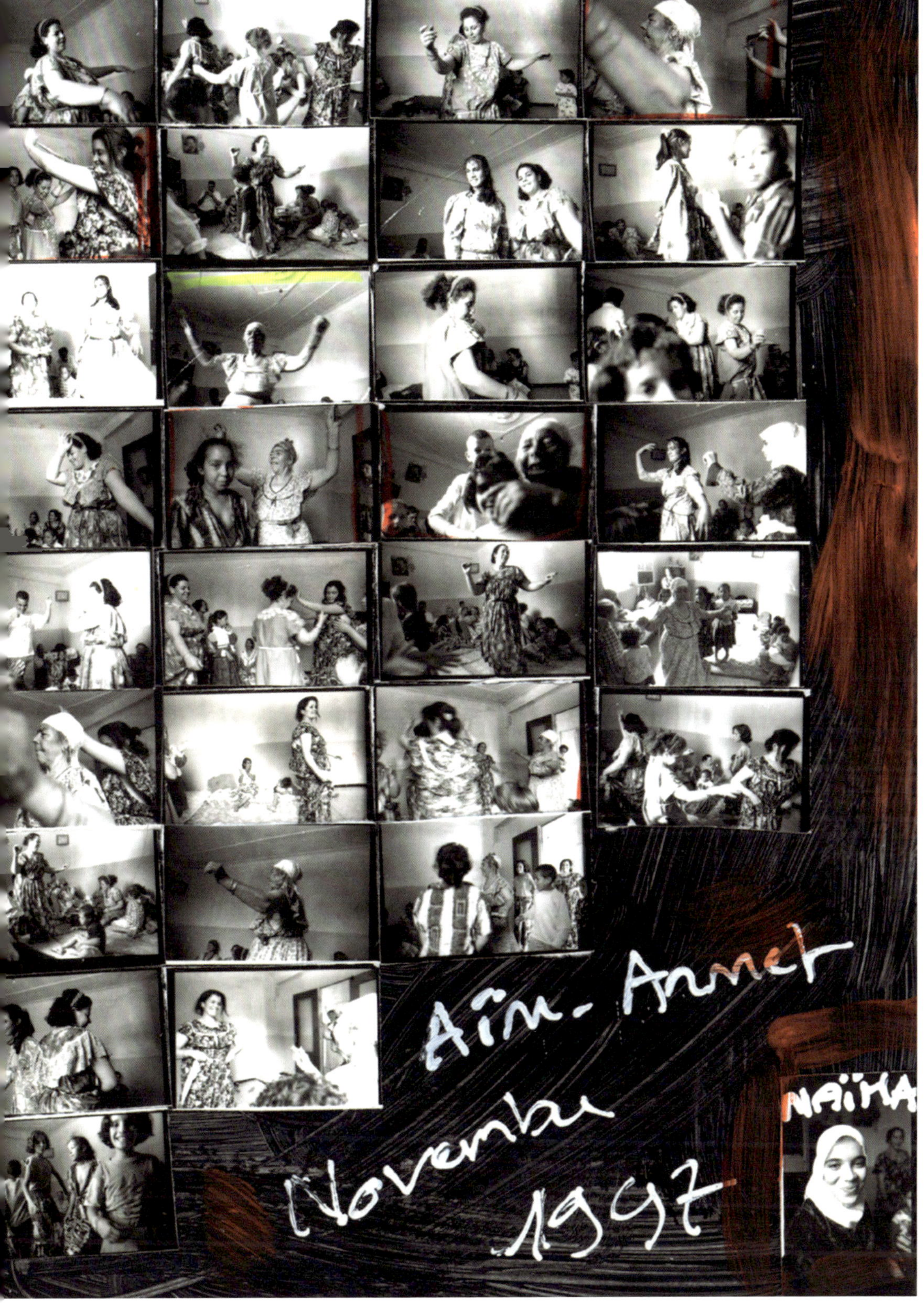
Aïn- Ahmet
Novembre
1997
NAÏMA

TITLE

# PARIS BOUT DU MONDE

COVER

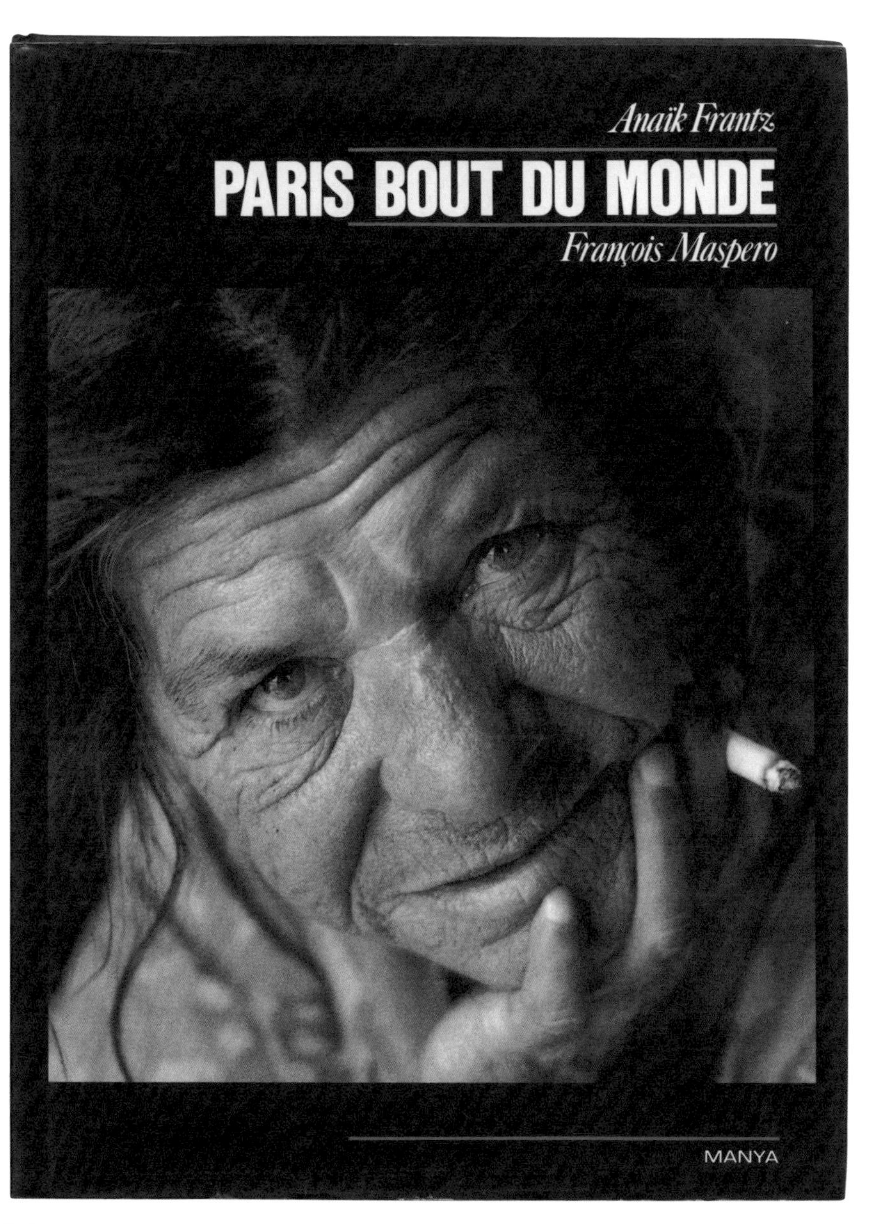

| ARTISTS | Anaïk Frantz and François Maspero |
|---|---|
| PUBLISHER | Manya |
| SPECIFICATIONS | — 95 pages<br>— first published in 1992<br>— size: 24 × 32 cm |
| SUMMARY | *Paris bout du monde* focuses on marginalized Parisians and highlights marginalized urban communities. This glossy album of photographs mostly taken by Anaïk Frantz and accompanied by a short text by Maspero features members of what Maspero termed as "Anaïk's family", photographed mainly within their living spaces. These are marginalized people – gypsies, poor whites, Asians and African Caribbeans. An unsettling intimacy is created.<br><br>Frantz has also collaborated with Maspero on *Les Passagers du Roissy-Express*, a book that deeply inspired Johny Pitts's work on the "Afropean" concept. The quality of Frantz's work, this undefinable "something", is the magic of B-side photography Johny Pitts infuses in this issue of *The Eyes*.<br><br>François Maspero, who was the first to publish Frantz Fanon's *Les Damnés de la terre*, once said of Anaïk Frantz's relationship with her photographic subjects: "I always used to say that I loved them, but I couldn't say why or how, I just did, like a natural reaction and attraction, certain that when I looked at them something happened, that they went straight to his heart ... Each of Anaïk's photos has a long story behind it. They never took people by surprise, they were never muggings ... the faces did not spring from nowhere only to melt back into anonymity: each one had a name, each one was linked to memories, confidences, meals, some shared human warmth or hours spent together. The stories were always 'to be continued ...' They had something in common with Arab tales or African palavers. They were photos that took their time." |
| BIOGRAPHY | Born in 1952, Anaïk Frantz is a French photographer who grew up in the 14th arrondissement of Paris. She worked in collaboration with François Maspero on *Paris bout du monde* and *Les Passagers du Roissy-Express* – both projects dealing with questions of transit and home, mainly concerning the Parisian suburbs. |

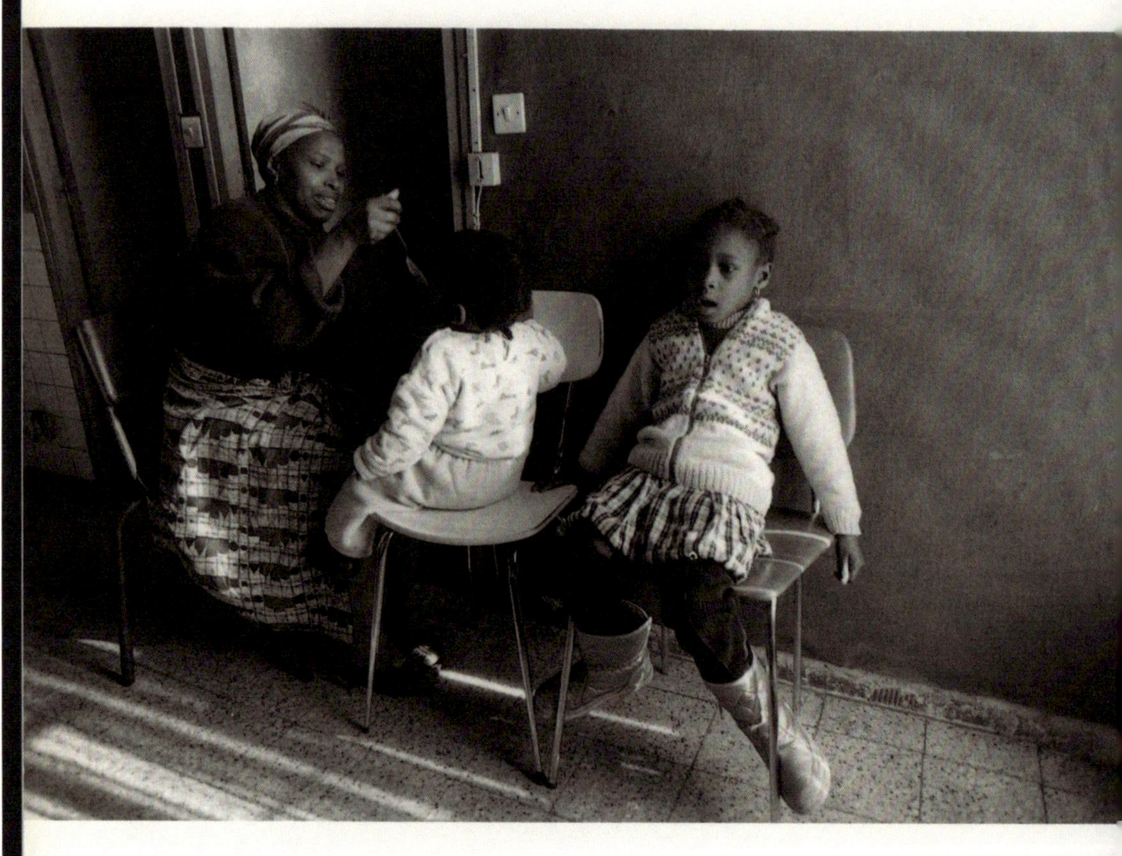

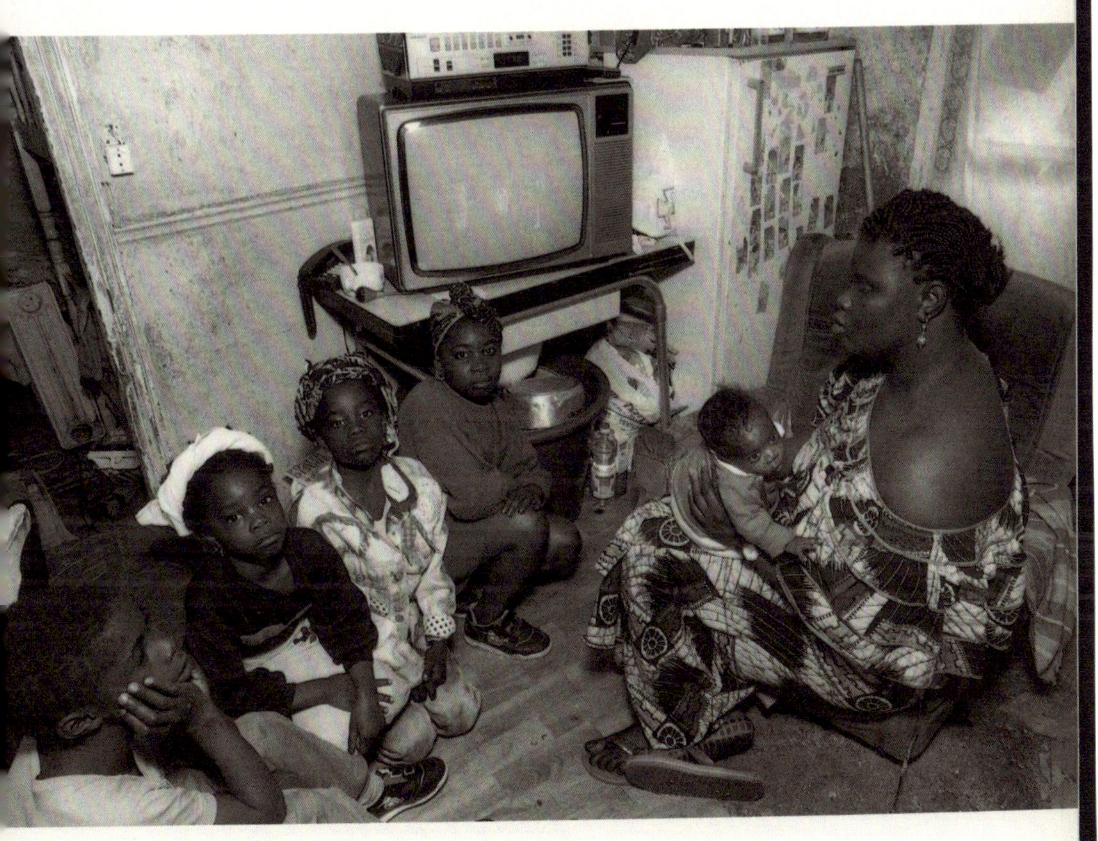

## 9

Quand elle a commencé à faire des photos, Anaïk habitait impasse de l'Ouest, dans le XIV$^{e}$ arrondissement. Ce n'était pas le Montparnasse des boulevards. Il y a tout un discours sur les villages de Paris qui relève du cliché pour syndicat d'initiative. Montparnasse – comme la Butte aux Cailles, comme Belleville ou la Chapelle – n'était pas un village. C'était Paris, dans ce qu'il avait probablement d'unique : ce mélange à nul autre pareil de familiarité et d'indifférence, où voisins de paliers et de rues étaient à la fois très proches et complètement étrangers. Assez liés par le côtoiement quotidien pour ne pas s'ignorer tout à fait, mais trop nombreux pour que la rumeur, la médisance trouvent à circuler sans se perdre. La gouaille, mot parisien, mode de relation spécifiquement parisien, marquait à la fois une distance et une solidarité. Fiers d'être parisiens mais suffisamment venus d'ailleurs pour inscrire dans cette fierté l'originalité d'avoir un voisin de palier parlant une langue impossible, moldo-valaque ou patagon. Concierge, artisan, bourgeois, épicier, artiste-peintre, acceptant l'autre tout en s'en moquant, quel qu'il soit : terreau d'élection pour les douaniers Rousseau, mais aussi pour tous ceux que, déjà, dans les quartiers mieux pensants on dénonçait comme « la lie de l'Europe » – en attendant celle du tiers monde. J'ai aimé ce Paris-là, et j'étais fier, moi aussi, que l'on y rêvât dans le monde entier. Aucune ville au monde et encore moins, naturellement, aucun village, n'ont été cela : la ville où toutes les différences pouvaient venir se fondre dans la chaleur d'une foule jamais réellement anonyme. Je crois qu'avec toute sa brutalité, sa misère ou ses vices, c'était là, et particulièrement à Montparnasse, le Paris du respect de l'autre.

Et je ne dirai jamais assez que j'ai la nostalgie de ce Paris-là.

On était dans la ville-lumière, mais comme dans l'œil du cyclone : on se disait au centre du monde et on était tranquille comme au bout du monde.

Je ne sais pas quand tout a commencé à changer.



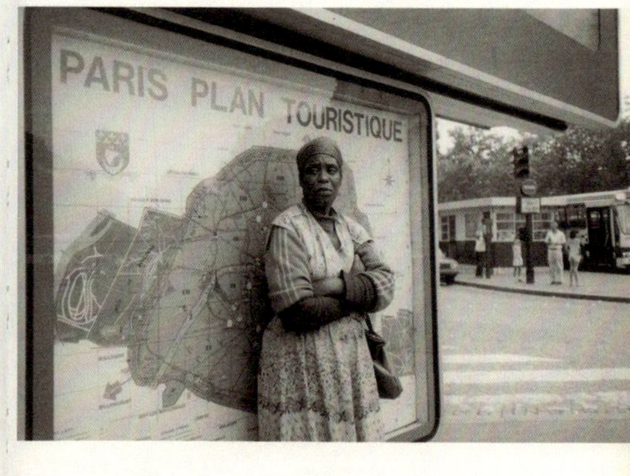




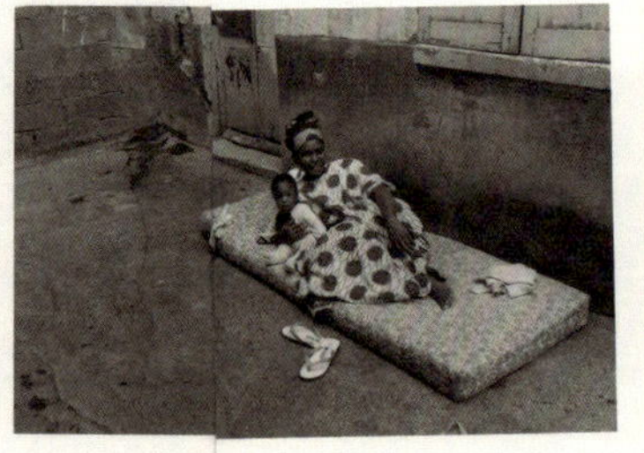

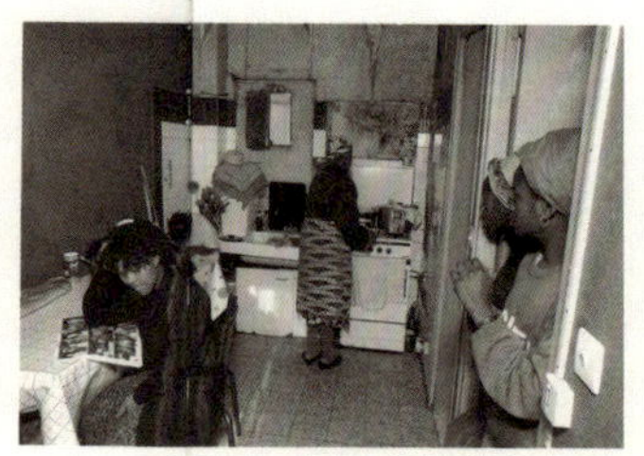

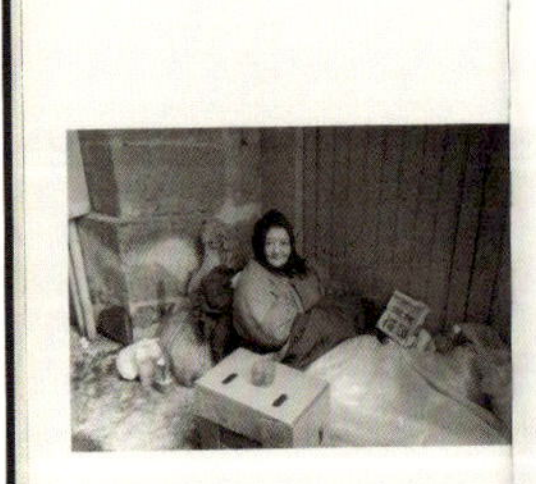

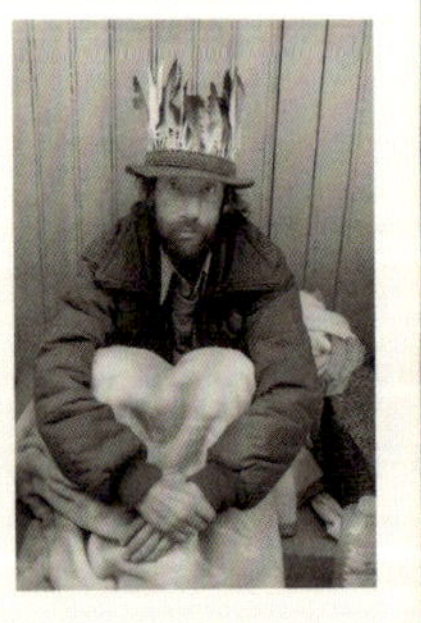

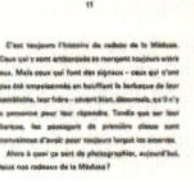

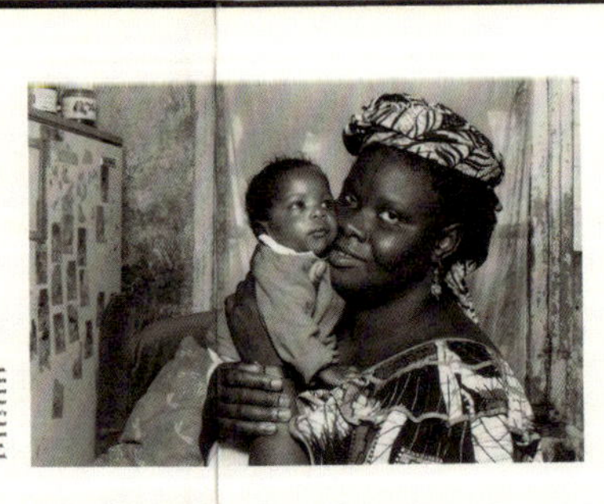

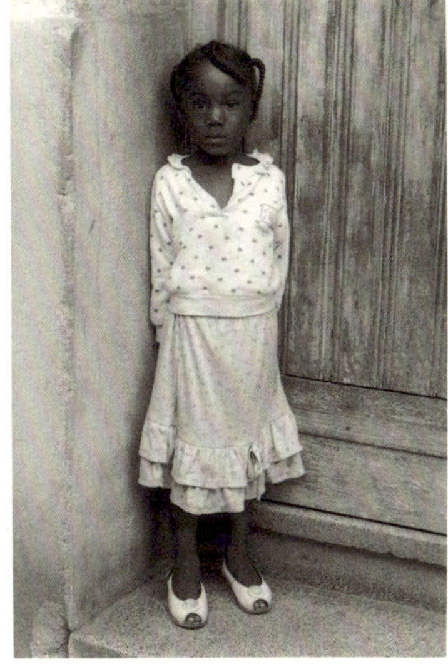

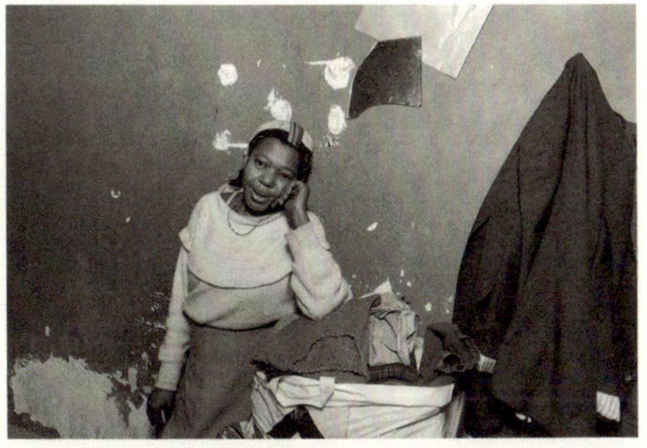

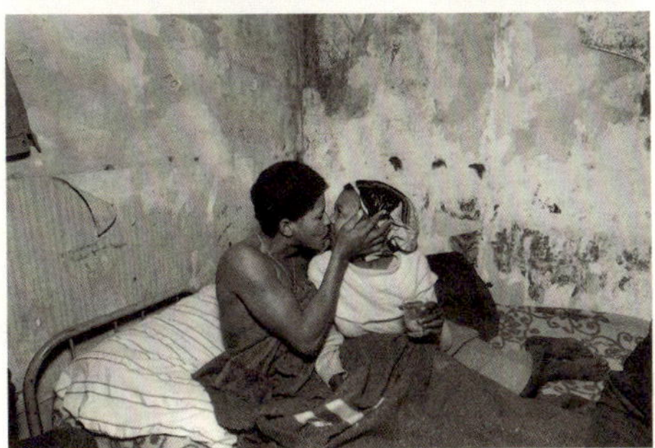





pas l'existence des bains-douches municipaux. Il fallait en finir. On en a fini : aujourd'hui tout le monde a l'eau chaude, tout le monde jouit de ce qu'on appelait « le confort moderne ». Sauf que ce « tout le monde » n'est plus le même : on a finalement réalisé ici, patiemment, avec toutes les formes de la société démocratique, le rêve de ceux qui, dans les années 40, sous les auspices de Vichy et des troupes d'occupation, expulsèrent en une matinée et avec un grand déploiement policier les trente mille « indésirables » du vieux port de Marseille avant de dynamiter le quartier. Mais on n'est pas des chiens. On n'est pas non plus Ceaucescu, cet affreux qui rasa le cœur de Bucarest, crime pour lequel, toutes les télévisions nous l'ont montré, on a bien fait de le fusiller (*sévèrement*, comme disait Francis Blanche) ; on est civilisé et, quand les comités de défense ont eu fini de s'époumoner, usés par leurs luttes de pot de terre contre pot de fer (encore une phrase cent fois entendue au coin des zincs), pris entre la lassitude, les promesses d'indemnités et l'intimidation, ils ont eu droit eux aussi, les vieux locataires de Montparnasse, à tout le confort moderne : on les a presque tous envoyés finir leurs jours dans des barres de stockage humain qui offrent toutes les garanties de l'hygiène. Un exil, ce relogement à quelques kilomètres à peine du quartier perdu ? Il est dans l'Histoire, c'est vrai, de pires déportations... Alors, pourquoi se plaindre, et au nom de quelle nostalgie rétrograde ? A quelques pas de l'impasse de l'Ouest, les façades de Bofill donnent au nouveau quartier une noblesse et une respectabilité que n'avait jamais eues l'ancien. Par le bus ou le RER, ceux qui ont vécu là, dans le lacis effacé des cours, des impasses et des culs-de-sac, pourront toujours revenir le dimanche pour s'en convaincre. Et retourner ensuite à leur F3, au trentième étage de la tour Machin, retrouver au bout du couloir rectiligne le décor final de leur vie, et qui est pour eux la vraie impasse, le vrai cul-de-sac, le vrai bout du monde.

Et puis si ça ne leur suffit pas, ils en auront bientôt un autre, de bout du monde, et tout neuf, à l'autre bout du RER : Disneyland.

Anaïk a vécu et photographié chaque épisode de cette histoire. Elle avait exploré le dédale des cours – celles qui abritaient les rassemblements des petits bookmakers et des parieurs clandestins, celles qui débouchaient sur des terrains vagues imprévus, connus seulement des chats et de leurs vieilles dames protectrices. Elle a suivi la marche des bulldozers. L'installation des chantiers, avec les ouvriers portugais ou maghrébins, vivant au cœur de la ville comme s'ils campaient sur un haut plateau désert. L'abandon des ateliers et des commerces, la formation de colonies provisoires dans les squatts, l'édification de précaires cabanes le long du chemin de fer. Le quartier n'en finissait plus de mourir, pour renaître çà et là et vivre d'une vie provisoire, menacée, spasmodique. Jusqu'au jour où, enfin, il s'est figé dans ses murs neufs.

On ne vit pas, on ne photographie pas cela sans colère.

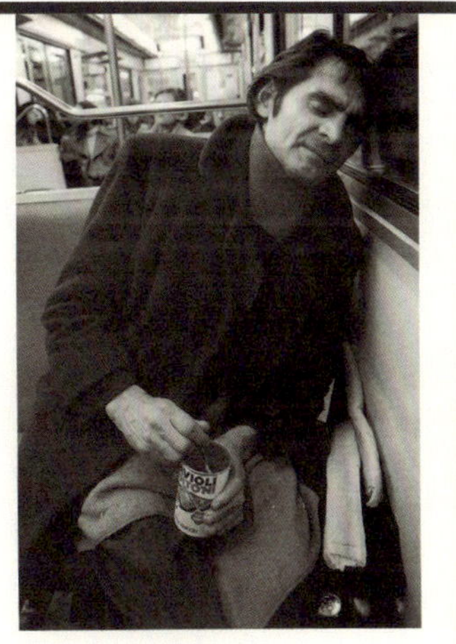

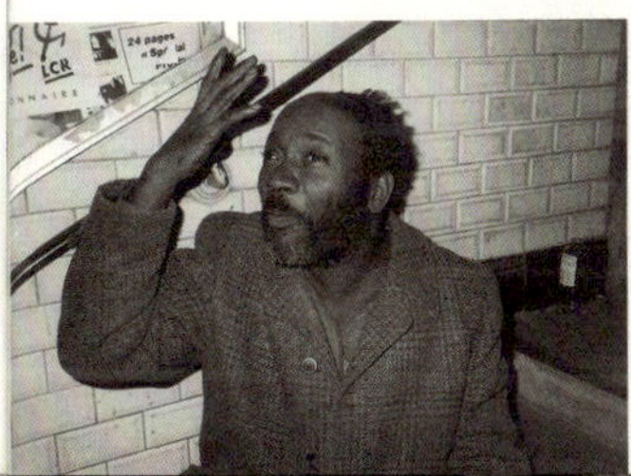

# TABITA REZAIRE

## INNER FIRE & SORRY FOR REAL

Tabita Rezaire was born in 1989, of Danish and Guyanese ancestry. She grew up in Paris and studied in France, Denmark and the United Kingdom at the Central Saint Martins art and design college in London. After living in South Africa, she chose to settle in French Guyana. Her work as a visual artist and video-maker is an extension of her reflections on colonial history and its contemporary ramifications, and takes a critical look at our global systems of information and communication. Her images and videos examine and twist the aesthetic codes of the internet, often addressing the discrimination and stereotypes that it propagates.

The series "Inner Fire" brings together five digital self-portraits. In an abundance of visual and cultural references, Tabita Rezaire recalls the contributions of Black culture and denounces the archetypes of "the Black woman" in terms of race, sexuality, spirituality, technology and capital. In the series "Sorry for Real_Sorrow", Tabita Rezaire ironically imagines the West calling on the phone to ask for forgiveness from formerly colonized countries.

Tabita Rezaire is represented by the Goodman Gallery in South Africa and in London.


*Inner Fire – Bow Down*, 2017
*Inner Fire – Make It Rain*, 2017
*Inner Fire – Pimp Your Brain*, 2017
*Sorry For Real_Sorrow For_Soul*, 2015
*Sorry For Real_Sorrow For_Heart*, 2015
*Sorry For Real_Sorrow For_Womb*, 2015
*Sorry For Real_Sorrow For_Land*, 2015

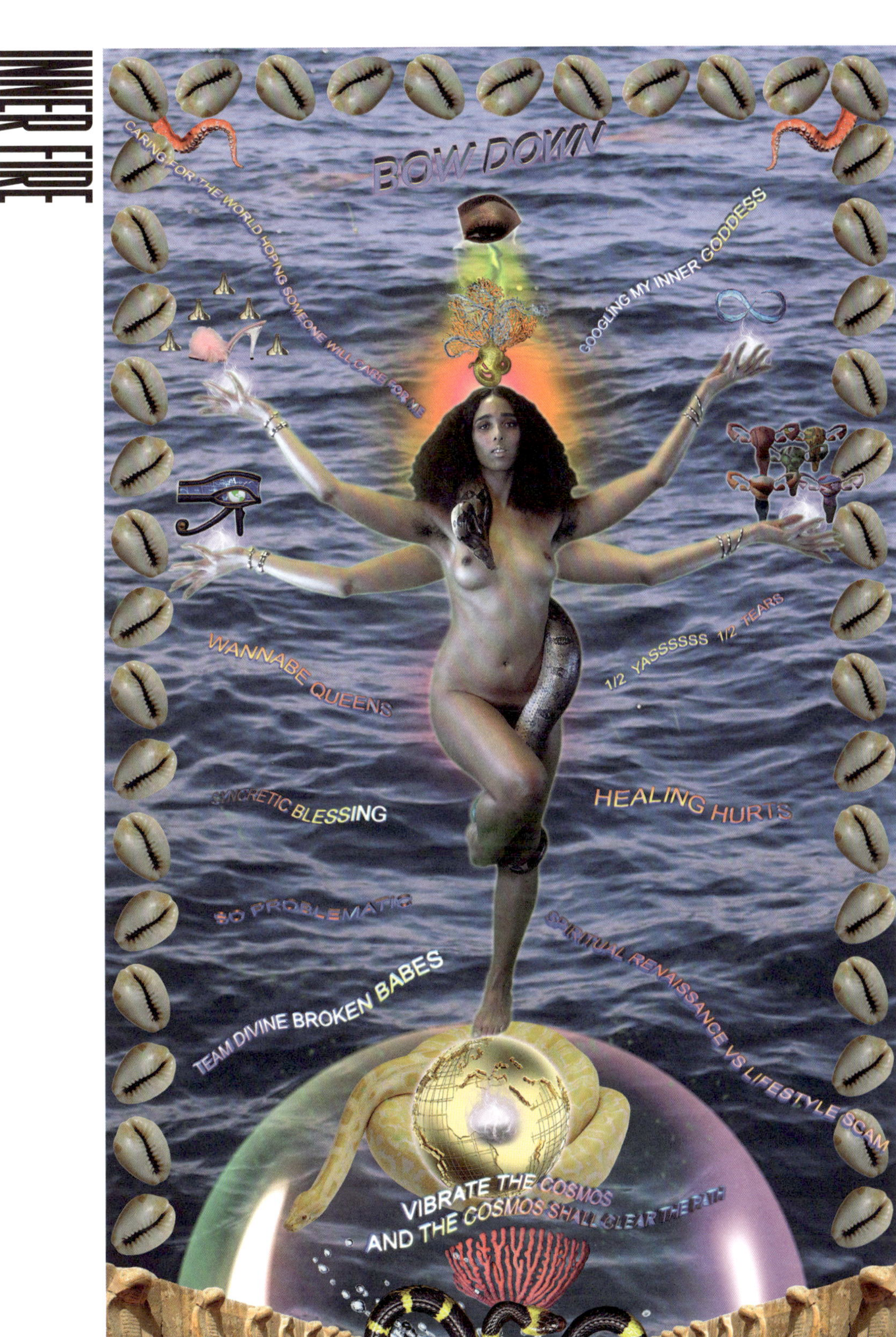
BOW DOWN
CARING FOR THE WORLD HOPING SOMEONE WILL CARE FOR ME
GOOGLING MY INNER GODDESS
WANNABE QUEENS
1/2 YASSSSSS 1/2 TEARS
SYNCRETIC BLESSING
HEALING HURTS
SO PROBLEMATIC
SPIRITUAL RENAISSANCE VS LIFESTYLE SCAM
TEAM DIVINE BROKEN BABES
VIBRATE THE COSMOS
AND THE COSMOS SHALL CLEAR THE PATH

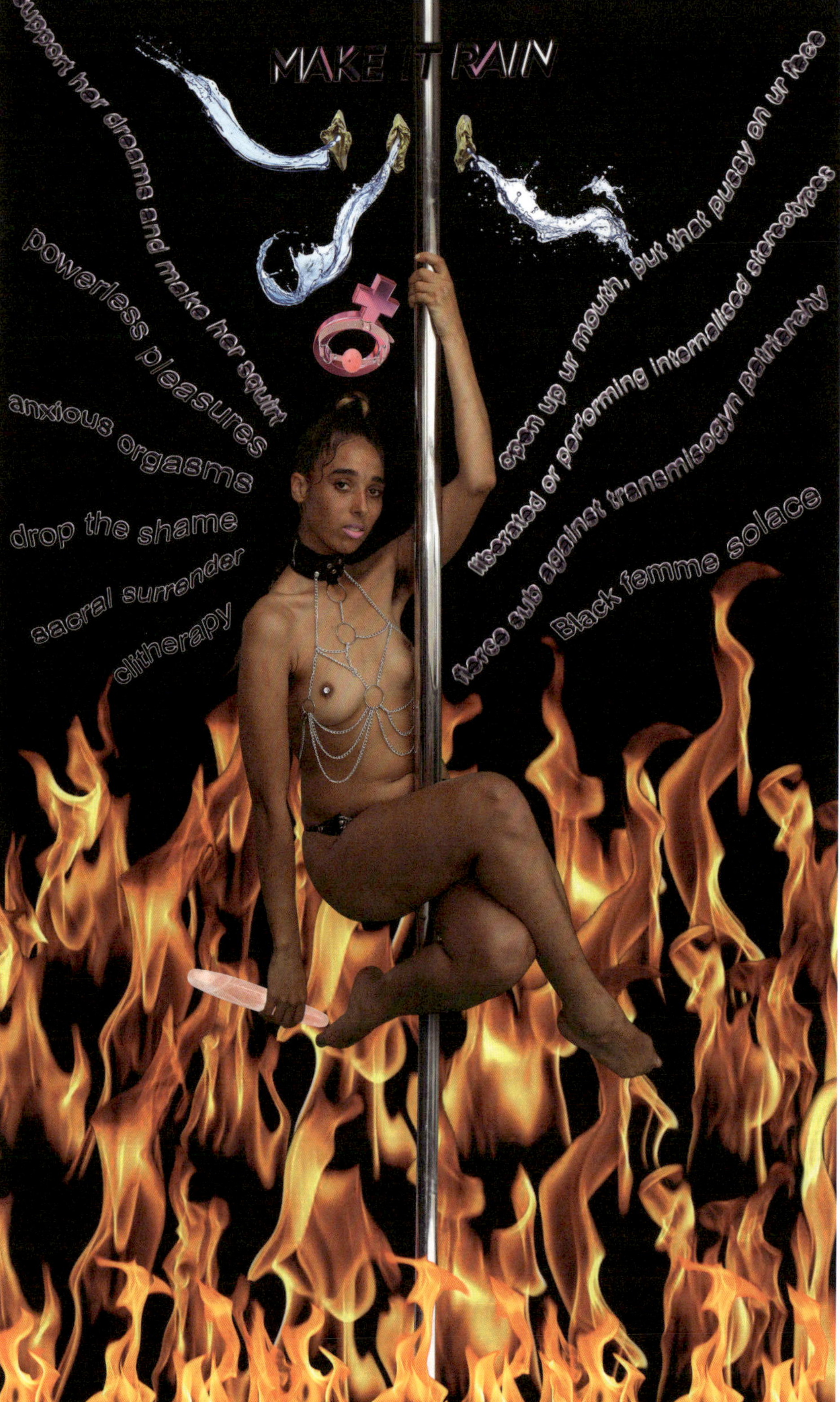
MAKE IT RAIN
support her dreams and make her squirt
powerless pleasures
anxious orgasms
drop the shame
sacral surrender
clitherapy
open up ur mouth, put that pussy on ur face
liberated or performing internalised stereotypes
fierce sub against transmisogyn patriarchy
Black femme solace

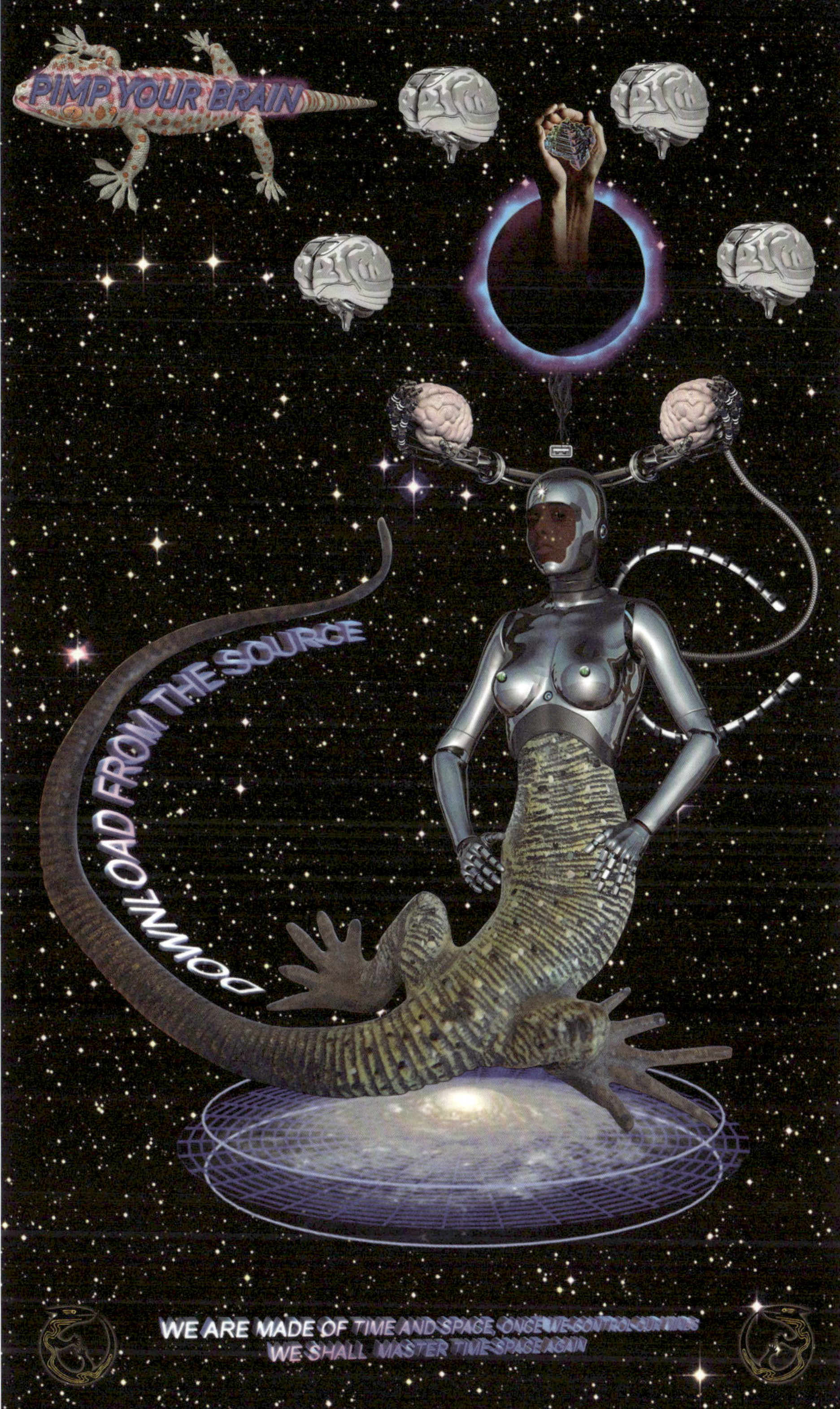
PIMP YOUR BRAIN
DOWNLOAD FROM THE SOURCE
WE ARE MADE OF TIME AND SPACE, ONCE WE CONTROL
WE SHALL MASTER TIME-SPACE AGAIN

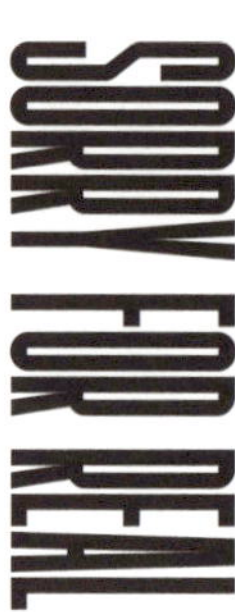


I wish to apologize for our domination, for creating a system that oppresses and subjugates, and for legitimizing our superiority and global hegemony.

I am calling to apologize on behalf of the Western world.

NO WHITE TEARS!

NOT TODAY!

9:41 AM

Western World

mobile

The Governor & Administrator of Entire Universe

WTF???

I GOT NO TIME FOR WESTERN SAVIORISM!

Decline

Answer

SO WHAT NOW? SHOULD I GIVE YOU A HUG AND PLAY THE GOOD N*****?

I apologize for slavery as we instructed genocidal actions upon indigenous communities and created the legal and financial policies necessary for the enslavement of Africans.

I apologize for creating the concept of race and consequently, hierarchies among people, cultures and knowledge systems.

My apologies for the 400 years of colonial domination and further control and prejudice over the emancipated.

I wish I could just delete contact. Move to trash!

So now we all forgive you and move on? LOL

Where's our gold?

Sorry for white supremacy as we institutionally perpetuate a system of exploitation and oppression on people of color for the purposes of maintaining and defending our wealth, power and privilege.

NEVER TRUST DEMONS!

Let me apologize for imperialist-white-supremacist-capitalist-hetero-patriarchy.

I apologize for forcing a gender binary on your communities, and for exporting misogyny, homophobia and transphobia.

So are you gonna stop killing us?

Do you want a cookie?

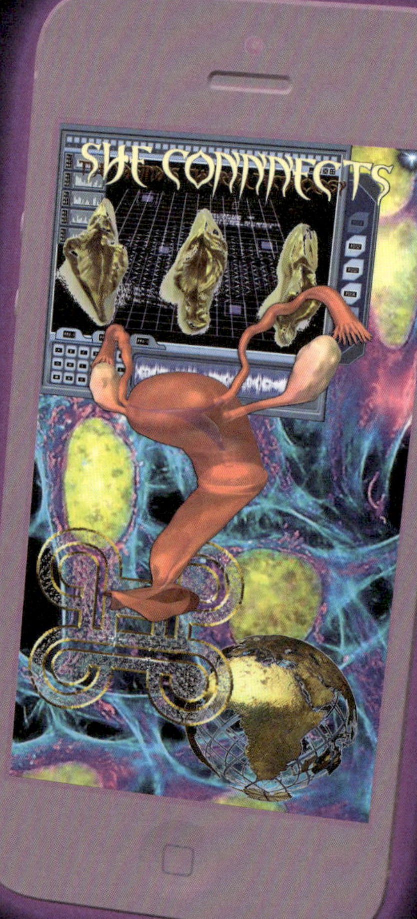


Sure his assistant scrolled through #intersectionality

To women I apologize for the lost knowledge of your wombs, for forcing you into a role of subjugation; for shaming your sacred sexuality, for making your menstruations impure, and for cursing birth and hiding its orgasmic secrets.

I apologize for sexual slavery, for rape culture, for biological warfare and for your traumatized genetic memory.

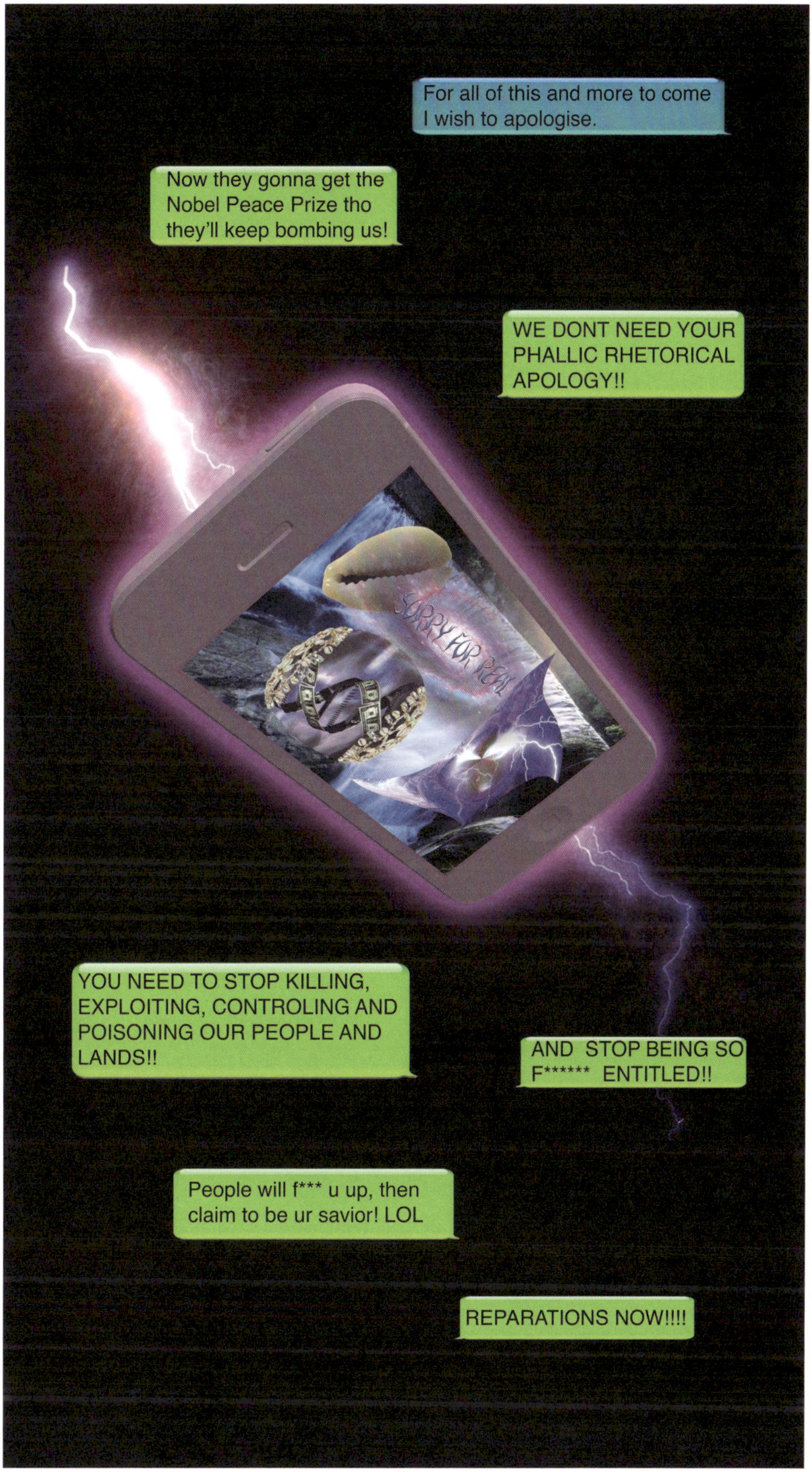

For all of this and more to come I wish to apologise.

Now they gonna get the Nobel Peace Prize tho they'll keep bombing us!

WE DONT NEED YOUR PHALLIC RHETORICAL APOLOGY!!

SORRY FOR REAL

YOU NEED TO STOP KILLING, EXPLOITING, CONTROLING AND POISONING OUR PEOPLE AND LANDS!!

AND STOP BEING SO F****** ENTITLED!!

People will f*** u up, then claim to be ur savior! LOL

REPARATIONS NOW!!!!

TITLE

# THE GHOSTS OF SONGS: THE FILM ART OF THE BLACK AUDIO FILM COLLECTIVE

COVER

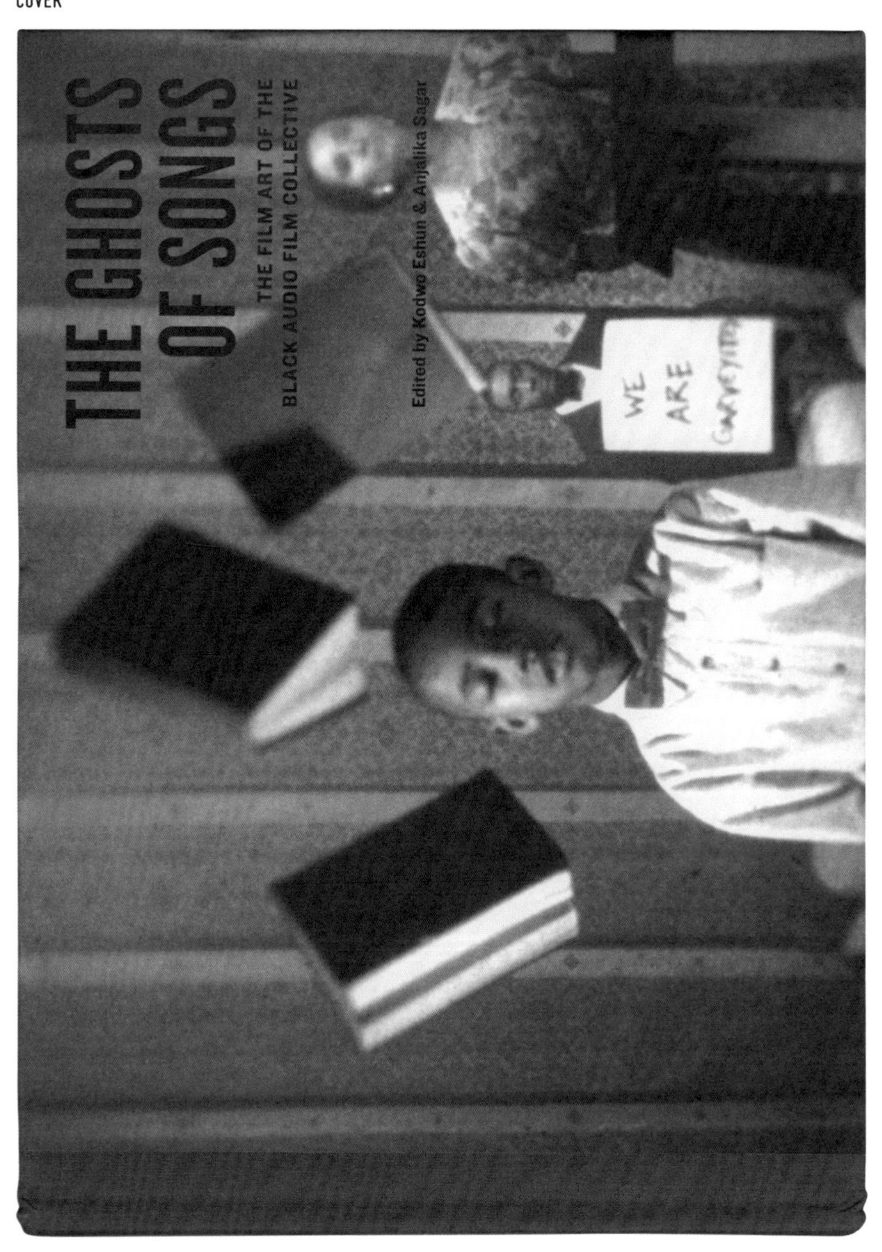

| | |
|---|---|
| ARTISTS | Kodwo Eshun and Anjalika Sagar (eds.) |
| PUBLISHER | Liverpool University Press |
| SPECIFICATIONS | — 256 pages<br>— first published in 2007<br>— size: 28.96 × 21.08 cm |
| SUMMARY | *The Ghosts of Songs*, edited by Kodwo Eshun and Anjalika Sagar, is the first book devoted to the work of the Black Audio Film Collective (BAFC). Richly illustrated (with many previously unpublished images), the book catalogues all the films, videos, installations, essays, manifestoes and statements of the collective. Contributions from artists, film-makers and academics highlight the group's innovative practice, elegant style and ground-breaking approach, influenced by psychoanalytic theory, debates on postcolonialism, and theorists such as Homi Bhabha and Stuart Hall. |
| BIOGRAPHY | The Black Audio Film Collective (BAFC) was formed in 1982 in London by seven Black British film-makers and multimedia artists: John Akomfrah, Lina Gopaul, Avril Johnson, Reece Auguiste, Trevor Mathison, Edward George and Claire Joseph, replaced by David Lawson in 1985. All had met while studying at Portsmouth Polytechnic in the UK. The collective was formed in the wake of the 1981 Brixton uprisings and in response to stereotyping of Black identities in the media. Until its disbandment in 1998, the BAFC had a major influence on film, music, fashion and culture. Working as a laboratory, the collective continued to experiment with new forms of film writing, pushing the boundaries of the documentary. |

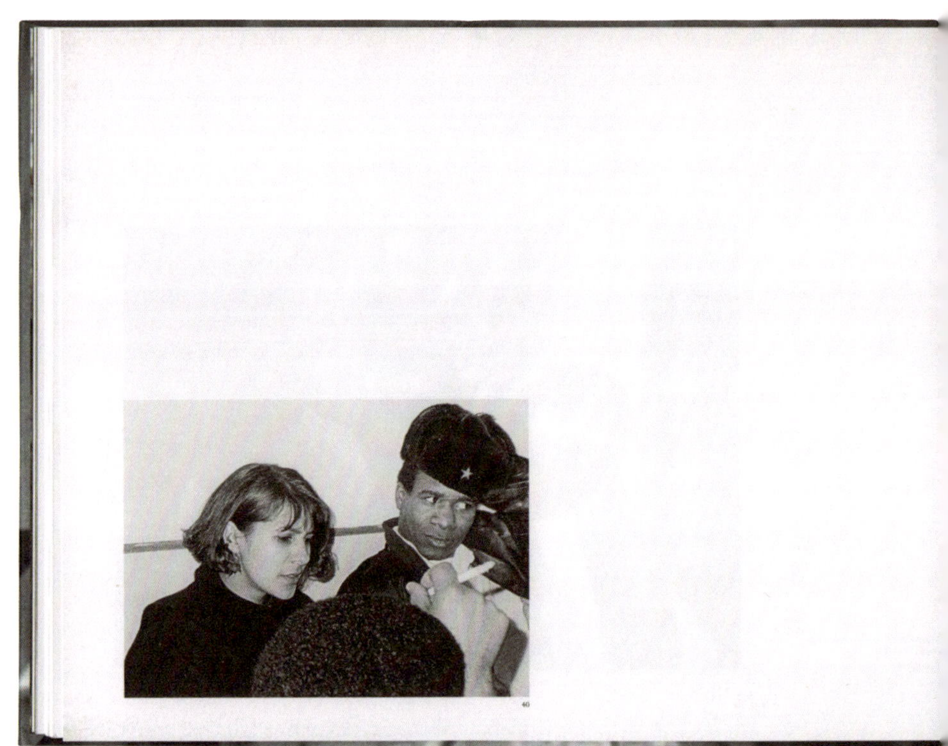

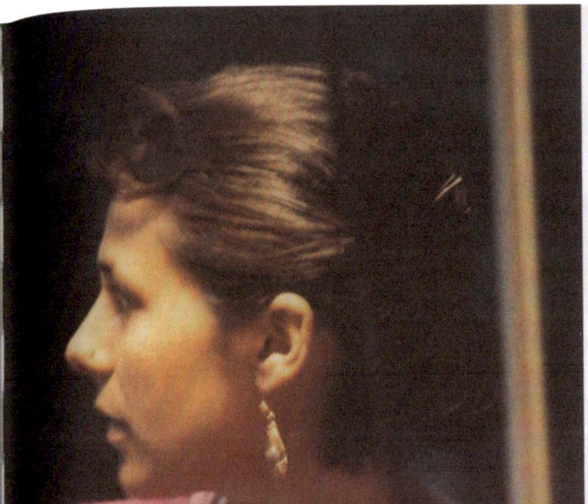

80

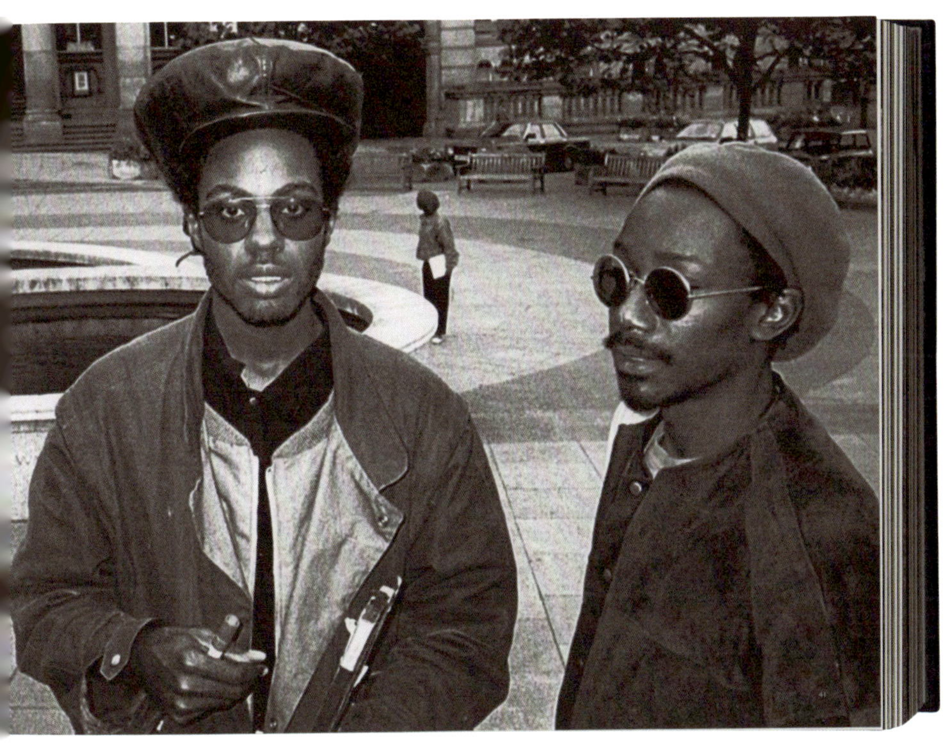

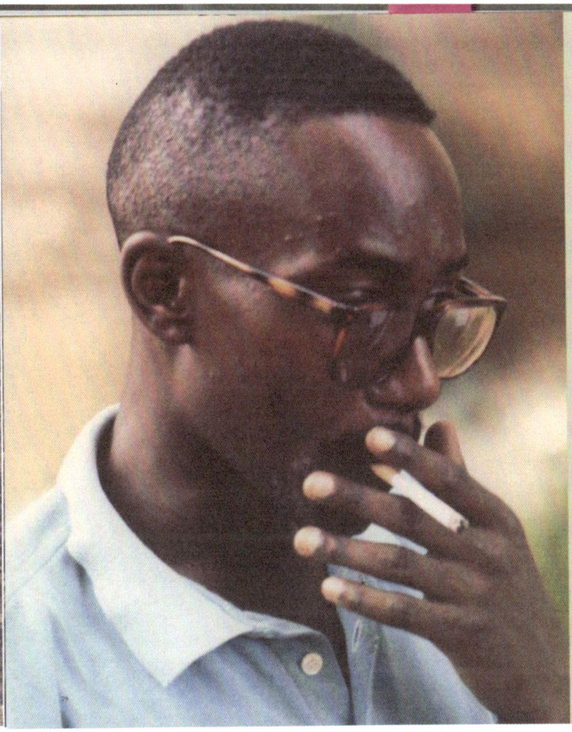

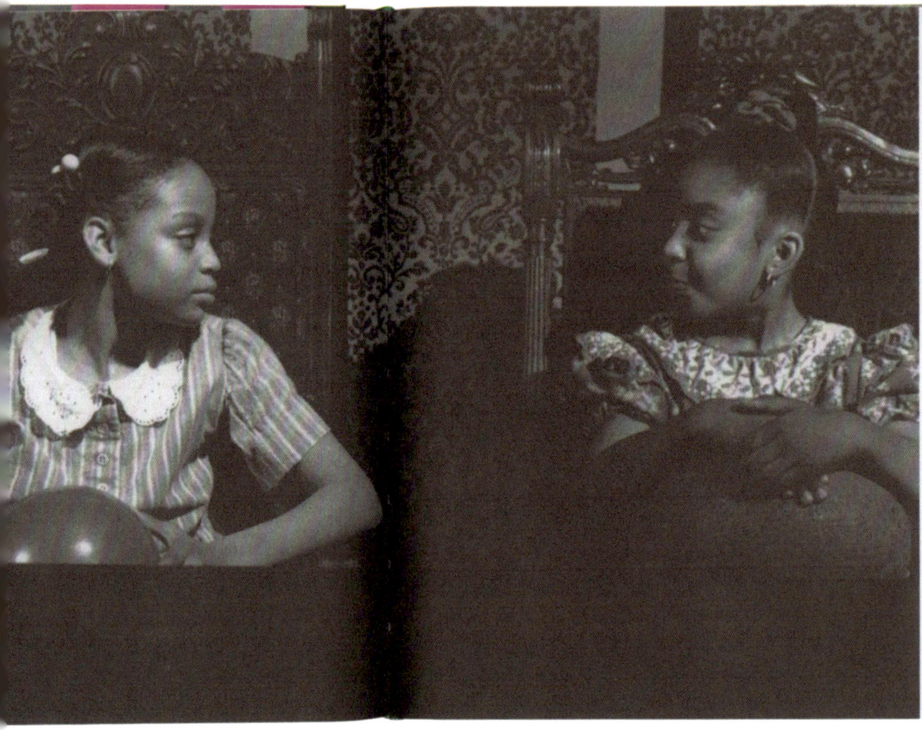

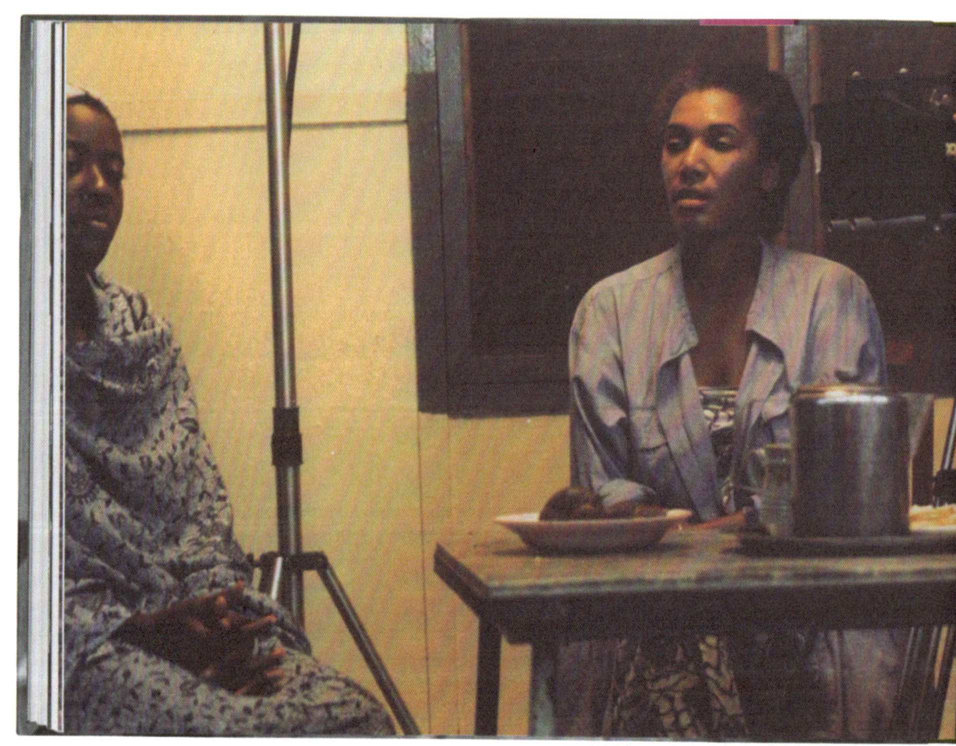

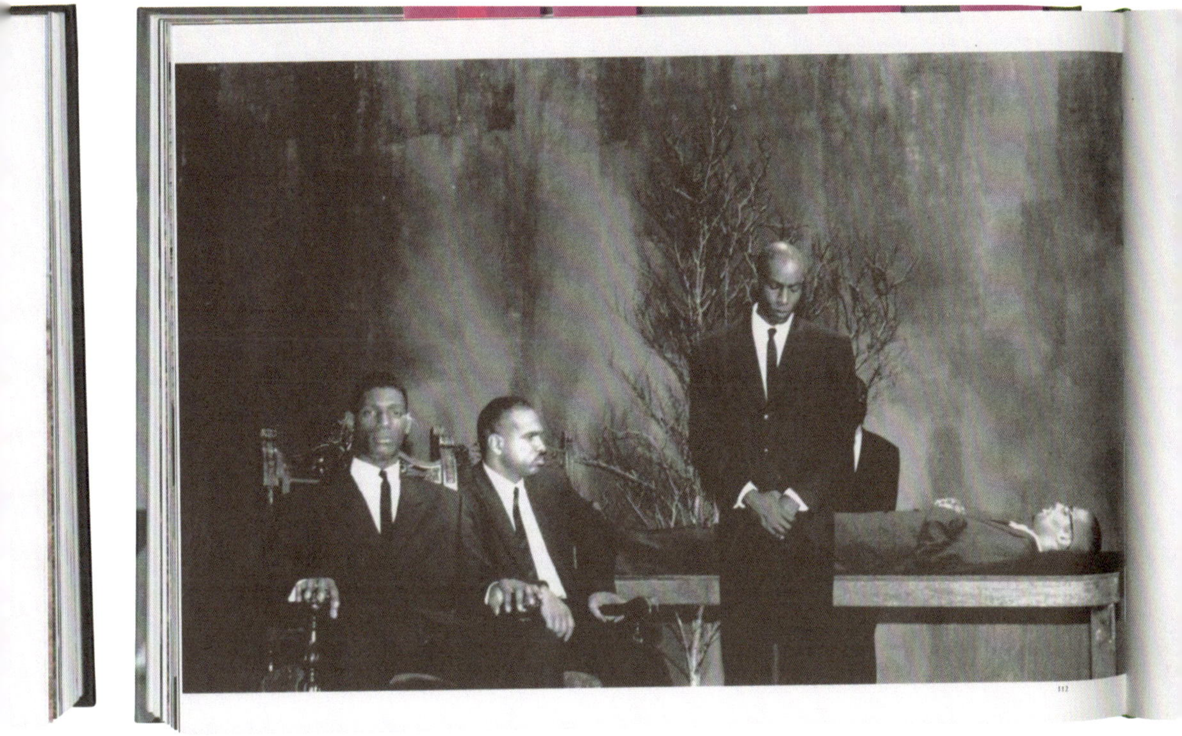

112

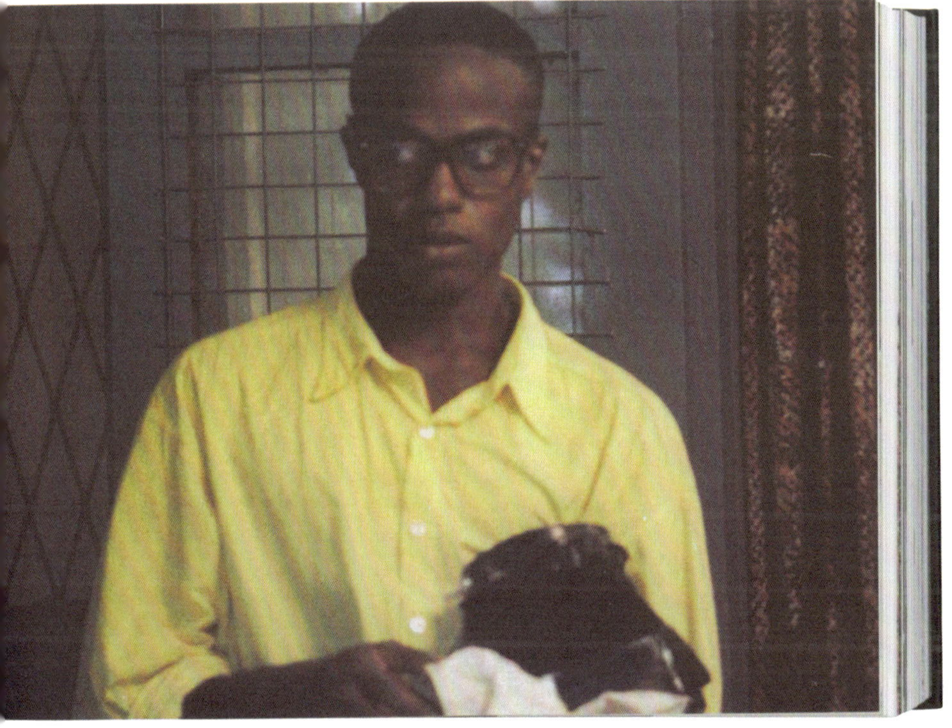

# WHAT DOES AFROPEAN MEAN TO YOU?

VITTORIO LONGHI
ITALIAN ERITREAN JOURNALIST

As an Italian raised in an all-white environment, I became aware of my Afropean identity quite recently, quite late.

And yet, the very notion of being a European of African descent should be more familiar to Italians than to any other people on the Old Continent. Until the end of the Roman Empire, the Mediterranean had been the centre of the world, at a crossroads between Africa and Europe, the Far and the Middle East. For aeons the *mare nostrum*, "our sea" in Latin, had represented an ideal bridge between peoples and cultures, a place where mixed-race identities meant richness, and beauty.

The modern period and the creation of a white-dominated Europe have turned the Mediterranean into a peripheral area. Europeans from the south, such as the Greek, the Italian and the Spanish, have now become the gatekeepers of the continent. Our main concern seems to be patrolling borders and preventing people from further south from crossing that millenary bridge. When I started researching my Eritrean roots, a few years ago, I asked myself: how could the long history of African European identity across the Mediterranean vanish so silently?

The answer lies in Europe's colonial history and the white privilege theories that justified the scramble for Africa, after the Atlantic slave trade.

From the early days of Italy's colonialism, the government considered the children born to Italian men and young Eritrean women as a threat to the purity of the white race. And if the Italians called them *meticci* with contempt, the Eritreans used the word *deqala*, in Tigrinya meaning both "hybrid" and "bastard". In 1940 Mussolini himself wanted a specific "law against the mixed", aimed at denying the right to citizenship to those children.

My grandparents Maria and Vittorio, on my father's side, were *meticci* too. They were born and raised in a segregated Asmara by their Eritrean mothers alone. The expression "African roots" has always remained unspoken in my father's family, like a sin. I wonder what Maria and Vittorio would think about the cosmopolitan notion that the word Afropean has today. But I have the feeling that they would encourage me to reclaim that definition for myself. With pride.

ELVAN ZABUNYAN
FRENCH CONTEMPORARY ART
HISTORIAN, LECTURER AND ART CRITIC

## Unbridged "Afropean"

> "Conceive of the expanse and its so-approachable mystery. Don't leave your shore for a journey of discoveries or conquest. Let the journey do that."[1]

In 2008, the artist Francis Alÿs made his piece *Don't Cross the Bridge Before You Get to the River*, questioning the possibility of reuniting both shores of the Strait of Gibraltar. Europe and Africa are 14 kilometres apart. The project intended to install a line of miniature sailboats that traced, on a scale of 1 kilometre, a bridge between the Spanish and the Moroccan coasts. The main protagonists were children and adolescents each holding a little boat in their hands – a boat made from colourful flip-flops and babouches. In the project presentation taken from a diary in which, since 2006, the artist noted down his various ideas but also his doubts regarding the feasibility of the project, Francis Alÿs wrote: "Should a line of kids leave Europe towards Morocco, and another line of kids leave Africa towards Spain, will these two lines meet somewhere in the chimera of the horizon?" The balance between continents and countries ("Europe towards Morocco", "Africa towards Spain"), and mostly the metaphor of that hybrid horizon, refer to the power of artistic imagination. Even if the physical encounter remains impossible, the symbolic power of these bodies in simultaneous contact with the Atlantic Ocean and the Mediterranean Sea is enough to grasp the importance of such an idea. Scientific research confirms that the European and African tectonic plates have been moving closer to one another for 70 million years; a movement of convergence continuing today, by 1–2 centimetres every year. Francis Alÿs's artwork tells of the possible collision between Africa and Europe. It considers a new continental configuration, a new, unbridged place for encounters: an Afropean configuration.

1 Edouard Glissant, *Traité du Tout-Monde*, Paris, Gallimard, 1997, p. 59.

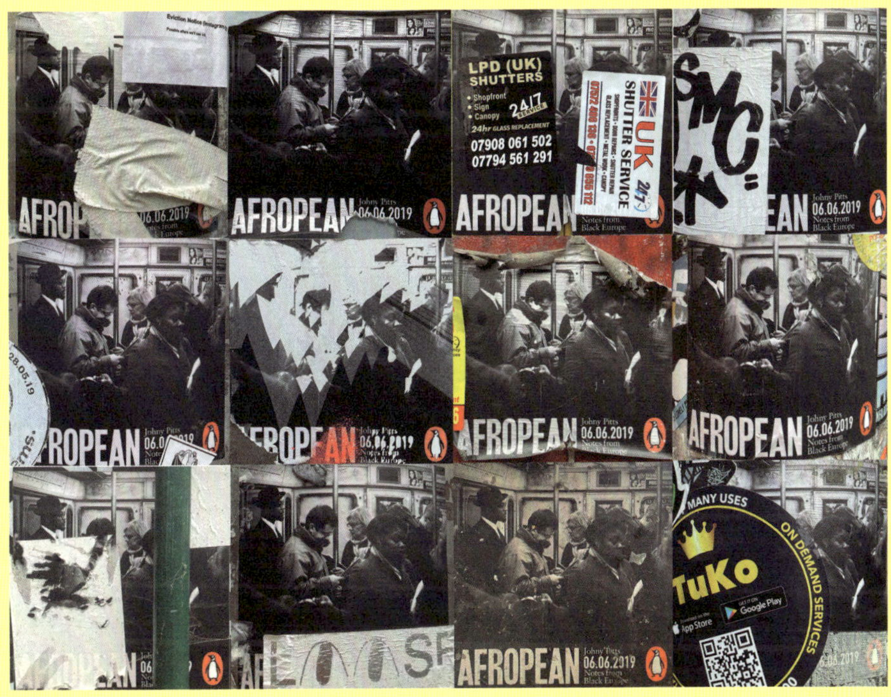


@Johny Pitts, *Guerilla Marketing*: Self Made Afropean stickers after two and a half years on the road, 2021

CARYL PHILLIPS
BRITISH KITTITIAN NOVELIST, PLAYWRIGHT AND ESSAYIST

"Afropean". It's a strange hybrid of "African" and "European". When I first encountered what I've come to regard as "Johny Pitts's word", I was intrigued. Of course, one can be of African origin and European as well, and what was needed was a nice, pithy word to neatly circumscribe this fusion. At first glance, Afropean would seem to quite brilliantly fit the bill. But there's something about the necessary brevity – the shrinkage, if you like – that feels a bit off. Which is perhaps why I'd never use the term to describe myself. I want to have it both ways. I want a word or phrase that points in the right direction – which Afropean does – but I also want a word or phrase that fully displays the cultural complexity that is being suggested. I'm not sure Afropean, in its brevity, does this. It's interesting to think of the United States, where in the space of less than a century people struggled to find a term that could be both appropriately descriptive and also suggest a broad, rich history. At the start of the century the word was "Negro", then "Coloured", then "Black", and finally "African American". It feels to me as though Afropean is part of a similarly long conversation in Europe, one that will finally offer up a word or phrase which will suggest our place in the continent. These things take time, but it is to Johny's credit that he has opened up that conversation.

THOMAS CHATTERTON WILLIAMS
AMERICAN JOURNALIST, CRITIC AND AUTHOR

One of the most pressing questions confronting Western democracies in the 21st century is and will continue to be, how are we to make our multi-ethnic societies *work*? Should we ever figure out the answer – not at all a foregone conclusion – we may then dare to extend the inquiry further still: and how might as many people as possible inside them flourish? It is this latter, more ambitious variation that is anticipated in Johny Pitts's captivating *Afropean*, a formidable, often beautiful account of travelling through pockets of Black and Brown Europe, and revealing traces of Africa in the wider societies where others would prefer to overlook them. Late in the book, when Pitts is fatigued and miserable from his voyages, unnerved even, he spots a lone Muslim kneeling in the ice in prayer before moving on to an internet cafe bustling with students from East and West Africa. He approaches several and attempts to draw them into political conversation, "as if to say, *I'm black, you're black, and I want to hear your story*". But they could not care less and rebuff him. "I realized that blackness wasn't such a conundrum to them," he reflects. This is perhaps because, where they come from everyone is as they are; the necessary contrasts do not exist. Where they find themselves now is, to Pitts's eye, both oppressive and also fundamentally ephemeral. "They weren't black students, they were just students," he observes. "And though it's true that *I* saw these students as black, it made me feel less sure of my own blackness than ever before, and less sure about the usefulness of any label when searching to understand my own identity or that of a community."

The day we can all achieve such an insight is the day we will finally, convincingly, answer these most pressing questions looming over our ever-more mixed-up worlds.

CLAUDE GRUNITZKY
FRENCH AMERICAN TOGOLESE
JOURNALIST, EDITOR AND ENTREPRENEUR

I met Johny Pitts in the Eurostar one day, when we were both travelling from London to Paris. He approached me because he recognized me from pictures he'd seen. He was familiar with the work I did with *TRACE Magazine*, and from the way he spoke about identity I immediately knew that we were kindred spirits. Even though his drawl revealed a Northern English accent, and I responded with a mid-Atlantic twang as a Togo-born and Paris-raised New Yorker, I recognized that we spoke the same language, as a result of our shared affinities.

He told me about the book he was working on, *Afropean: Notes from Black Europe*, and I was drawn to his cross-border approach to documenting the Black experience all over Europe. I could relate to the term Afropean because I was one of them. When I was growing up in Paris as a teenager, French people would always ask me what my country of origin was. They still do, in fact. The French Republic is supposed to be "indivisible", but many white French people have a habit of asking people of colour where they are really from, as if citizens were supposed to be classified into two categories, European French (meaning white citizens) and non-European French (people like me).

I loved the term Afropean because I saw how it described people like me, Europeans of African descent who love Europe but are often stigmatized in European countries. With *TRACE Magazine*, I created a cultural publication that always claimed a clear focus on Black identity and how we Black people are somehow able to relate to other cultures in Europe, in America and in other parts of the world, even if we are sometimes made to feel like second-class citizens. I believe we Afropeans will become an increasingly meaningful force in Europe and in Africa, because our hybrid identities speak to the new transcultural world we are now entering.

MINNA SALAMI
FINNISH NIGERIAN JOURNALIST
WWW.MSAFROPOLITAN.COM

Estrangement from one's family, for no other reason than racial categorization, is a stinging experience. The first time I learned that was as a child staying at my grandmama's house in Ibadan in Nigeria. Grandmama didn't speak English and I didn't speak Yoruba. There were different routines and customs to mine. For the first time in my life, I felt distinctly European. Other factors were at play too. I lived in Lagos, a cosmopolitan city, and Ibadan is a historic Yoruba city. But I became aware of my European heritage because it created a barrier between me and my ancestry. It estranged me from my identity as a Nigerian.

The second clear memory of sharp estrangement was also with my grandmother, except this time with my Finnish one, Mummo. My mother, aunt and I were visiting Mummo's sister in a small town in Finland. We were eating traditional cakes and coffee. As family conversations often do, the discussion veered into memories – of the Winter War, of previous family gatherings. The sense of racial alienation again hit me acutely and unexpectedly. I had just spent weeks of my summer holiday as part of a four-woman quartet with my mum, aunt and mummo. I could not have felt more at ease. Yet, that afternoon, that sense of being inherently Nigerian – which had escaped me in Ibadan – made me feel different and alien. I felt disassociated from my Finnish identity.

Perhaps it wasn't simply racial categorization that estranged me from my family. Instead, I lacked a language to describe myself with. I now wonder if the word Afropean, with its diagnostic and reconciliatory tenor, could have made my alienation in both situations less jolting.

"Only where there is language is there world," the poet Adrienne Rich said. The term Afropean "worlds" experiences like mine. It makes room for pluralist, hybrid, borderless Blackness while crucially, also, interrogating why Blackness is an estranging conduit of identity in the first place. If I could return to my childhood self, I would gift her the term Afropean and so gift her "worlds". Worlds, where she could be African, European and Afropean.

ANNE LAFONT
FRENCH ART HISTORIAN, RESEARCHER AND DIRECTOR OF STUDIES AT THE ÉCOLE DES HAUTES ÉTUDES EN SCIENCES SOCIALES (EHESS)

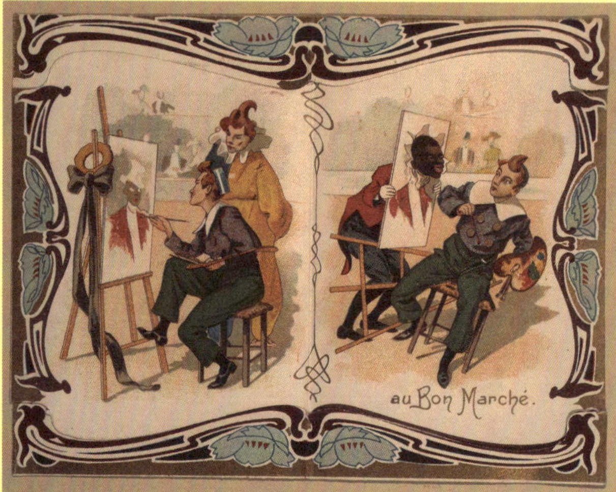


*Les clowns Guguss et Chocolat*, back of the advertising card for the Bon Marché. Courtesy Bibliothèque nationale de France, Département des Estampes et de la Photographie.

*Afropeanity*
*The search for the term that will best convey the experience.*

I had never yet rubbed shoulders with the notion of "Afropeanity", which is more an invitation to scrutinize individual identity than the material and symbolic construction specific to art and images (on which my work as a researcher is based), and which had led me to the stimulating notion of "Afrotrope", conceptualized by friends Huey Copeland and Krista Thompson. However, this invitation to consider the notion of Afropeanity immediately brought back this late-19th-century advertising vignette, where the department store Le Bon Marché – located a stone's throw away from the EHESS[1] where I work – takes advantage of the popularity of the French clown "Chocolat" to caricature his face, and the delicious dread of his unexpected eruption. The supposedly improper nature of his face is used to manufacture a portrait intended to provoke the mocking laughter of the viewer thus won over to the Bon Marché brand. The Black character decidedly does not fit, overflows, cracks, tears, even destroys the two-dimensional code of the painting.

This, in any case, is one first interpretation of the vignette.
It seems to me, however, that a second one can be considered, which probably escaped Le Bon Marché, and marks the moment with the advent of Afropean; in other words, that one moment when, in the image itself, the role of the observer and the observed, the one who targets and the one who is targeted, shifts. And Chocolat, prey of the artist and of the department store, carries out a reversal, crosses the canvas and comes alive, offering a Black and masculine version of the myth of Pygmalion who saw his statue, object of his love, come to life. Having broken into the other side of the social border embodied by the canvas, Chocolat now takes his destiny and his image into his own hands, in Paris, in the heart of Europe, equipped with the Western frame and clothes – not without a conspicuous African feature, the colour of his skin, but standing up then and there in a world whose codes he possesses. For Chocolat holds with both hands the frame that kept him out of sight on the image to the left, while the white clown has vanished on the image to the right and the painter of Le Bon Marché, clinging to his palette and brushes, topples over. This two-stroke playlet, typical of the popular imagery of the denigrating cliché, is, in spite of itself, subverted by an implicit meaning that opens the way to Afropenanity – if understood in the sense that it is a matter of holding on to the frame of one's visibility in the heart of the modern metropolis.

1 School for Advanced Studies in the Social Sciences

MARIE DAULNE AKA ZAP MAMA
BELGIAN ZAIRIAN SINGER AND COMPOSER

I grew up in a part of Brussels known as Matongé, where my mother had cosmetics stores. The area takes its name from a market in Kinshasa in the Democratic Republic of Congo, and is where the African community in Brussels would congregate. It served as a marketplace and space to party, and everything was mixed, from the way we used language, which would be a mix of French with Lingala, to the style of dress and the music people would dance to.

However, at a certain point, I realized that I was part of a world that you couldn't find represented in the institutions – a part of Belgium that seemed to exist outside of anything "official". You could say it was like the B-side of Brussels.

"Afropean", then, is not only a landscape but a state of mind, a term I used like "African American", to show that we exist. There is something futuristic about the term, I think, because it gives a name to what is happening everywhere – in a way, we are all part of a fusion, mixed culturally or through fashion; everybody is inspired by one another, but too often we limit ourselves to being this or that. But when you know your history, and you learn the anthropology of the human being, you realize just how mixed we all already are, and how much more mixed we will be.

Through music I could bring this fusion to the surface, and conjure this Afropean world. Take people on an adventure; I can bring listeners to the forest of the Pygmies in the Congo using the humour of a person from the West, and vice versa – that was the concept of Afropean, it was in a way an act of translation. Even people with no African or European descent, they recognize in my work something that feeds them.

In the 1990s, Zap Mama started to have success with a new kind of people – people who connected with something that gives them a place to meet. Artists, musicians, writers, poets and photographers often attempt to propose the world in another way, one that touches people with a feeling before they start thinking. It's something that moves them intuitively and guides them. People often say to me "I felt it", and when I ask what they mean, they can't explain it, they just feel it – and I think that's what artists are: people who can connect with the invisible world. In Africa they would call that the spirit, who would give you the inspiration and you write it down. When Johny Pitts came with the Afropean book I felt that finally we have an extension, a new chapter in the story. We are born to create this landscape that can be a realm where everybody feels at home.

# DÉLIO JASSE

Délio Jasse was born in 1980 in Luanda, Angola. In the early 2000s, he learned screen printing in Lisbon. His artistic practice is based on the use of archival documents and found images bearing clues to past lives. Working on the materiality of photography, he develops his printing techniques and often uses historical photographic processes such as cyanotype, platinum-palladium or Van Dyke printing. These processes allow him to subvert the reproducibility of the photographic print by obtaining subtle variations each time.

In this series, the artist attempts to deconstruct the colonial gaze and restore dignity to the mostly anonymous people depicted in the photographs. The postcolonial subject is a fluctuating subject, as the author Paul Gilroy suggests, a subject that is both rooted and routed.[1]

Series produced in 2021 during an artistic residency at the Nogueira da Silva Museum (Braga, Portugal).



1 Paul Gilroy, *The Black Atlantic: Modernity and Double Consciousness*, London, Verso, 1993, p. 133.

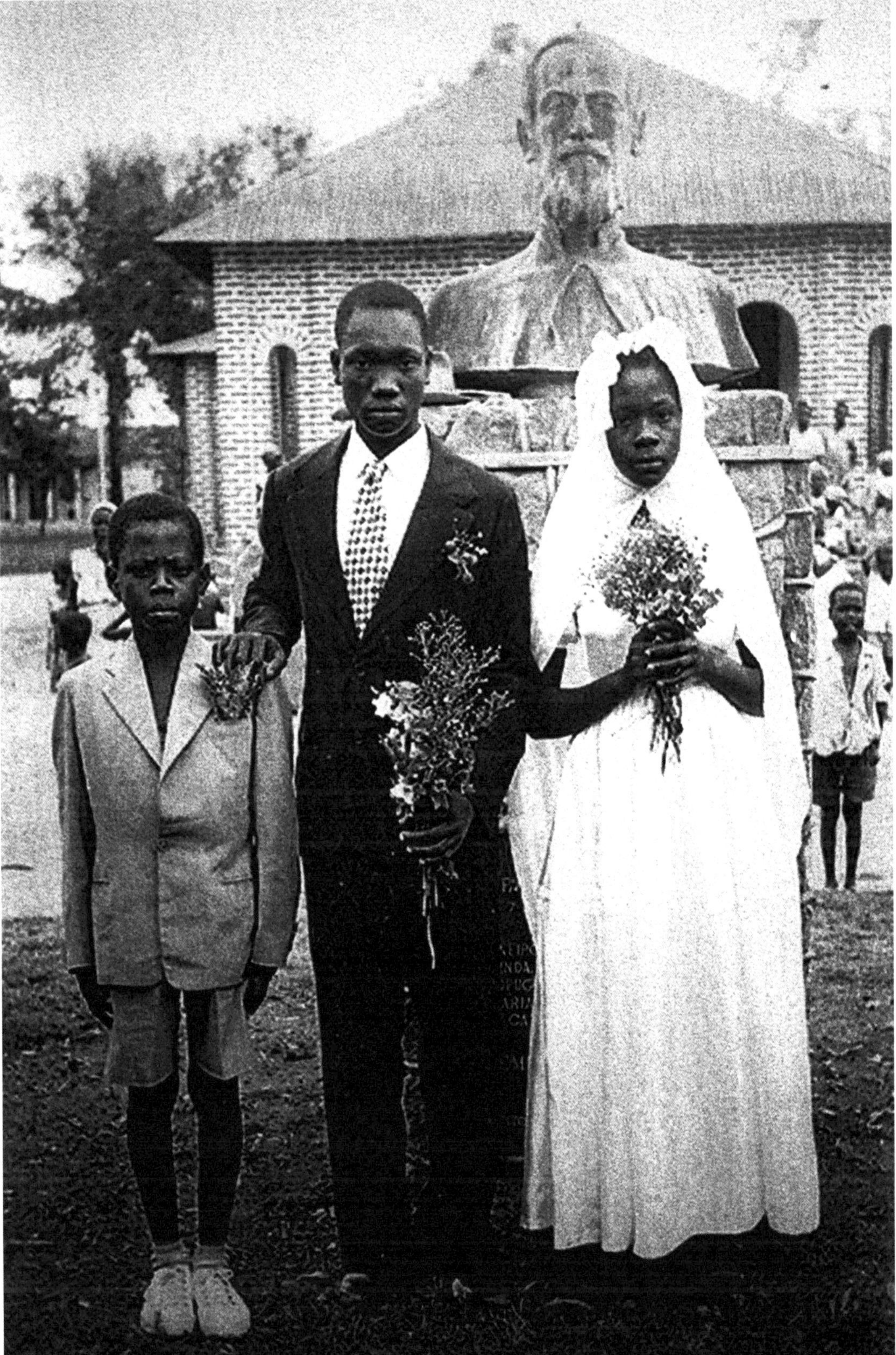

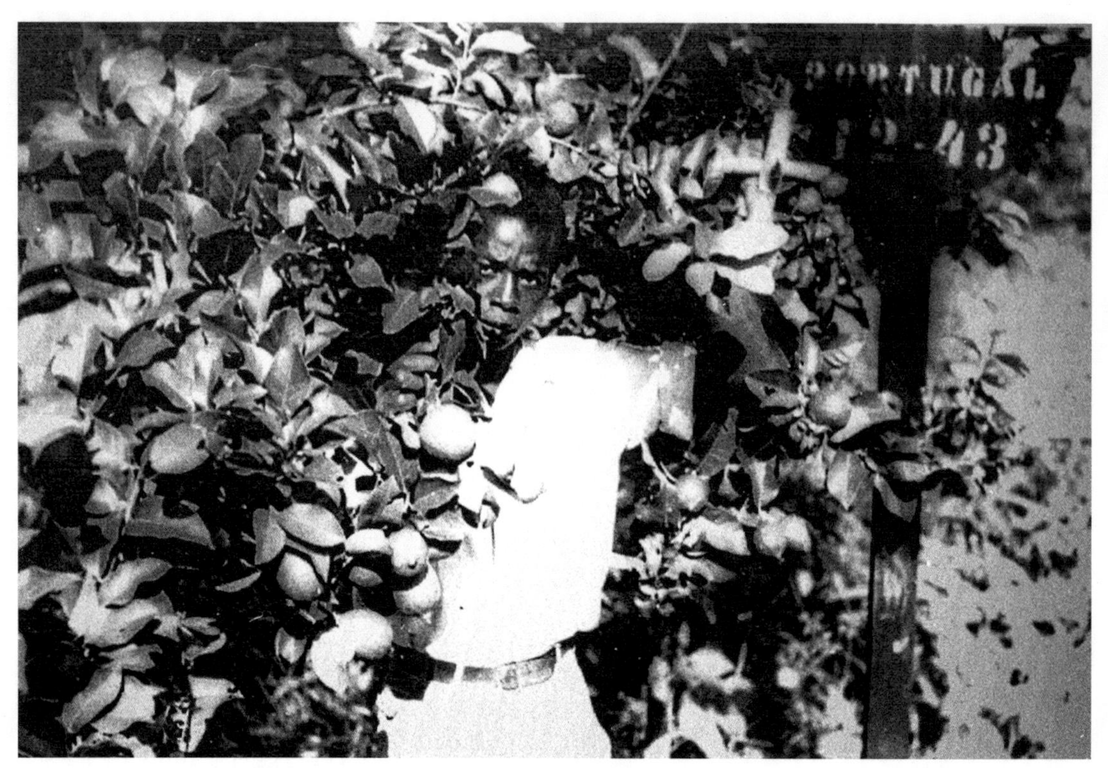
PORTUGAL
19-43

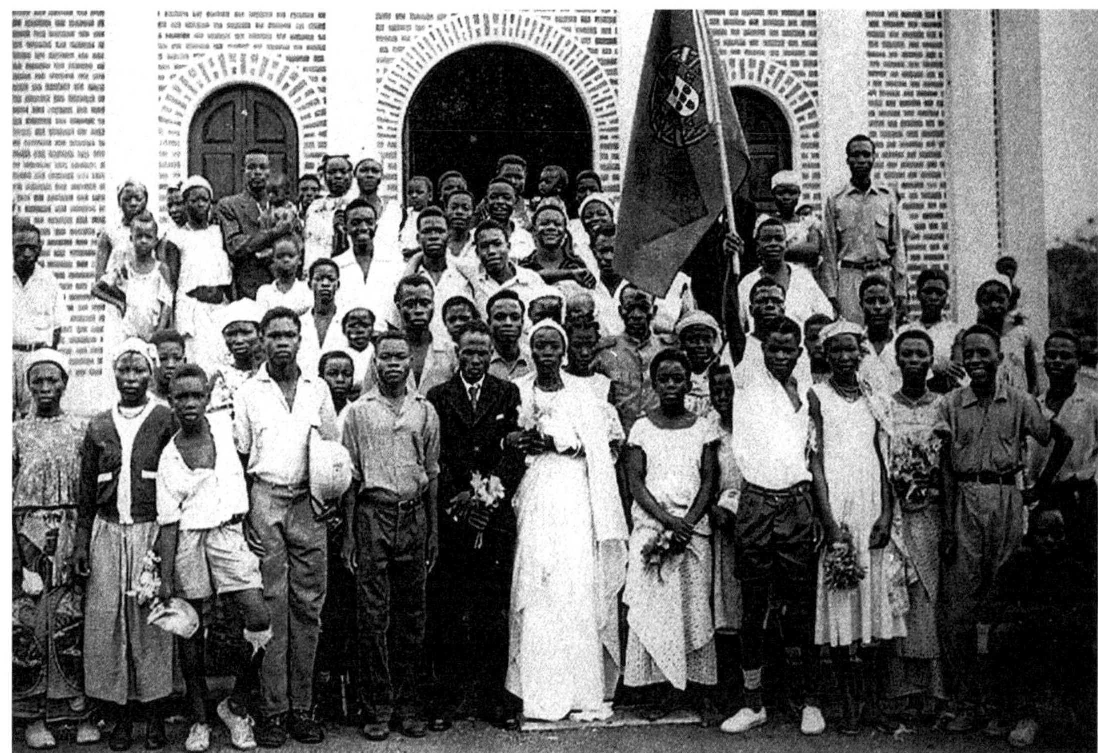

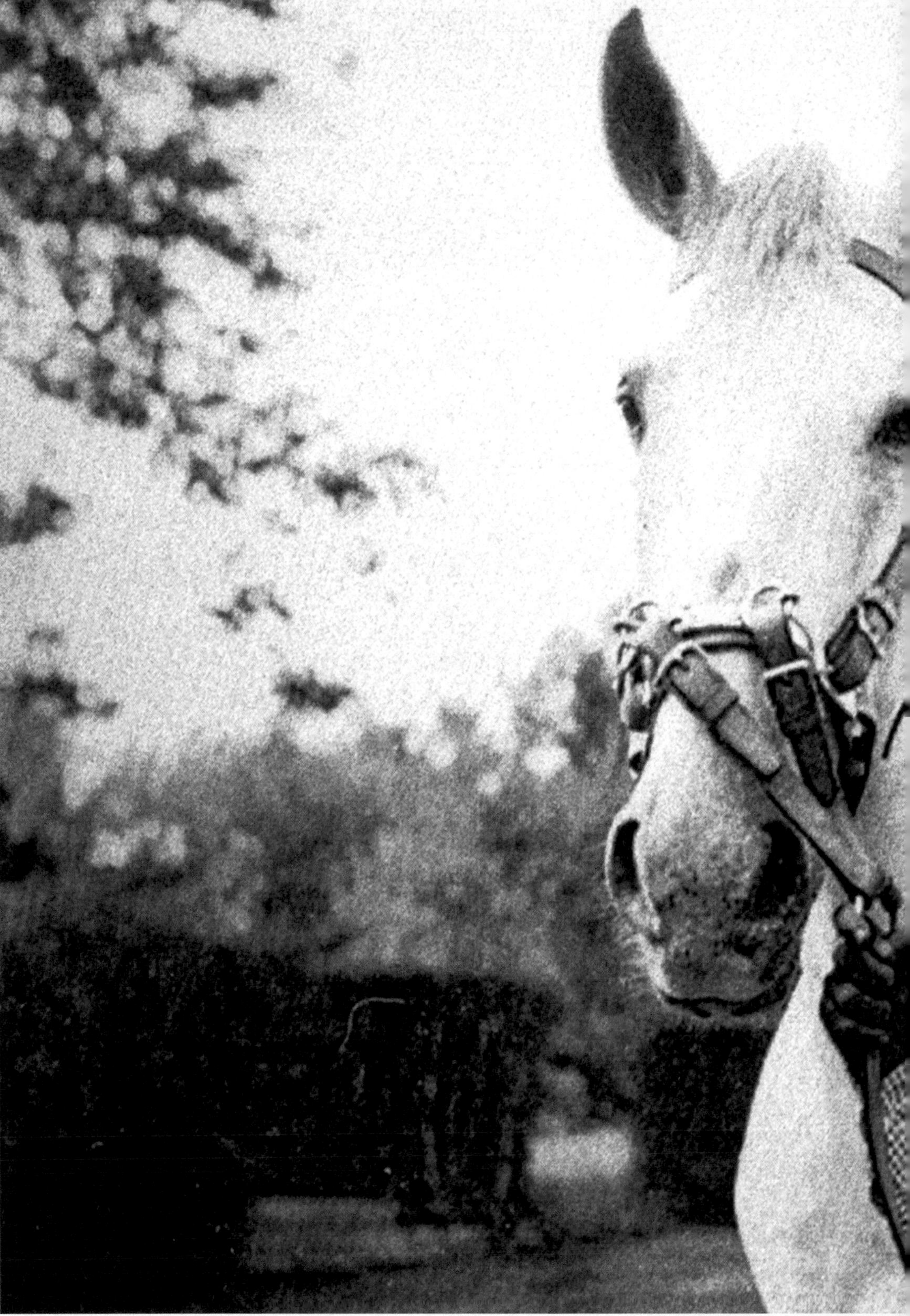

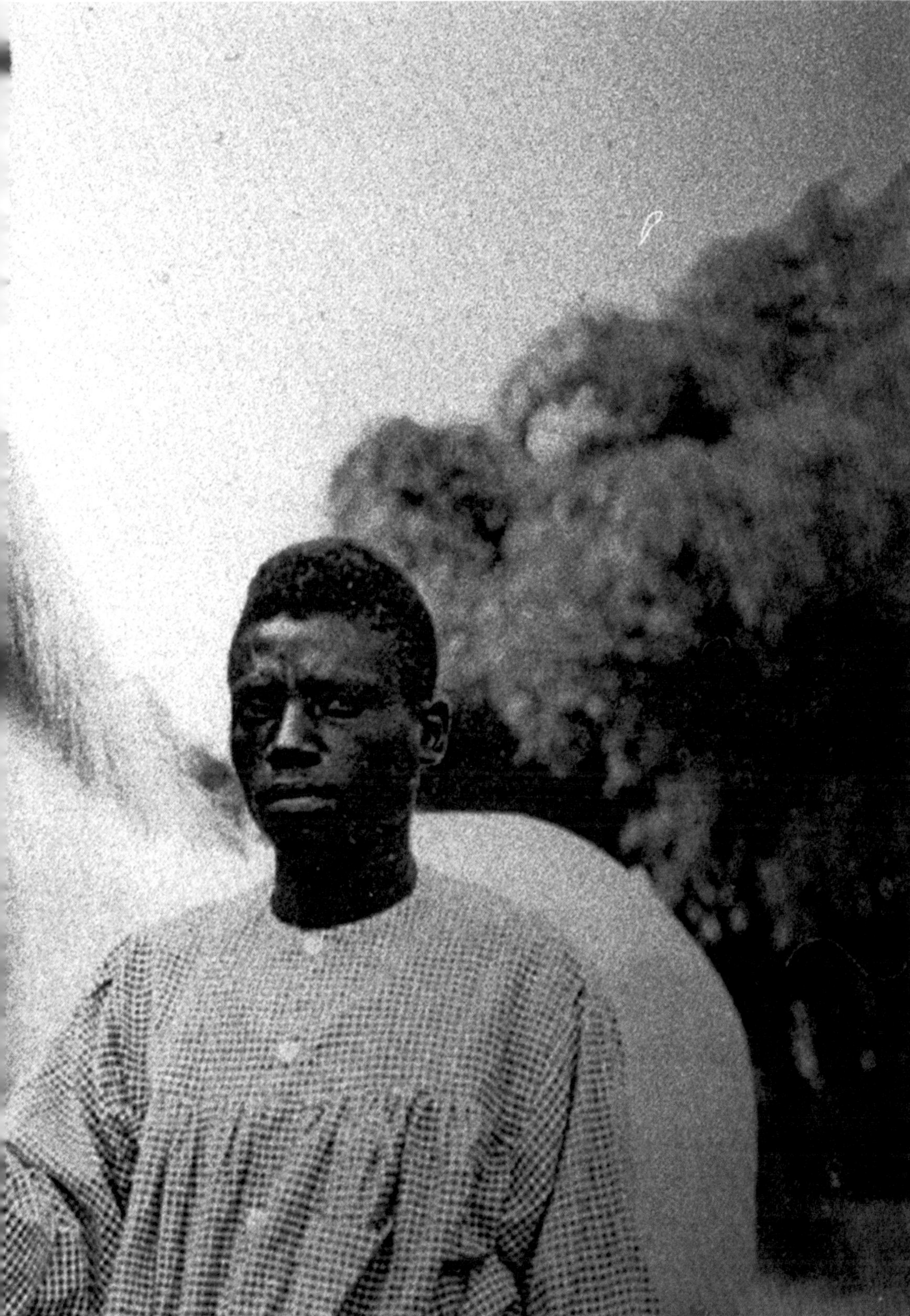

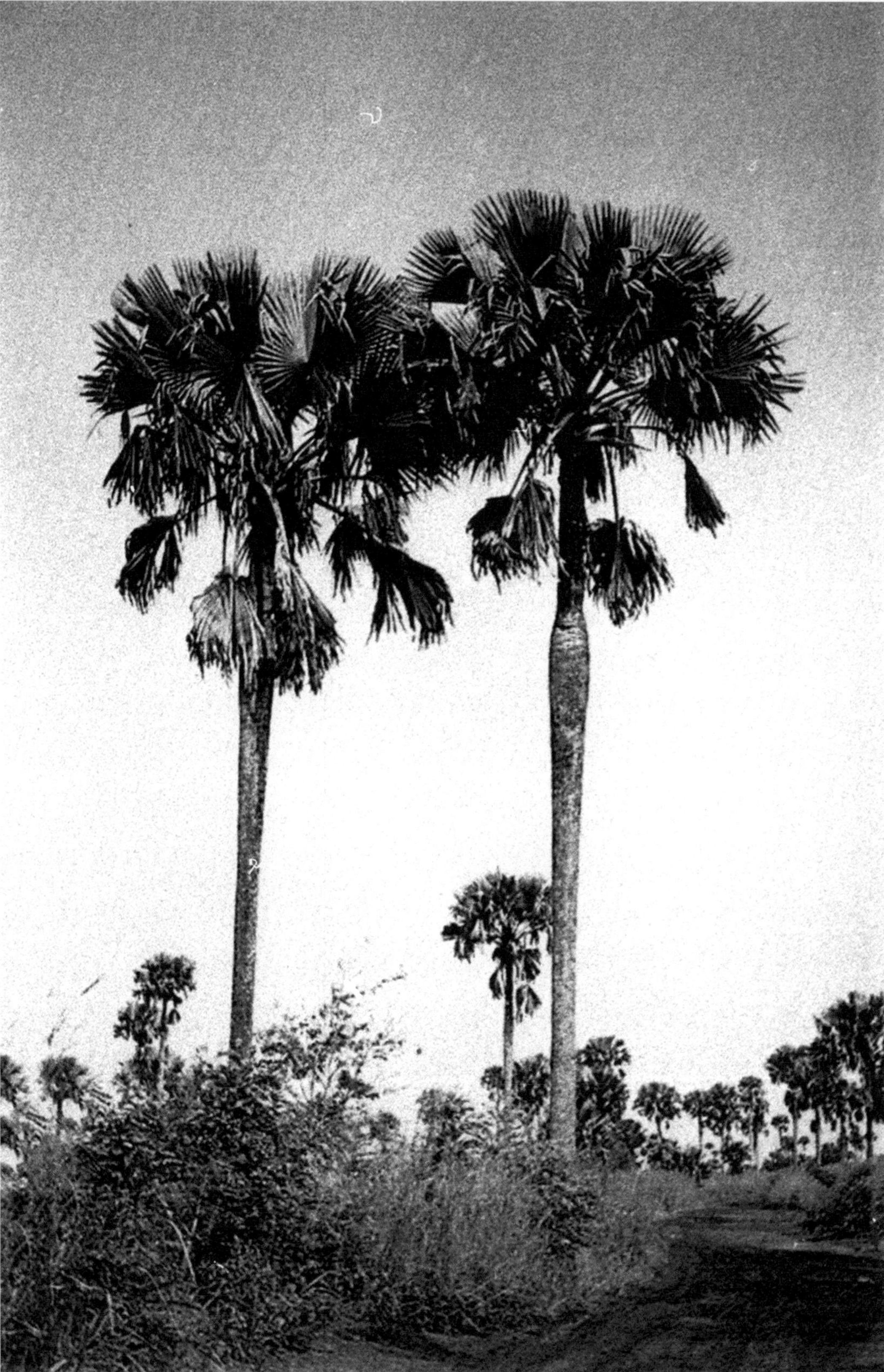

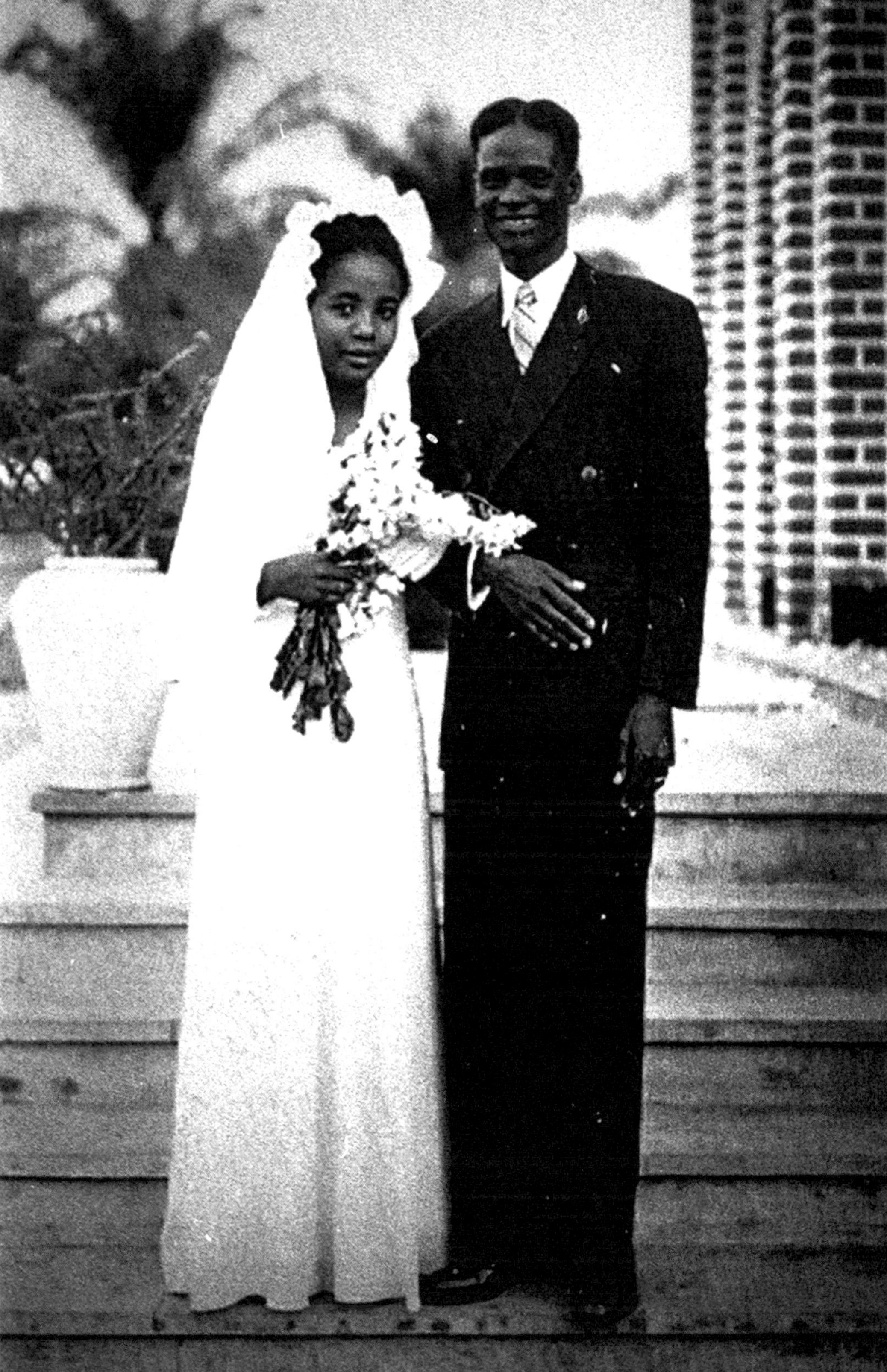

# MAUD SULTER

## SYRCAS

Maud Sulter (1960–2008) was an artist and writer of Ghanaian and Scottish heritage. She was awarded an MA in photography in 1990. In her artistic career she focused on photomontage and portraiture. Throughout her career, she aimed to "put Black women back in the centre of the frame" in European art and history. She researched the representation of Black women in Scotland in the 16th century, Jeanne Duval in 19th-century Paris, and Black women in Germany in the inter-war period, speaking out against the occlusion of Africa and the African diaspora. Photographer, poet, playwright, essayist, teacher and curator, her work was many-layered and deeply committed.

The "Syrcas" series consists of 16 handmade photomontages, reproduced and enlarged, accompanied by her poem "Blood Money". In each of these photomontages, Maud Sulter juxtaposes canonical images from the history of classical European art and photography with African art objects, masks and statuettes. With "Syrcas", she intends to "bear witness to the Black experience during the Holocaust" and to create, in the face of the genocides and ethnic cleansings of the 20th century, "a reminder of individual responsibility".


*Voyager: Je lui parlais du film lorsque le téléphone sonne*, 1993
*Noir et Blanc: Un*, 1993
Noir et Blanc: *Deux*, 1993
*Duval et Dumas: Dumas*, 1993
*Duval et Dumas: Duval*, 1993
*Hélas l'héroïne: Quelques instants plus tard, Monique cherchait sa brosse à cheveux*, 1993
*Hélas l'héroïne: Vous parliez de moi?*, 1993

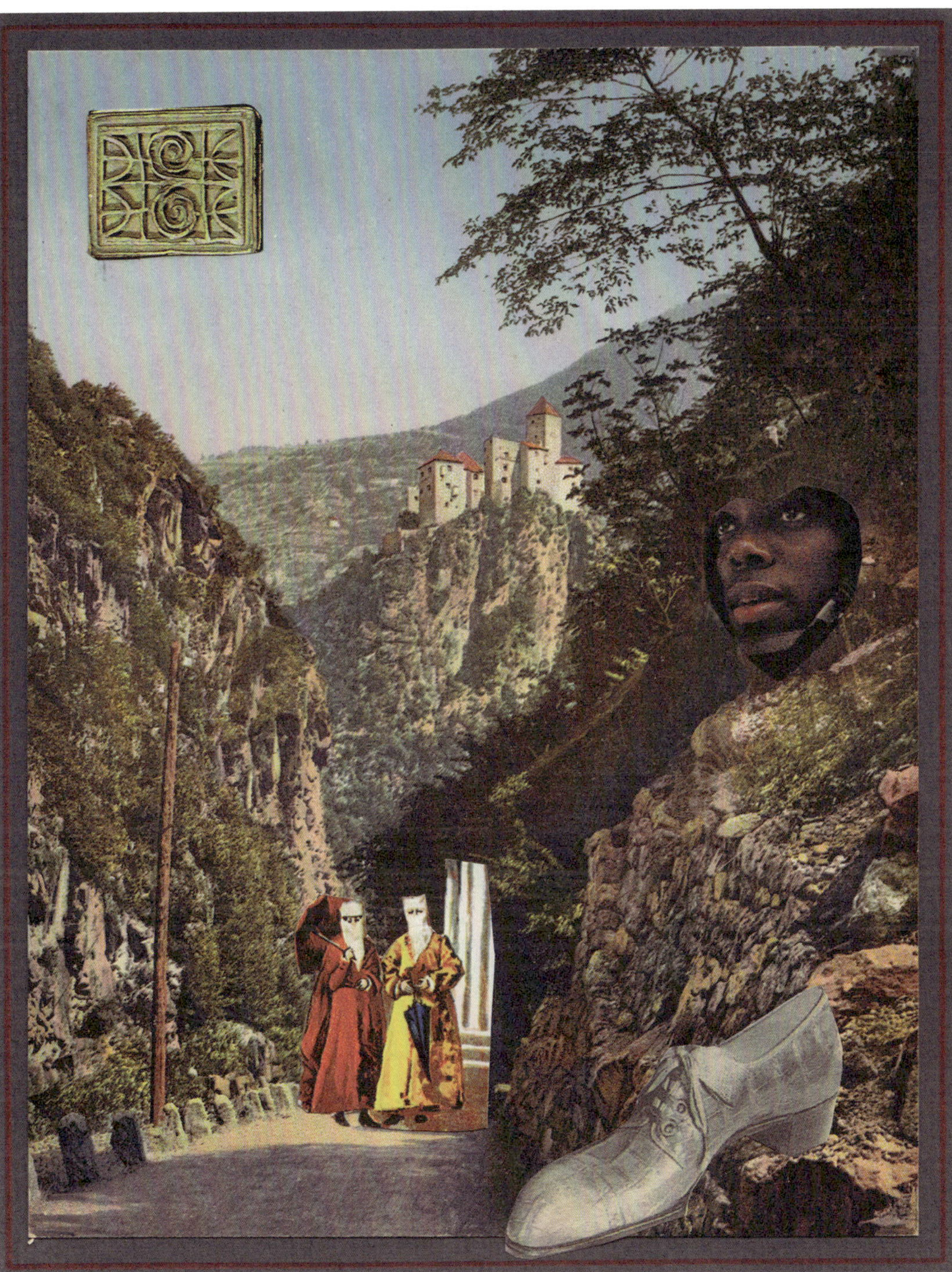

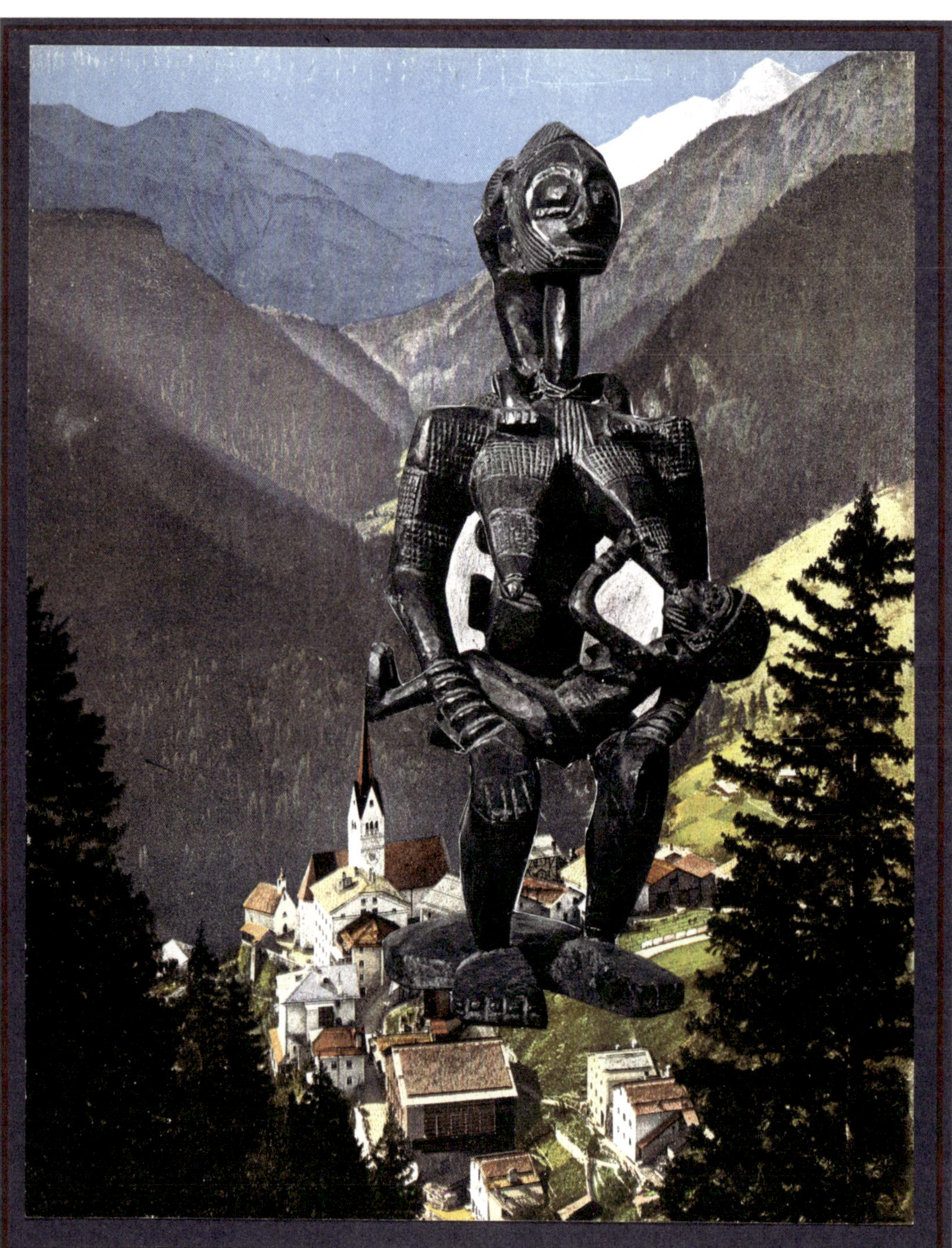

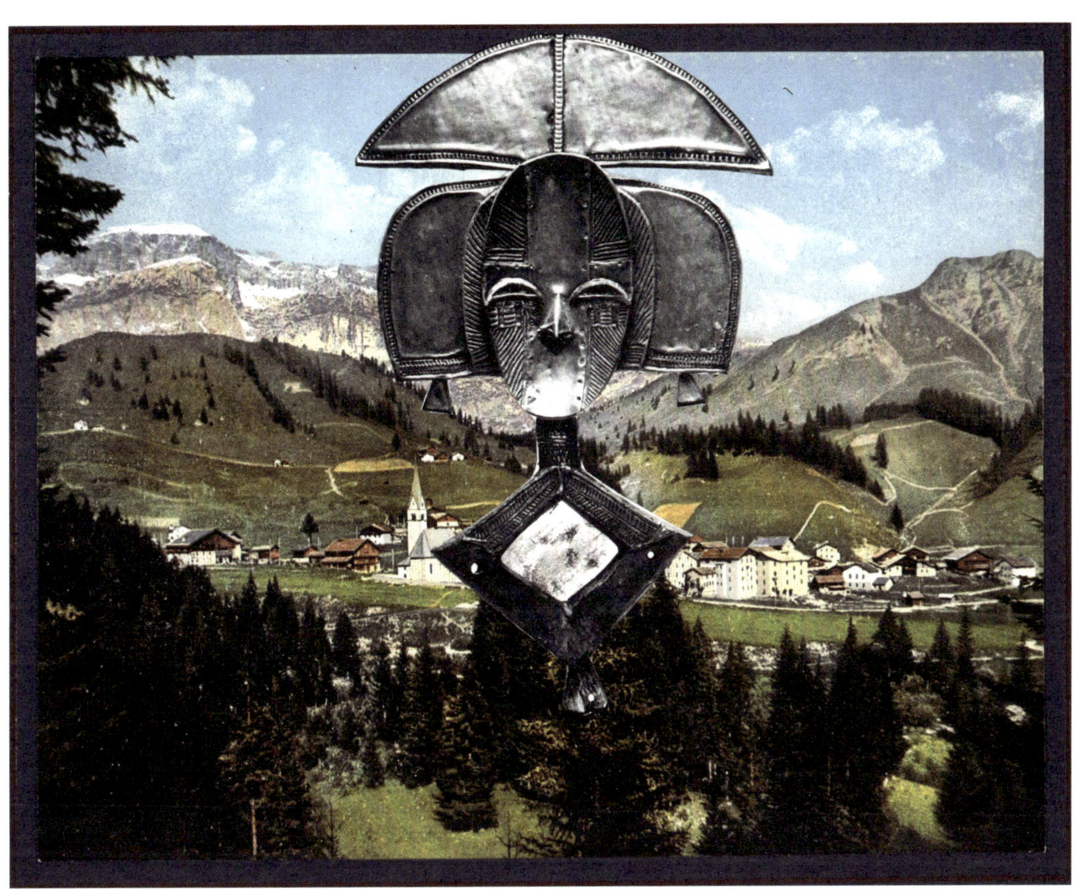

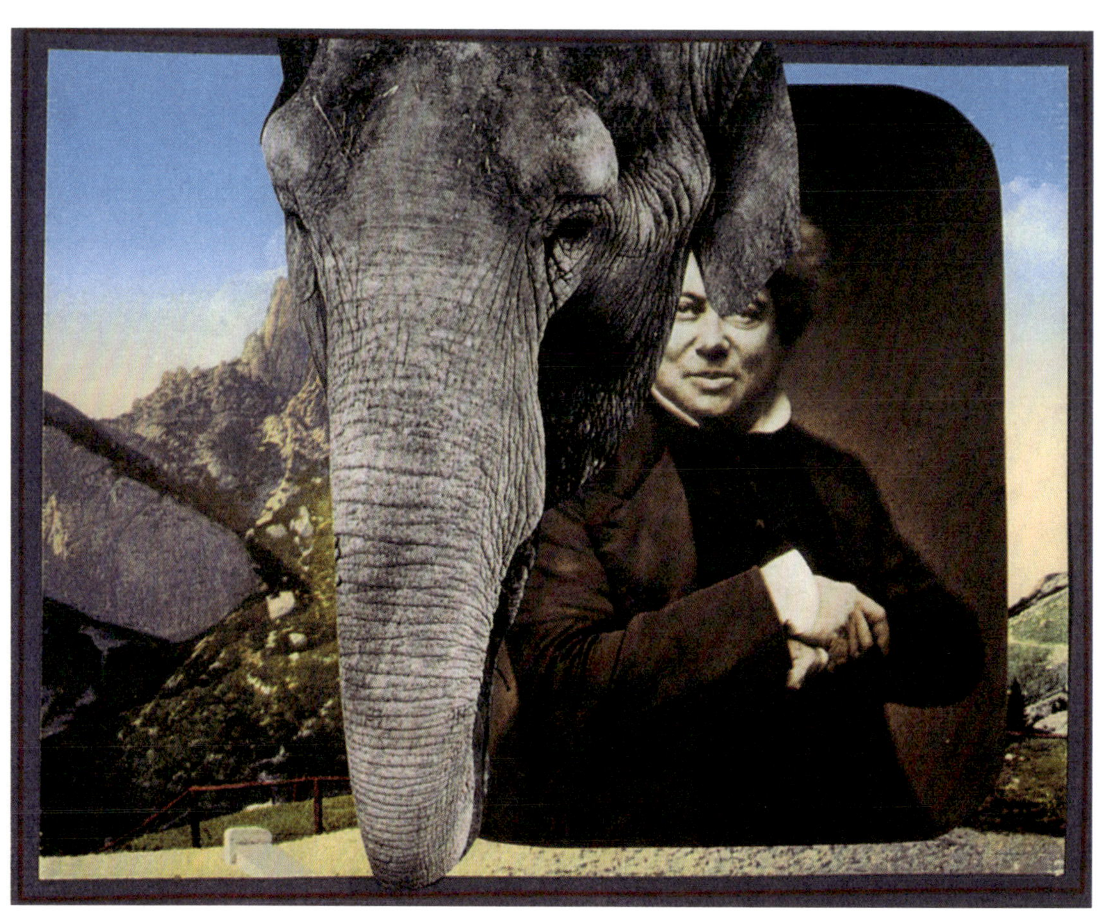

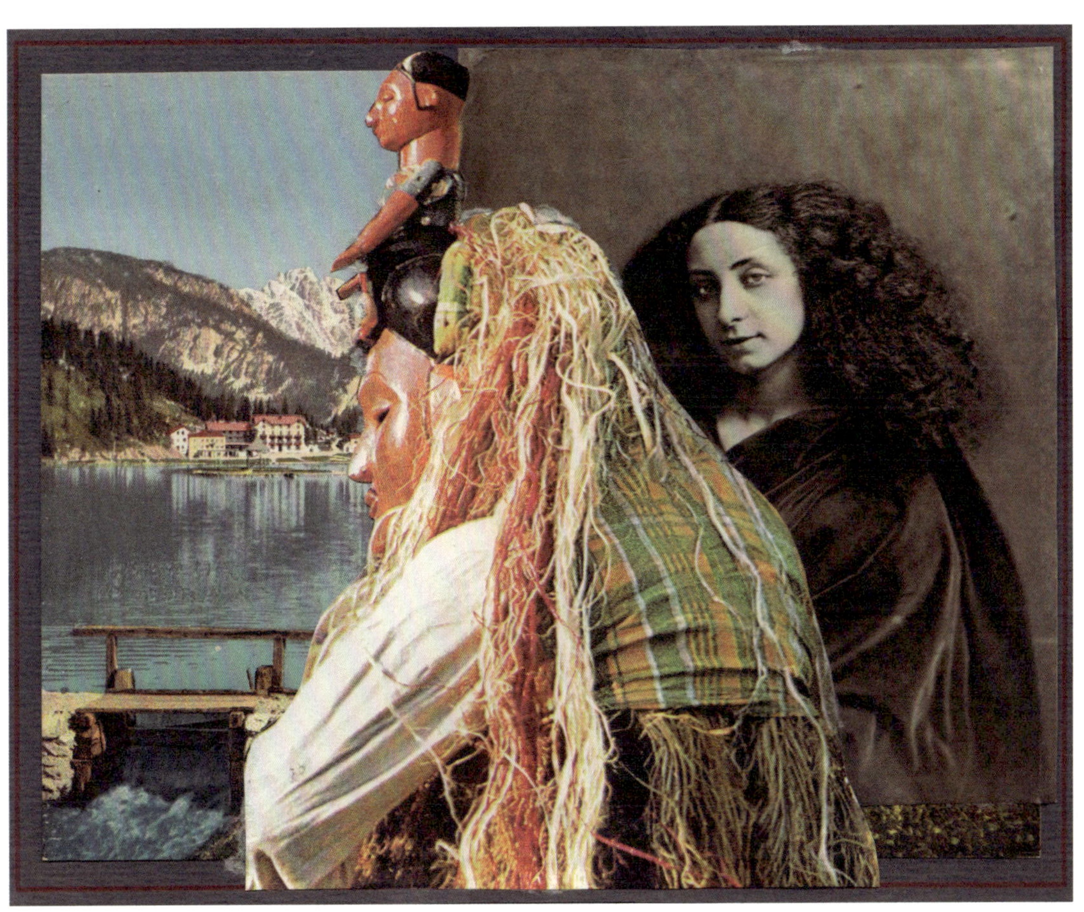

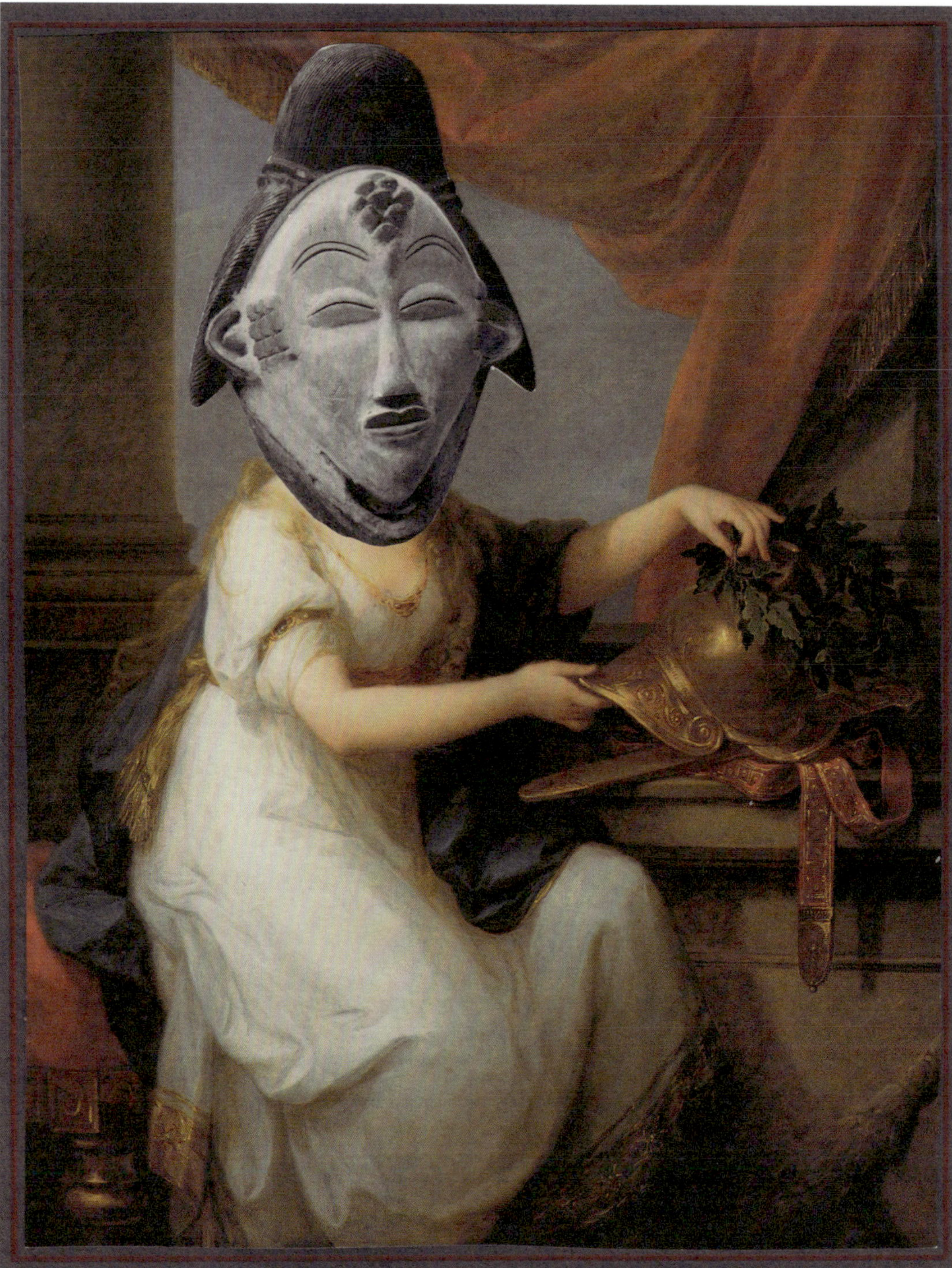

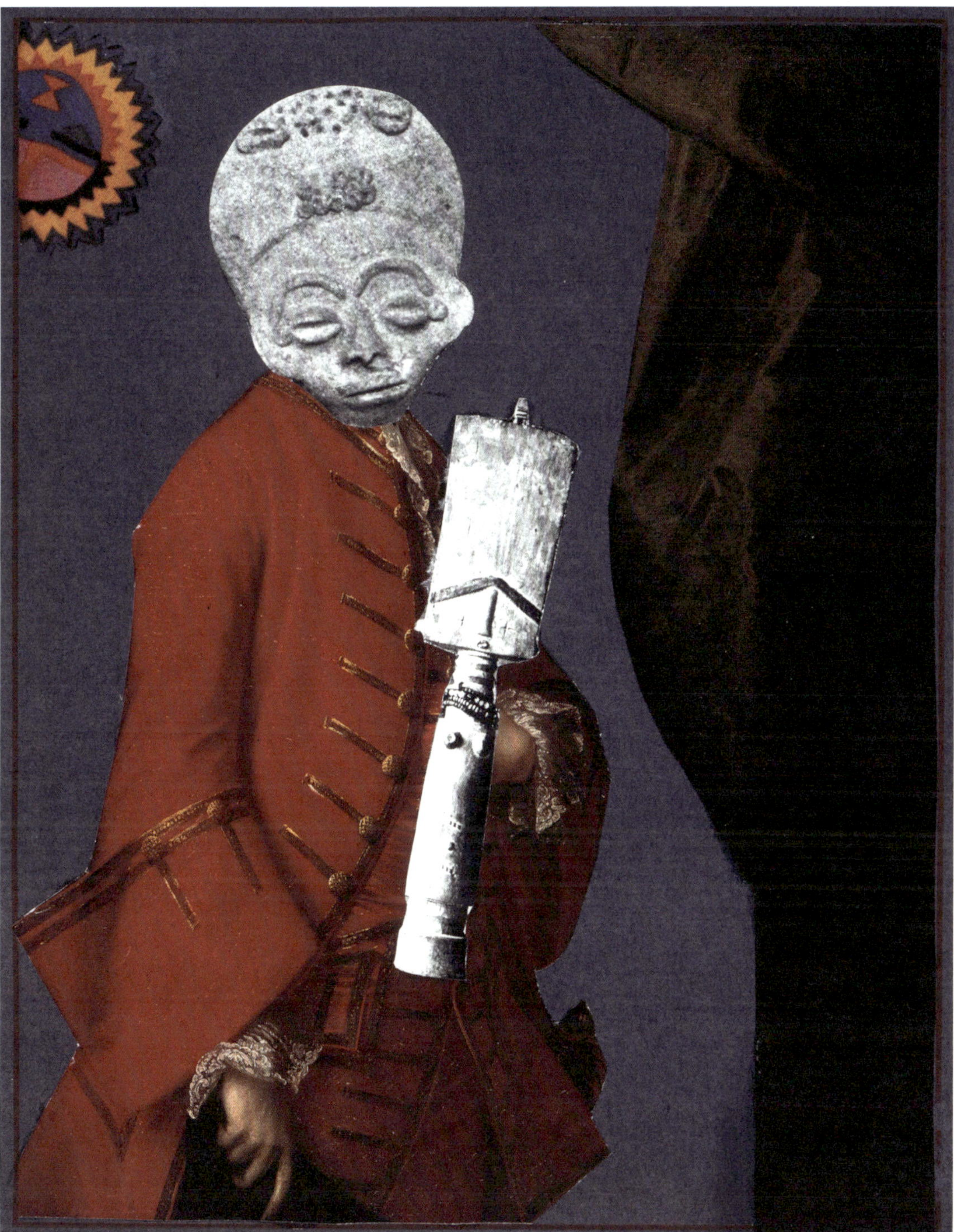

TITLE

# BISO BANA YA POTO

COVER

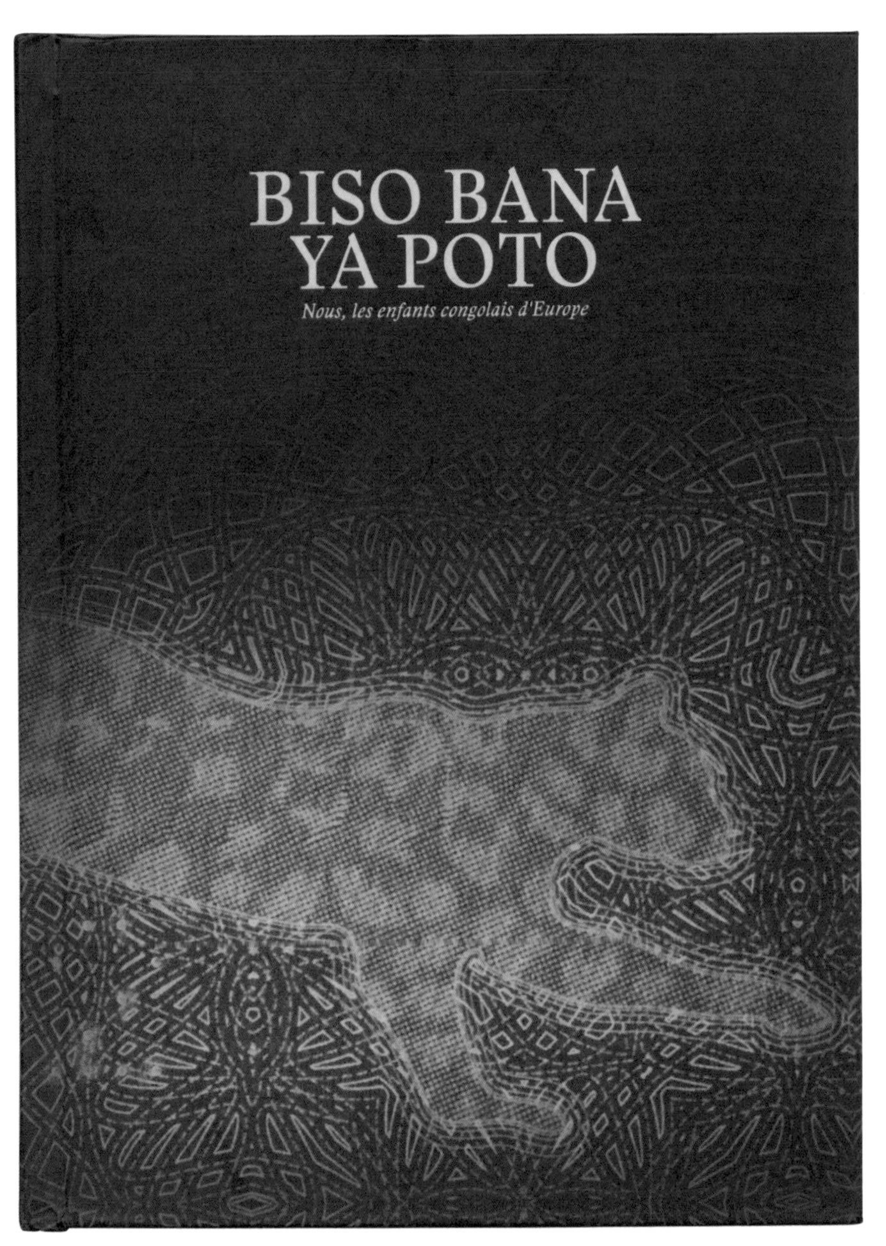

| | |
|---|---|
| ARTIST | Claudia Ndebele |
| PUBLISHER | Claudia Ndebele |
| SPECIFICATIONS | — 209 pages<br>— first published in 2020<br>— size: 18 × 25 cm |
| SUMMARY | *BISO BANA YA POTO* deals with the question of identity and connection with culture of Congolese origin. The book brings together archival photographs, mostly taken from photo albums, and testimonies of Europeans of Congolese origin. The title, which means "We, the Congolese children of Europe", refers to an expression commonly used by the diaspora to designate children with family members who have remained in the country of origin.<br><br>Claudia Ndebele writes in her book: "Growing up with two cultures often leads us to put one aside. So, the culture of our country of origin only manifests itself in certain situations. What is our relationship with it, us Congolese children living in Switzerland? I have chosen to highlight this link with African, and more particularly Congolese, roots in this personal work." |
| BIOGRAPHY | Claudia Ndebele was born in Switzerland in 1989. Her parents are from the Democratic Republic of Congo. She graduated from the Geneva University of Art and Design (HEAD) and works in the field of graphic arts as a freelancer for cultural institutions while developing her personal projects. |

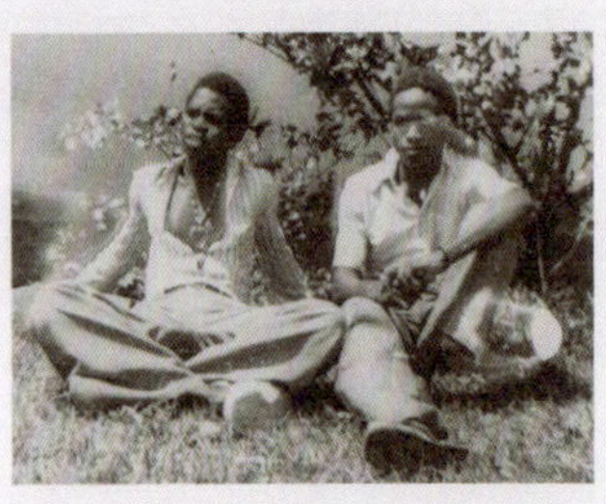

Le temps d'une réflexion, d'une prise de décision.

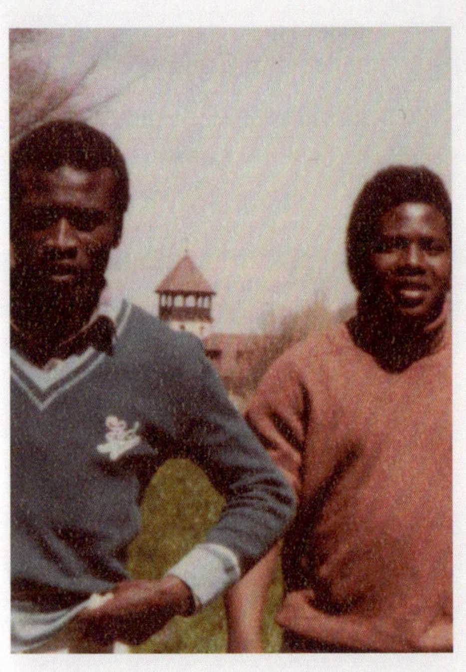



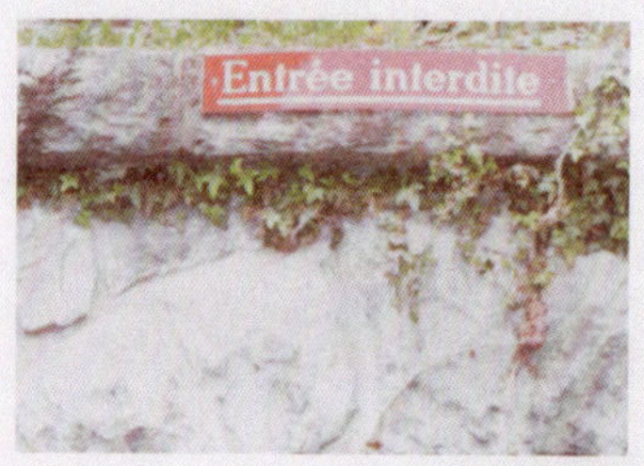


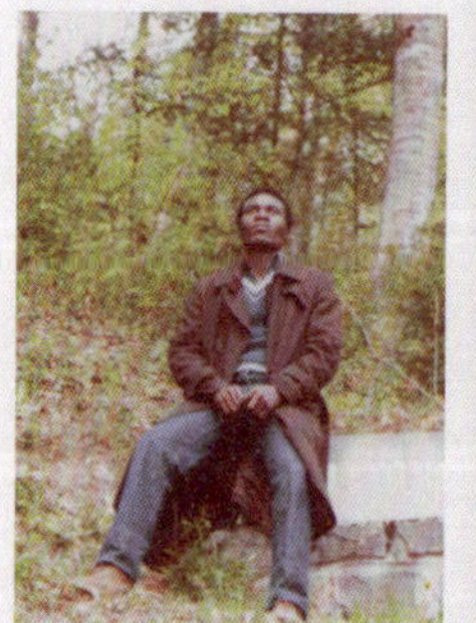

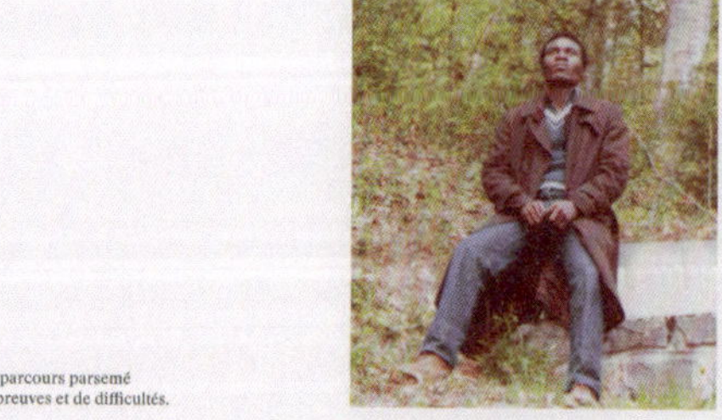

Un parcours parsemé d'épreuves et de difficultés.

Livret pour étrangers C / Ausländerausweis C

L'autorisation d'établissement n'est valable que pour le canton qui l'a délivrée. Tout changement de canton néces - site une nouvelle autorisation. Il est conseillé de de-mander cette nouvelle autorisation au nouveau canton avant son départ et de ne pas changer de domicile avant de l' avoir obtenue. Deux semaines avant l'échéance du délai de contrôle , le présent livret doit être remis aux autorités compétentes pour renouvellement.
L'étranger est tenu de déclarer son départ lorsqu'il change de canton ou lorsqu'il quitte la Suisse.
L'autorisation d'établissement prend fin lorsque l'étranger annonce son départ ou séjourne effectivement pendant six mois à l'étranger; sur demande présentée au cours de ce délai, celui-ci peut être prolongé jusqu'à deux ans.
L'étranger est tenu de présenter son livret sur réquisition des autorités.

Die Niederlassungsbewilligung gilt nur für den Kanton, der sie ausgestellt hat. Ein Kantonswechsel ist bewilli - gungspflichtig. Dem Ausländer wird empfohlen, das Gesuch vorher beim andern Kanton einzureichen und erst nach Erhalt der Bewilligung umzuziehen. Der Niedergelassene muss seinen Ausländerausweis zwei Wochen vor Ende der Laufzeit der zuständigen Behörde zur Erneuerung der Kontrollfrist vorlegen.
Beim Wegzug in einen andern Kanton oder ins Ausland hat sich der Ausländer abzumelden.
Die Niederlassungsbewilligung erlischt mit der Abmeldung oder wenn sich der Ausländer während sechs Monaten tat - sächlich im Ausland aufhält; stellt er vor deren Ablauf das Begehren, so kann diese Frist bis auf zwei Jahre verlängert werden.
Der Ausländer ist verpflichtet, seinen Ausländerausweis den Behörden auf Verlangen vorzuweisen.

Ausgestellt durch: Etabli par: Rilasciato da:
Service de la population / Secteur Etrangers

Lausanne, le 31 octobre 2007 / RM

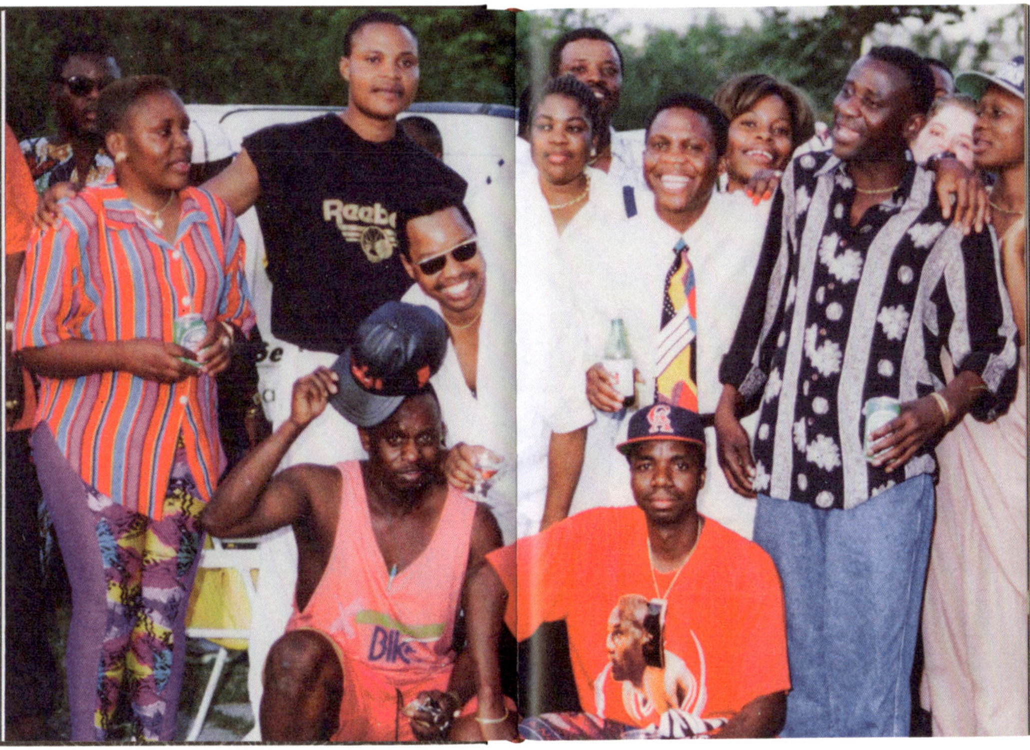

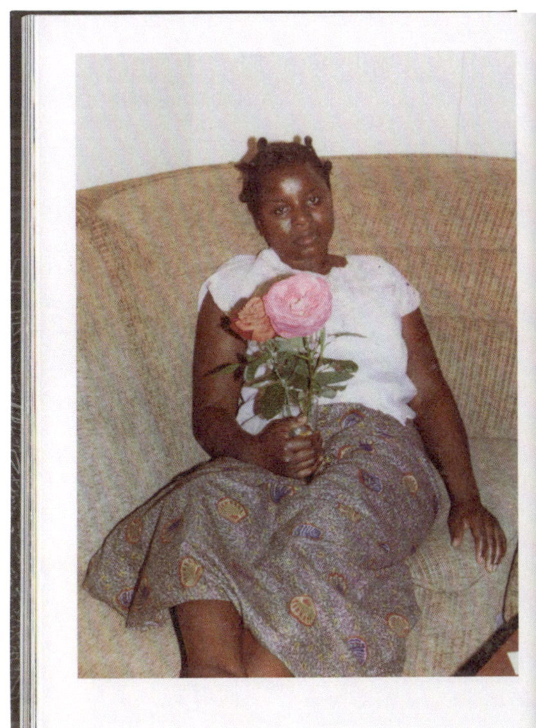

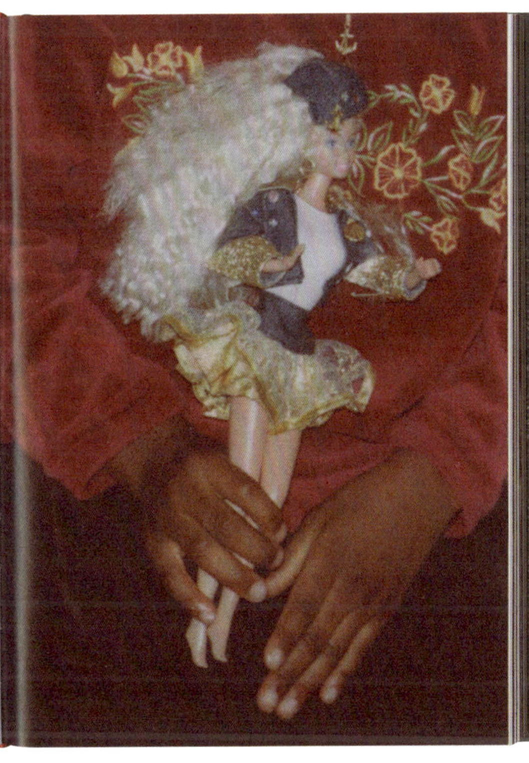

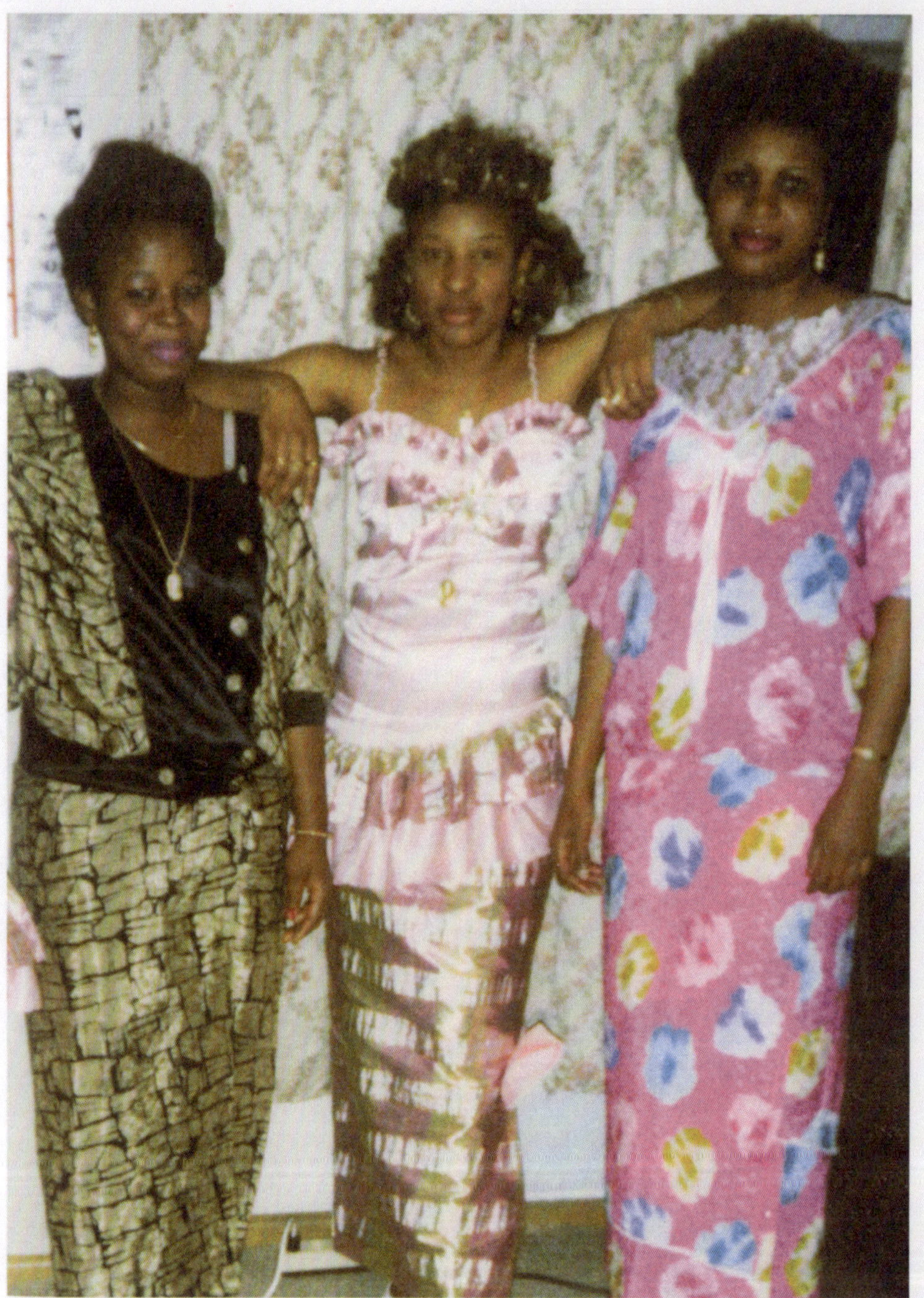

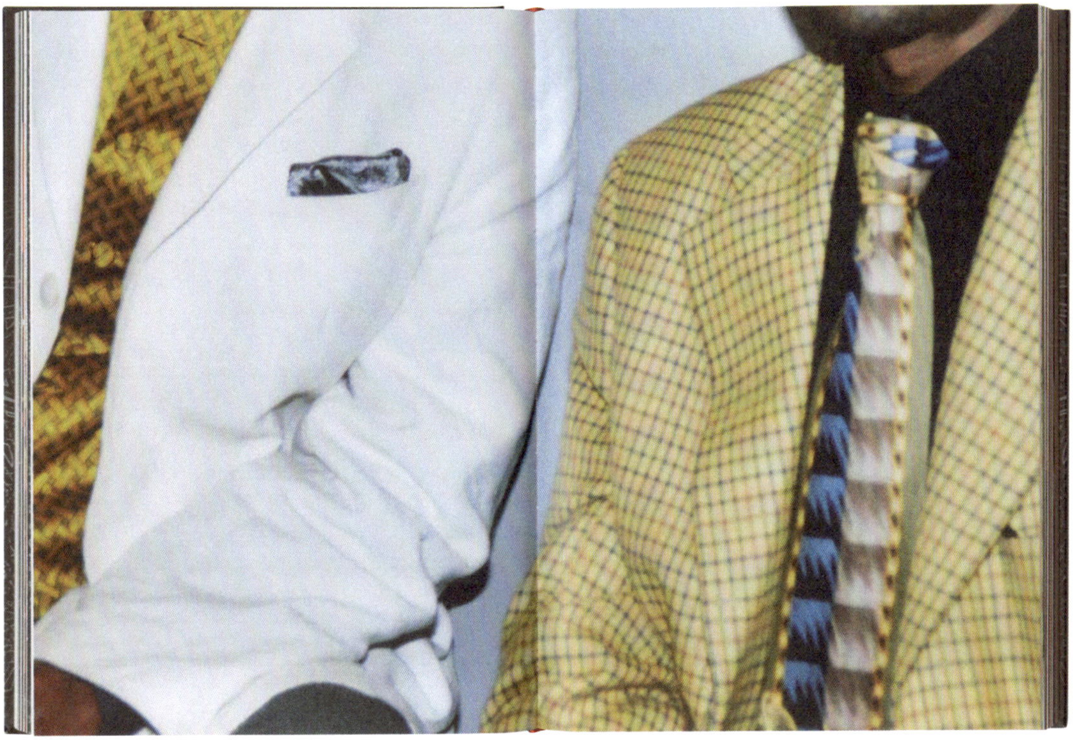

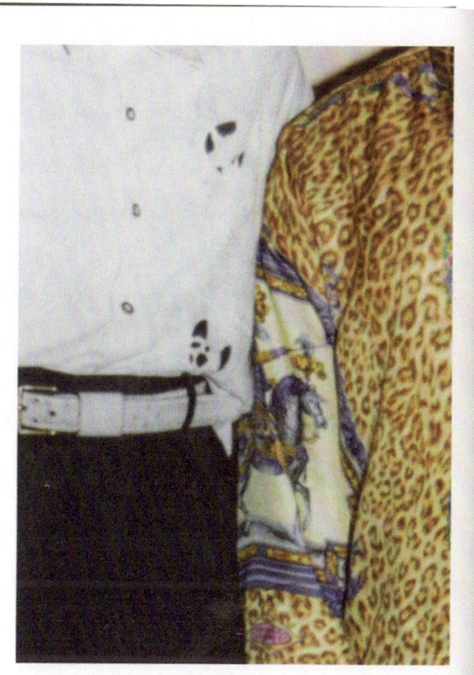

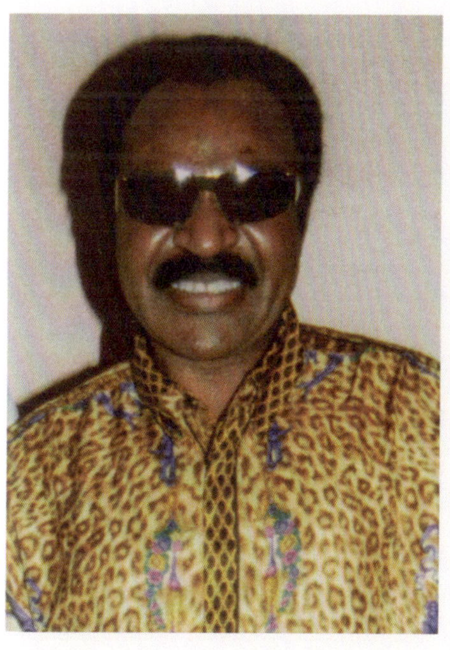

« Mama, je dois remplir un formulaire. On me demande mes origines, qu'est-ce que je mets ? »

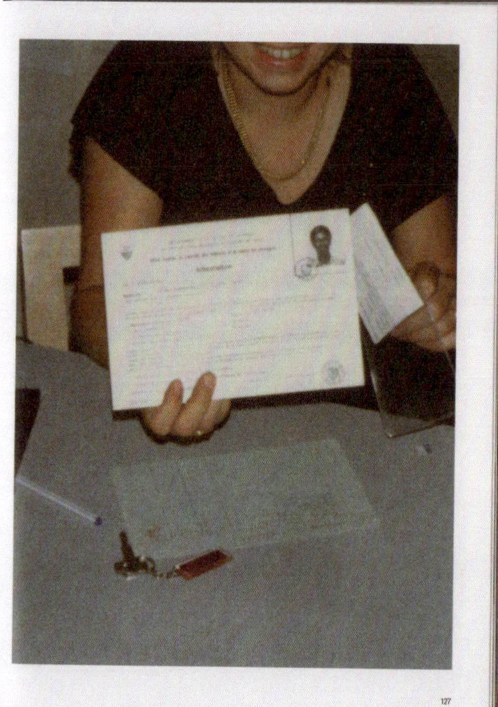



« Pour pays d'origine, tu mets République démocratique du Congo et pour commune d'origine, Montreux »

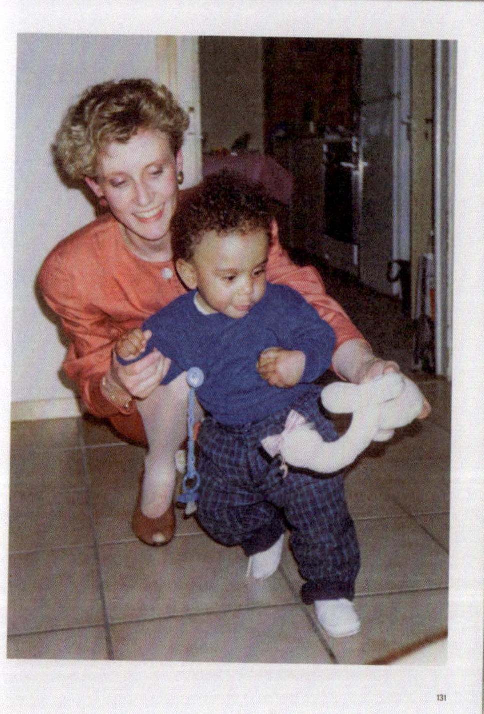

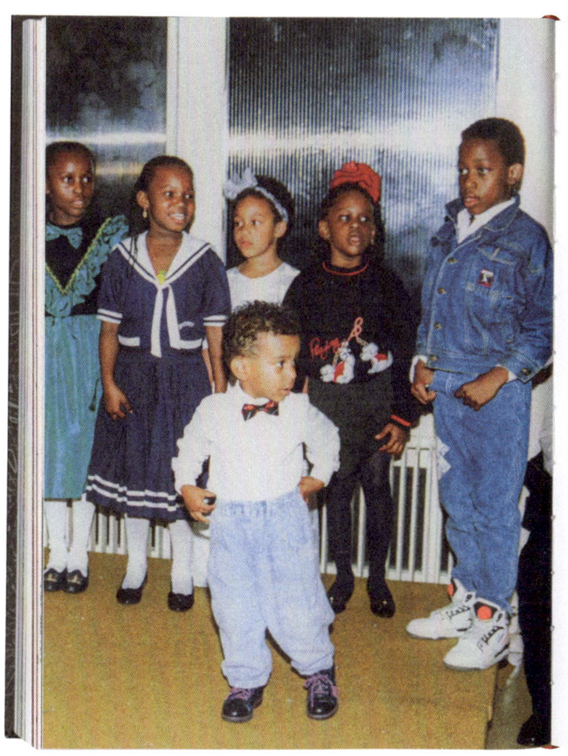

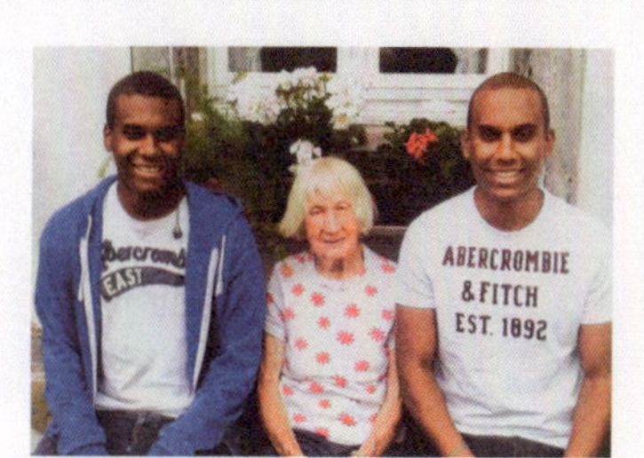




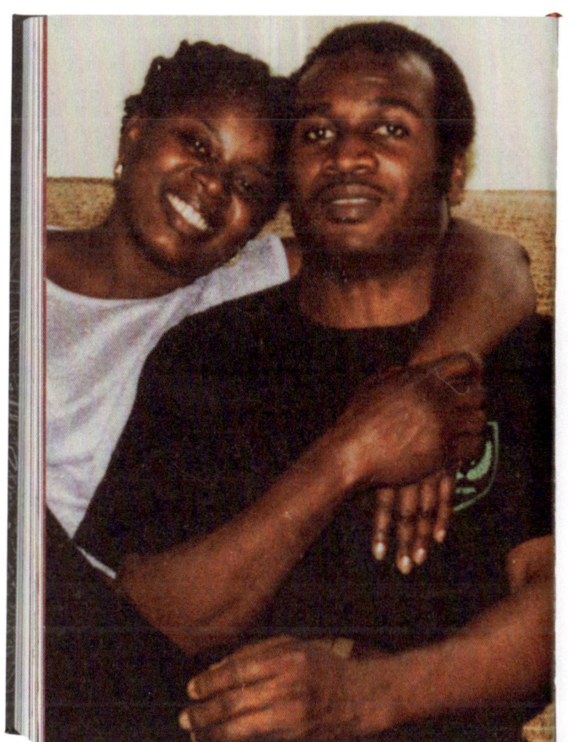

# 30 ANS QUE MES PARENTS SONT EN SUISSE

# MARVIN BONHEUR

## THIS IS LONDON

Marvin Bonheur was born in 1991 in Paris. He grew up in various towns in Seine-Saint-Denis, where his family, who came from Martinique, had settled in the 1960s. After a BEP (vocational diploma) in printing and a baccalaureate in computer graphics communication, he instinctively turned to photography, using his camera "like a sheet of paper, to write". In 2014, he began his "Alzheimer" series to immortalize the places of his childhood that are dear to him and to give an account of ordinary life in the "neighbourhoods" by giving a different vision from those broadcast by the media. The very favourable reception the series received encouraged him to continue this documentary and autobiographical work with "Thérapie" and then "Renaissance". Together they form "La Trilogie du Bonheur".

The series "This is London" was made between 2019 and 2020, during several stays in the capital of England. It was born from the desire to discover the hidden side of London, a city that Marvin Bonheur knows indirectly through English rock, new wave and drill music. Equipped with his 35 mm film camera (the colours of which remind him of his family's photo albums), he went to the working-class neighbourhoods of Stratford, Brixton, Camberwell and Kennington and took portraits of the inhabitants he met, most of whom were immigrants – strangers and artists whose daily lives he shared for weeks.


*Double Cup Kase*, 2020
*Hood House*, 2020
*Fierté*, 2020
*BIGGA*, 2020
*Vinch*, 2020
*Tax Team*, 2020
*Sooty*, 2020
*2pounds50*, 2020
*Sans relâche*, 2020

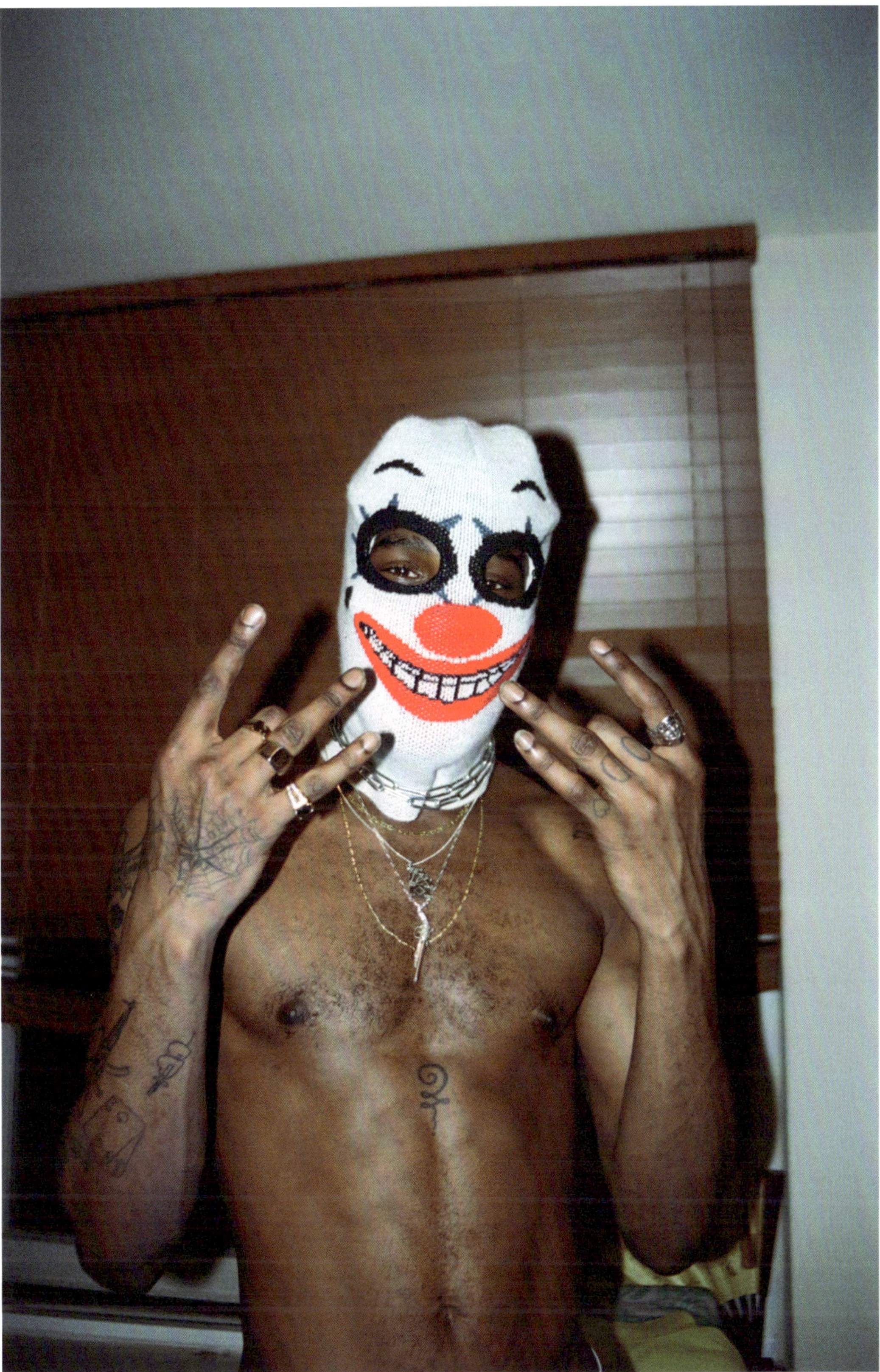

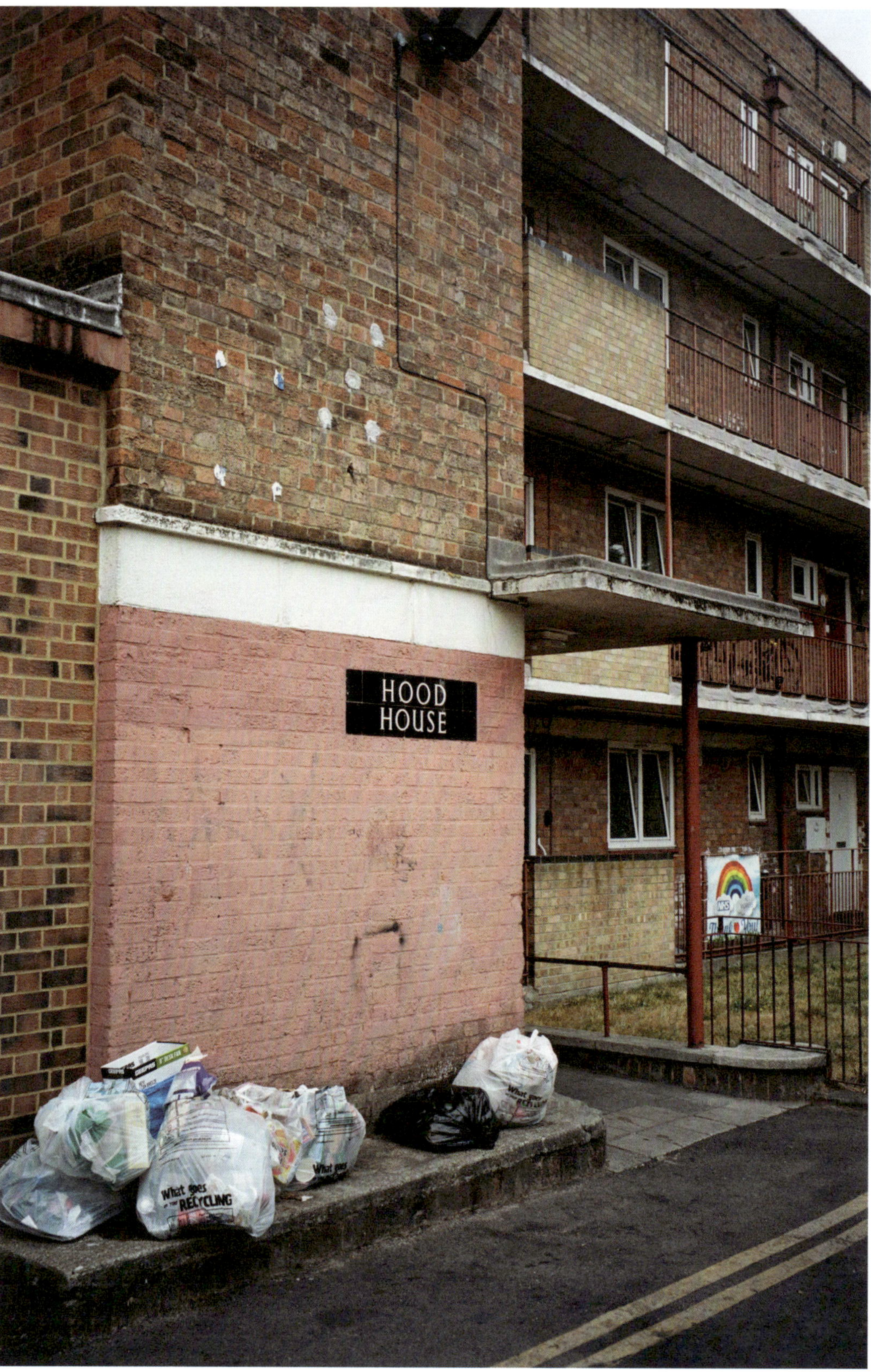
HOOD
HOUSE

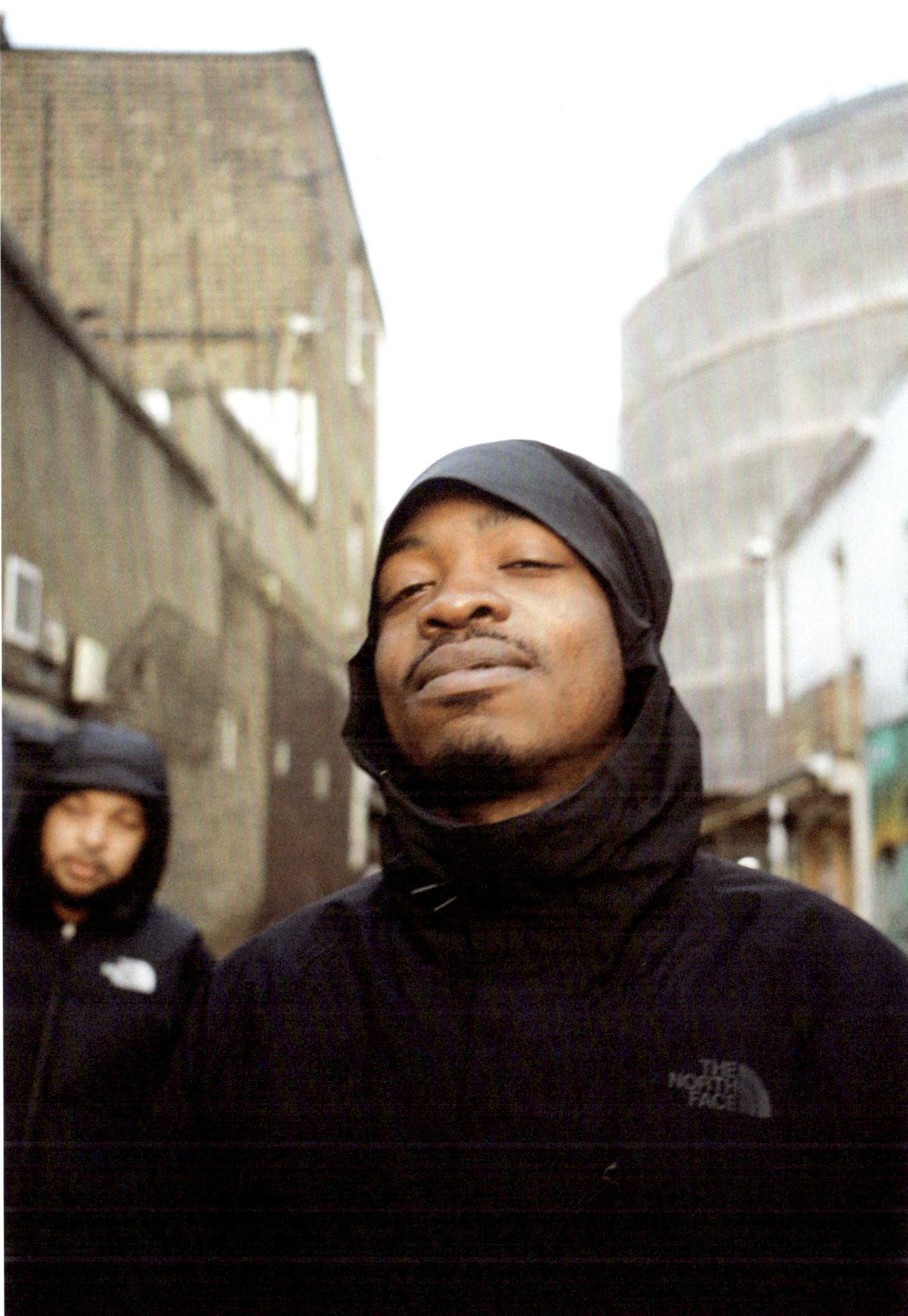
THE
NORTH
FACE

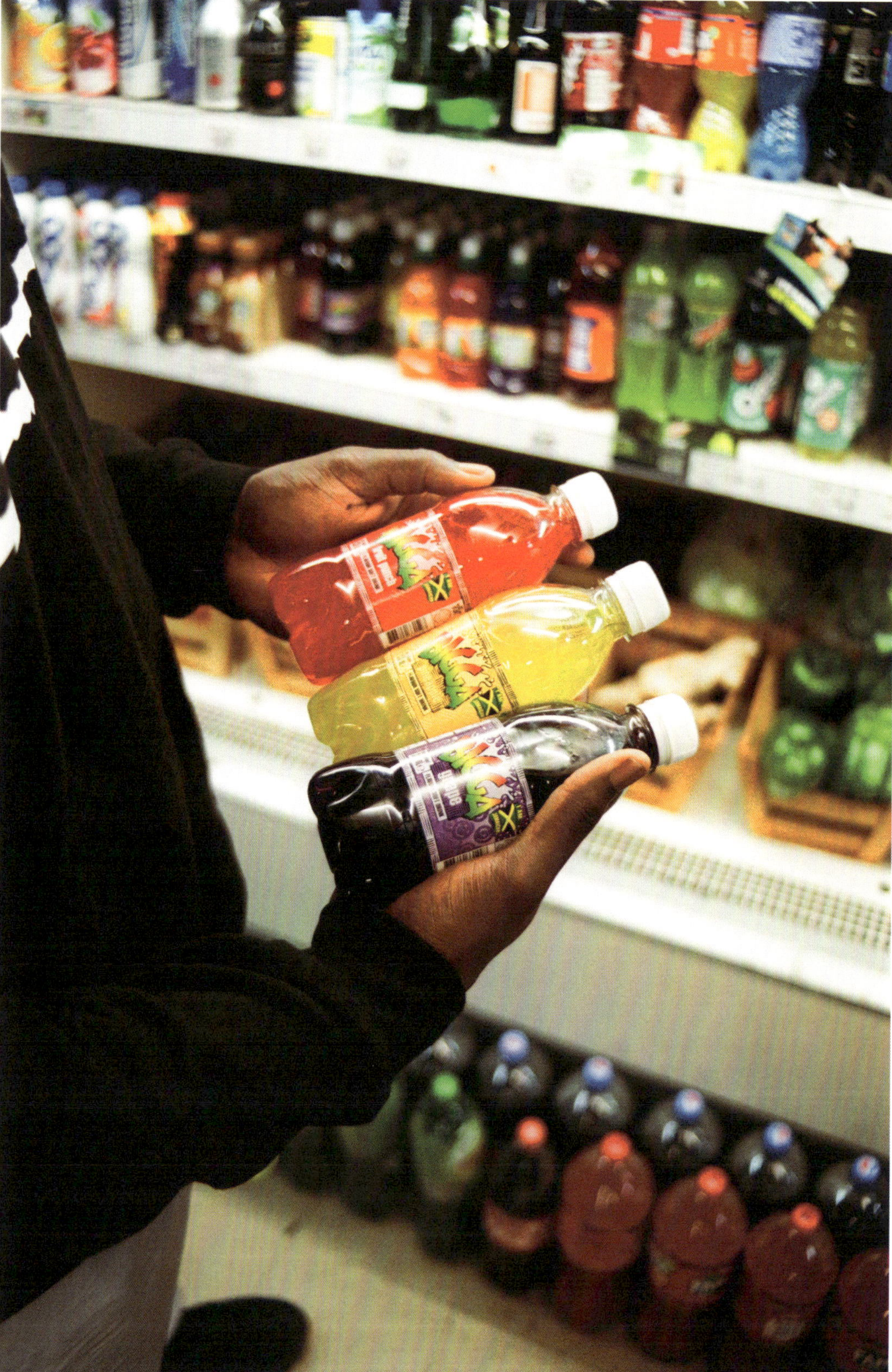

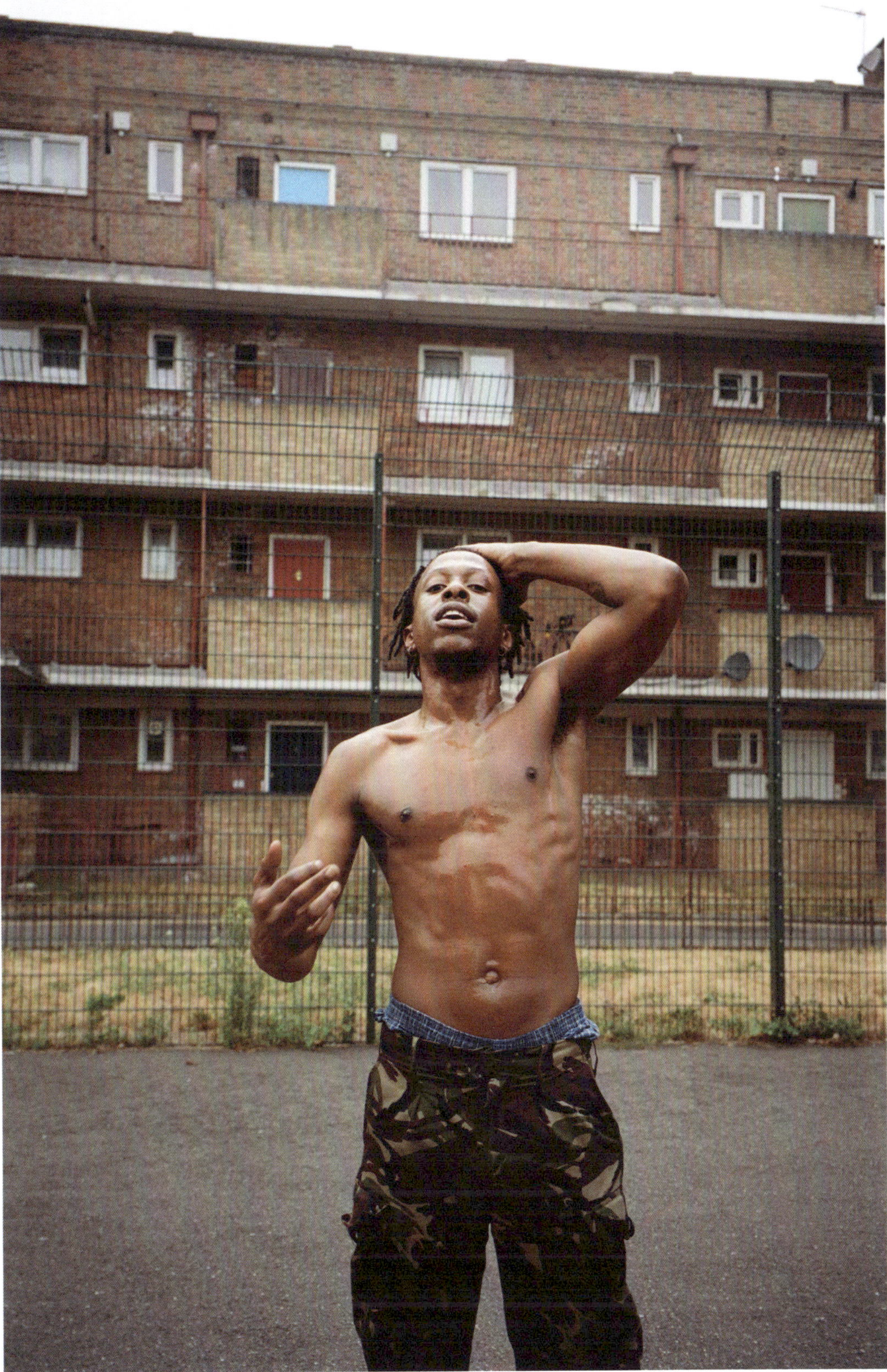

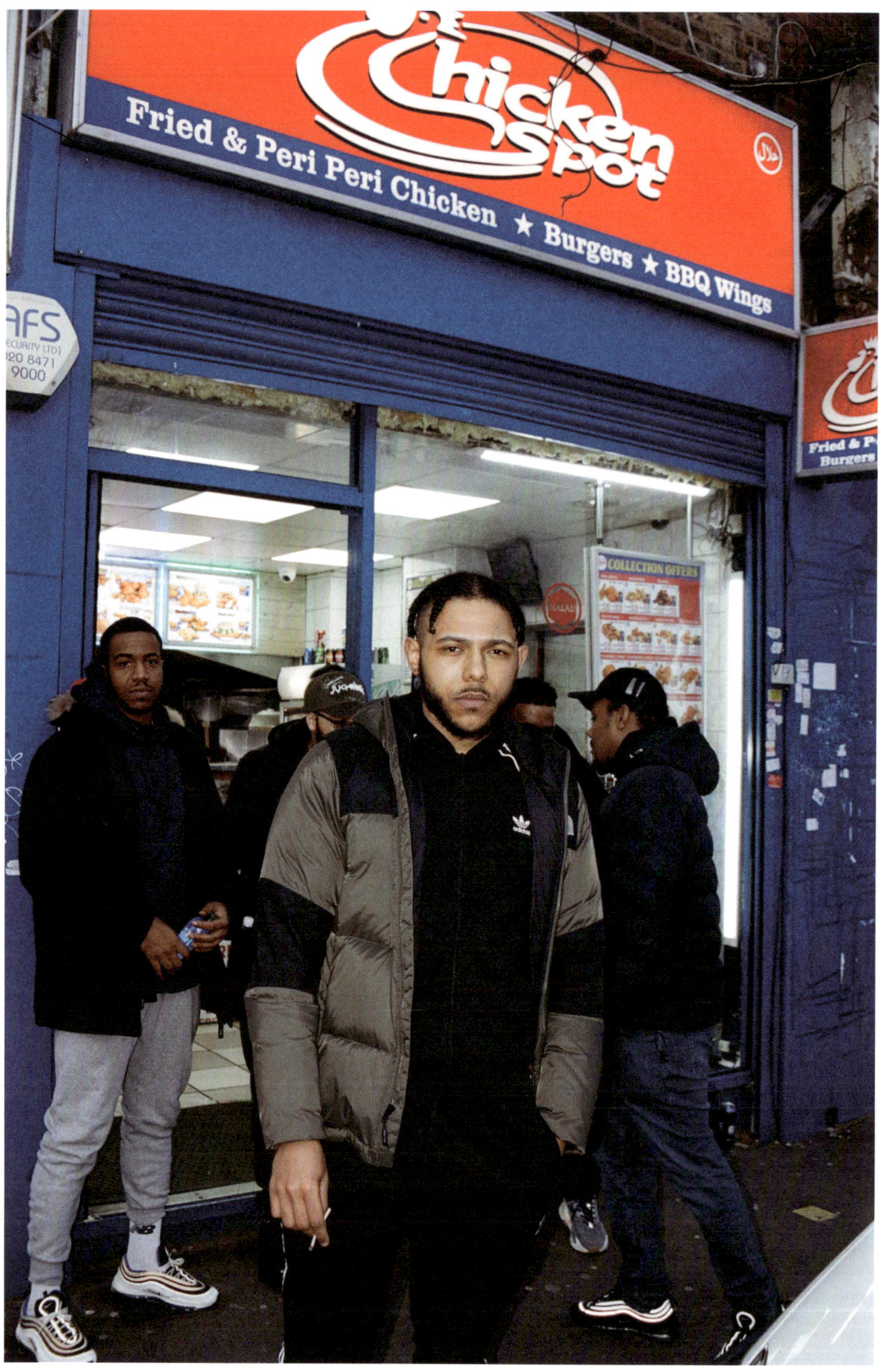
Chicken Spot
Fried & Peri Peri Chicken ★ Burgers ★ BBQ Wings
AFS
COLLECTION OFFERS
HALAL

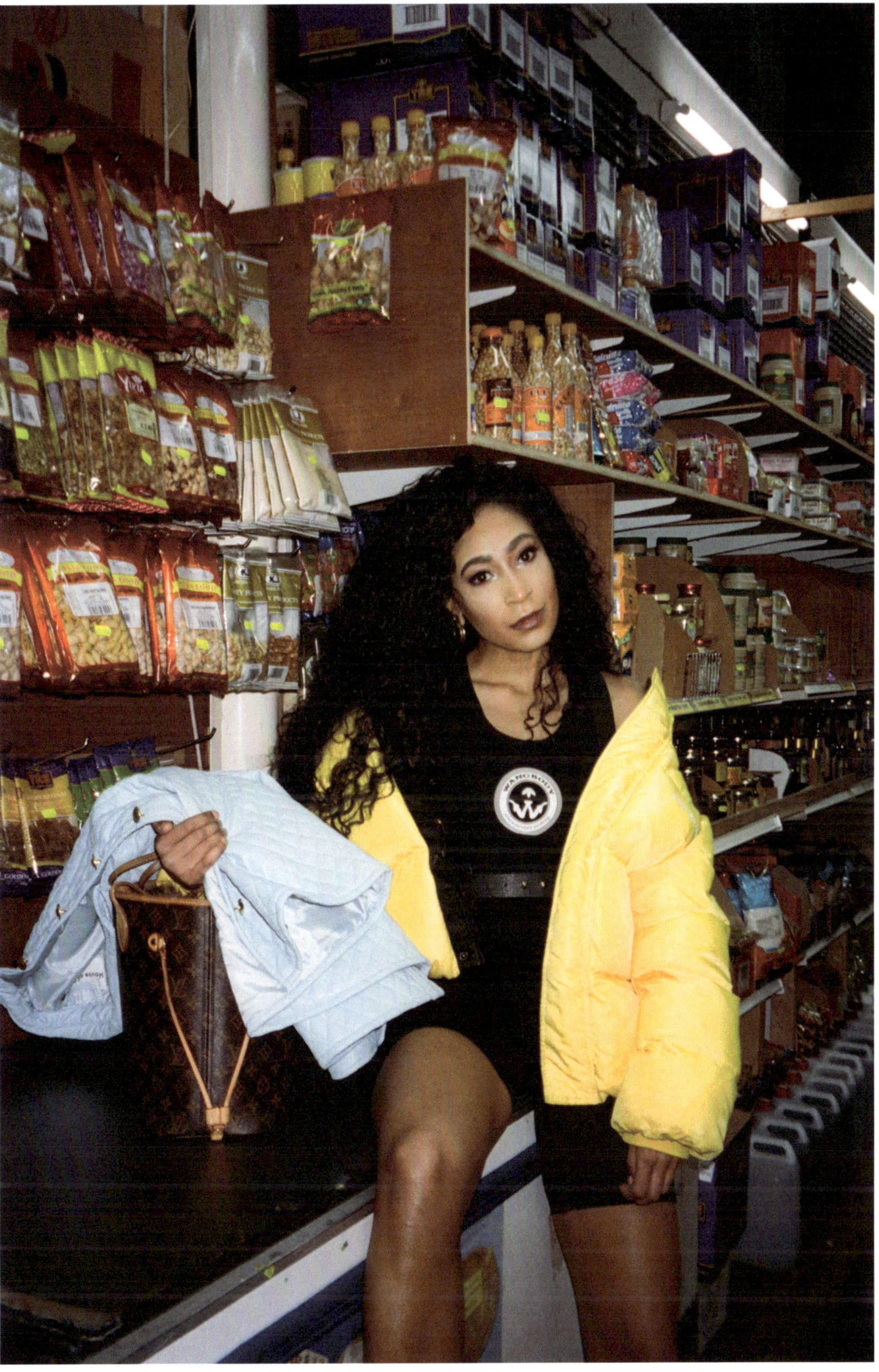

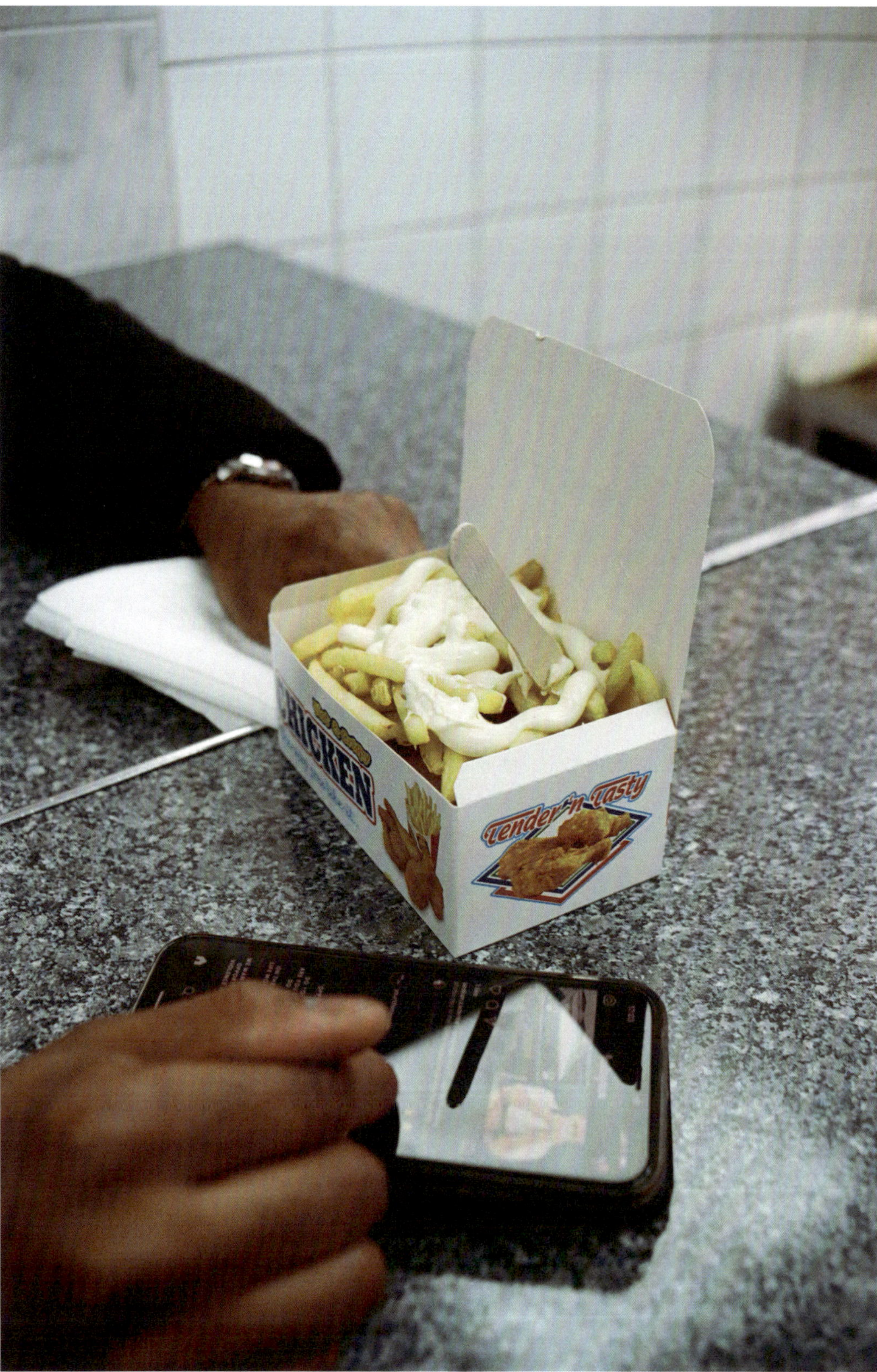
CHICKEN
Tender 'n Tasty

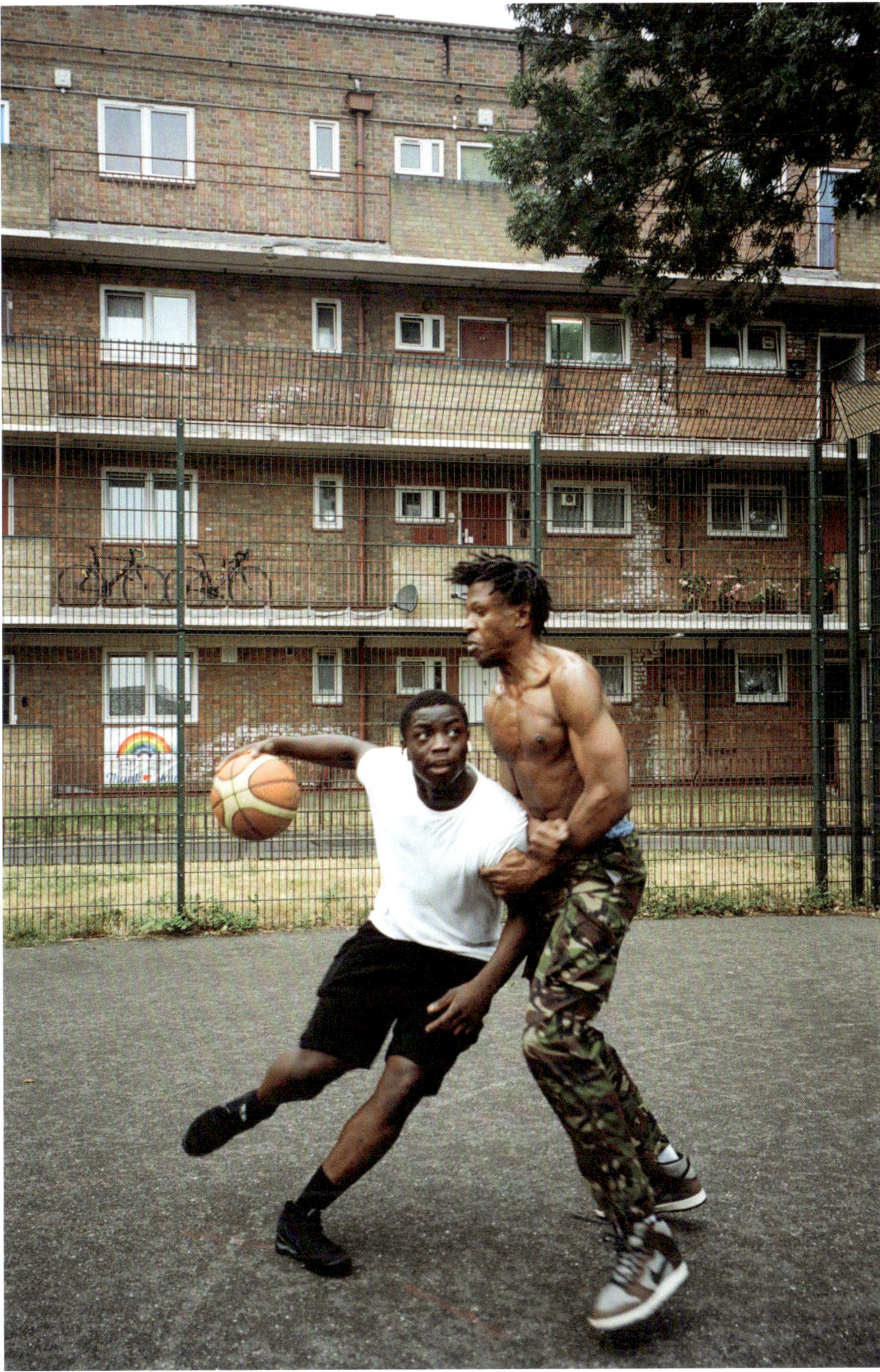

TITLE

# A SERIES OF UTTERLY IMPROBABLE, YET EXTRAORDINARY RENDITIONS

COVER

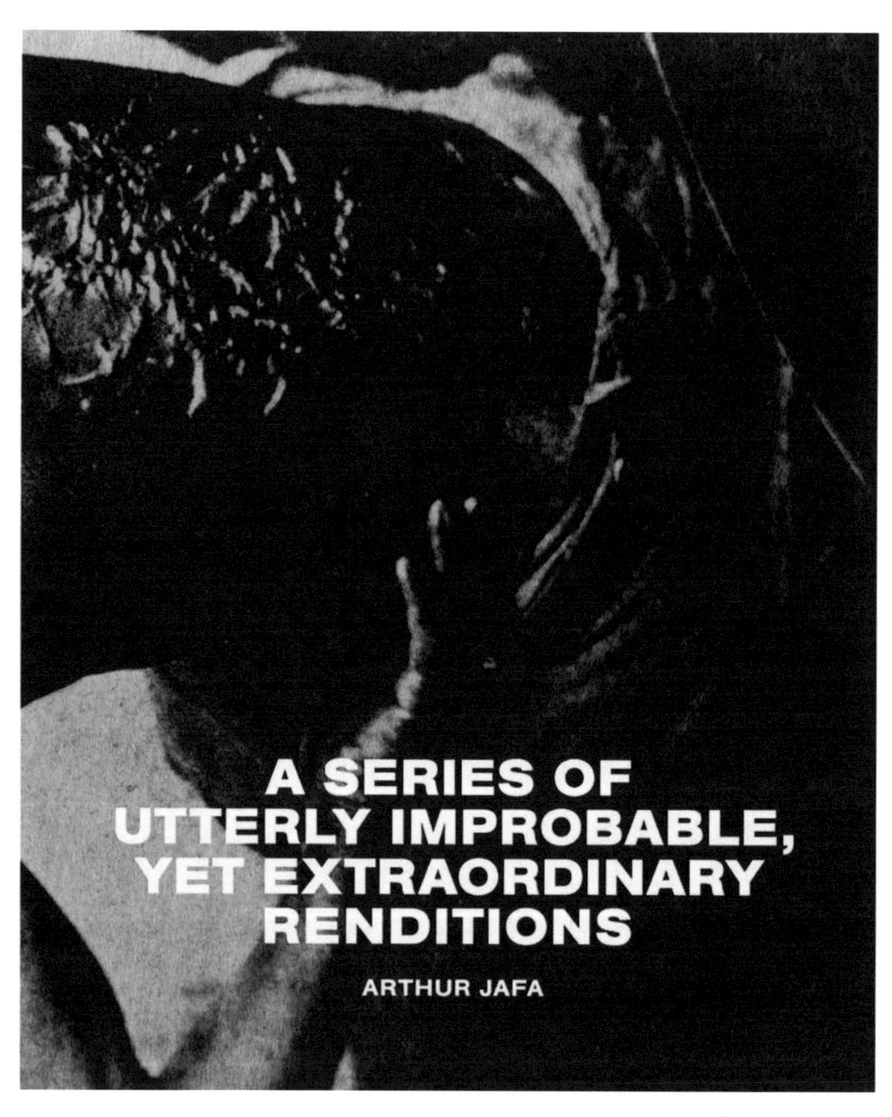

| | |
|---|---|
| ARTIST | Arthur Jafa |
| PUBLISHER | Verlag der Buchhandlung Walther König |
| SPECIFICATIONS | — 848 pages<br>— first published in 2018<br>— size: 27.94 × 34.29 cm |
| SUMMARY | *A Series of Utterly Improbable Yet Extraordinary Renditions* is representative of Arthur Jafa's artistic practice, halfway between appropriation, juxtaposition and montage. The book presents a multitude of images taken from video sequences about race, conflict, the cosmos and nature. Texts by writers, philosophers and artists such as Hilton Als, Jean Baudrillard, Amiri Baraka, Judith Butler, Samuel R. Delany, Gilles Deleuze, Félix Guattari, Fred Moten and Cecil Taylor punctuate the book and converse with the images. |
| BIOGRAPHY | Arthur Jafa was born in 1960 in Tupelo, Mississippi. He is a graduate of Howard University in Washington, where he studied architecture. A director and cinematographer for the past 30 years, he has collaborated with many directors, including Spike Jonze, Andrew Dosunmu and Haile Gerima. He co-founded the film studio TNEG, "whose aim is to create a Black cinema as culturally, socially and economically central as Black music in the 20th century". His multidisciplinary artistic practice has evolved over the decades to challenge dominant cultural assumptions about identity and race.[1]<br><br>1 We use the term "race" here not to refer to a scientific concept differentiating human groups, but to a historical, social and cultural construction. |

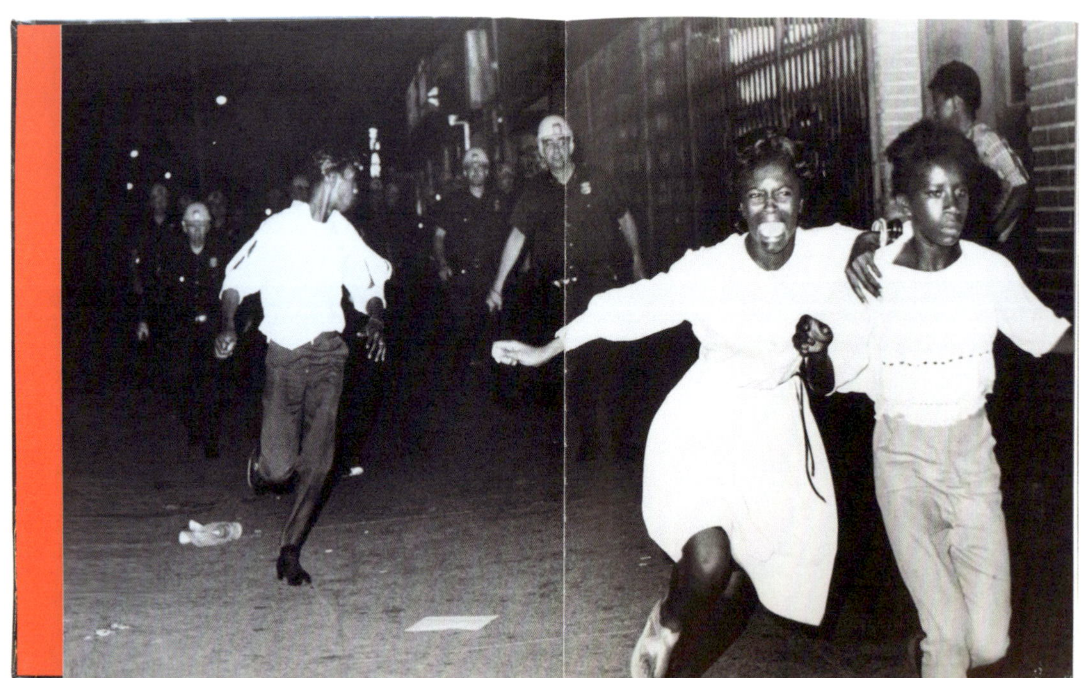

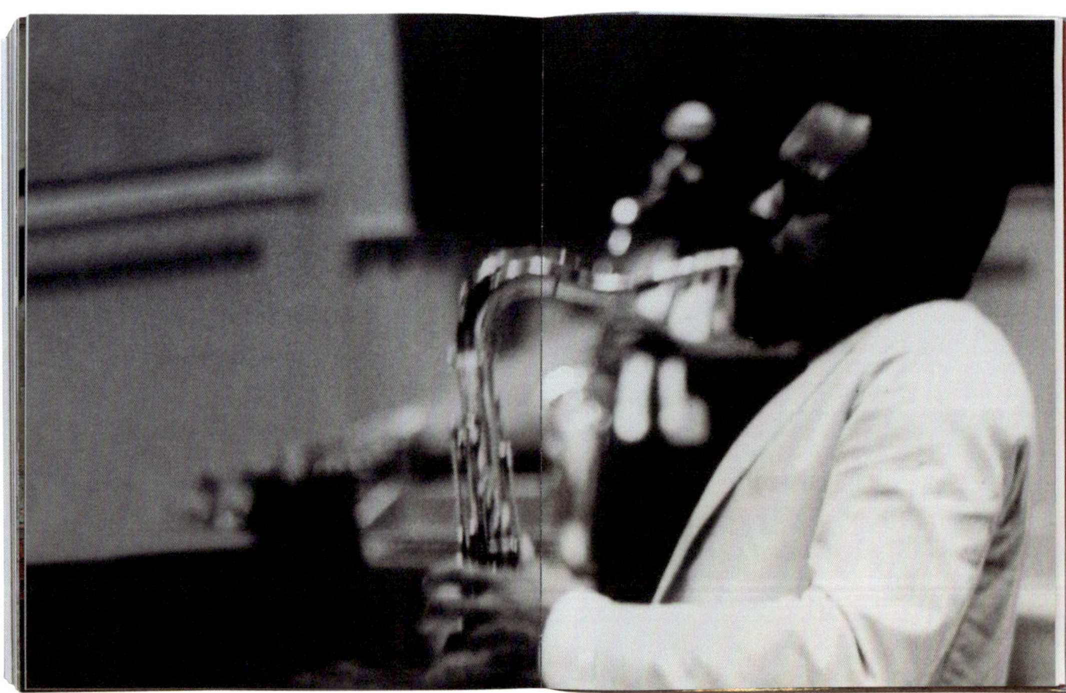

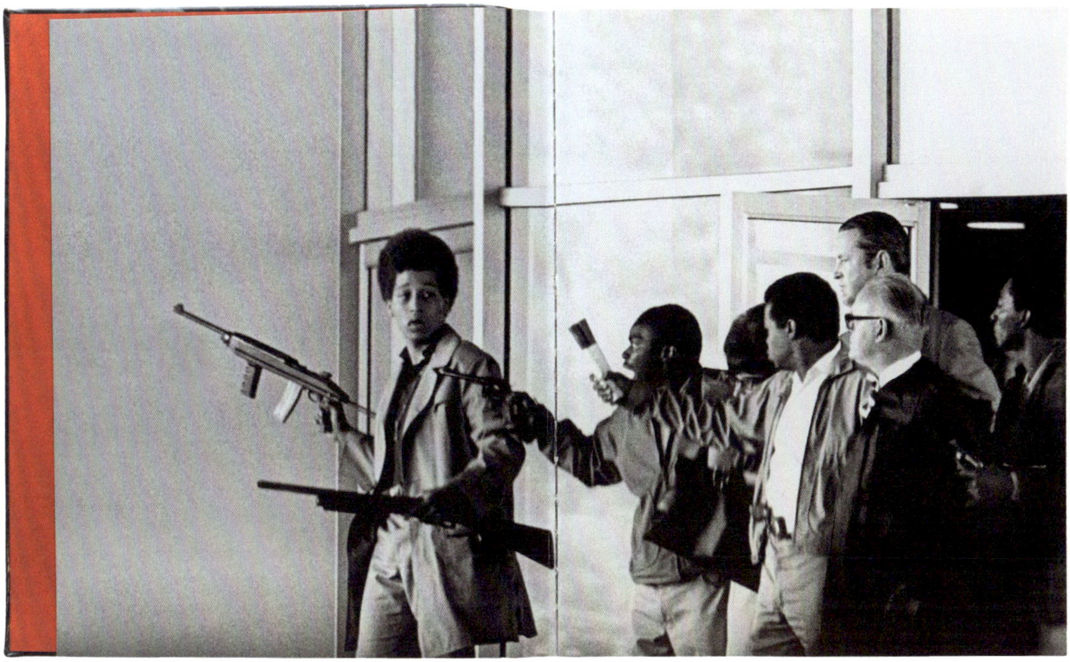

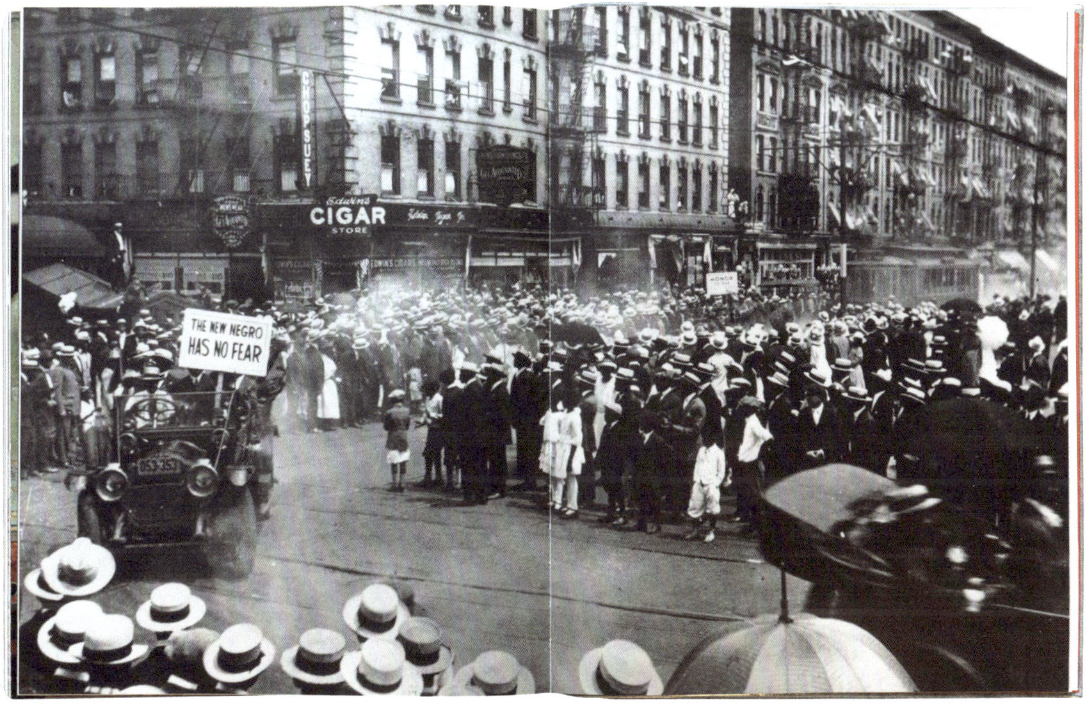

CHOP SUEY
Edwin's CIGAR STORE
THE NEW NEGRO HAS NO FEAR

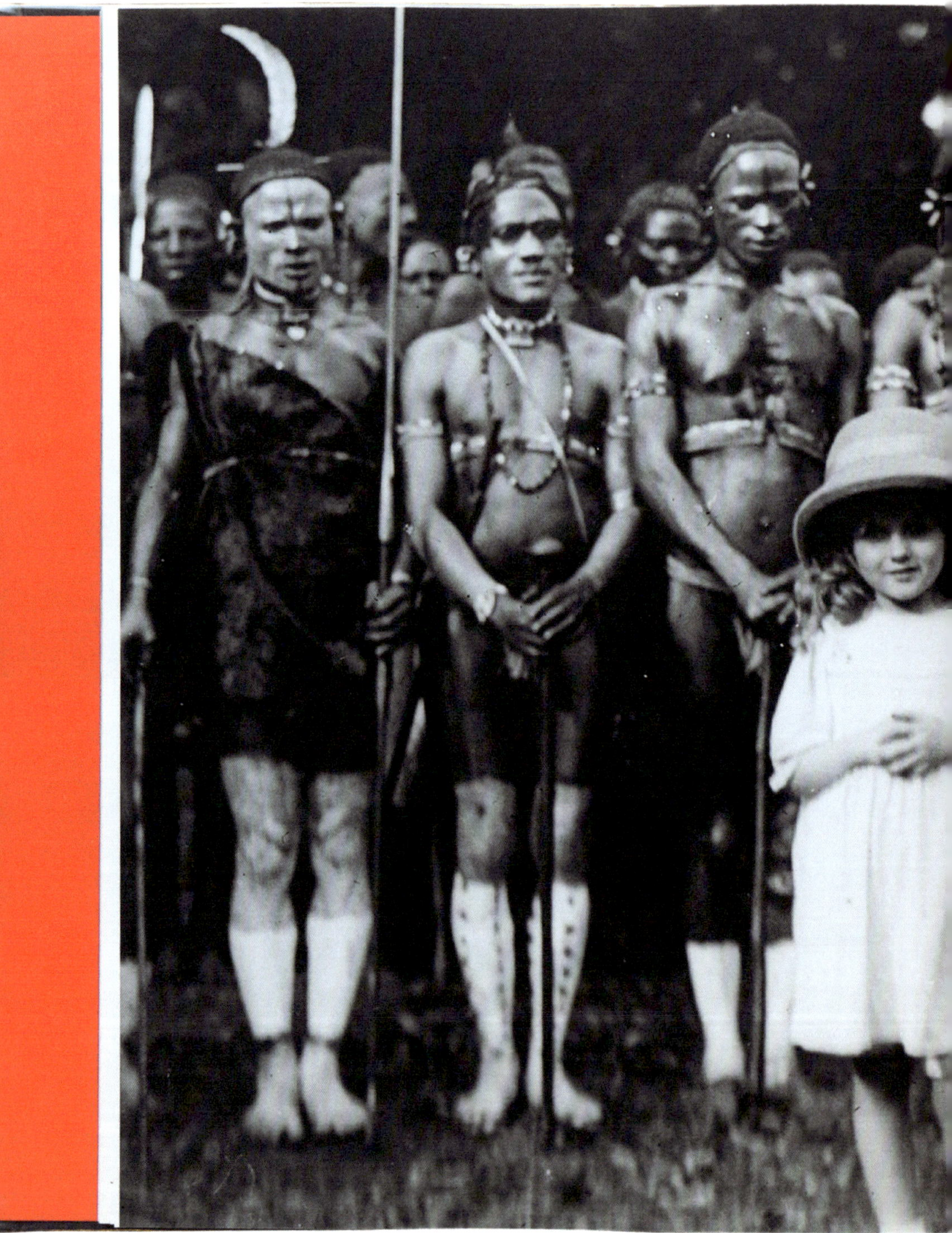

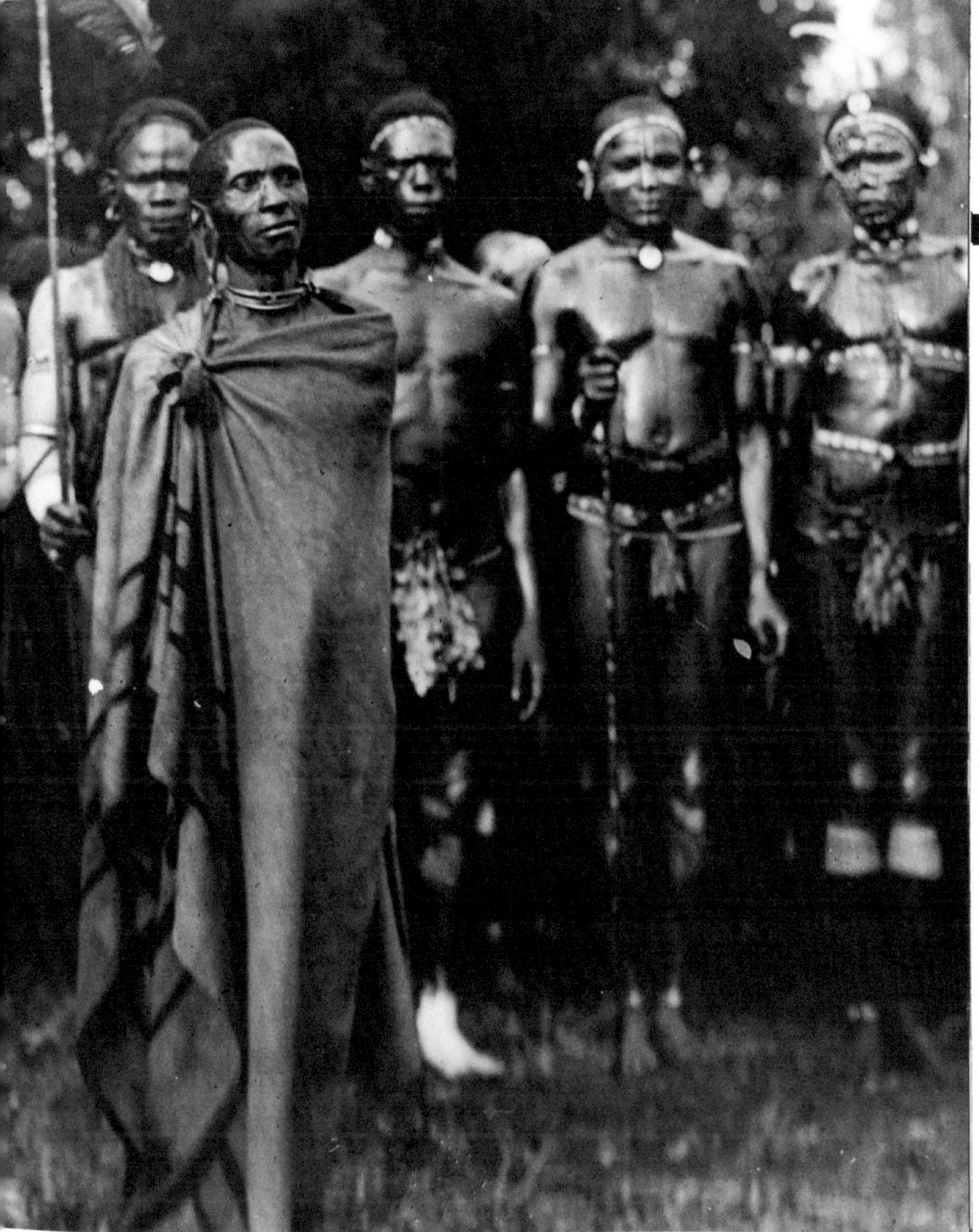

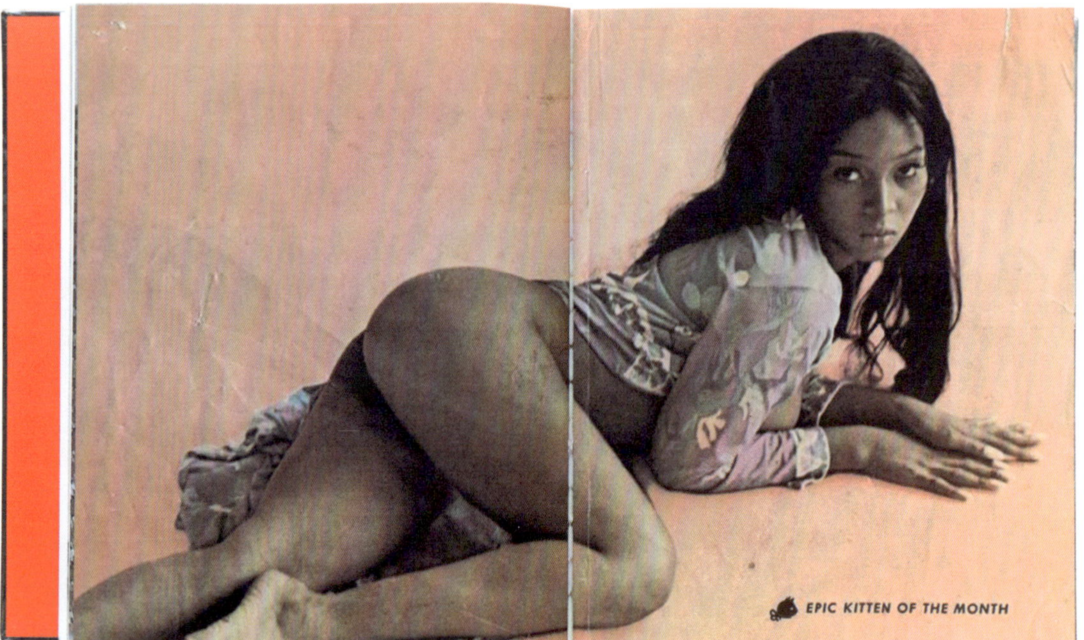
EPIC KITTEN OF THE MONTH

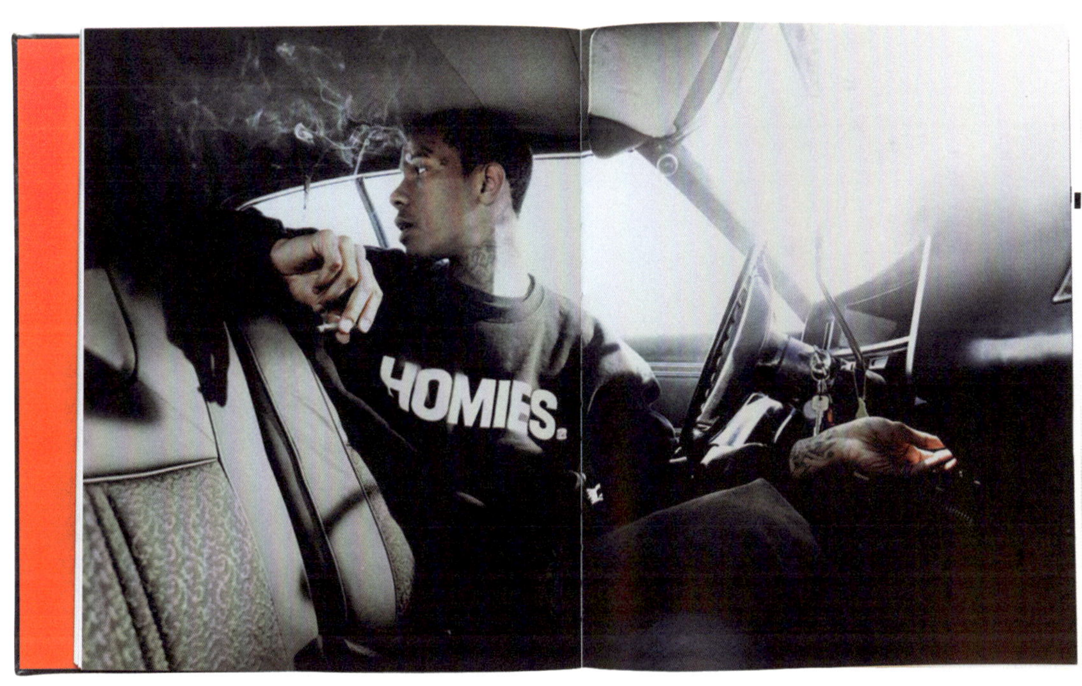
HOMIES.

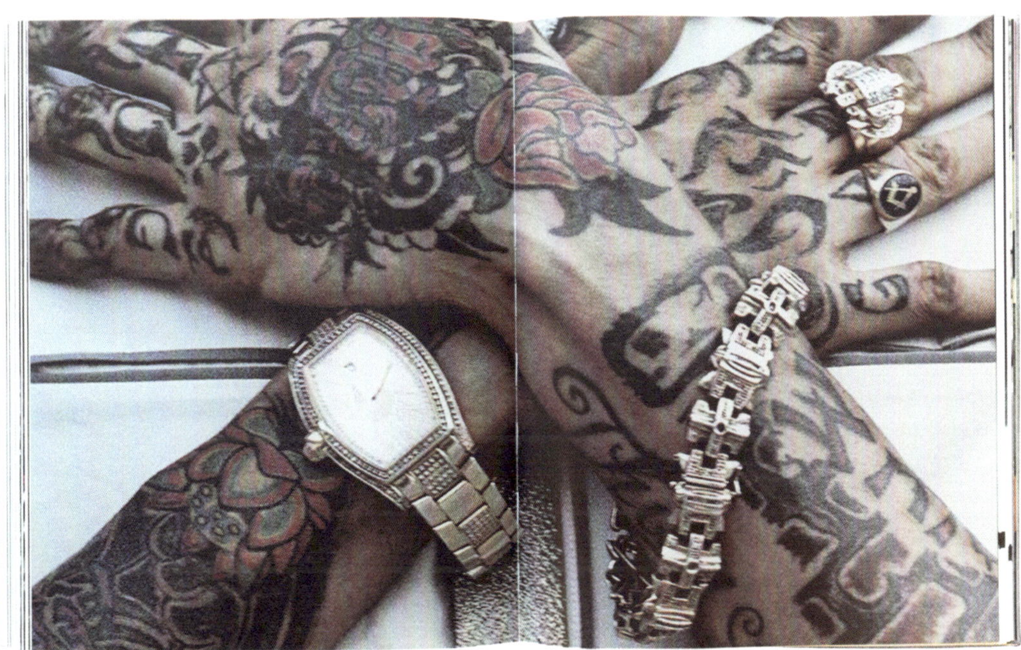

# SOFIA YALA RODRIGUES

Sofia Yala Rodrigues was born in Lisbon in 1994. Her grandparents, of Angolan origin, arrived in Portugal in the early 1950s and 1960s. Her childhood was lulled by the stories of both grandfathers who worked in the Portuguese merchant navy. With a background in African studies and anthropology in Lisbon, she decided to study film and photography at the University of Derby to further develop her practice.

Yala's artwork explores archival material combined with unexpected encounters in life. Her art conveys storytelling bringing in different times, textures and layers. The material process is based on photography, but Sofia enjoys testing and presenting her work with the photographic medium alongside other formats and compositions. Collage allows her to represent, in her own words, the hybrid and fragmented dimension of her identity. Her work focuses on collective memory and the decolonization of narratives and history. She currently lives and works between England and Portugal. She participated in the 2021 edition of Circulation(s), the European emerging photography festival.

The series "Playing with Visual Fragments", "Type Here to Search" and "The Body as an Archive" consist of digital collages. More specifically the series "The Body as an Archive" collects documents such as ID photos, passports, correspondence and recent photographs of the artist that are assembled, juxtaposed or superimposed. The title refers to the interplay between fiction and reality, between family history and unofficial history.


*Playing with Visual Fragments*, 2021
*The Body as an Archive*, 2020/21
*The Body as an Archive*, 2020/21
*Type here to search*, 2020
*The body as an archive*, 2020/21
*Type here to search*, 2020
*The body as an archive*, 2020/21
*Untitled*, 2021
*Untitled*, 2021

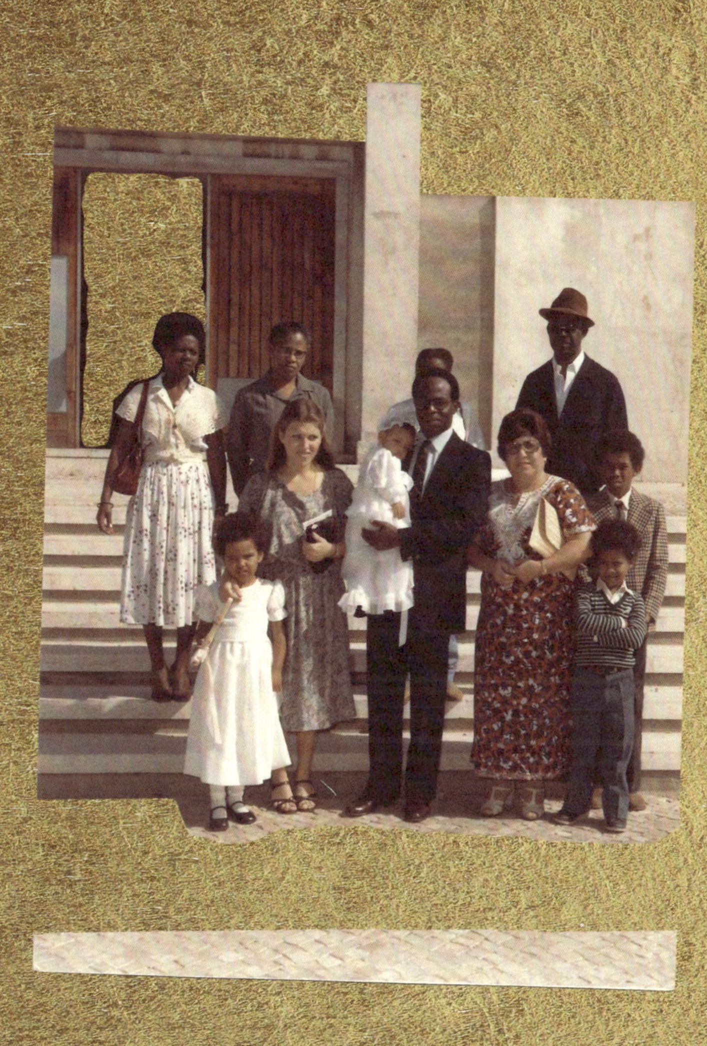

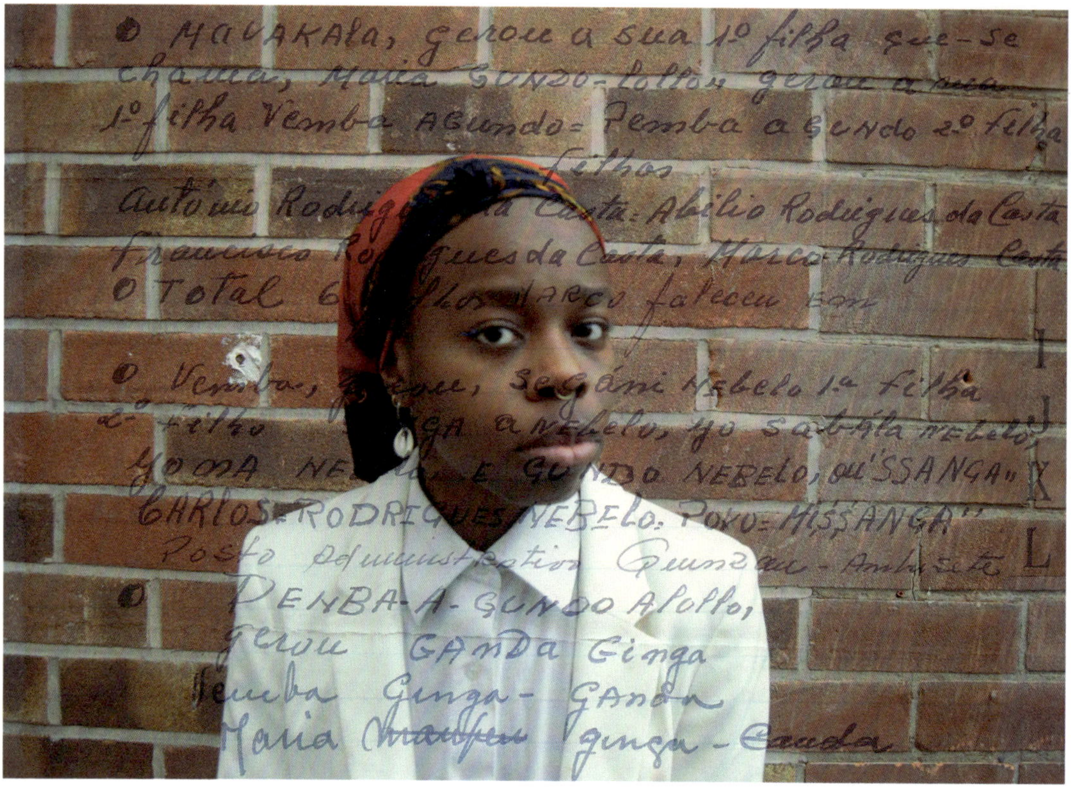

o Mavakala, gerou a sua 1º filha que-se chama, Maria Gundo-lollo; gerou a sua 1º filha Vemba Agundo= Pemba a Gundo 2º filha
filhos
António Rodrigues da Costa: Abílio Rodrigues da Costa
Francisco Rodrigues da Costa, Marco Rodrigues Costa
O total 6 filhos Marco faleceu em

o Vemba, gerou, Segámi Nebelo 1ª filha
2º filho [illegible] Ginga a Nebelo, yo Sabála Nebelo,
Yoma Nebelo e Gundo Nebelo, ou "Ssanga"
Carlos Rodrigues Nebelo: Povo= Missanga"
Posto administration Quenzau - Ambrizete
o Pemba-a-Gundo Alollo,
gerou Ganda Ginga
Vemba Ginga - Ganda
Maria ~~[illegible]~~ Ginga - ~~Ganda~~

I
J
K
L

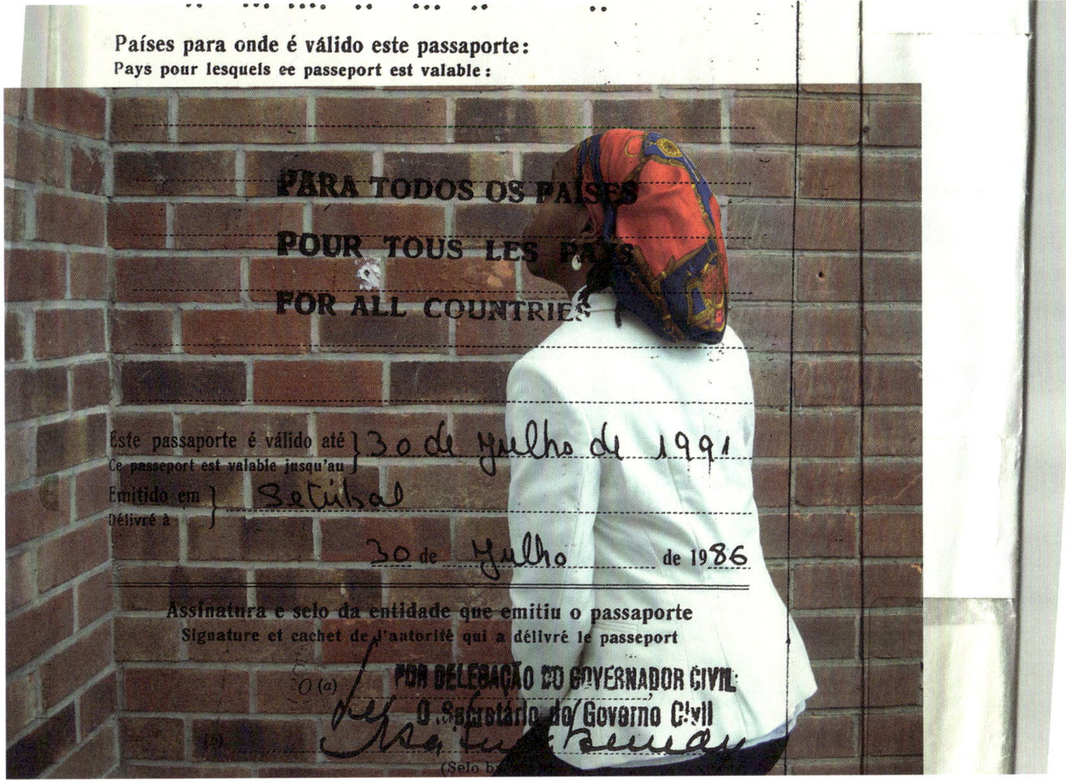

Países para onde é válido este passaporte:
Pays pour lesquels ce passeport est valable :

PARA TODOS OS PAÍSES
POUR TOUS LES PAYS
FOR ALL COUNTRIES

Este passaporte é válido até } 30 de Julho de 1991
Ce passeport est valable jusqu'au

Emitido em } Setúbal
Délivré à

30 de Julho de 1986

Assinatura e selo da entidade que emitiu o passaporte
Signature et cachet de l'autorité qui a délivré le passeport

O (a)

POR DELEGAÇÃO DO GOVERNADOR CIVIL
O Secretário do Governo Civil

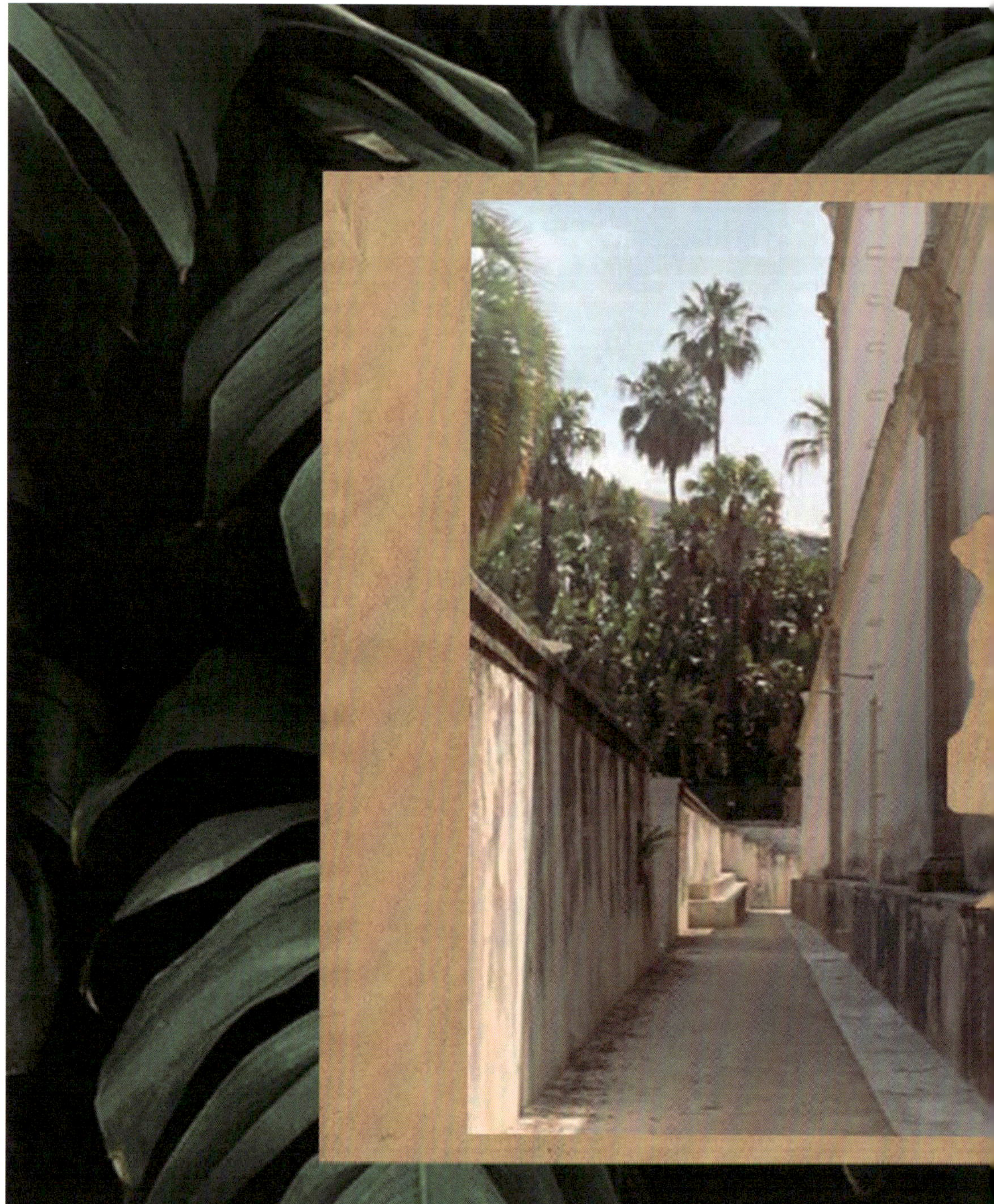

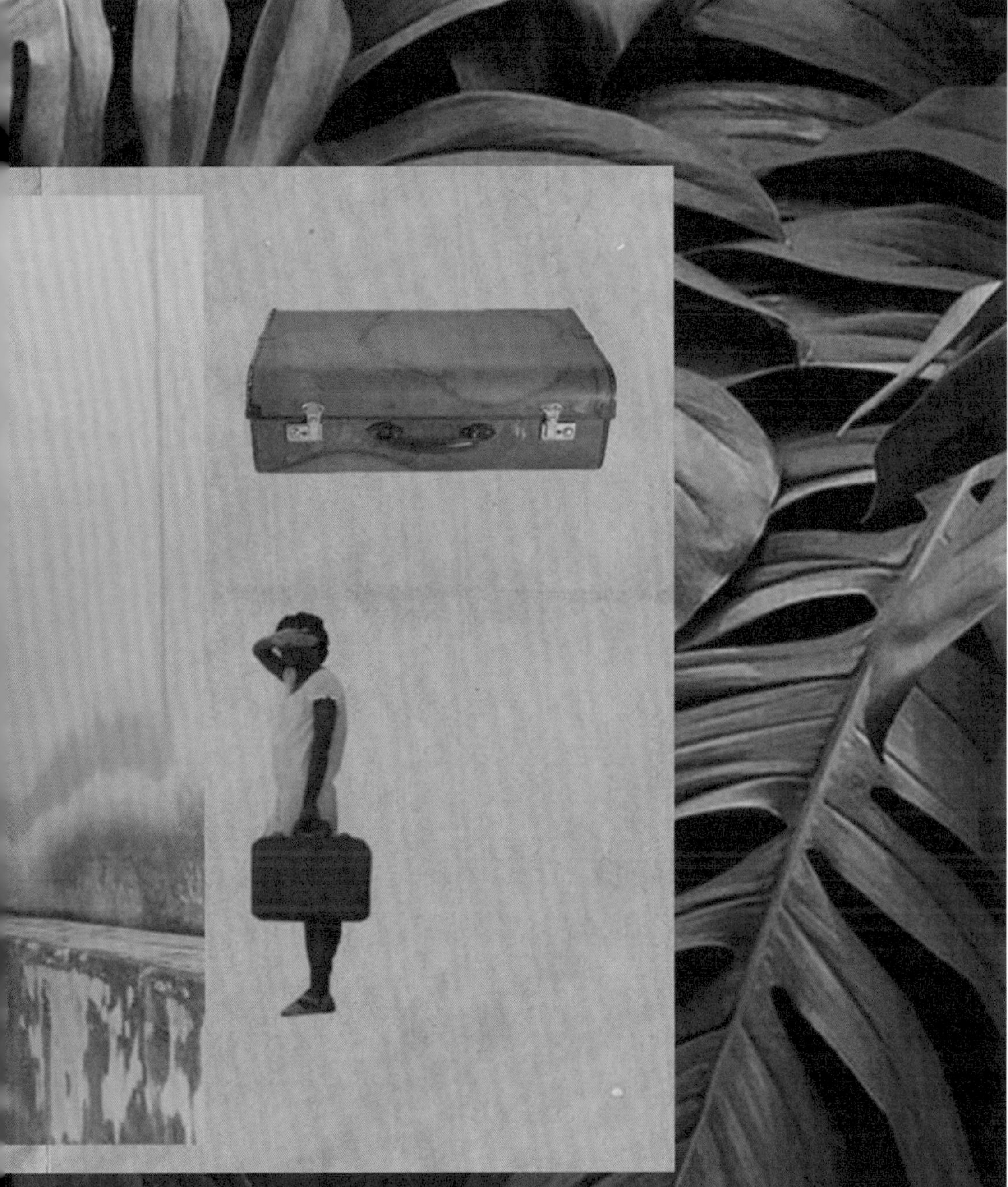

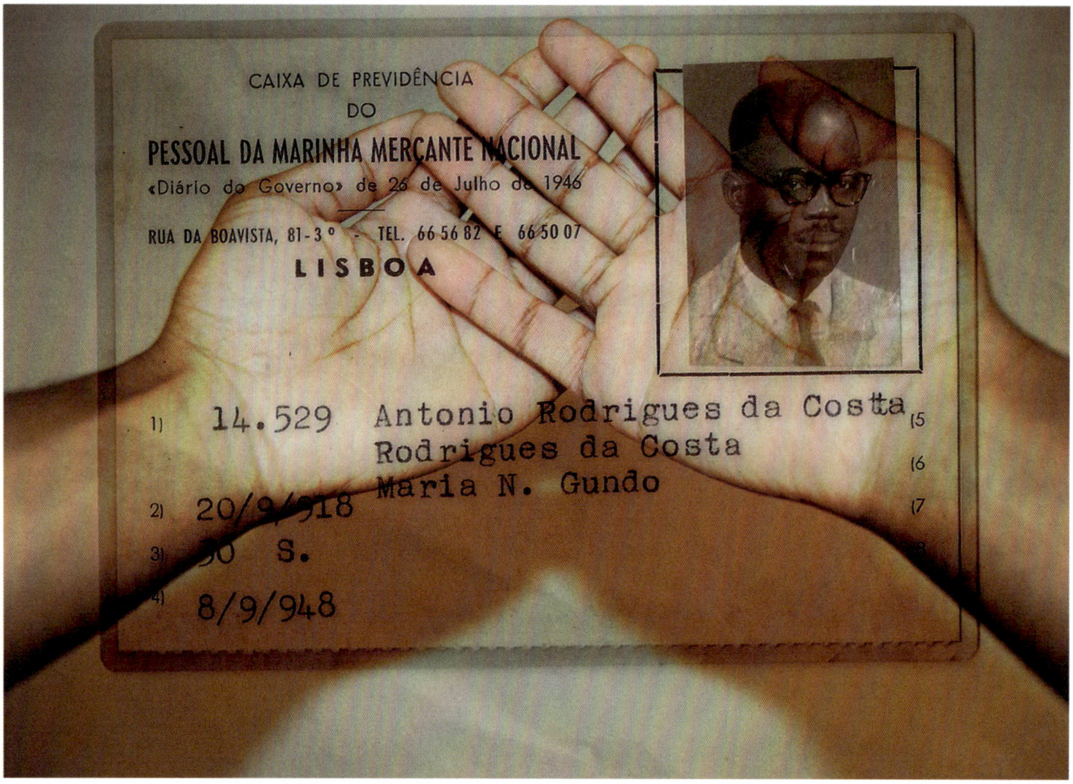

CAIXA DE PREVIDÊNCIA
DO
**PESSOAL DA MARINHA MERCANTE NACIONAL**
«Diário do Governo» de 26 de Julho de 1946

RUA DA BOAVISTA, 81-3.º - TEL. 66 56 82 E 66 50 07
**LISBOA**

1) 14.529 Antonio Rodrigues da Costa (5
Rodrigues da Costa (6
Maria N. Gundo
2) 20/9/918 (7
3) 30 S.
4) 8/9/948

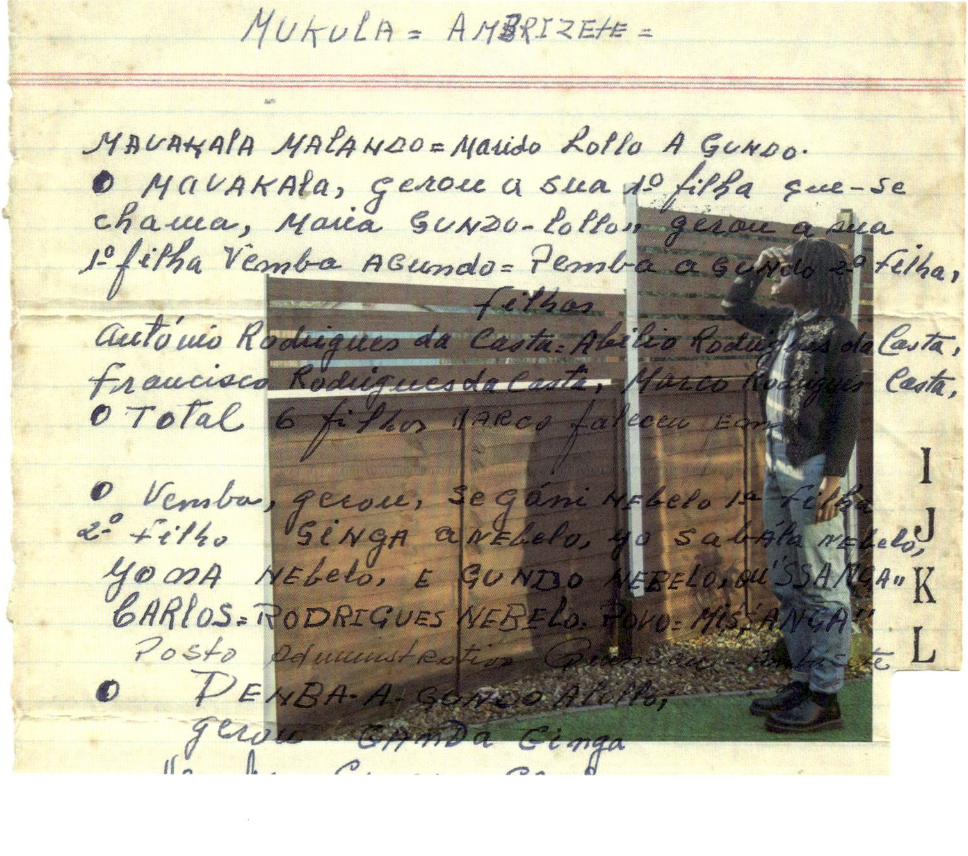

MUKULA = AMBRIZETE =

MAVAKALA MALANDO = Marido Lollo A Gundo.
• MAVAKALA, gerou a sua 1º filha que-se chama, Maria GUNDO-Lollo, gerou a sua 1º filha Vemba AGundo = Pemba a GUNDO 2º filha,
filhos
António Rodrigues da Costa = Abilio Rodrigues da Costa, Francisco Rodrigues da Costa, Marco Rodrigues Costa, O Total 6 filhos MARCO faleceu Em

• Vemba, gerou, Segámi NEBELO 1ª filha 2º filho SINGA a NEBELO, yo sabála NEBELO, YOMA NEBELO, E GUNDO NEBELO, "MISSANGA" CARLOS = RODRIGUES NEBELO. POVO = "MISSANGA"
Posto Administrativo Quinzau - Ambrizete
• PENBA-A-GUNDO Alollo,
gerou CAMBA Cinga

I
J
K
L

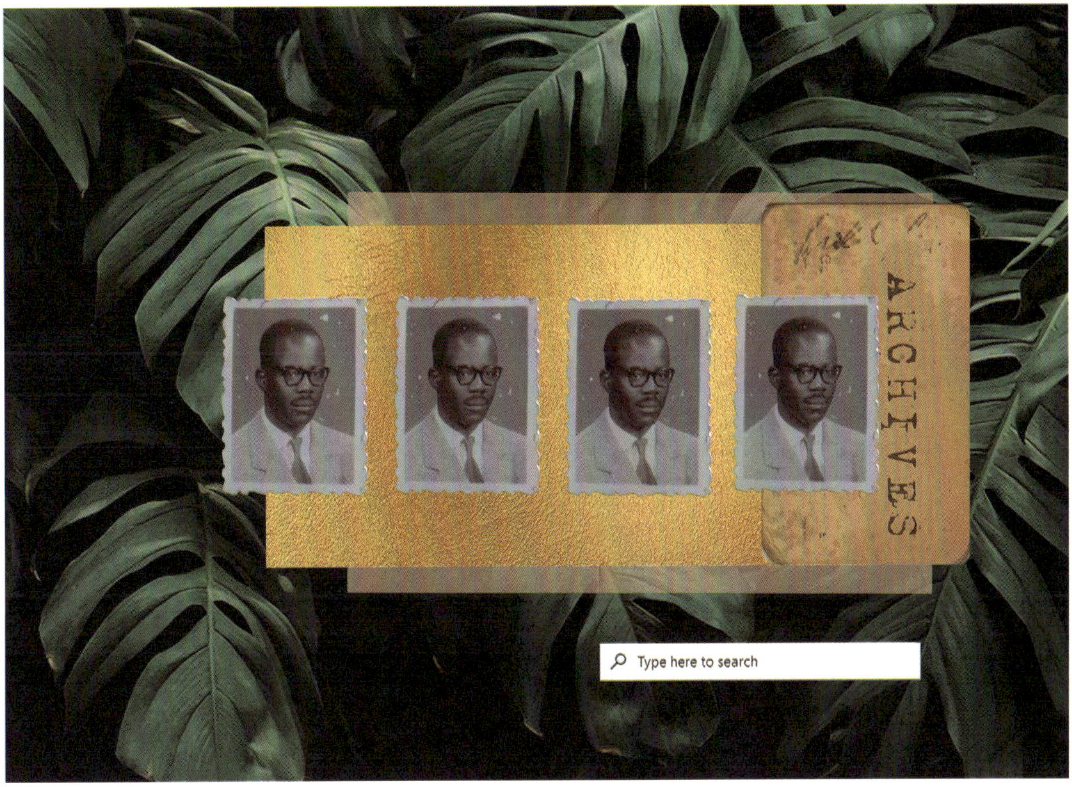

ARCHIVES
Type here to search

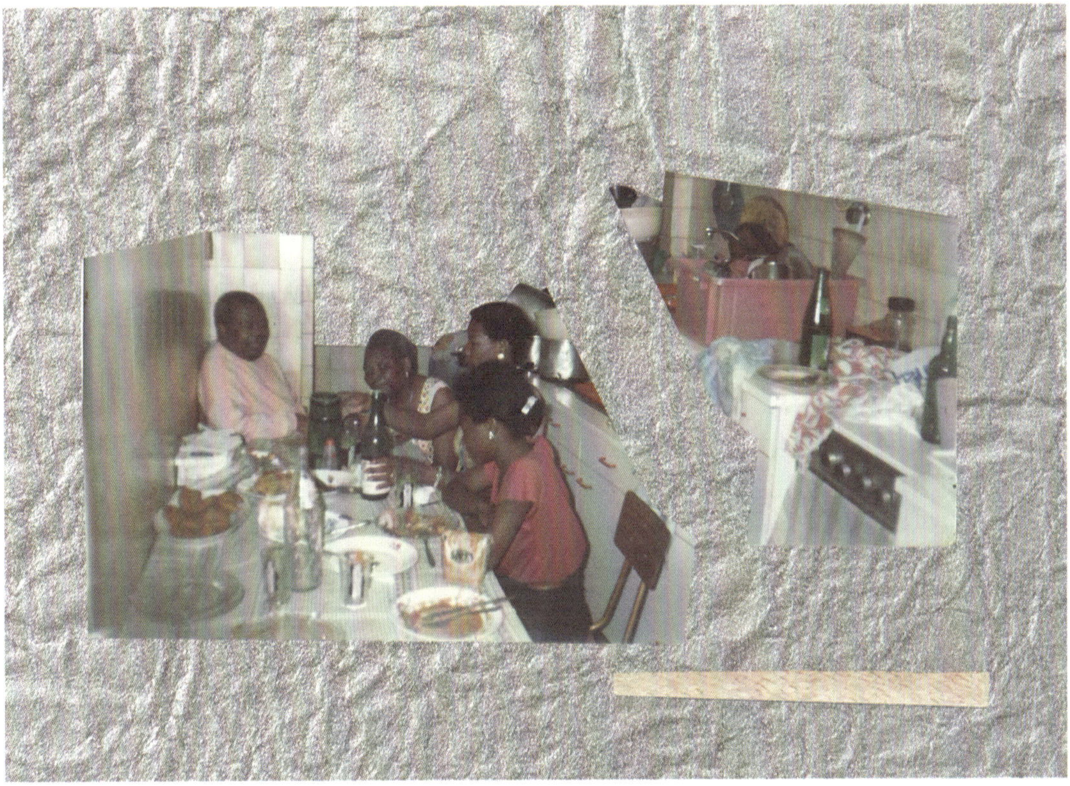

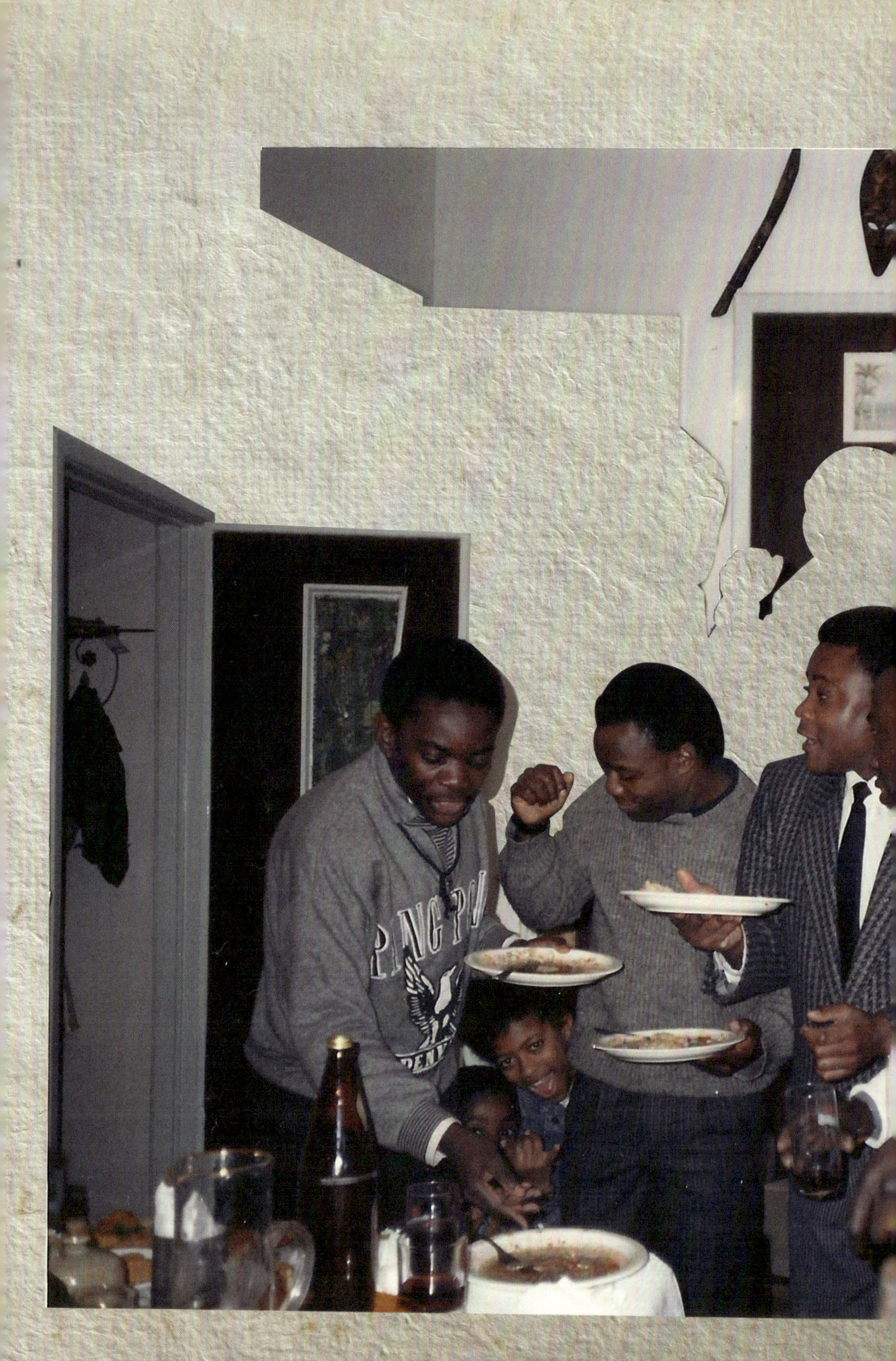

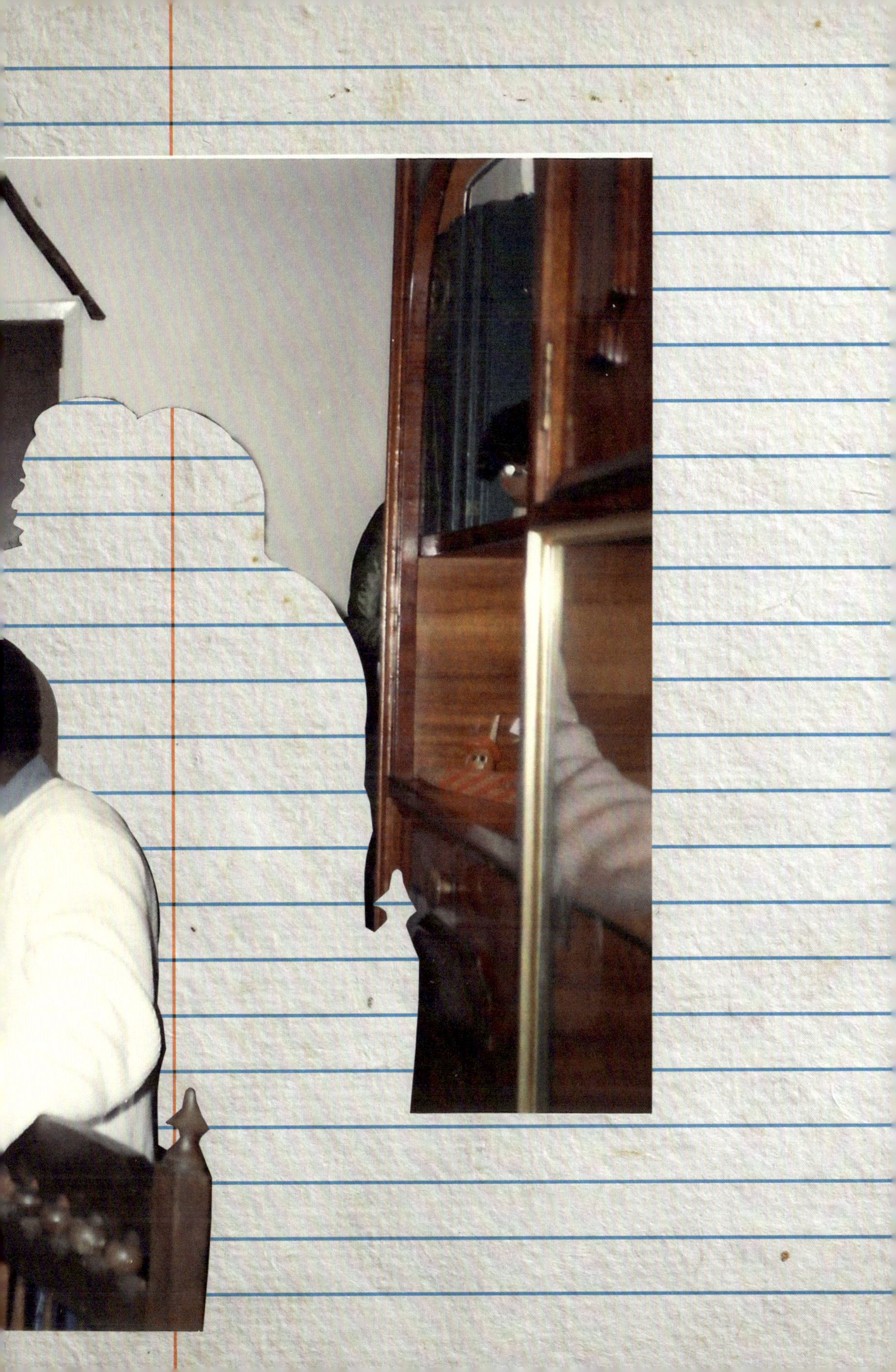

The Photocaptionist is a photo-literary platform that promotes the marriage of photographs and words through editorial and curatorial projects. The platform operates both online and offline.

For this issue, The Photocaptionist presents a taster of "Home is not a Place", a collaborative work in progress between Johny Pitts and the poet Roger Robinson. Taking Roy DeCarava and Langston Hughes' seminal book *The Sweet Flypaper of Life* as its cue, the project focuses on the layered identities and experiences of the Black British community at the start of the 2020s. Both for and from the community, it will be published as a book by William Collins in 2022, with photographs produced in the field of the Ampersand / Photoworks Fellowship.

Poems : Roger Robinson
Images : Johny Pitts
Courtesy of the artists and Photoworks


*Union Jack Cap*, Peckham High Street, 2021 (from the series "Home Is Not a Place")
*Club Cassiopeia*, Berlin, 2010 (from the series "Afropean")
*Another Kind of Life*, Barbican, 2018 (from the series "Home is not a Place")
*Bouna & Zyed Memorial* (A Portable Paradise), Clichy-sous-bois, 2010 (from the series "Afropean")
*If You Can Dream Then Anything Is Possible*, Peckham High Street, 2021 (from the series "Home Is Not a Place")
*Man and Flowers*, Bristol, 2021 (from the series "Home Is Not a Place")
*New Europe*, Baker Street Station, London, 2013 (from the series "Afropean")
*p h o t o m e m o r i e s*, Gillingham, 2021

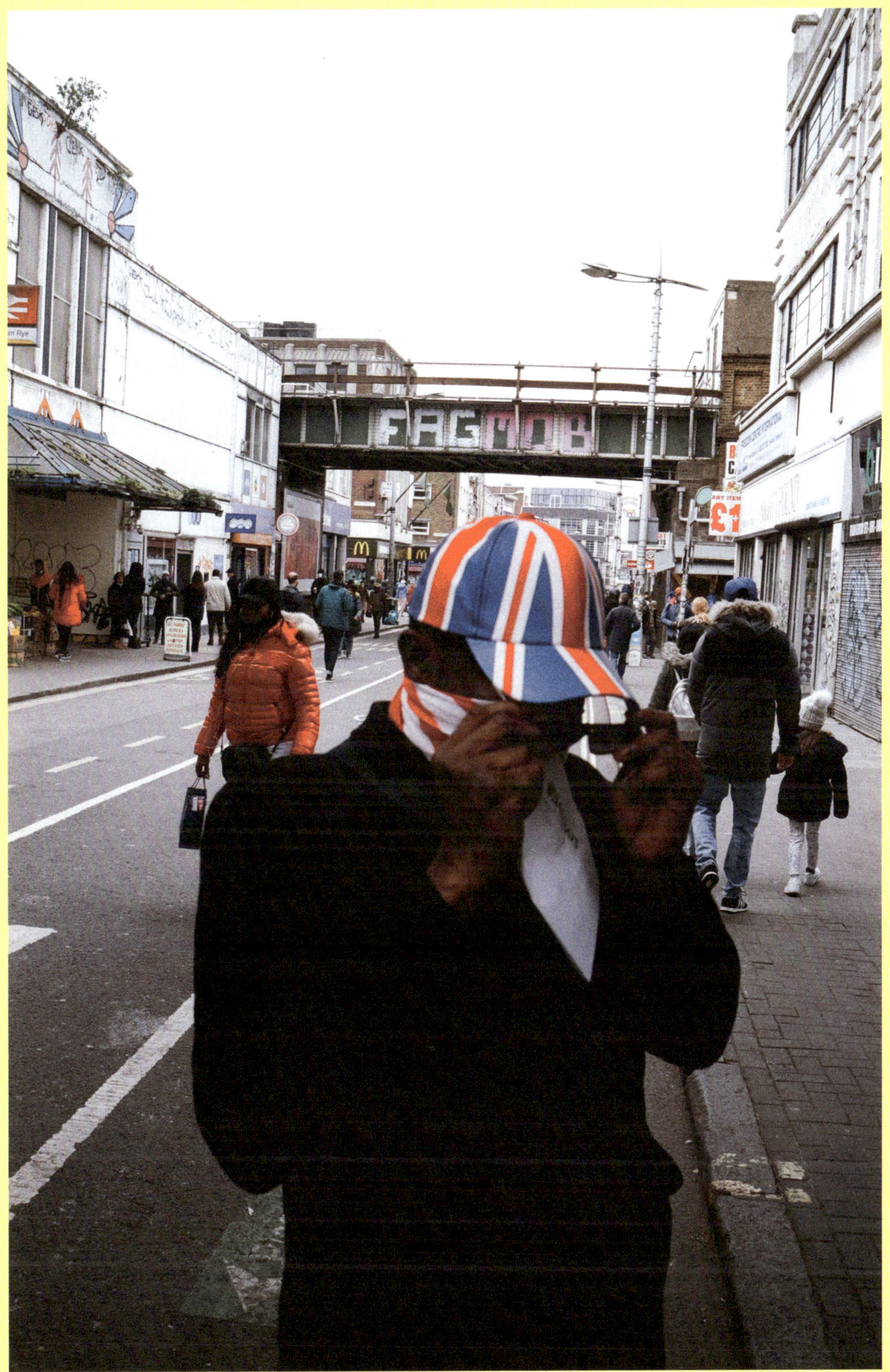
FAGMOB
ANY ITEM
£1

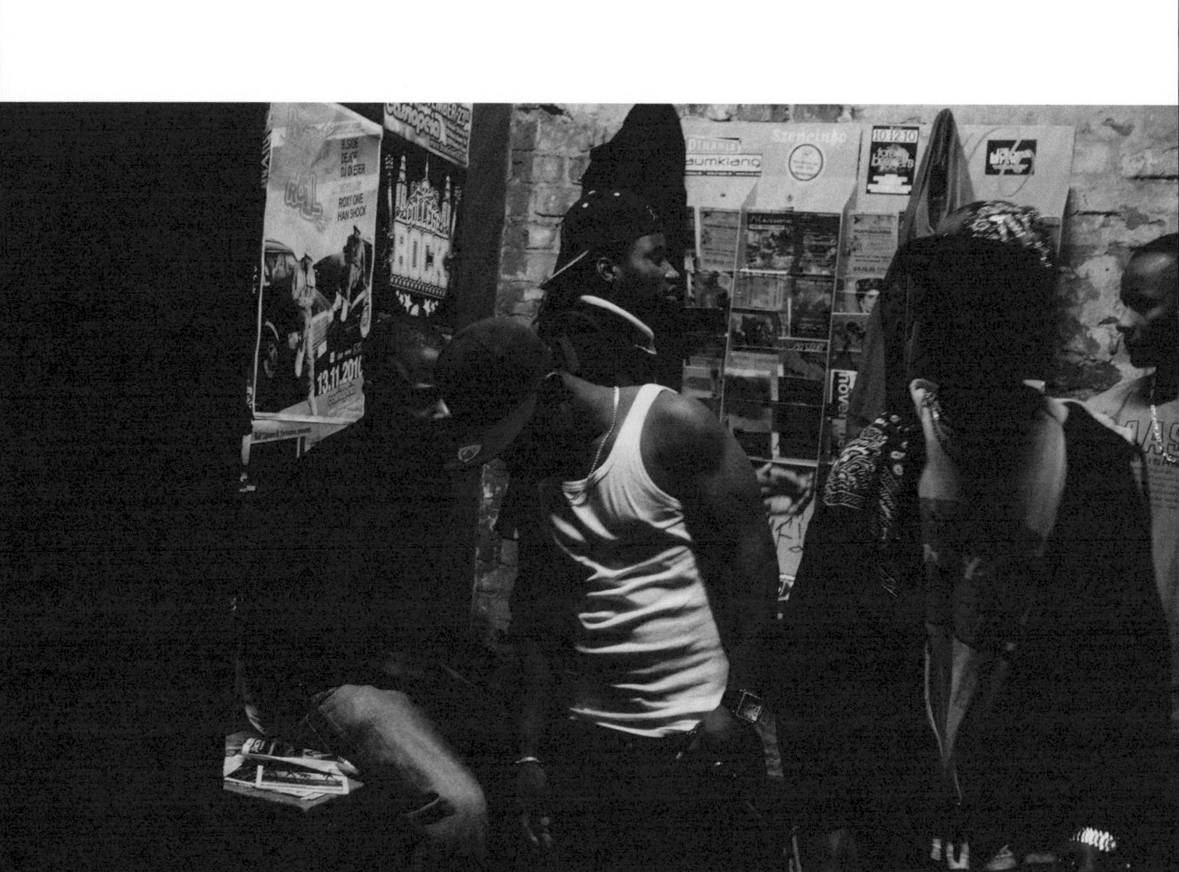
ROXY ONE
HAN SHOCK
ROCK
13.11.2010
10.12.10

Aba Shanti Sound System

Aba Shanti Soundsystem could shake the trauma out of you with pure bass sound. During the hundreds of years of trauma, Black people had became accustomed to particular frequencies of bass and certain rhythms of drums to relieve all their generational hurt. Certain rhythms became very valued by them. These healing frequencies became wailing blues and jazz in America, became whispering samba in Brazil, became soca in Trinidad and became, and became, and became. Now Aba Shanti, he had every principal healing frequency on 45 vinyl. It is said that he lives in a big house but sleeps only in one room, as every other room holds black 45s (bathroom included). As with anything else, soon White people heard of the healing and felt like they had to get some, even though they were not sure of the illness that they were suffering but they knew that something was not right; but the frequencies spoke differently to them. It made them dance but, a dance that made them grieve the transgressions of their generations. It made them cry hysterically with a deep, deep sorrow and drop out from the system and twist their blond flowing hair into dreadlocks. Healing still, but healing different ills.

Benin Security Guard at the V&A[1]

When the last visitor has left and the chefs from the restaurant have given him some dinner to eat later from a takeaway tray. When the cleaners have donned their thick winter coats and black and purple berets. When all the display screens have been turned off, and the museum is dark and still, the security guard heads for the African artefacts room. The first thing he goes for is the Benin crown. It fits him perfectly, like it was made for his head, the rose gold against his dark-brown skin. Next he picks up the wooden armband denoting a South African leader, sliding it over his security shirt. Then he takes the indigo adire cloth and wraps it around his waist and stands in front of the autumn colours of the Wissa Wassef[2] Egyptian tapestry, pulls out his phone and takes a selfie. Tomorrow he'll be back for another shift, pulling strands of ancient African culture into a moment. It's the only thing he looks forward to.

1 Victoria and Albert Museum
2 Ramses Wissa Wassef (1911-1974) was an Egyptian architect and designer, professor of art and architecture at the Faculty of Fine Arts in Cairo. He was also a potter and weaver, crafts that he taught to many of Egypt's disadvantaged children.

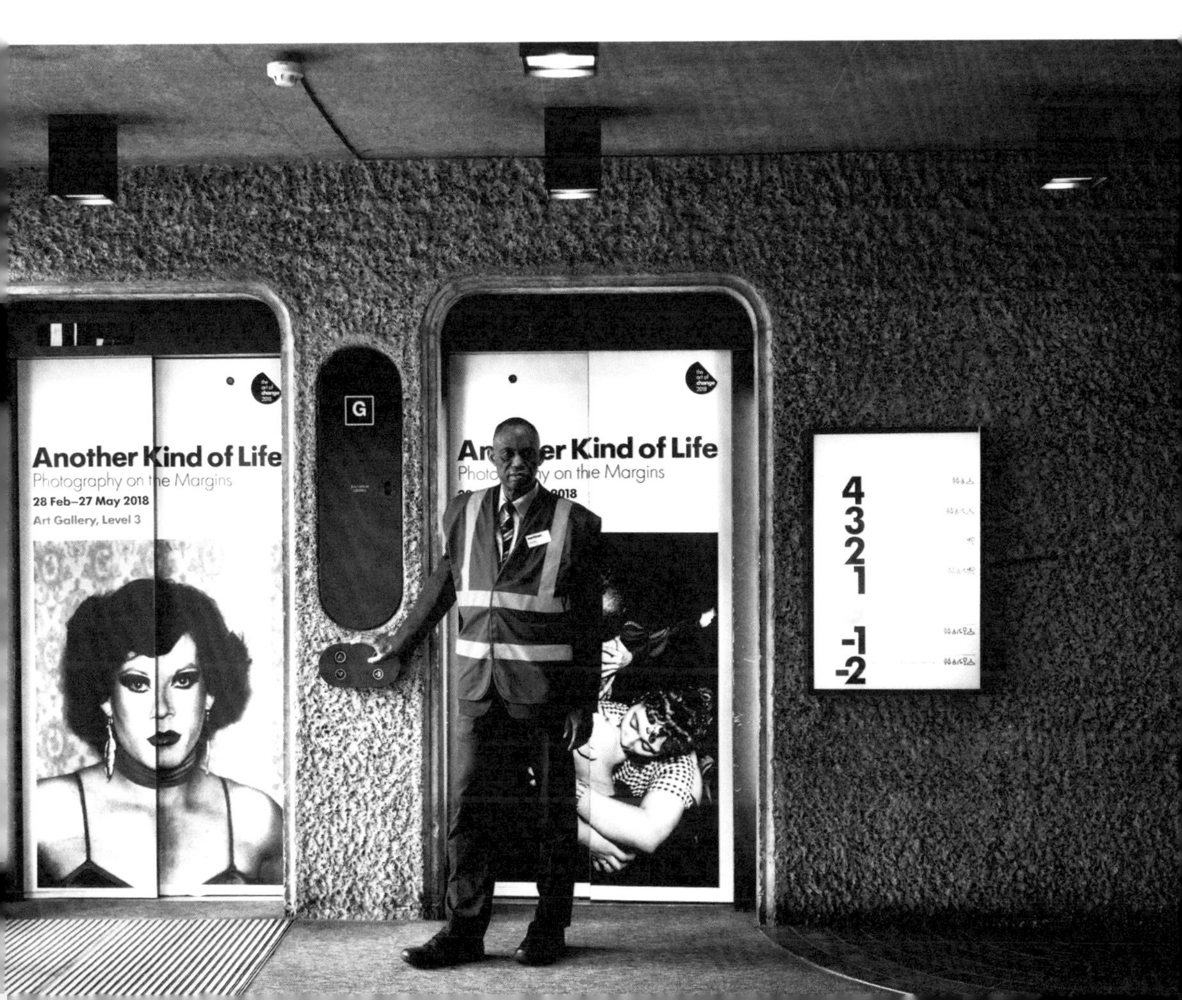
Another Kind of Life
Photography on the Margins
28 Feb–27 May 2018
Art Gallery, Level 3
G
4
3
2
1
-1
-2

# Caribbean Food Shop Sign Sonnet

BBQ Chicken, Brown Stew, Curry Chicken, Fried Chicken, Jerk Chicken, Fried Fish, Ackee and Saltfish, Butter Bean and Saltfish Callaloo, Steam Fish, Curry Goat, Oxtail, Cowfoot, Stew Beef, Peas, Lamb Chops, Pepper Prawn, Rice and Peas, Plain Rice, Roast Breadfruit, Fried Plantain, Carrot Cake, Sweet Potato Pudding, Banana Cake, Fruit Cake, Bun and Cheese, Festival, Dumpling, Porridge, Red Peas Soup, Chicken Soup, Fish Tea, Angel Juice, Carrot Juice, Peanut Punch, Guinness Punch, Sorrel Drink.

Just because it's on the sign doesn't mean you can buy it.

Just because we are smiling doesn't mean we stay silent.

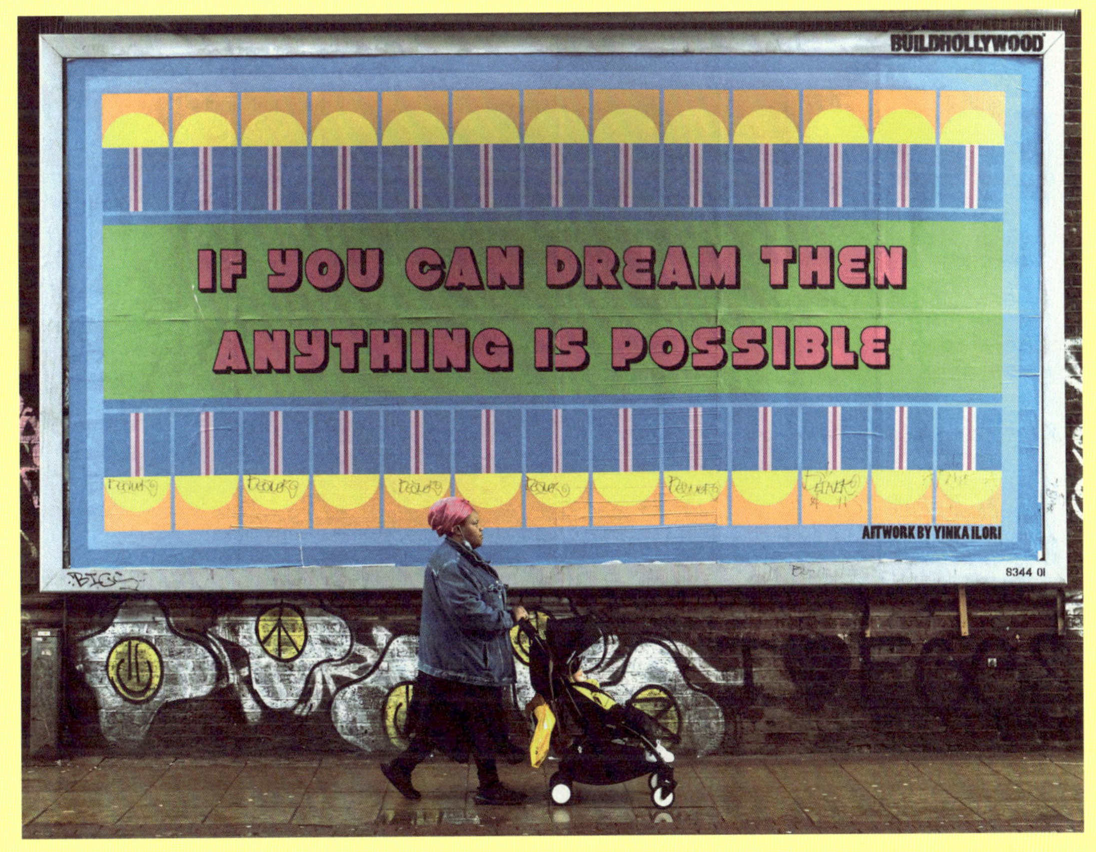
BUILDHOLLYWOOD
IF YOU CAN DREAM THEN
ANYTHING IS POSSIBLE
ARTWORK BY YINKA ILORI
8344 01

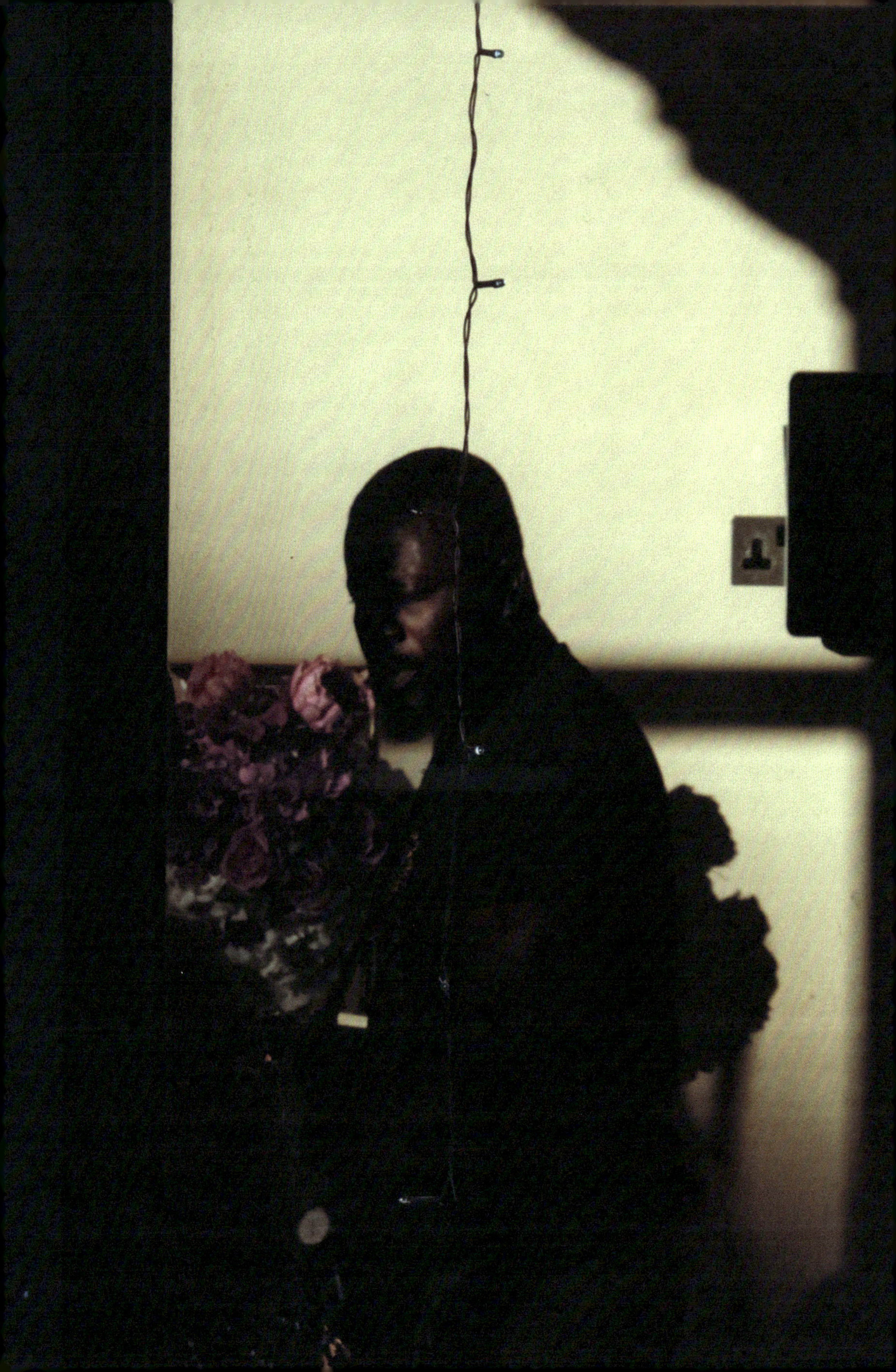

## Halos

The lamplights are softened into halos
floating below a tracing paper moon.

Illuminated puddles and main roads
are fog haunted, and side streets atmosphered

in this light. A simple parked bus
turns woolly mammoth then fort;

perhaps this is the work of smudged light
to soften the world and expand our story;

or maybe to dull the world into a new story
from each yellowed window, the days' survival.

And from each day's survival the drift into dreams,
a reset, a hazy forgetting,

much like this town being bathed this night
in fog and the morning becoming anew.

# The New Black Europe

The New Black Europe is a series of enclaves within enclaves in main cities. Some places they live in soar up past the clouds as a tenement tower and others exist as hotel rooms up dark wooden spiral stairs, in unlikely town centres with walls stained by cigarette smoke and wine-stained carpets. No matter the abode, they all have garlic, oil and iron pots filled with gravy-thick stewed meat.

It is not uncommon to witness in a crowd of grey and black macintoshes, a resident of the New Black Europe, walking down a high street. in the blustering rain with a large, open, bright cherry-red umbrella, and a pair of oxblood sandals. His body expertly wrapped (like a Black Gandhi) in bleached white cotton. Black skin glowing with shea or cocoa butter.

A symbol of a lost empire. They have no time for the yellowed curling pages of the colonizer's history book; and even though they are not united by marches or civil wars, they unite by garlic, salt, oil, skin, cloth and knowing nods.

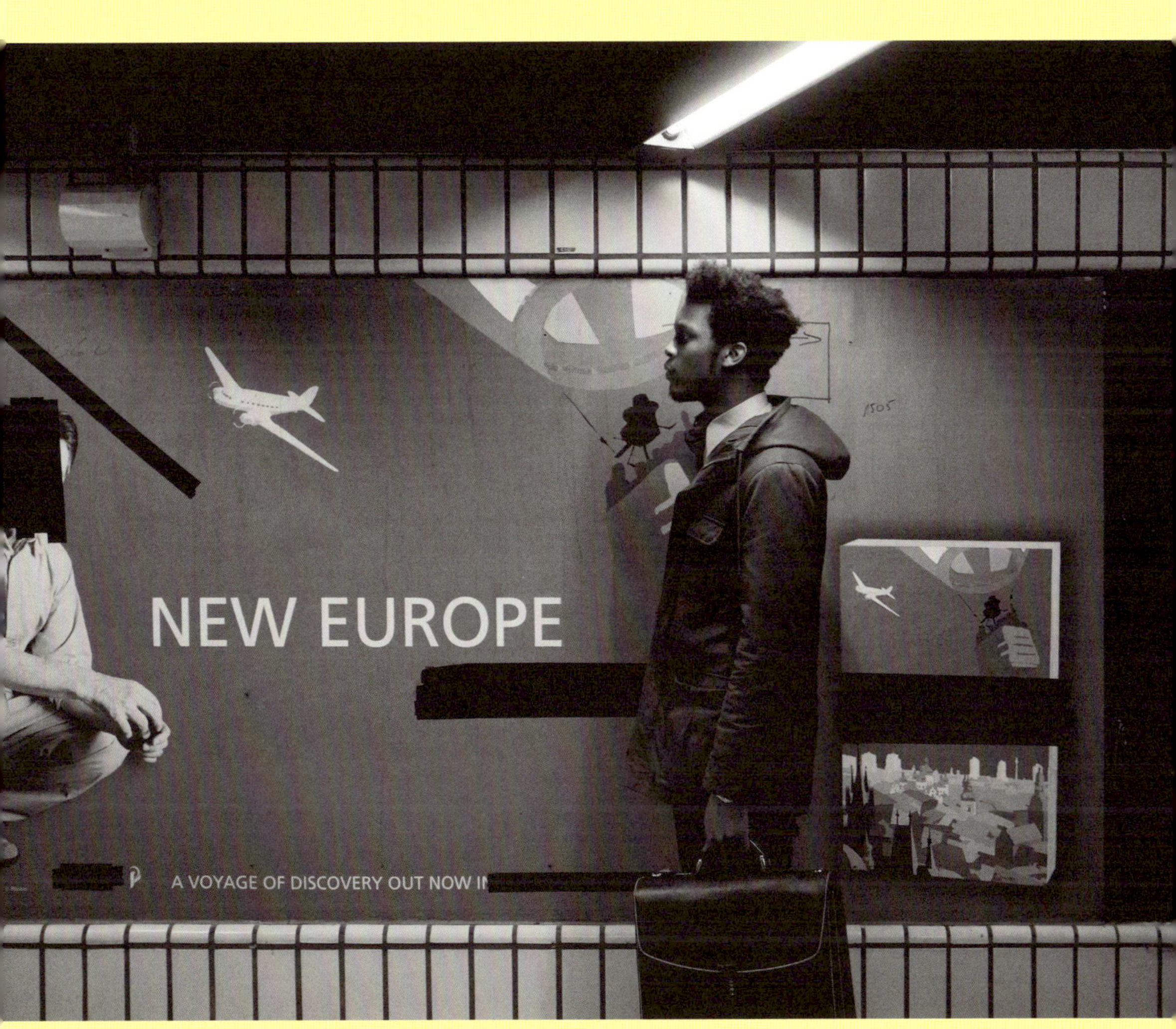
NEW EUROPE
A VOYAGE OF DISCOVERY OUT NOW IN

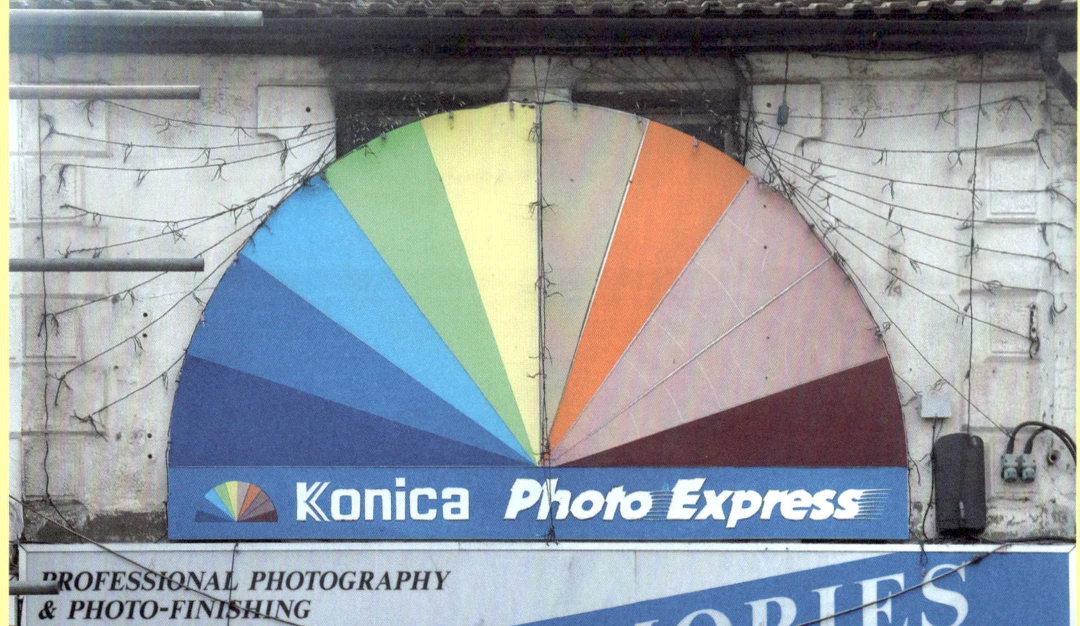
Konica Photo Express
PROFESSIONAL PHOTOGRAPHY
& PHOTO-FINISHING
PHOTO MEMORIES
KENTS PREMIER IMAGING CENTRE
COMPUTER DESIGN
& IMAGE MANIPULATION
MASTER
PASSPORT
Visas
Bus pass
ID cards
Driving licence
PORTRAIT STUDIO
dpd

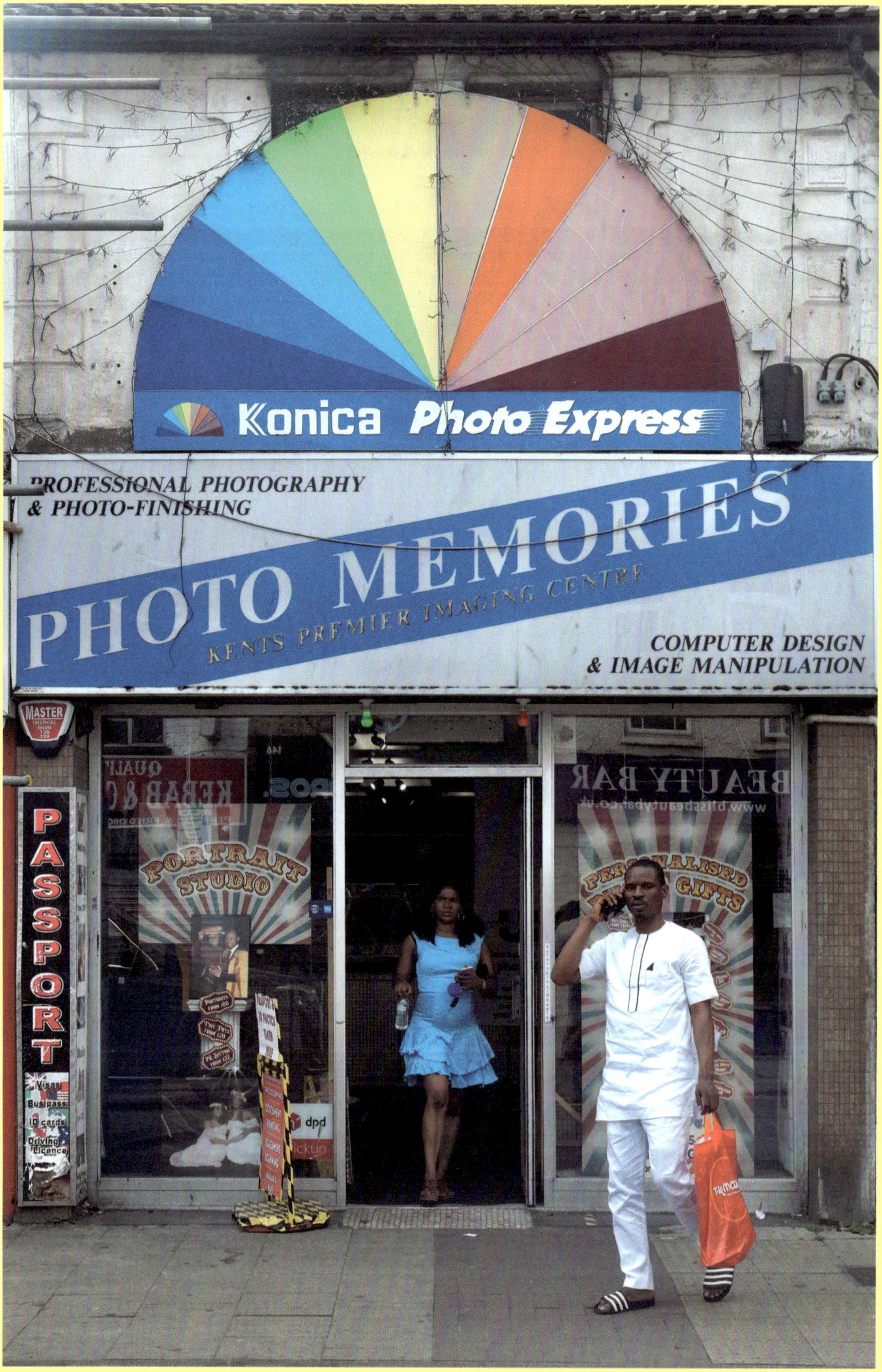

Every year, *The Eyes* offers its readers a cross-cutting vision on a contemporary social subject. This free and engaged editorial approach exists thanks to the support of loyal partners who are also close to the artists of today. This section is devoted to the programmes they carry out and the projects they support.

Contents:

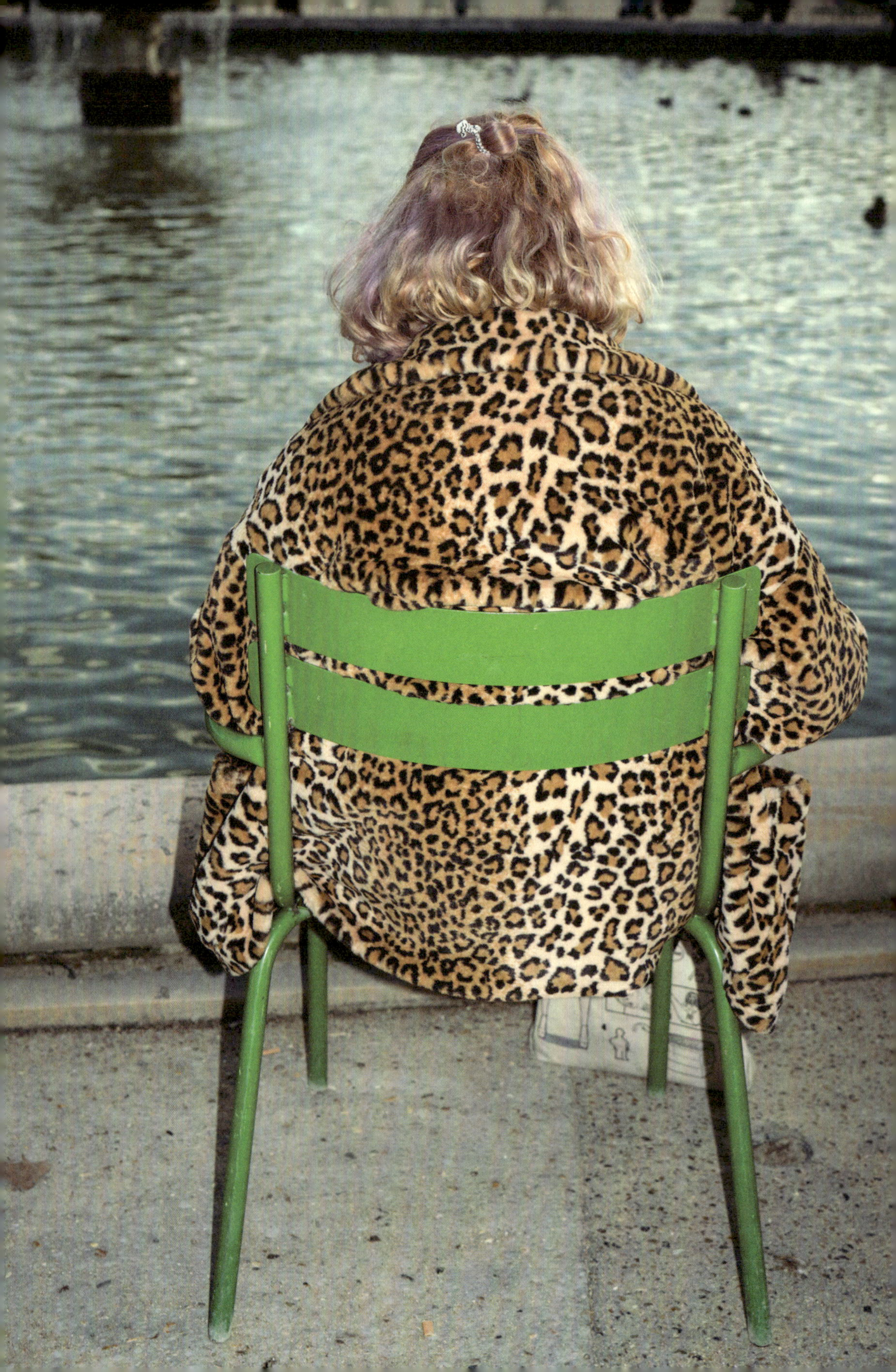

# FANTASY PARIS, FANTASTIC PARIS

A single format, pages with rounded corners, a colourful linen cover enhanced with a small-sized photograph: the Fashion Eye books are as elegant to look at as they are pleasant to hold in hand. Focused on the themes of travel, art and fashion, this collection conceived by Louis Vuitton reflects the brand. Created in 2016 by Julien Guerrier, it now holds close to 30 books on a host of cities, regions and countries: Venice, New York, the French Riviera, Monte Carlo, Saint-Tropez, Morocco, Japan, Shanghai, etc. An invitation to travel to distant or nearby dreamlike destinations, but also to more unusual parts of the world such as Iran, along the Silk Road or on an expedition on the mythical *Orient Express*.

The collection alternates between internationally established photographers, past and present, and emerging talents: Cecil Beaton, Saul Leiter, Helmut Newton, Adolph de Meyer, Kourtney Roy or Sarah Moon. And while some of the images come from archives, others are recent, produced via cartes blanches offered to the photographers.

Paris now holds a special place in the collection, with already three volumes dedicated to the French capital. And understandably so, as the city has always been a favourite subject for many photographers ever since the advent of the medium – not to mention the humanists who relished the capital. After a dive into the archives of Jeanloup Sieff for a black-and-white edition, two new publications have recently been released: one authored Melvin Sokolsky, the other, Feng Li, respectively born in New York in 1933 and in China in 1971; on one hand, a "historical" perspective with "Bubble" and "Fly", two fashion commissions for Harper's Bazaar made in 1963 and 1965 that include unpublished colour images recently unearthed and rediscovered by their author; on the other, an unclassifiable contemporary expression, mixture of street photography and burlesque, the result of a four-month residency in the French capital.

As foreigners, Melvin Sokolsky and Feng Li both took a fresh look at the eternal subject. Using wide shots, Sokolsky turns the city – Paris in "Bubble" and Saint-Germain-en-Laye in "Fly" – into a proper character. In the case of Feng Li, the capital is considered more like a decor. Driven by the human, the photographer roamed the city looking for the unusual: "My purpose is not to give my point of view about this city or that country. I'm only interested in human beings, be they Chinese, French or Berliners, because they all share a certain universal complexity that could be described as humanity," he explains in the interview published in this volume.

*Paris*, Melvin Sokolsky
Louis Vuitton Éditions
Fashion Eye
2021
&
*Paris*, Feng Li
Louis Vuitton Éditions
Fashion Eye
2021

Images:
Melvin Sokolsky and
Feng Li

Text:
Sophie Bernard

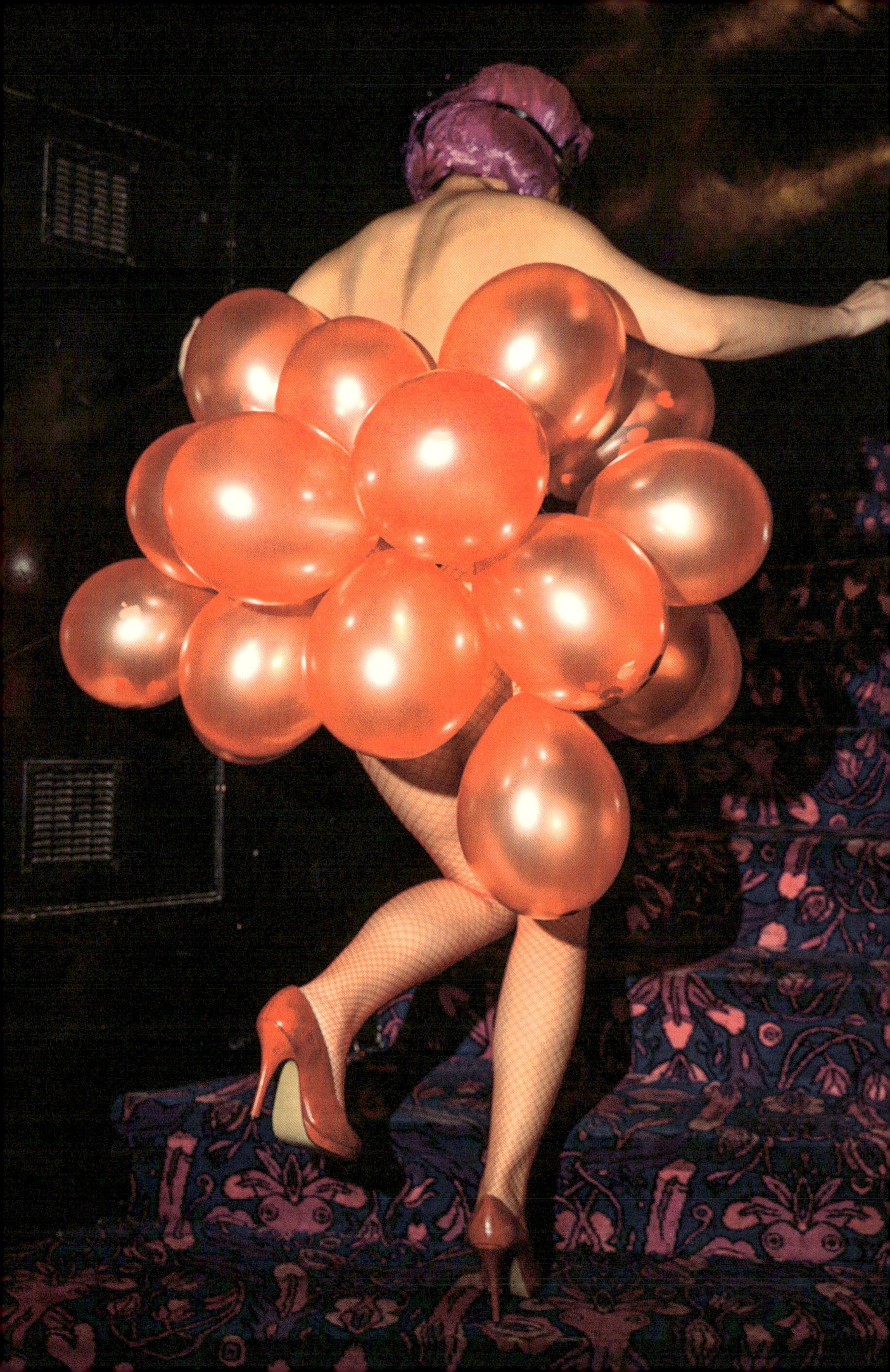

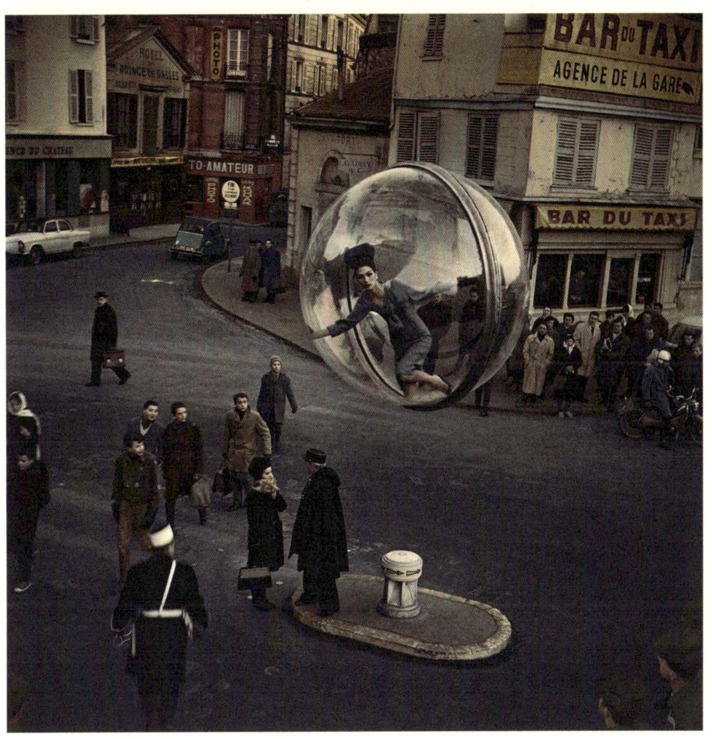


While both Melvin Sokolsky and Feng Li play with the symbols of Paris, their perception is very different, even opposite. With the bridges, the River Seine, the stairs and the Parisian rooftops, the American photographer depicts a romantic atmosphere wrapped in all the finery of humanist photography; while the Chinese artist, as is usual with him, humorously and mischievously plays with the monuments. So while the real Eiffel Tower makes a few appearances in the 90 images gathered in the volume, what is mostly noticeable are its miniature avatars that he found along his strolls. Whether he sets his lens on the Iron Lady, the Louvre Pyramid, the Arc de Triomphe or the banks of the Seine, Feng Li's perspective is systematically shifted, an encounter with the absurd. Thanks to the use of the flash, he transforms the real into magic, emphasizes the bizarre and surprises us. Away from the cliché, he makes a living stage of Paris where the bodies seem to play hide-and-seek with his lens, as if engaging in a strange choreography within the urban environment, and turning the constraints of the image into an asset.

Melvin Sokolsky's images also hold their bit of madness ... With him, we note a great mastery of the staging in "Bubble", realized on site, and of the composition in "Fly", which is the result of photomontages. Melvin Sokolsky certainly is astute. His imagination has no limit, at least not in terms of technique. Yes, Paris will always be Paris, but no "déjà vu" here, neither with Melvin Sokolsky nor with Feng Li.

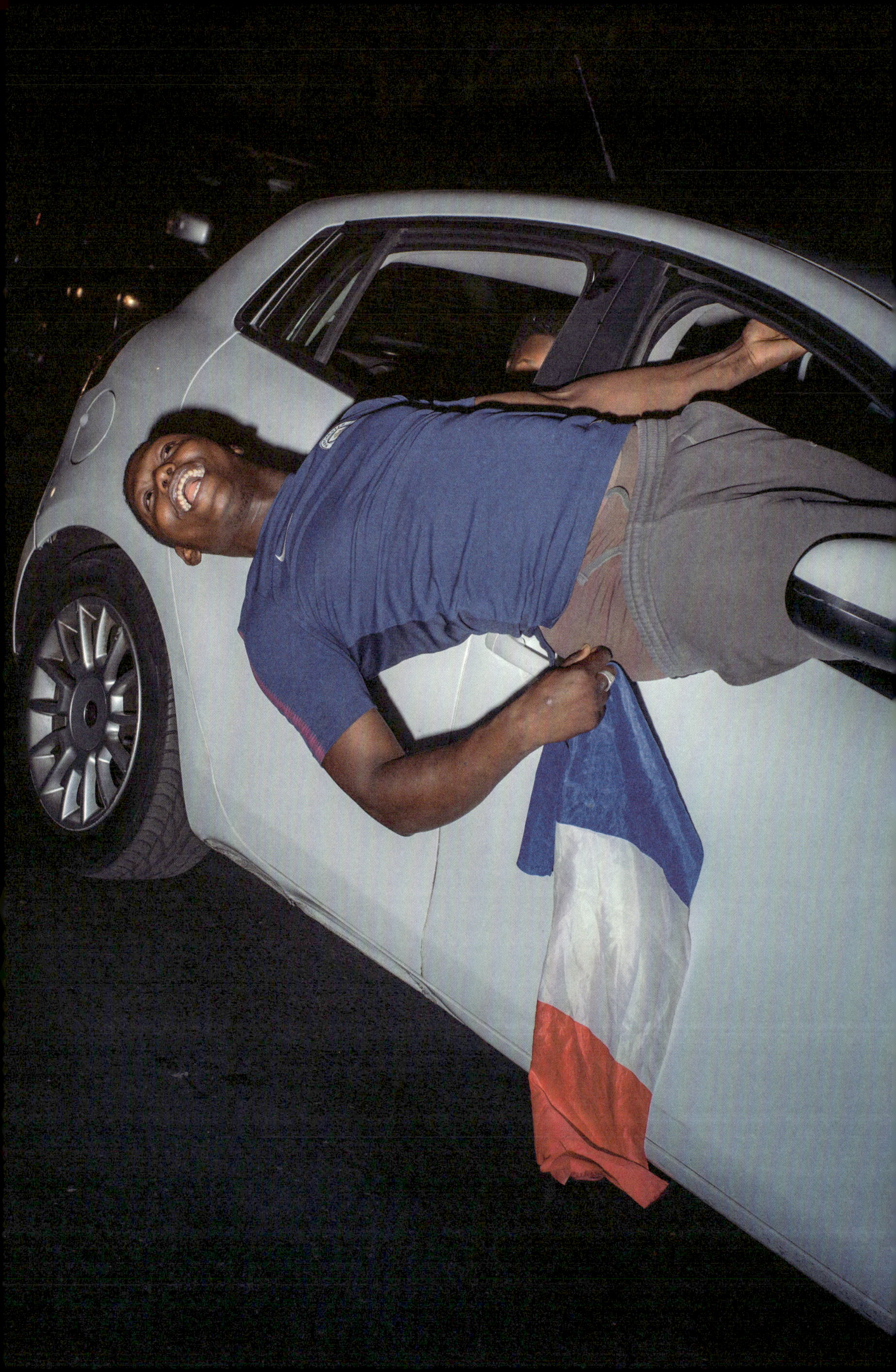

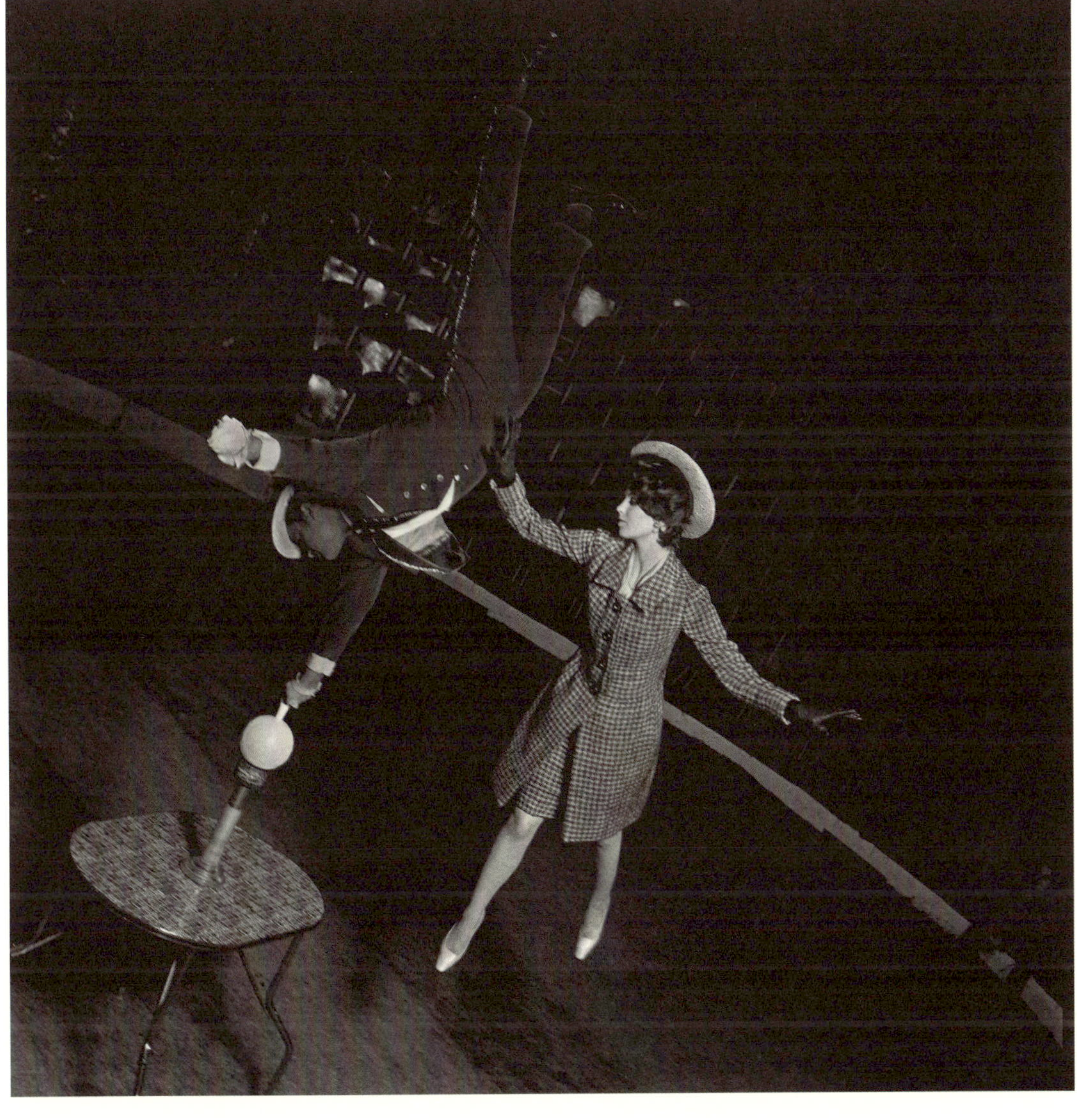

# PRAISE OF NATURE

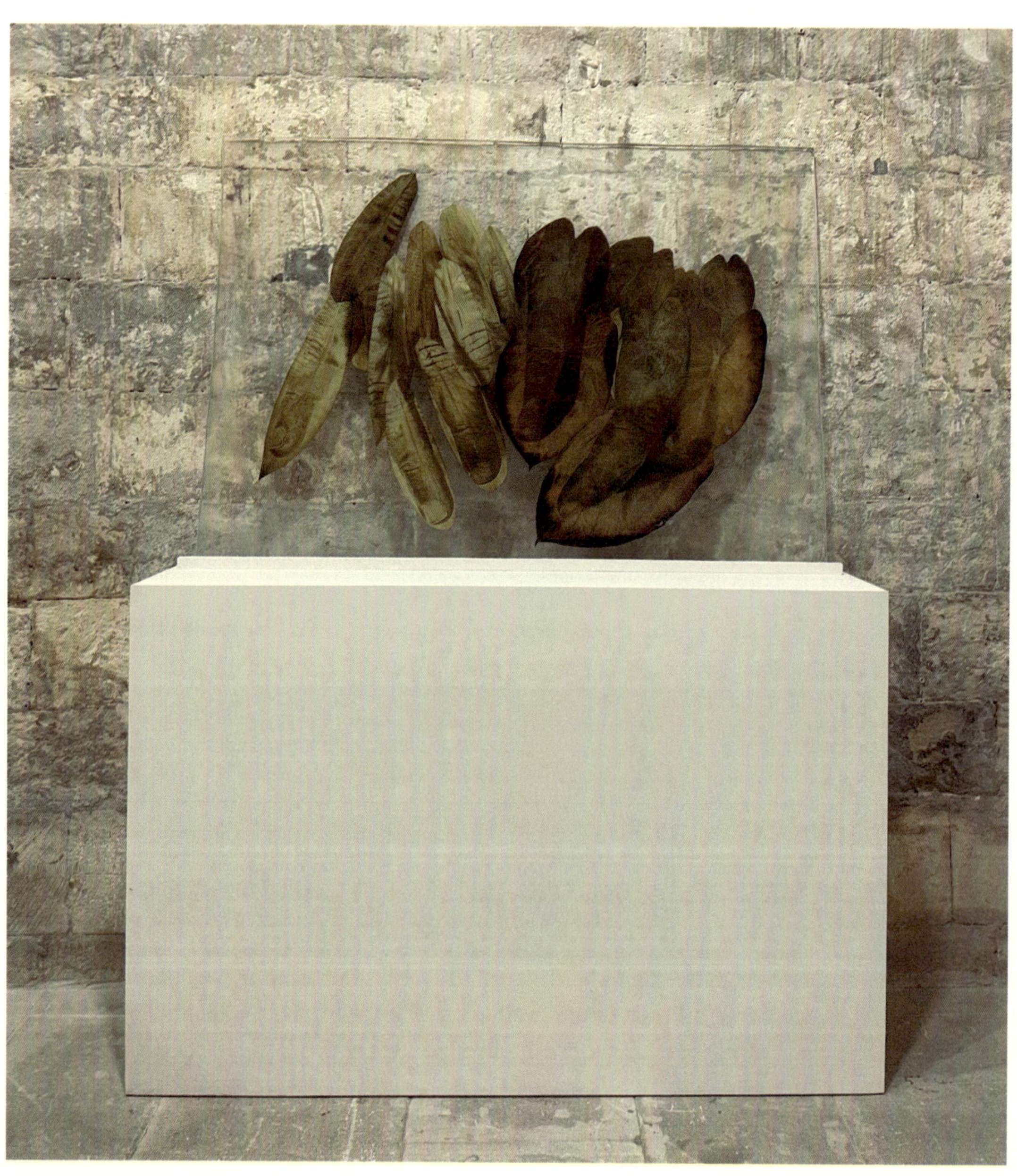

# ODE TO LIGHT

Images:
Almudena Romero
series produced in the framework of the BMW Residency

Text:
Vincent Marcilhacy

*The Pigment Change*, published by BMW Arts and Culture/de l'air, des livres, 2021.

The BMW Residency is a carte blanche given to a photographer every year since 2011, in association with GOBELINS, l'École de l'Image. Dedicated to photographic innovation and transmission, the BMW Residency encourages experimentation and research into new means of expression and photographic approaches.

For this 10th edition, Almudena Romero has developed both an experimental and scientific approach to natural photographic production, focusing on pigmentary changes, with an ecological and societal focus.


Exhibition "*The Pigment Change*"
by Almudena Romero at the Rencontres d'Arles in the framework of the BMW Residency.
*The Pigment Change, Chapter III: Family Album*
*The Pigment Change, Chapter III: Family Album*
*The Pigment Change, Chapter II: Offspring*
*The Pigment Change, Chapter I: The Act of Producing*

"My interest today is in the work of Stefano Mancuso, an Italian researcher who established a neurobiology laboratory in Florence. Through plant neurobiology, he is demonstrating the dynamics of plants' neural system. Plants too might be able to produce art ..." Almudena Romero takes us into a parallel world, a world where photosynthesis is at the heart of the writing and creative process. Why produce more, wonders the artist, whether material work or ourselves on earth? What is our sustainable future, then? In trying to understand how photosynthesis works, Almudena Romero questions our role on the planet, through the awareness of environmental protection as much as the materiality of the image, whose original nature must be preserved.

The majority of the series presented here are the result of a carte blanche invitation extended by the BMW Residency to the artist for one year to carry out her unique experiments. In the industrial sector strongly impacted by environmental issues and threats, BMW is looking for alternatives and a path to a more virtuous model, particularly with ambitious targets to reach a share of at least 50% of electric vehicles sold each year by 2030. This goal has been pursued by the German automotive group through the programme RE:THINK, RE:DUCE, RE:USE, RE:CYCLE. By supporting artists who are committed to these social issues, the BMW Residency thus encourages dialogue on these key issues and its own role towards a sustainable environment.

Her interest in plants began with her grandmother, whose garden was teeming with an extraordinary variety of species. Almudena Romero later became a specialist in 19-century techniques, processes that would become her speciality as a photographic artist. It was in fact in the 19th century that this research into vegetal photography began: colour photography is the result of scientific research into natural pigments, an avenue ultimately abandoned in favour of chemical

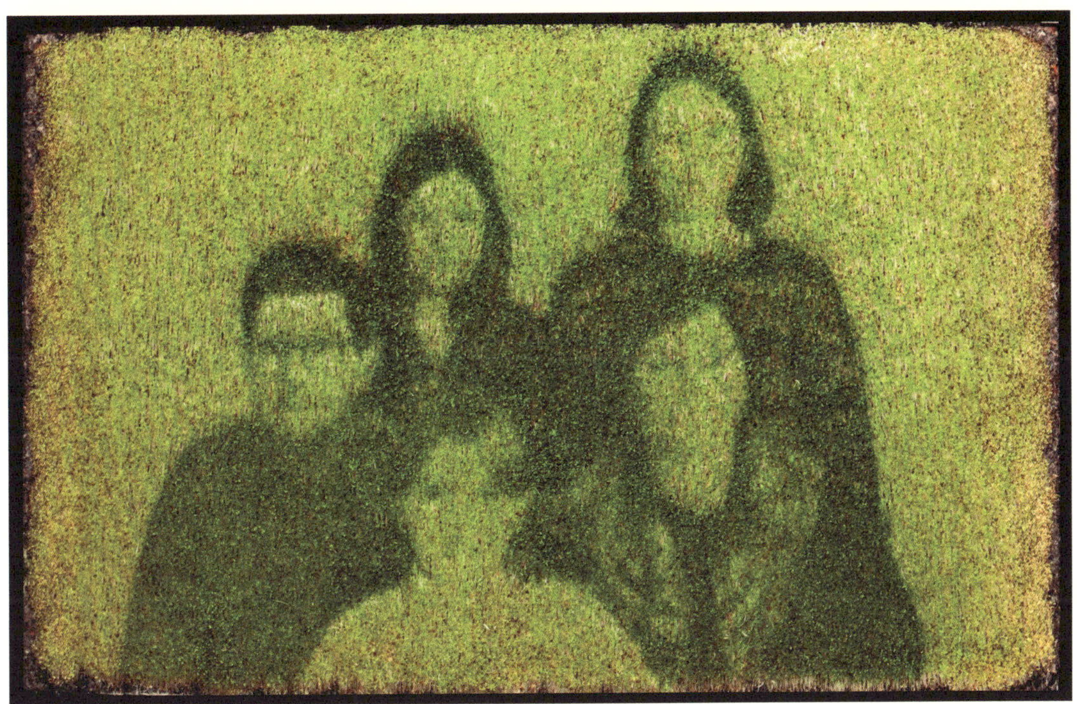

photography. Romero resumes this research by taking it further through the use of living matter.

In her early series, such as "The Act of Producing", Romero questions the need for her own production when faced with environmental issues. These are photographs of her hands directly revealed on petals and leaves, and subsequently fixed in natural resin – pine resin having the property of being able to filter light and stop the evolution of living matter. She found the species conducive to her experiments in her grandmother's garden – where all plants seem to want to grow. She then explored various techniques, such as the application of a negative on petals by transparency using a translucent layer or glass; the petal then takes the light that will whiten the pigments, requiring five days of exposure under the great Spanish sun ... Or the projection on a sheet that must drink water and receive sunlight to stay alive; the leaf transforms UV energy into chemical energy that will modify the pigment of the chlorophyll.

In the series "The Pigment Change", produced as part of the BMW Art & Culture Residency, Almudena Romero uses the natural photosynthesis function of watercress to evoke the fragility of family memory. By projecting a family archive on a panel covered with cress seeds, she uses photosynthesis to reveal the image before letting it disappear again: the parts receiving the most light produce the most chlorophyll, unlike the less-illuminated areas, which remain paler.

“It took me a lot of time to find a seed with satisfactory results, one that allows for details.” “The Pigment Change” imposes a revelation process of the image in which any detail counts for the artist. Since there is no soil and only seeds, it is necessary to select the watercress seeds that will be best suited. Then, the quality of the water is essential: unsatisfactory in Paris or London, where Romero has worked, it is the water in her grandmother’s garden that enabled a reduced revelation time of the image, from 10 days down to 3, and finer results. To produce the watercress piece presented at the Théâtre Antique for the opening week of the Rencontres d’Arles, Almudena Romero transported 12 litres of water from her native countryside by BlaBlaCar [French carpooling platform] ...

In another series, Almudena Romero used a plant that produces only two leaves over the span of its life. Every day for 30 days she made an image of the leaf growing. The artist invites us to a metaphor of the process of natural development, to reflect again on a sustainable future that should, like plants, respond to natural elements and phenomena. By returning to the essence of the image, writing with light; by taking the time to observe evolution, what nature teaches us; and finally by questioning our responsibility when confronted with the state of the world, Almudena Romero meticulously demonstrates how art can actually encourage us to make *Homo sapiens* evolve in the face of the world (or monster, we might even say, in light of sustainable development problems) that he created and in which he tends to retreat.

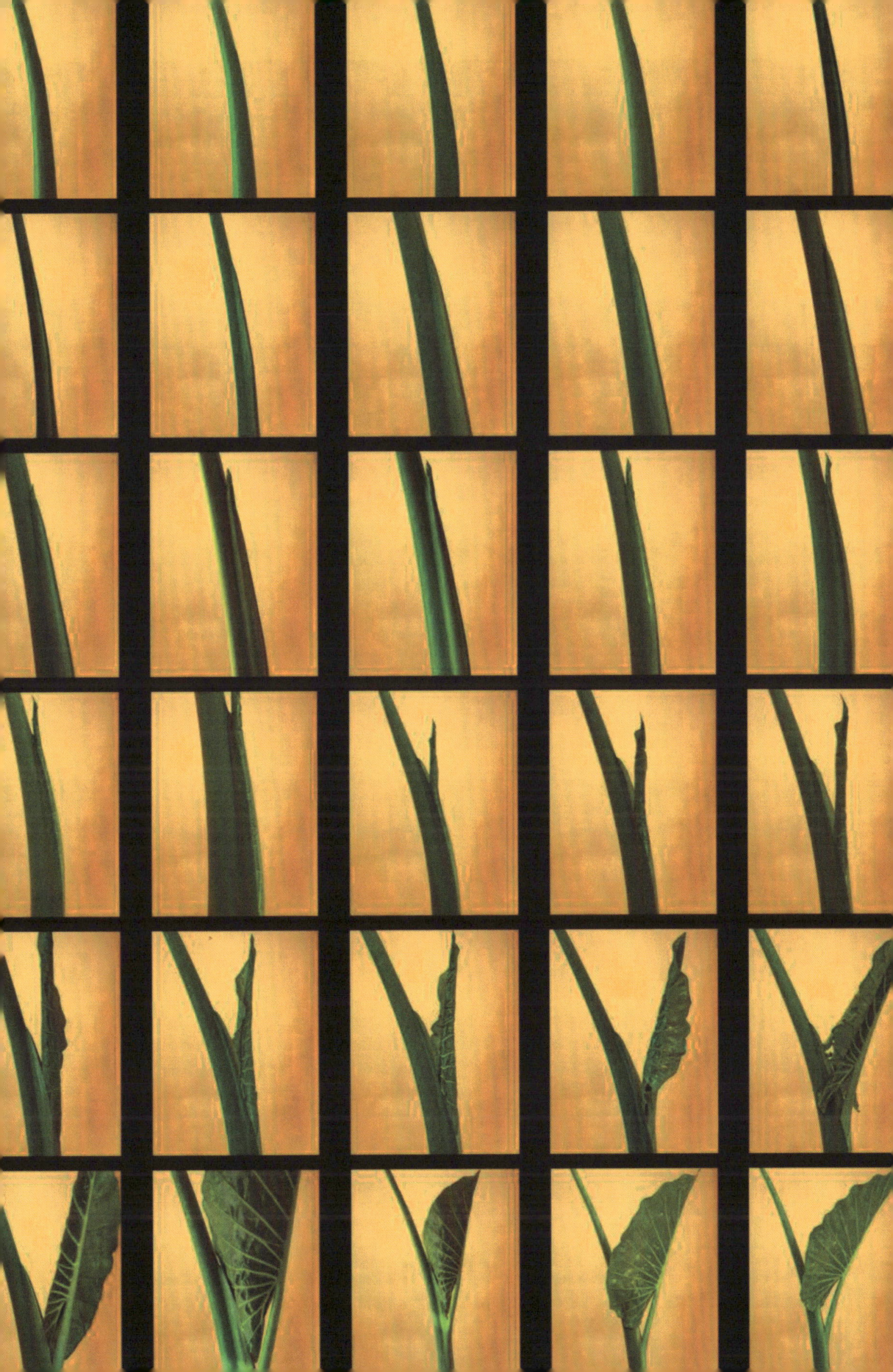

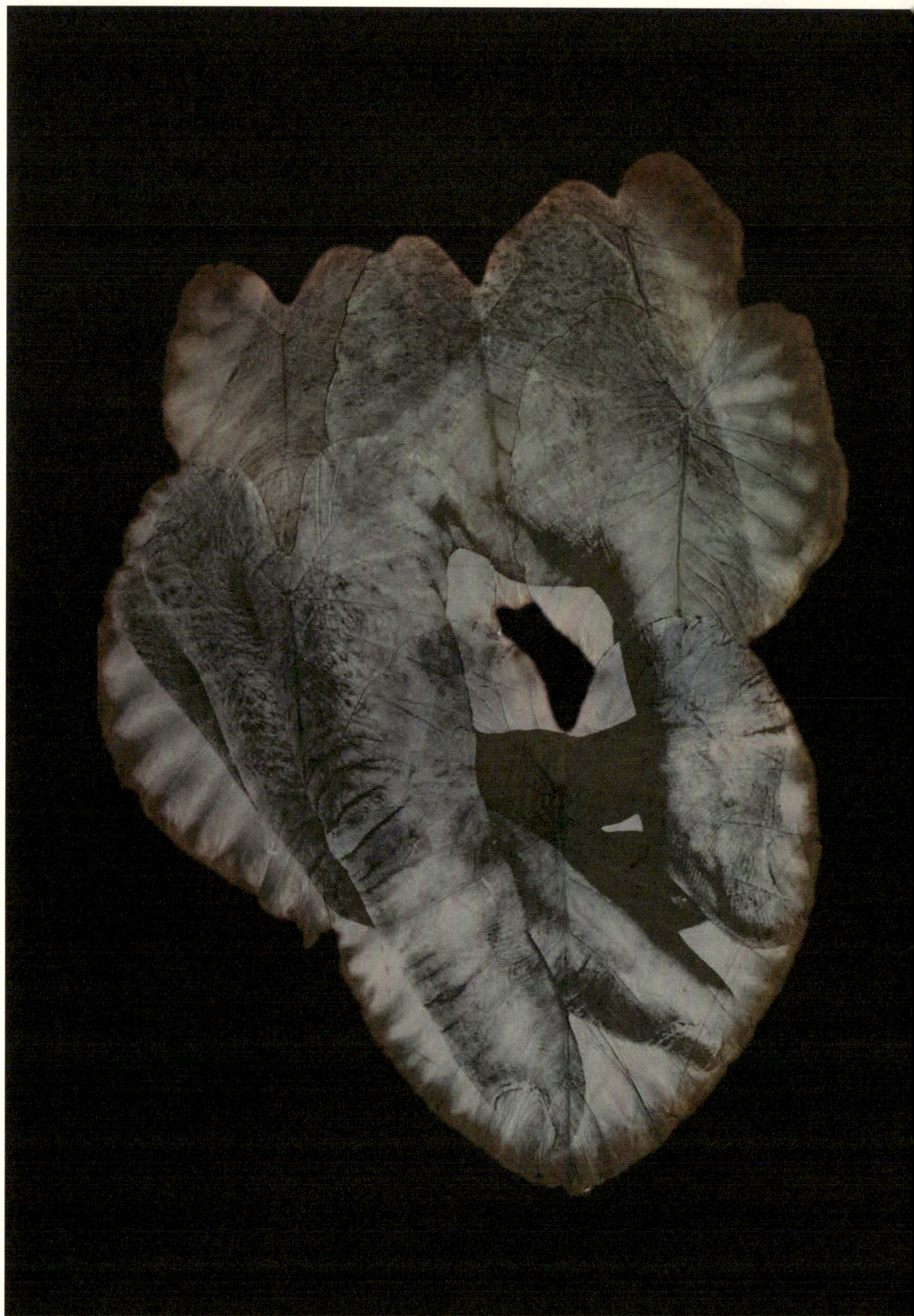

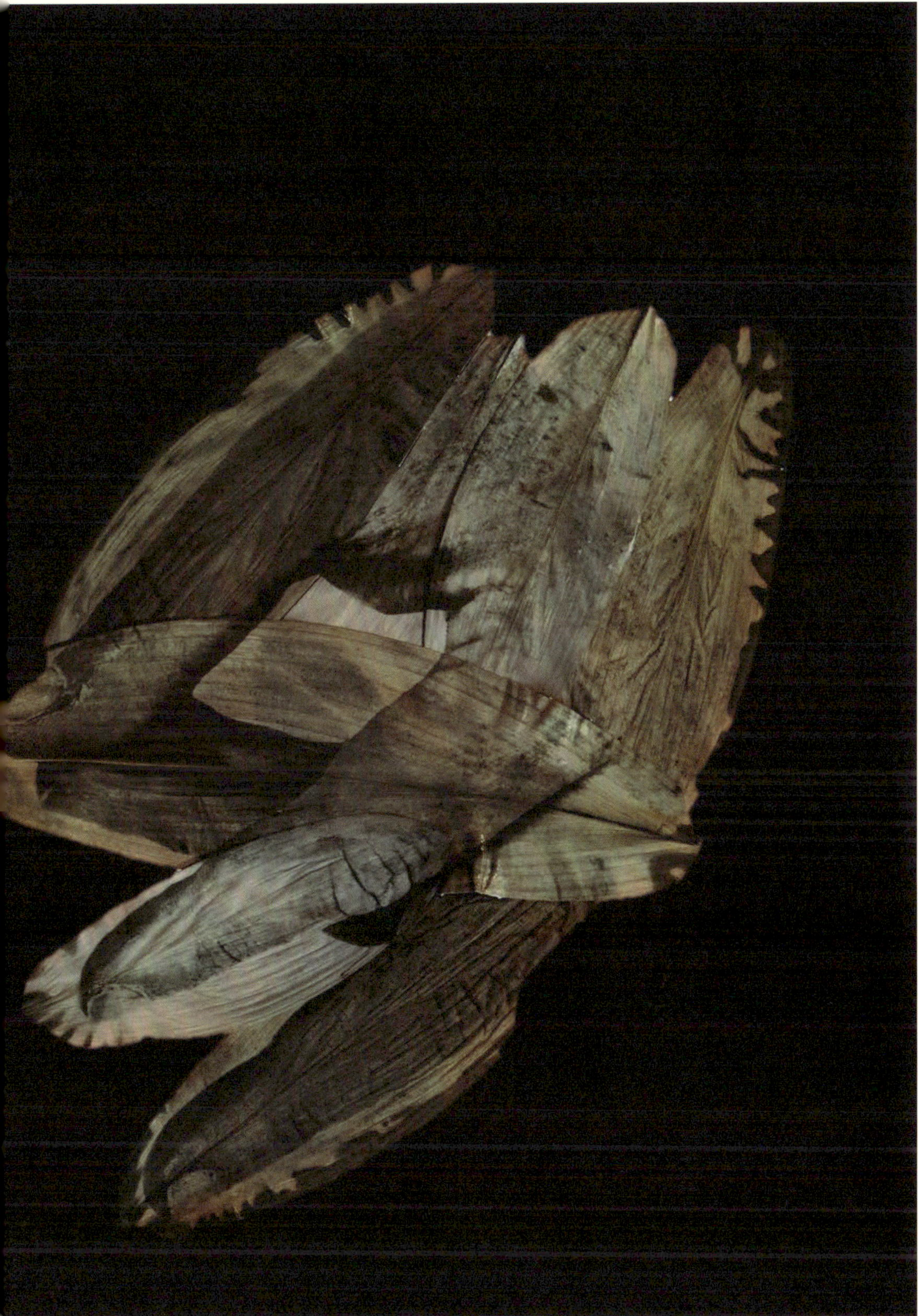

# THE ONE WHO KNOWS HOW TO GIVE A VOICE TO VENUES

Images:
Gosette Lubondo

Text:
Valentin Marceau

To be introduced to Gosette Lubondo's photography is to be introduced to the representation of waking dreams, those that we all live in a present inhabited by traces, memories, our imagination. Each of her images is an imaginary journey. As her gallerist Pierre Daybert writes about her work, "ultimately, her imaginary travels are an invitation to our own wanderings through time". These photographs animate our own experience of the past through imaginary journeys, where, far from showing us the way, Lubondo invites us to escape, even if it is clear that the power of heritage and personal history lies at the heart of her artistic approach.

She discovered photography at the age of 14 by replacing at short notice the official photographer (a man) for a family celebration whose organizer, a woman, had decided it had to be a women-only event. That was a revelation for her, one that she would quickly choose to perfect with her father. And in an equally original way, she chose to make it her profession by enrolling at the age of 18 at the Académie des Beaux-Arts in Kinshasa, against her father's wish for her to register,


Carte blanche, Maison Ruinart, 2021
Carte blanche, Maison Ruinart, 2021
*Imaginary Trip*, 2016
*Imaginary Trip II*, 2016

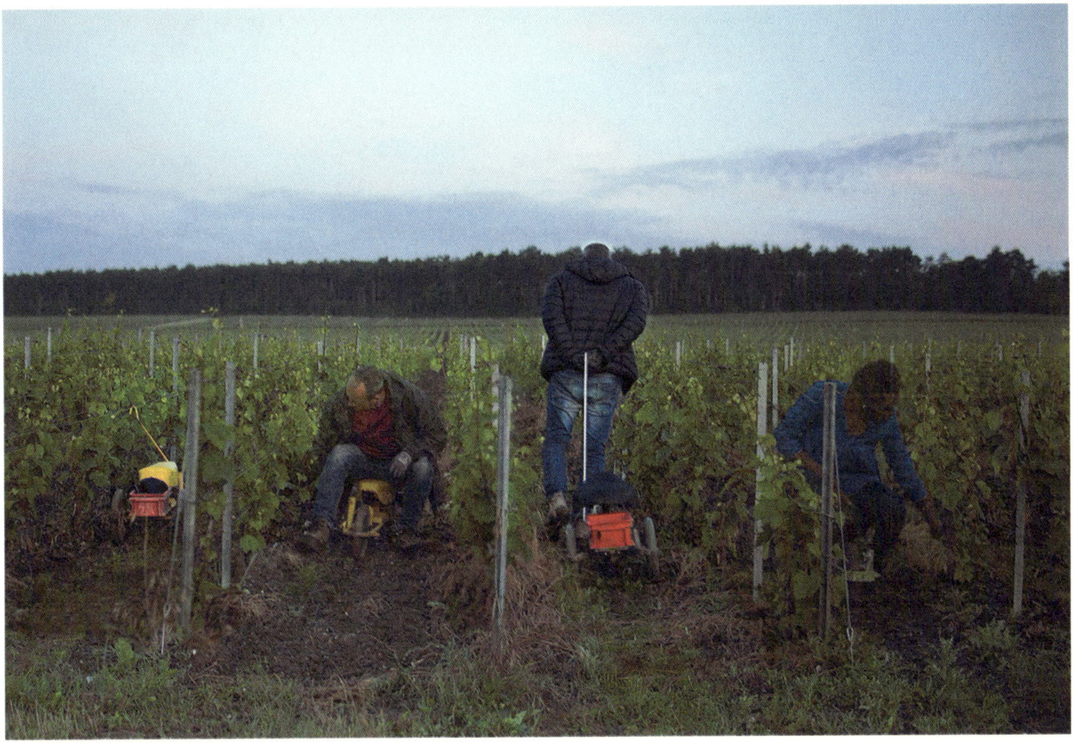

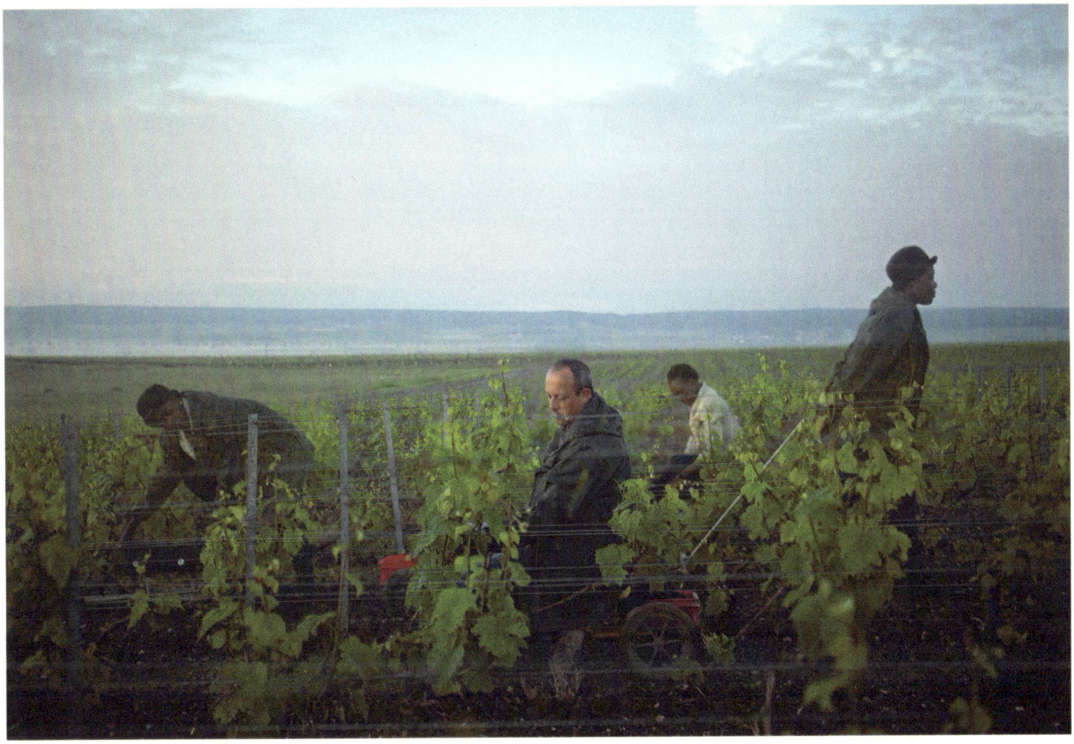

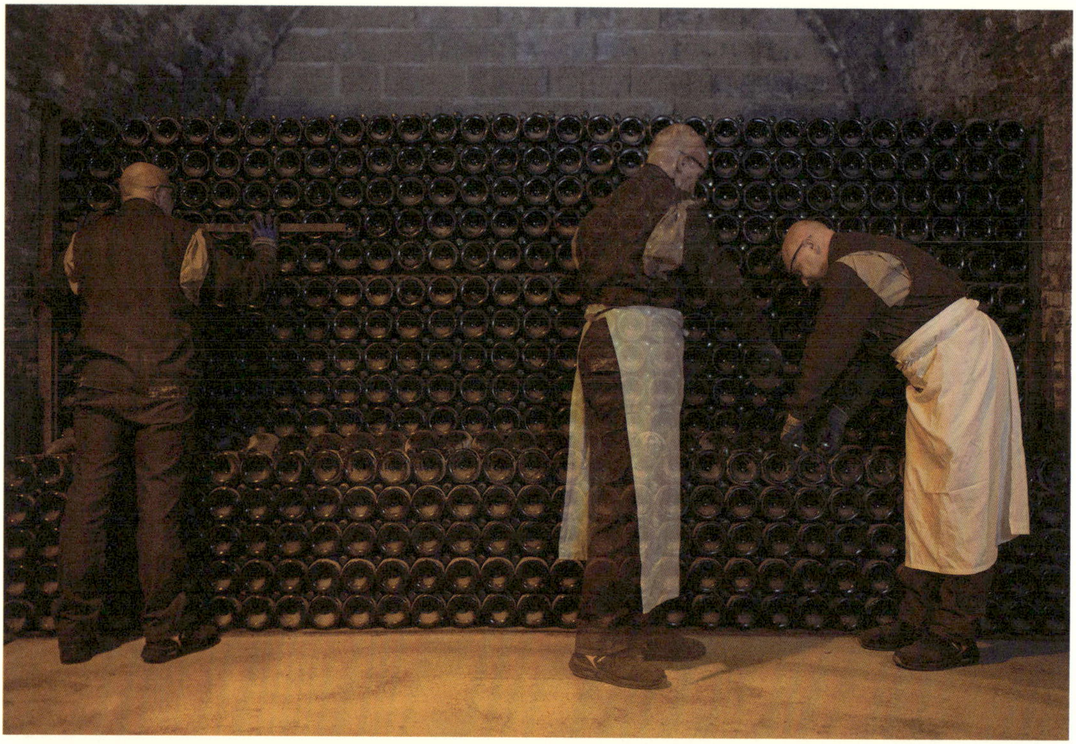

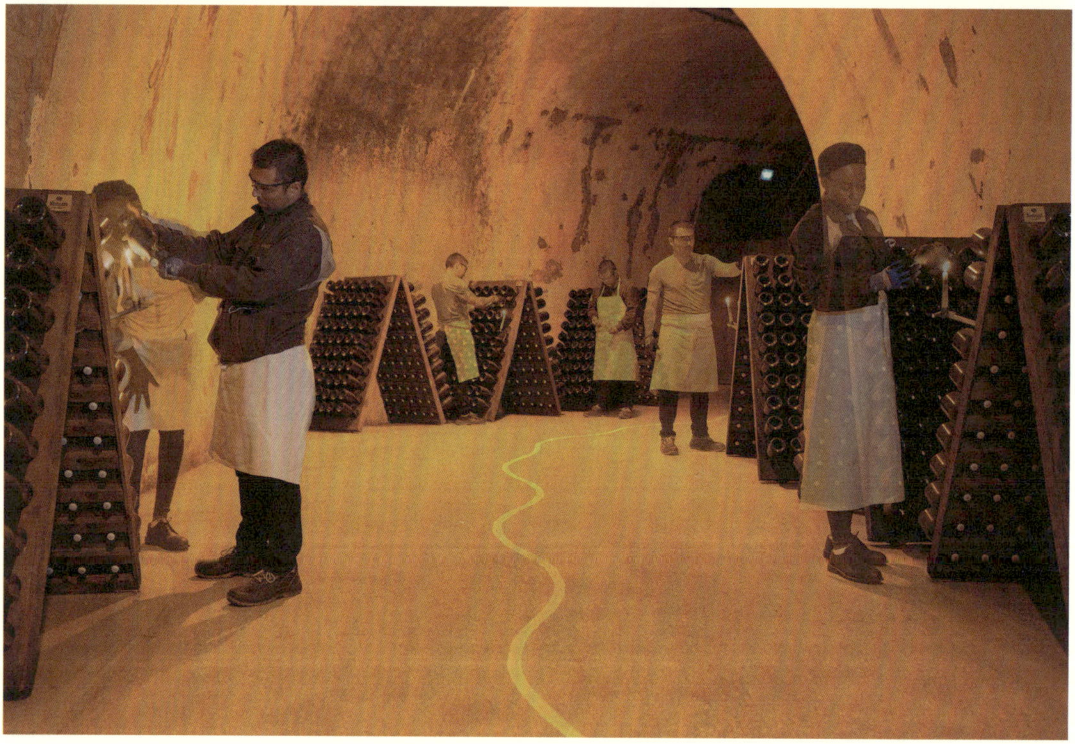

that same day, at the nearby Institute of Communication. This should not come as a surprise considering that her father's uncle was one of the very first Congolese photographers at the end of the 19th century, and that it was Gosette Lubondo's own father, Gaston Yana-Mambu Diakota, who took over after his uncle. Lubondo has since patiently forged a strong and coherent artistic identity in which she explores the memory of once-remarkable places that have now fallen into oblivion.

Champagne Ruinart offered their latest carte blanche to such an independent and intuitive personality. As in most of her series, in which the artist visits landmarks of her personal history or of the memory of Congolese history, Gosette Lubondo wants to bring the know-how infused through generations of craftsmen into the images she delivers of her stay in Champagne. Often, here again, the people – the craftsmen at Maison Ruinart – appear in a ghostly manner, through overprinting or double printing, almost evanescent. Such a ghostly – even mystical – tone in some of her work is, so to speak, a trademark for Gosette Lubondo, coupled with an intense personal involvement in many of her photographs. It was in 2016 that she decided to establish this device and started producing the series that would reveal her, "Au fil du temps" (As time goes by). She took hold of a disused train in the Kinshasa railway station and conceived a staged project by introducing characters to explore both the memory of the place and the aesthetics. By setting herself in a coach, Lubondo renders mobile what has been abandoned over the years, suspending the exalting promises of the journey. In another series, "Imaginary Trip II", this time it's an old school founded in 1936 by a Christian congregation that she takes over, a school that has deeply marked the personal trajectory of several generations of inhabitants in what is now called Kongo Central and their descendants. Most of the time, her compositions suggest suspended or frozen movements. The viewer is uncertain of what they are seeing, questioning the existence of the venues, looking for elements about their real history, what they are hiding from us or what they are preserving for us. Ruinart does not escape the project of this artist, who, calmly and with unstinting humility, has come to question the living of these environments, from the lungs to the brain, scrutinizing their memory in the transparency of the bodies and the breathing of the stones.

Christine Barthe, who recently showed the artist at the Musée du Quai Branly, tells of the singular, enigmatic dimension in Gosette Lubondo's work when she writes that "her images possess the charm of the legend, and a power of fascination driven by seducing colours, the apparent simplicity of the forms and the mystery of a meaning that suddenly escapes the viewer". This is no doubt one of the characteristics of these emerging artists in the creation of great works. Gosette Lubondo is building a personal body of work that, while focusing primarily on shedding light on the history and reality of her native Congo, nevertheless illuminates far beyond, thus acquiring an almost universal quality.

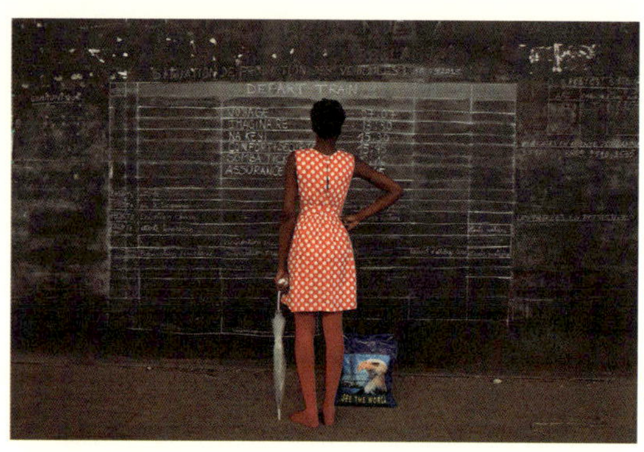
DEPART TRAIN
ASSURANCE
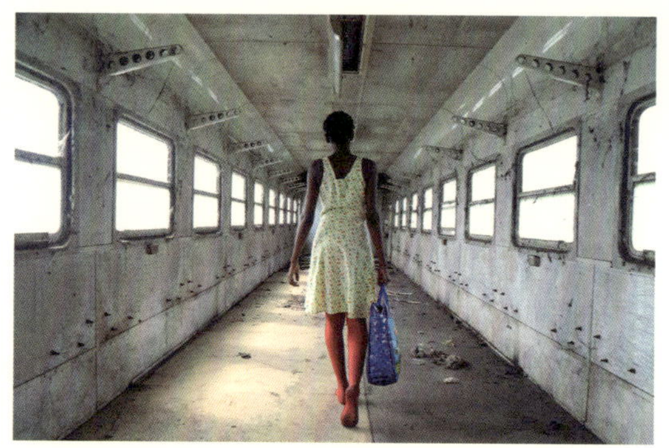
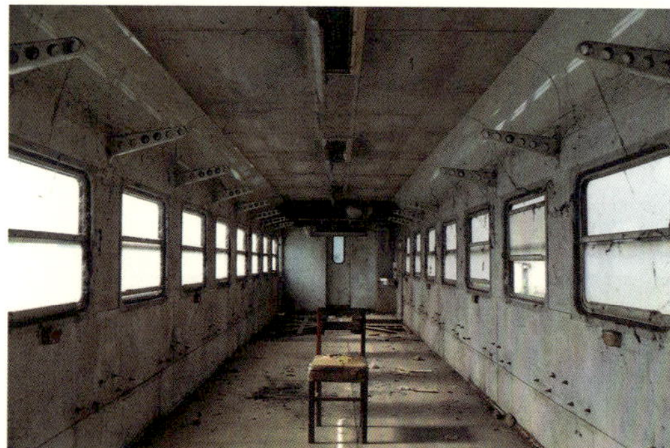
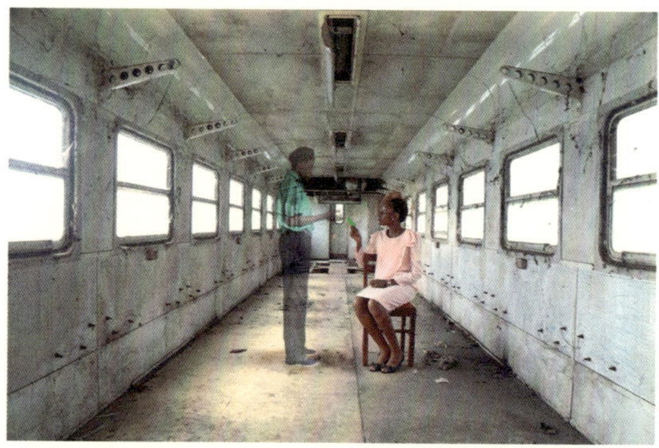
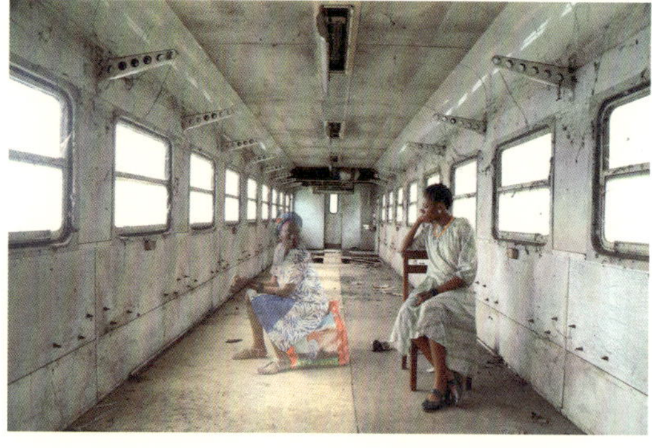
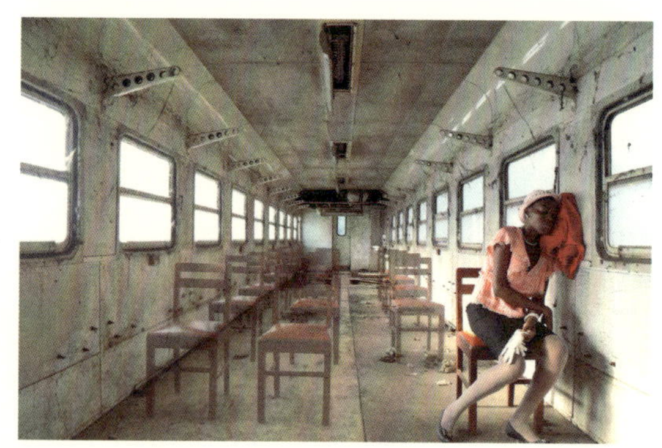

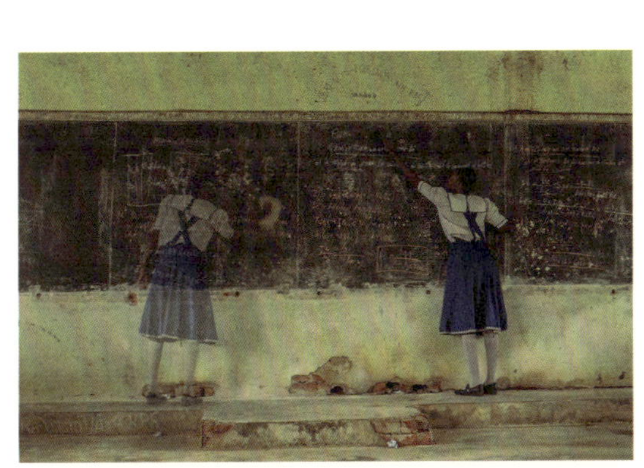
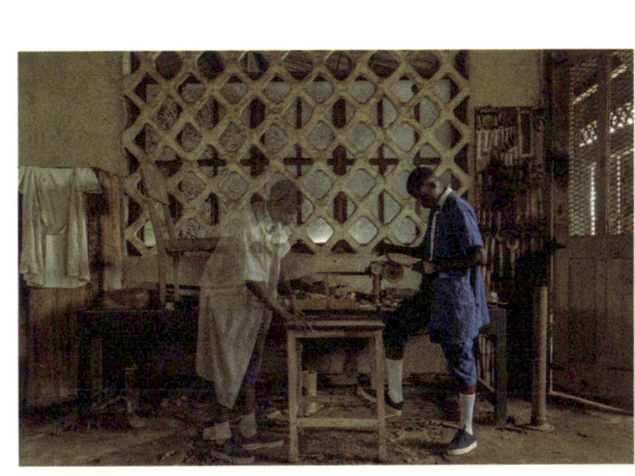
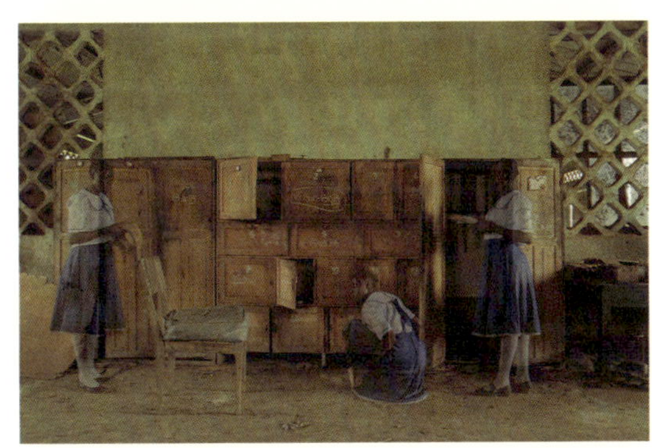
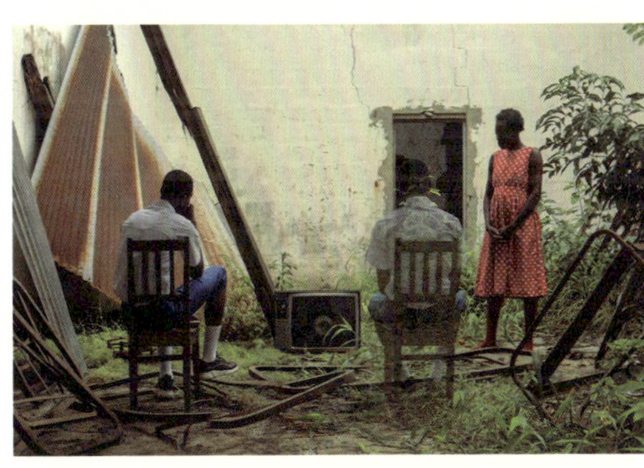
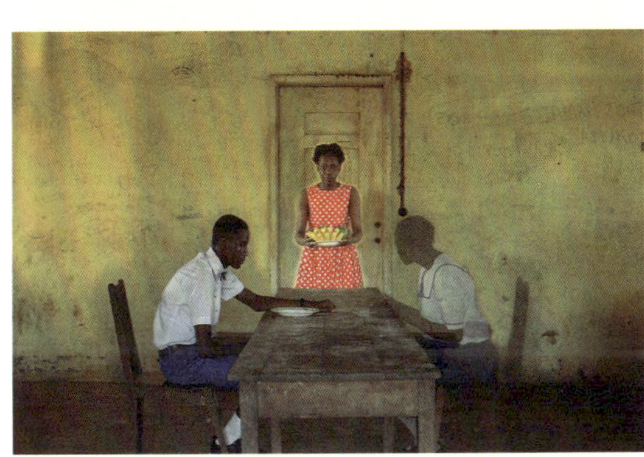
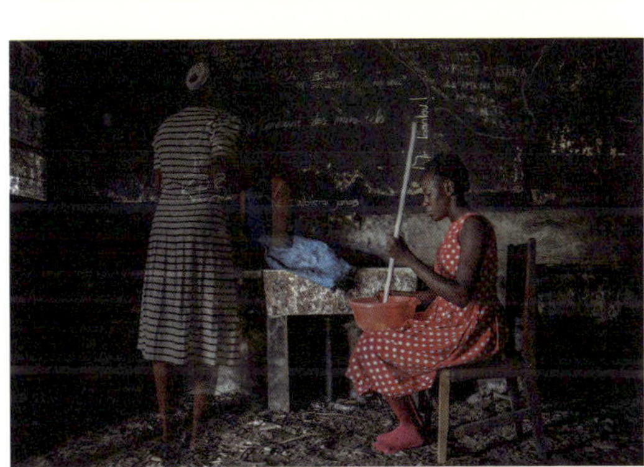

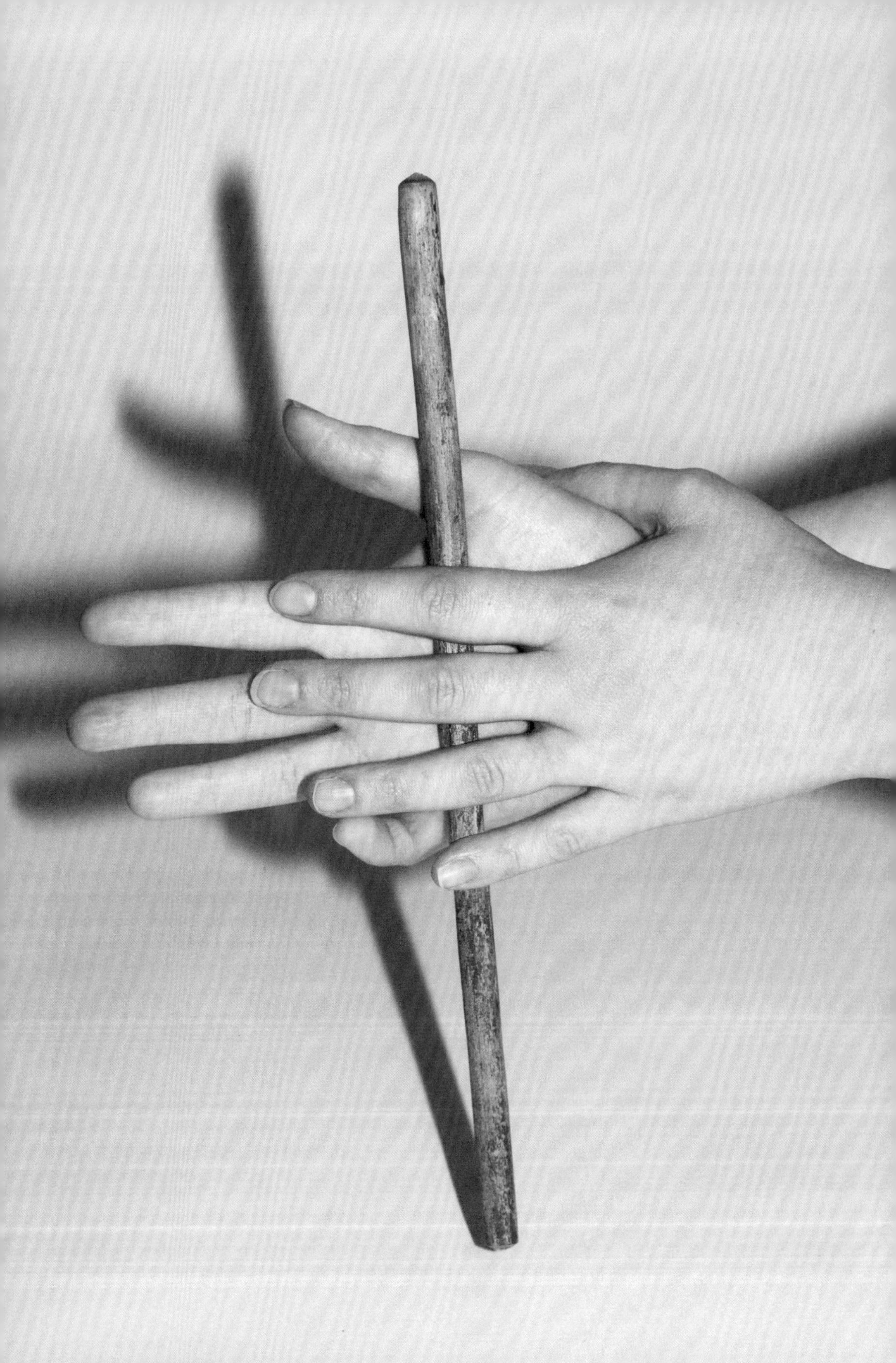

# CHANGING TIMES

Images:
Artists and curators invited in the field of the Parallel Programme

Text:
Rémi Coignet

*Changing Times:*
*Art Facing a New World*
The Eyes Publishing, 2021

Parallel is a platform that brings together creative European organizations committed to promoting cross-cultural exchanges and mentorships in order to set new standards in contemporary photography

Page 230: © Thomas Wynne, *I Send Forth, I Promise*
Page 233: © Glorija Lizde, *Fearless Youth, Petrijevci*
Page 234: © Agata Wieczorek, *Artefacts*
Page 235: © Aad Hoogendoorn, *The Logo of the Institution Formerly Known as the Witte de With Center for Contemporary Art in Rotterdam*, 2020
© Negar Yaghmaian

Observing the diversity of the answers provided by the artists gathered in this volume when questioned on the notion of "changing times" can only bring to mind Giorgio Agamben's definition of contemporaneity: "The anachronism that allows us to seize our time in the form of a 'too early' that is also a 'too late', of an 'already' that is also a 'not yet'."[1] Indeed, it is between 'too late' and 'too early', between memory and anticipation, that the present of their work lies.

Too late for Glorija Lizde, who delves into the story of her grandfather, enlisted at the age of 15 in 1943 by the nationalist, fascist and anti-Semitic movement of the Ustaše, and wonders: "In what way should we be involved in the consequences of crimes that we have not witnessed?" A past that she anchors to the present by appropriating the autobiography of her grandfather, by finding the locations of tragedy and by making use of the self-portrait as a mask. What Lizde confronts is, to use the controversial expression of Hannah Arendt, the banality of evil.

Artist and curator Laura Konttinen questions the use of family albums by today's artists – precisely the anachronism noted by Agamben. It is when this photographic object is devalued (having lost its value of use and exchange) that it is symbolically revaluated by art.

The balance between too late and too early is precarious for Inês Marinho and Negar Yaghmaian, who revive the ancient practice of correspondence art, and for whom the anticipation of the recipient eagerly awaiting their correspondence is contemporaneous with the memory of the sender. These letter writers recreate a temporality of exchanges in our age of instant communication.

Artists and curators Seda Yildiz and Cihad Caner participate in a debate as timely as it is polarized on the museum institution, its function and its functioning. A debate in which the very notion of memory is an issue serving antagonistic objectives.

Resolutely oriented towards anticipation are Agata Wieczorek and Thomas Wynne.

The former is concerned with the virtualization of our very bodies under the effect of technology, which Jacques Ellul has described as a process that, having eluded humans, enslaves rather than benefits them.[2] Wieczorek, however, elegantly and shrewdly overturns her own proposition, pointing to the alienation that access denial can create. For example, the prohibition of the right to have an abortion in Poland today.

The latter contemplates the probable colonization of space. Toying with the "evidential" quality of photography, Wynne dialectically articulates Thomas More's *Utopia*, the paranoid visions of Philip K. Dick (thanks to which it is assumed that space colonization will inevitably turn towards penal colonies) and a critique of a Promethean conception of science. Between parable and prophecy, the artist invites us to "an enlightened catastrophism".[3]

The work of Ana Zibelnik offers an open end to this reflection about time and change. By questioning the ontology of photography and its relationship to life – of which it is both a sample and a distancing (killing), she opens, as Joanna Zylinska points out, a perspective that might not necessarily be pleasing but is certainly transcendent: there will be a future, with or without us.

1 Giorgio Agamben, *Qu'est-ce que le contemporain?*, Rivages, 2008.
2 Jacques Ellul, *La Technique ou l'enjeu du siècle, 1954*, Economica, 2008.
3 Jean-Pierre Dupuy, *Pour un catastrophisme éclairé*, Seuil, 2002.

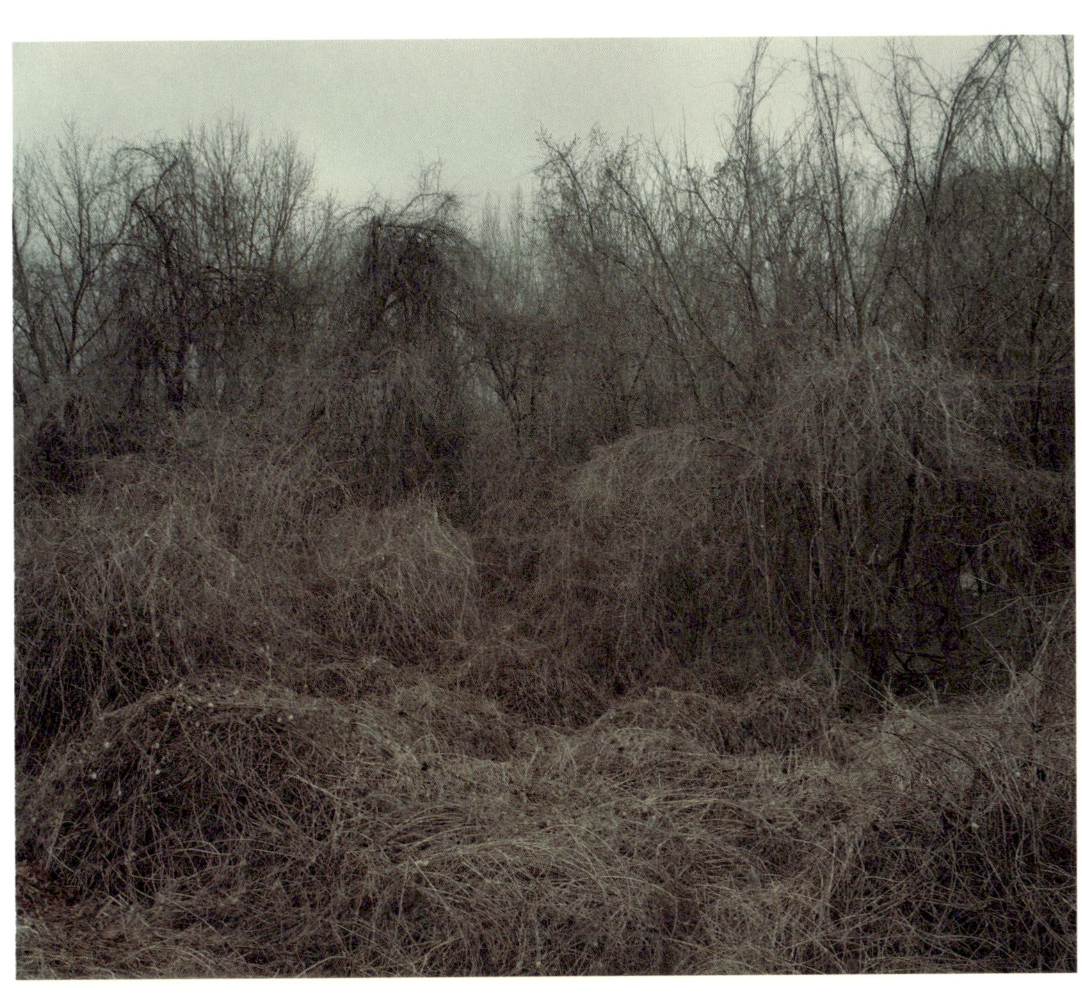

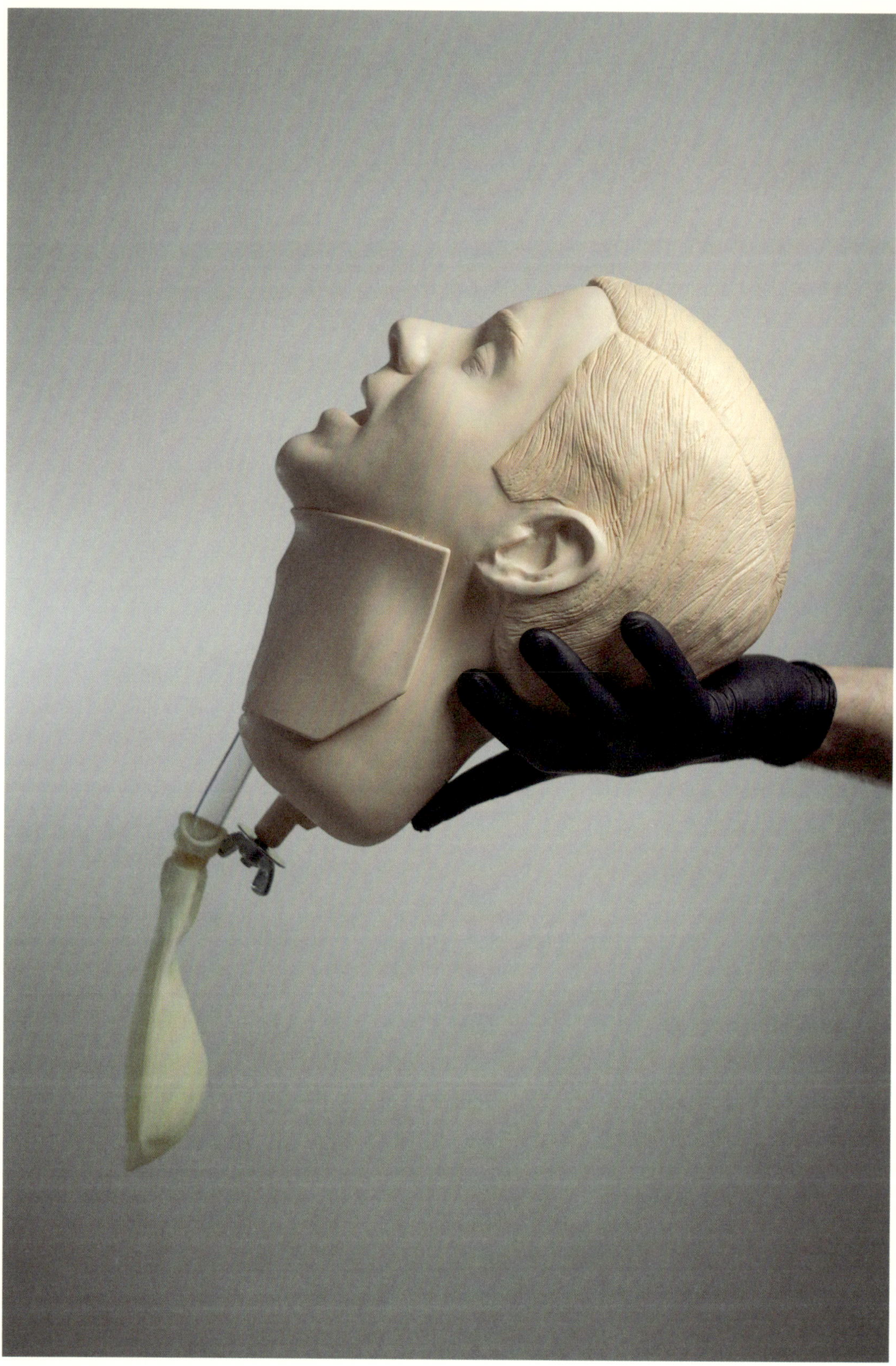

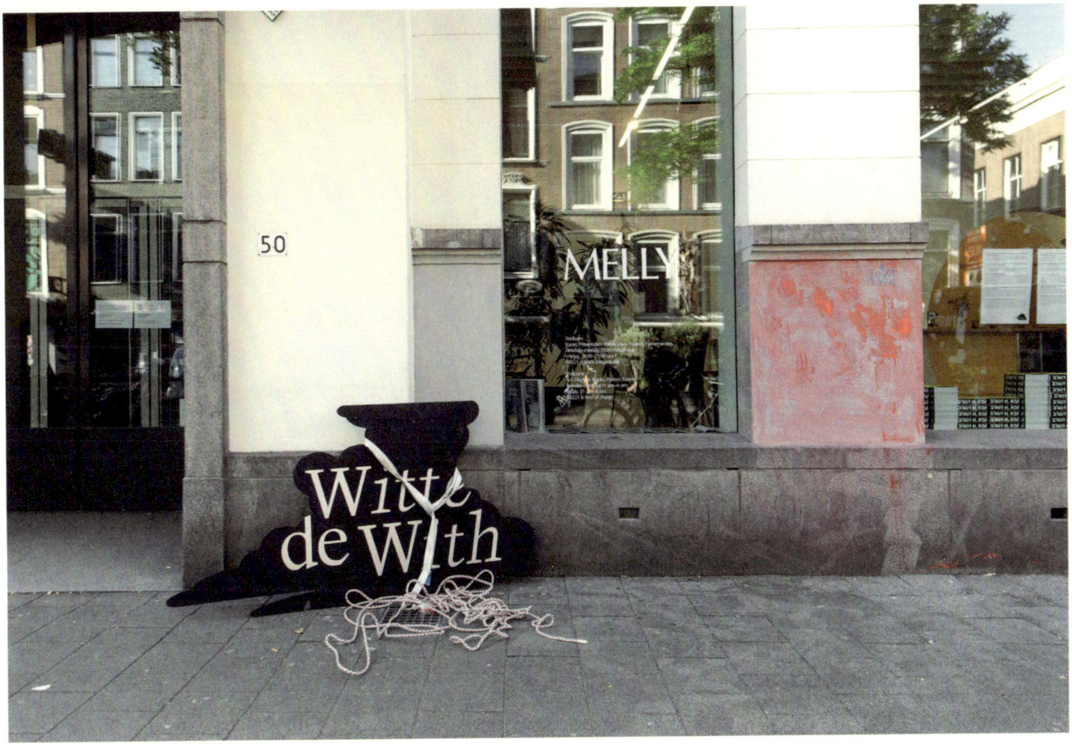

50
MELLY
Witte
de With

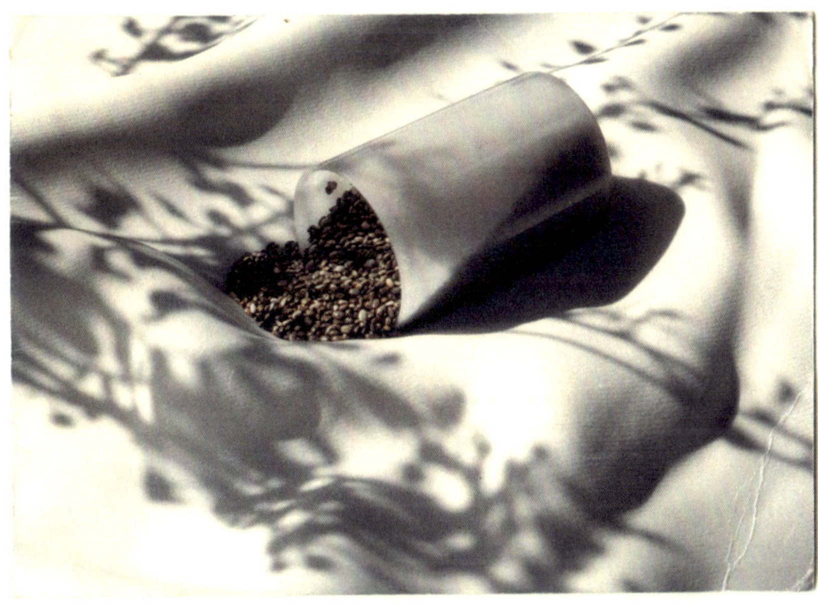

# SUPPORTING

# IMAGE CREATORS

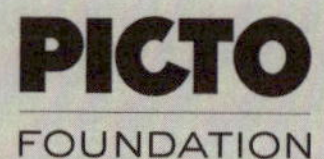

# THE INTERNATIONAL MEETING PLACE FOR PHOTOGRAPHY

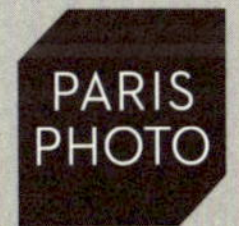

A PATRON
COMMITTED TO

CONTEMPORARY
PHOTOGRAPHY

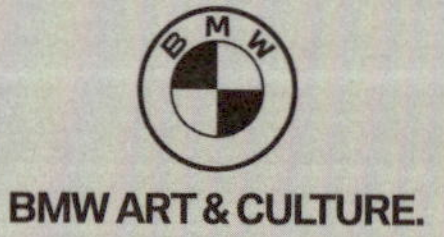